Refried Elvis

Refried Elvis

The Rise of the Mexican Counterculture

ERIC ZOLOV

University of California Press

BERKELEY   LOS ANGELES   LONDON

University of California Press
Berkeley and Los Angeles, California

University of California Press, Ltd.
London, England

Library of Congress Cataloging-in-Publication Data

Zolov, Eric.
    Refried Elvis : the rise of the Mexican counterculture / Eric Zolov.
      p.   cm.
    Includes bibliographic references and index
    ISBN 0-520-20866-8 (alk. paper). — ISBN 0-520-21514-1
    1. Mexico—Civilization—20th century. 2. Mexico—Politics and
government—1946–1970. 3. Mexico—Politics and government—
1970–1988. 4. Youth movement—Mexico—Mexico City—
History—20th century. 5. Rock music—Mexico—History and
criticism. 6. Music and society—Mexico—History—20th century.
7. Politics and culture—Mexico—History—20th century. 8. Social
values—Mexico—History—20th century. 9. Nationalism—
Mexico—History—20th century. I. Title. II. Title: Rise of the
Mexican counterculture.

F1235.Z65   1999
972.0893—dc 21   98-7968

Printed in the United States of America
9 8 7 6 5 4 3 2 1

The paper used in this publication meets the minimum requirements of
American National Standards for Information Sciences—Permanence
of Paper for Printed Library Materials, ANSI Z39.48-1984.

To Emmy, Sal, and Tacho

Contents

Illustrations

Acknowledgments

In a fundamental sense, the origins of this project date to my years as an undergraduate at Colby College. Therefore it is only appropriate that I acknowledge the support of a 1986 Walker Scholarship summer grant which allowed me to begin research on what eventually became my senior honors thesis at Colby. Through the University of Chicago I received a summer travel grant from the Latin American Studies Center, which enabled me to do preliminary research in 1991. A predissertation Mellon Foundation grant funded research during the summer and fall of 1992. Funding for my stay in Mexico City during 1992–1994 came from a U.S. Information Agency Fulbright grant, which I stretched to the best of my abilities. I was also fortunate to receive a teaching position at the Universidad de las Américas in Mexico City, which allowed me to extend my original research schedule. I am deeply grateful to Harvard University for an Exchange Scholar Fellowship during 1994–1995, which provided the opportunity to use the library facilities and finish writing the dissertation. Invaluable institutional support during revisions has come from the University of California, Davis, the University of Puget Sound, and Georgetown University.

Of the many people who have contributed to the transformation of this thesis, I wish to thank first and foremost my dissertation committee: John Coatsworth, Friedrich Katz, Michael Geyer, and Leora Auslander. Their astute comments and insights, coupled with unwavering support for the project, are immensely appreciated. From Mexico, I wish to extend my thanks in particular to the following people and institutions: the Reyes Mota family, for their love and generous hospitality over the years; Manuel Ruiz, who generously lent his time and gave me access to his early rock 'n' roll collection; Ramón García, who also generously lent his time and his native rock collection; Sergio García, for private screenings of various underground films; Federico Arana, for lending me numerous photographs and other materials from his private archive; Andrew Paxman of *Variety*; Carlos Martínez Assad, Ilán Semo, and José Luis Reyna, for their early comments and encouragement; Leticia Medina and José Enrique Pérez Cruz of the Archivo de la Difusión Cultural, Universidad Nacional Autónoma de México; the Cámara Nacional de la Industria de Radio y Televisión, for its rich coffee and repeated access to its newsletter, though not, unfortunately, to its archives; the people at Radio Educación, the Filmoteca de San Ildefonso, and Polygram Records; the Sotomayor family, for access to various rock 'n' roll films, and, finally, to Pete Cecere of the U.S. Information Agency, for his wit and wicked mouth, but especially for his accumulated personal archive.

Of the many friends and colleagues who have also offered their criticisms, I wish to thank in particular the following: participants in the Mass Culture Workshop at the University of Chicago (1991–92), in the History–Political Science Workshop at Harvard University (fall 1994), and in the Latin American History Discussion Group at the University of California, Davis (spring 1996); Fernando Calderón, Jean Franco, Stuart Ewen, Glen Kuecker, Anne Rubenstein, Claudio Lomnitz-Adler, William Beezley, Mauricio Tenorio-Trillo, Jeremy Baskes, John Lear, Alex Saragoza, George Yúdice, and Juan Flores. I am particularly indebted to Deborah Pacini-Hernández, whose critical reading of the dissertation for University of California Press substantially helped influence the final manuscript. Special thanks also go to Mitchell Blank for access to his 1960s archive, Rogelio Agrasanchez Jr. of Latin Nostalgia, for lending me a copy of the film *Juventud desenfrenada* and to Bill Belmont of Fantasy Records for his assistance in garnering copyright permissions and especially for our conversations about rock music in Mexico. One of the advantages (as well as pitfalls) of this kind of project is that nearly everyone has a tidbit of information to share. For all of you who have passed on to me articles, interviews, photographs, musical selections, books, and other paraphernalia of the rock counterculture from abroad and at home—thank you so very much. This project is certainly the better for your generosity.

I also wish to gratefully acknowledge the support and guidance of my editors and production staff at the University of California Press, William Murphy, and Sarah K. Myers for her meticulous copyediting. Your editorial skills, accessibility, and friendship have helped make this process as smooth and enjoyable as possible.

Finally, I would like to thank my families here and in Mexico. Your support—whether unspoken, verbal, or material—has helped to keep the spirit and direction of this project alive and well. Special thanks go to my wife and *compañera*, Emmy Avilés Bretón, whose enthusiasm often encouraged me to keep the faith during trying moments. Her insights into Mexican popular culture, along with other suggestions and criticisms, are reflected in the final project. Also, her tireless determination to help transcribe numerous taped interviews (often poorly recorded) cannot go unmentioned. Our cats, Sal and Tacho, bore with this project in their own style, and so to all three is dedicated the final product.

I hope to have produced a book that consolidates a wealth of information within a theoretical framework that rings true, both to academics and to participants. For both minor and major oversights, I accept full responsibility.

Introduction

This is the story of how Mexico's "Revolutionary Family"[1]—in its political, cultural, and social manifestations—became irrevocably frayed. Because my focus is largely urban centered, and on Mexico City especially, the story is necessarily biased. By focusing on the social and cultural transformations wrought by rapid modernization during the 1950s and 1960s, it largely ignores the still overwhelming (though no longer majority) rural population in favor of an analysis of the new middle classes. Mexico's peasantry appears, but mostly in the guise of urban migrants, the new lumpenproletariat struggling to assert a voice from the margins. Still, the 1968 student movement, which forms the basic point of reference for this story, was in itself an event centered in the nation's capital and drew its ranks from the middle classes.[2] Mexico City is by no means an encapsulation of Mexico as a whole, nor can "middle-class values" adequately encompass the question of ideology, but the student movement—despite its geographical circumscription—had a profound effect on the nation at large. The challenges to one-party rule that the students raised were indeed national challenges, affecting Mexicans well beyond the center of the country.

The crisis of authority that the Mexican regime faced in 1968 had its parallel in the middle-class family, which also experienced the conflicts of youth dissent. As such, 1968 was a social and cultural event as much as a political one. From this perspective, the student movement's challenge to the dominant political structure reflected less a spontaneous organizational response to repression and the wastefulness associated with the staging of the Olympics than a cumulative crisis of patriarchal values. The student movement of 1968 was not the start of a new historical consciousness but its pivotal event, a fulcrum that articulated the restlessness and rage for much of the youth of a middle class which had come of age during Mexico's acclaimed modernizing "miracle" and which afterward opened the floodgates of cynicism and everyday resistance to a political system bent on maintaining control.

But, as the title of the book suggests, this is also a story about rock and the countercultural revolts that exploded around the world during the latter half of the 1960s. We do not normally associate Mexico with rock music. And yet for Mexican middle- and upper-class youth who came of age in the 1960s Elvis Presley, the Beatles, and the Rolling Stones were household names, as were Emiliano Zapata (whose name was later borrowed by a Mexican rock band), Francisco Madero, and Benito Juárez. In this study rock music functions as a keyhole into modern Mexican society, allowing us to view and discuss the crisis of revolutionary nationalism that coincided with the rise of rock 'n' roll itself. By following what may be called the commodity thread of rock music—identifying how producers, consumers, and state gatekeepers wrestled with the definition of rock's production and reception—we discover an important vehicle for exploring a critical moment of late-twentieth-century capitalism. In the process we encounter the myriad ways in which global patterns of commodity exchanges are reconfigured locally and in turn projected back into a "global ecumene."[3]

The concept of the Revolutionary Family is a convenient and fitting metaphor for the overarching framework of the new political and ideological machine that arose from the ashes of revolutionary war and caudillo infighting in Mexico during the 1920s. Baptized by President Plutarco Calles in 1929 in the name of "revolutionary unity," the notion of such a political family coincided with Calles's founding of the Partido Nacional Revolucionario, precursor of the modern-day Partido Revolucionario Institucional (PRI). As a leader of the so-called Sonoran Dynasty that came to power after 1920, Calles's understanding of Mexico's postrevolutionary situation was astute. Without some political means for incorporating the disparate and often conflictual social forces and leadership that vied for political access and power, Mexico risked returning to a situation akin to that of the mid–nineteenth century, when regional bosses (only now mobilized by the events of revolution) directly challenged a central political authority. The political party that Calles founded thus built on the logic of a centralizing polity (ably accomplished, but with disastrous consequences, by one-man dictatorship under Porfirio Díaz from 1876 to 1910), while providing ample opportunity for political mobility. It was a system in which all principal roads led back to the party: deviations from the corporatist pathway were costly, if not deadly. When Lázaro Cárdenas came to power in 1934 and accelerated many of the revolutionary goals, such as land reform, workers' rights, and nationalization of resources, which had stalled by the late 1920s, he nonetheless was indebted to the corporatist political system put in place by his predecessor. Cárdenas's calculated mobilization of peasants, workers, and the middle classes not only depended on this nascent party structure but, moreover, deepened that structure by leaving a legacy of loyalist incorporation by these social groups. By the time Cárdenas stepped down from power in 1940 the groundwork had been laid for a development path of mixed capitalist growth in which domestic and foreign (mainly U.S.) investment could readily count on the organizing and repressive arm of the official party to provide a "stable" economic climate.[4]

No lasting political project, of course, is viable without a strategy for inculcating a common identification with the nation-state, and in this regard Mexico's ruling political party established important trademarks for other revolutionary and populist regimes. If in political terms the Revolutionary Family meant a relinquishing of individual claims to power in exchange for political access and resources meted out by a centralizing party, the project of constructing a consensual *vision* of postrevolutionary Mexico was equally far-reaching. Out of the chaos of revolution—and a history of caudillo uprisings throughout the nineteenth century—Mexico proved to be the stablest among Latin American nations. While Argentina, Brazil, and Chile, for instance, all passed into the twentieth century without major revolutionary upheaval, each experienced dramatic divisions in its national polity that ultimately resulted in prolonged military dictatorships. A multitude of factors account for this, of course, but the unifying strength of Mexico's revolutionary nationalism was unquestionably a defining feature of the nation's political stability and economic growth into the 1960s.[5] What kind, if any, cultural hegemony the official party achieved has been a matter of recent scholarly debate: where and when did legitimization "succeed" or "fail"? That such answers are by no means self-evident attests to the sophistication of state efforts as well as to the richness of Mexican cultural life.[6] But what does seem clear is that out of the chaos of revolution a stable political order reemerged, one that rested on more than violence and coercion to undergird its legitimacy.

The ideological state-building project was remarkable not only for its boldness but also in the complexity of the negotiated responses it in turn inspired. Beyond a heralding of folkloric culture (*lo mexicano*) and the racial valorization of a mestizo-driven "Cosmic Race," the postrevolutionary regime faced the task of rewriting the historical memory of the revolutionary experience itself. As Ilene O'Malley has written, "[t]he Mexican regime's use of the revolution as a symbol to unify the nation contradicted one of the most obvious characteristics of the revolution—its disunity."[7] By eliding the fact that the most significant leaders of the revolutionary struggle—Madero, Zapata, Villa, and Carranza—often fought different, contradictory battles against common enemies as well as one another, the new ideology propagated during the 1920s and 1930s meant to mystify the revolutionary process itself and thus to obscure the meaning of its outcome. This involved a re-presentation of that historical event as a depoliticized and yet gendered narrative, in which virile leaders joined forces to lead a glorified peasantry and working class to victory against a common enemy (that is, the old regime and imperialism). Hence the peasant leader Emiliano Zapata, defeated on the battlefield and later assassinated by the victorious Carrancista faction, acquired a "Christ-like, martyred image," whereas his arch enemy, Venustiano Carranza, became known as "the Father of the 1917 Constitution" and "a symbol of law" in the official discourse.[8] Victors and vanquished thus shared the stage as national heroes, their images and (perhaps less successfully) memories sanitized and re-presented as official history: the unified Revolution.

As the *official* party of the Revolution (capitalized to enhance its mythic status), the PRI became the "family home" in which postrevolutionary "squabbles" were resolved through rewards and punishment. At the head of this home stood, of course, the presidential father figure, to whom all disputes were directly or ultimately submitted. Octavio Paz has written about this metaphorical father and its implications for patriarchal authoritarianism in Mexico: "Behind the respect for Señor Presidente there is the traditional image of the Father. . . . In the center of the family: the father. The father figure is two-pronged, the duality of patriarch and *macho*. The patriarch protects, is good, powerful, wise. The *macho* is the terrible man, the *chingón*, the father who has left, who has abandoned a wife and children. The image of Mexican authority is inspired by these two extremes: Señor Presidente and Caudillo."[9] This notion of the president-cum-father of the nation was by no means unique. The dictator Porfirio Díaz himself had certainly accomplished as much, and the image of the benevolent caudillo is legend in Latin American politics. What the Mexican case achieved, however, was the *institutionalization* of the president as patriarch (passed along from one personality to the next via an electoral process, however flawed) and the official party as domestic council.

This metaphorical family was a reflection of and in turn served to reinforce an image of the stable family unit itself. The idealized family of the postrevolutionary order was one in which the father was stern in his benevolence, the mother saintly in her maternity, and the children loyal in their obedience. Faith in the father's ultimate commitment to the progress of the family—even when that father had been corrupted by temptation and error—excused his mistakes and pardoned his sins. Undergirding this sense of pardon was the vision of the mother figure as saint and sufferer, whose moral superiority and spiritual strength acted as glue for the ultimate stability of the family—and by extension the nation (as did the Virgin of Guadalupe, Mexico's semiofficial patron saint). It was no coincidence that Mother's Day became an official state holiday just after the revolution.[10] This patriarchal idealization of order permeated virtually every aspect of official nationalism—from muralism, to public monuments, to mass-media imagery—causing any challenges to the gendered order to be viewed as deviant if not subversive. As one author has recently put it, "[f]or better or worse, Mexico came to mean machismo and machismo to mean Mexico."[11]

This cultural framework, which superimposed a patriarchal ideology on a mythologized (though very real) revolutionary struggle, was nevertheless challenged and contradicted by everyday reality among Mexico's poor. If this was true in the countryside, where campesinos contested the political terms of land redistribution and restrictions on religious worship, it was equally true in the cities—especially the capital—to which rural migrants were lured in search of economic betterment and survival. The very dislocations wrought by modernization destroyed family stability and exposed the empty nature of state paternalism. In the capital the proliferation of an urban underclass not only altered the architecture of the city by introducing the shantytown in the midst of capitalist progress but, furthermore, posed an affront to the very notion of order that lay at the heart of the patriarchal state.[12] The poor were seen as *dis*-orderly by middle-class society, not only in their lack of material wealth but also, and more fundamentally, in their lack of *buenas costumbres*, a class- and gender-laden notion implying "proper upbringing."

While economic conditions and state policy produced important disjunctures between official ideology and material reality for the majority poor, for a growing middle class the revolutionary promise of a better life was coming true. Mexico's import-substitution industrialization strategy, which offered tariff protections and state subsidies for native industries, also underwrote an expansive consumer culture by keeping down the price of foodstuffs and energy. Sheltered by state protection, Mexican industry produced many of its own substitutes for basic consumer imports, but protective barriers also encouraged the emergence of transnational subsidiary operations ostensibly under majority Mexican ownership (though often on paper more so than in practice). While the new consumer culture was shaped by Mexican industry, it was thus also deeply engraved with the trademarks and imagery emanating from corporate culture in the United States, whose cars, television and radio sets, film and music personalities, foodstuffs, and fashion styles were being exported around the world. As Jonathan Kandell describes the post–World War II decades in his biography of Mexico City, *La Capital:*

> Throughout the capital, fast-food outlets serving hamburgers, hot dogs, and pizza vied with taco stands. Baseball crowds rivaled those at bull-fights and soccer matches. Supermarkets stocked their shelves with Kellogg's Rice Krispies, Campbell's soups, Coca-Cola, Heinz catsup, and Van Camp's Boston baked beans. Neon signs flashed a lexicon of U.S. corporate names: Ford, General Motors, Chrysler, Zenith, General Electric. Blue jeans became the uniform of the younger generation, rich and poor. A hit parade of rock 'n' roll competed with Mexican "corridos" on the radio. *Ozzie and Harriet, Leave It to Beaver, Mannix, Dragnet, The Lone Ranger,* and many other American television series had a loyal following. Hollywood relegated Mexican films to the more decrepit movie houses. Even Christmas became Americanized: in department stores, adoring youngsters sat on the lap of a red-coated, white-bearded Santa Claus; at home, stockings were hung over the fireplace, and gifts were piled under fir trees festooned with pulsing lights and cotton snow fluffs.[13]

But it was not simply a question of economics: the middle classes relentlessly pursued these products and the values that accompanied them. Conspicuous consumption became a mark of the middle classes' own modernity and a sign of the nation's advancement not only in material terms but also in the more abstract sense of development itself. As the Mexican novelist José Emiliano Pacheco describes in his short story "Battles in the Desert," about middle-class life in the capital just after the end of World War II:

> In the meantime, we modernized and incorporated into our vocabulary terms that had sounded like Chicanoisms when we had first heard them in the Tin Tan movies [Mexico's comic star of the period] and then slowly, imperceptibly, had become Mexicanized: *tenquíu, oquéi, uasamara, sherap, sorry.* . . . We began to eat *hamburguesas, páys* [pies], *donas, jotdogs.* . . . Fresh juice drinks of lemon, jamaica, and sage were buried by Coca-Cola. . . . Our parents soon got used to drinking *jaibol,* even though at first it tasted to them like medicine. Tequila is prohibited in my house, I once heard my Uncle Julian say. I serve only whisky to my guests: We must whitewash the taste of Mexicans.[14]

As the bicycle had during the Porfiriato (the period of late-nineteenth-century growth under the dictator Porfirio Díaz), the automobile now became the sign of the modern times, and Goodyear—as much so as the PRI itself—a benefactor of that modernity.[15]

This growth of the middle classes was the boastful accomplishment of the PRI (renamed for the last time in 1946), and by the late 1950s the official party drew increasing accolades from U.S. businessmen and State Department officials for the "Mexican Miracle" that was under way. The so-called miracle combined low inflation with a stable exchange rate to produce annual growth rates of more than 6 percent for more than twenty years and a per capita growth rate of more than 3 percent for the same period.[16] Such phenomenal growth, generated especially by the expansion of industry, directly affected but was disproportionately borne by labor and the peasantry, whose real incomes declined during this period.[17] Constrained on one side by corrupt union officials beholden to the PRI and on the other by the threat of violence to suppress independent organizing, Mexico's urban and rural proletariat found themselves squeezed between a rapacious capitalist sector and the lack of democratic recourse. Indeed, the real miracle lay in the fact that the corporatist structure of the PRI had succeeded in stabilizing the cities and countryside through a combination of carrot and stick tactics, while virtually eliminating the possibility of politics outside the official party of the Revolution. This is not to suggest that independent challenges to PRI control did not arise; Mexico's postrevolutionary narrative is full of such instances. But the PRI proved extremely effective at mobilizing its corporatist clients to rally around it, while not hesitant to use force where necessary. Moreover, through its direct and indirect control over the mass media the PRI manipulated a discourse that combined a revolutionary mythology with the promises of modernity, all aimed at sustaining a middle-class consensus and thus preventing any direct questioning of the PRI's authoritarian politics.

The ruling party spent countless sums erecting monuments, staging celebrations, and mouthing words in praise of Mexico's revolutionary heroes and accomplishments. In fact, such was its commitment to upholding Mexico's revolutionary heritage that the PRI positioned itself to be seen as synonymous not only with the Revolution but—in adopting the national colors as its own and underwriting all celebratory discourse of the nation—with national identity itself. Mexican cultural critic Carlos Monsiváis has identified this as "state control over the signification of [what it means] to be Mexican,"[18] a pronunciation that both is an overstatement and has the ring of truth to it. While the PRI literally had its fingers in every available cultural, social, and economic activity — Octavio Paz would later label the party a "philanthropic ogre" [19] — there were signs that it was reaching a point of diminishing returns. For by the late 1950s the PRI's official nationalism had begun to generate a backlash not only among artists and intellectuals — not to mention workers and peasants who fought for more material gains — but also among a new middle-class generation of youth for whom Juárez and Zapata were more ossified heroes of the official party than living emblems of liberation. Mexico's nationalism, once heralded for its cosmopolitanism and vibrancy, was now being charged by critics as insular, authoritarian, "dead." [20] The Revolutionary Family continued to serve as the dominant discursive vehicle for rallying nationalist sentiment among the populace, but an incipient cynicism had entered.[21] And with this cynicism came a questioning of the patriarchal values at large: Must the voice of the father-president always be authoritative? It was with this question that Mexico's middle-class youth began to lay the foundations for a broader attack on the postrevolutionary order itself, not so much to overthrow it but to transform it into something more responsive and less authoritarian.

As an epitome of postwar consumerism rock 'n' roll introduced a questioning of the social order that reverberated throughout Mexican society in the so-called *rebeldes sin causa,* a catch-all phrase lifted from the James Dean film (shown and later banned) that heralded the new youth culture. Many Mexicans viewed the rise of rock 'n' roll as an imperialist import from the United States, a reaction similar to that in other societies around the world.[22] But clearly the issue was more complicated. On one hand, rock 'n' roll was associated with challenges to parental authority and wanton individualism. On the other hand, however, the new youth culture also appealed to many adults' perceptions of what it meant to be modern, to have access to global culture. Alan Knight has proposed that "a tide of cultural Americanization" — in which U.S.-influenced mass media forms redirected the shape and content of revolutionary culture — took place after 1940 and ultimately served the interests of the PRI. Knight's assumption is that a "dominant Western culture (or anticulture?) of commercialism and consumerism, of mass media and mass recreation" [23] depoliticized Mexico's populace, rendering a national culture linked more by a shared appreciation of comic books and television than by revolutionary activism. The mass media did indeed create a new series of reference points for the national identity that, on the face of it, were anything but political. But to view this as "the triumph of a bland cultural consumerism" [24] greatly overlooks the contested nature of mass culture (even when produced through the filter of an authoritarian regime) and its usefulness as a vehicle for counterhegemonic strategies. The 1950s may have witnessed the ascendancy of mass-media culture, but this emergence also marked the beginning of a new ideological questioning of authoritarian practices, not its death knell.

The mythologizing of national heroes within a patriarchal value system that emphasized respect for political authority was a common denominator of the modern nation-state. In a fundamental sense, Mexican reality had much in common with other capitalist and socialist regimes during this period. Built on ideological foundations of heroic nationalism spurred (or reconstructed, as the case may have been) by World War II, numerous political regimes around the world were characterized by similar strategies of nation-state formation and cultural hegemony, despite often broad differences in national character and political economy. Another common denominator was the ubiquitous presence of rock 'n' roll and the related student and countercultural protest movements that shook the foundations of many regimes at the end of the 1960s.[25] Yet while we readily acknowledge the place of rock music in our own countercultural protests in the United States, we have come to assume that rock is *our* cultural heritage rather than part of the global patrimony. In fact, since its initial mass distribution, in the late 1950s, rock 'n' roll culture has been disseminated via capitalist and underground channels throughout the world, embedding itself in local cultures in ways that came to have profound results. In one sense, the spread of rock 'n' roll culture had an effect elsewhere which was similar to that in the United States: intergenerational conflict, repudiation of authoritarian values, liberation of the body, accelerated consumerism. But where rock music entered nationalist, developing nations (including the Eastern bloc countries), it was adopted by youth (as well as some parents) as an agent of modernity, even while it was frequently condemned by government officials and the intelligentsia as an agent of imperialism.

In virtually every urban center around the globe that was large enough to proffer access to a record player and electronic amplification, local rock 'n' roll imitators sprang up. In a kind of universal pattern, musical expression began with "cover" renditions of U.S. pop hits that not only replicated the instrumental arrangements of Elvis Presley, Bill Haley, and others but also, at least initially, mimicked the guttural sounds of English-language lyrics. (By the end of the 1960s most bands were writing their own music in their native language, though Mexico was an exception to this.) In short, the baby boomer, rock 'n' roll generation that in the United States we have come to associate as the precursor of our 1960s cultural explosion was, in fact, a global phenomenon. Local articulations of this phenomenon were exceedingly diverse yet showed important consistencies across cultural and geographical divides.[26]

Around the world, rock music thus served as both wedge and mirror for societies caught in the throes of rapid modernization. Rock was a wedge in the sense that it challenged traditional boundaries of propriety, gender relations, social hierarchies, and the very meanings of national identity in an era of heightened nationalism. (This is not to say that rock was always "progressive," as it could also serve to reinforce social hierarchies and gender relations.) Yet rock was also a mirror reflecting the aspirations and anxieties of societies in pursuit of an elusive sense of "first-worldism," whether in emulation of or competition with its standard bearer, the United States. For instance, in the Soviet Union officials initially banned the twist but then reversed themselves and began to sponsor homegrown alternatives "that were modern and exciting but also rooted in Soviet traditions."[27] The effort failed: the twist and other Western dance and musical styles prevailed. But the issue that affected the Soviet Union was not dissimilar from that which affected Mexico and other nations; namely, how the state could contain the modernizing effects of the youth culture without losing control over its disruptive, countercultural, wedge element.

Mexico played a distinctive role in this process of rock 'n' roll's transnationalism. In other contexts rock 'n' roll imitators were often repressed, or perhaps one or two especially talented artists gained the privilege of a record contract. In Mexico, however, the rock 'n' rollers were outwardly embraced by local and transnational capitalist interests, found endorsement (at least partially) from the regime, and discovered a level of fame that catapulted them into national and international stardom. By the mid-1960s Mexican rock 'n' roll had become an integral element of a modernizing aesthetic, lending credence to the nation and the world at large of the economic "miracle" at hand. Mexico was not alone in cultivating a rock 'n' roll youth culture among Latin Americans. Argentina, especially, also produced a vibrant rock 'n' roll scene during the 1960s, as did other countries.[28] Yet Mexico established a level of commercialization during the early 1960s that distinguished it from other developing nations and that made its own rock sound widely recognized throughout much of Latin America.

How can we account for this? Certainly Mexico's proximity to the United States played an important role: access to the new youth culture was greater and role models were closer (Bill Haley and even The Doors performed in Mexico City); and the track to stardom was that much more evident. Culturally speaking, Mexico's shared border and the prominence of various rock musicians of Mexican origin (for example, Ritchie Valens and Carlos Santana) also lent an "insider" sense of participation. Another factor was the development of Mexico's mass-media industry, not only its transnational element but also the dominance by the conglomerate Telesistema (now Televisa), which was ably poised to exploit the sudden demand for youth culture. Finally, Mexico's unique political stability—in contrast with the populist swings, revolutionary insurrections, and military coups that characterized much of the rest of Latin America during the same period—clearly provided breathing room for a consumer-driven youth movement to flourish.

Rock music established itself as a crucial reference point in Mexican society, a signifier of cosmopolitan values and a bearer of disorder and wanton individualism. It was never neutral. By conducting a detailed analysis of rock music's production, distribution, and reception this study thus offers a unique view of the rising expectations and mounting contradictions of Mexico's modernizing "miracle." The first chapter explores the sudden impact of an imported youth culture in the late 1950s and the social conflicts that accompanied it. Editorial commentators decried the collapse of buenas costumbres while drawing the connection between disobedience in the home and social challenges to the PRI by dissident workers and other groups. By the end of the decade new legislation aimed at restricting the content and distribution of "offensive" mass culture was in place, but capitalist interests were already exploring ways of profiting from the demand for rock 'n' roll.

Chapter 2 describes the containment of rock 'n' roll via its Spanish-language domestication, thus rendering a sanitized version of a raucous import. Spanish-language *rocanrol* came to embody the modernizing aspirations of a middle class in ascendancy, but stripped of the offensive gestures of defiance that defined the original. Contained at the level of production, rock 'n' roll's consumption nonetheless had begun to transform the social values of everyday life by challenging the established parameters of an authoritarian society. This was especially the case after 1964, when rock 'n' roll dropped its boyhood charm and began to adopt a more explicitly irreverent posture, as heralded by the impact of the Beatles and other groups that followed in their wake.

By the time of the 1968 student movement, the subject of chapter 3, rock music had become an inextricable part of the urban landscape throughout Mexico City. While rock performance played only a minor direct role in the movement itself (unlike in the United States, where rock had acquired an overt political function), every student was nonetheless aware of its presence. More importantly, many of the values that were grounded in the incipient countercultural movement (called La Onda)—and even though these values were partially coopted as "fashion" by the culture industry— permeated the student revolt. This was reflected as much in the long hair of many participants as in their language and expressed contempt for hege- monic values. This countercultural discourse—also influenced by the ro- manticized image of Che Guevara and his revolutionary calling—directly contributed to the emergence and direction the student movement took. At the height of the student protests, government tanks and troops ended the movement in a massacre at the site known as Tlatelolco. Crushed was a democratic challenge to authoritarian rule on the eve of what was other- wise planned as President Gustavo Díaz Ordaz's crowning achievement of his administration: the staging of the Olympic games (a first for a develop- ing nation). Though the student demonstrations had taken place almost exclusively in the capital, their voices and the repression that silenced them reverberated throughout the nation. With the repression, the student movement came apart. In effect, the PRI had salvaged an image of stability in the eyes of the world—but at an extremely high domestic cost.

Chapter 4 follows the countercultural trajectory of these student ener- gies in the wake of the massacre. One of the most salient manifestations of the counterculture was the proliferation of a native hippie movement, the *jipitecas.* Where a government-pliant press had once seen the student pro- testers as a threat to social stability, now a new alarm was raised by the pros- pect of youth dropping out of society altogether. Even more alarming was their apparent imitation of foreigners, who began to arrive in ever-greater numbers as a result of their own escapism. At the same time society con- demned this twin countercultural explosion-invasion, however, the culture industry was gearing up to make a profit from the rising demand for rock music and its accompanying paraphernalia.

Chapter 5 thus explores the commercial, musical, and ideological impli- cations of a new wave of Mexican rock musicians, dubbed La Onda Chicana. Anxious to align themselves with a global rock movement, on one hand, and to disassociate themselves with Mexico's earlier "contained" rock suc- cesses, on the other, these youth sought to invent a musical and stylistic ex- pression they could call their own. In dramatic fashion, a rock culture that had been as much associated with elitism as it had with antiauthoritarian- ism before Tlatelolco was transformed into a vibrant outlet for defiance, dis- illusionment, and discovery. But there was one problem: this new wave of bands sang almost exclusively in English, even while writing its own lyrics.

The subject of chapter 6 is a massive rock festival in the fall of 1971 that drew an estimated 150,000–200,000 people and reflected the culminating moment of Mexico's rock counterculture. Popularly known as Avándaro, the festival generated an immense backlash against a generation that the left viewed as "mentally colonized" and the right saw as socially degenerate. The new political regime under President Luis Echeverría (1970–1976) took advantage of this backlash to further its own agenda of cultural nationalism, part of a broader strategy of "democratic opening" aimed at reincorporating leftist critics. Thus, despite moderate amounts of capital invested in promoting Mexican rock, the state demanded the mass media's withdrawal, while underwriting support for a Latin American folk-protest musical revival. At the same time, live rock performance was pushed into the barrios, where it was nurtured by the lower classes that reclaimed it as a movement for their own social rage.

Chapter 7 explores one of the hidden ideological forces at work in the transformation of cultural values: the U.S. Information Agency (USIA). Accused by many radicals and intellectuals of fostering an agenda of Americanization throughout the world, this chapter suggests ways in which the USIA was both an active participant and an ignorant bystander in the cultural revolts that were linked, directly and indirectly, to U.S. protest values.

In a brief concluding chapter we continue to follow the trajectory of native rock music as it reemerges from barrio culture to present itself as a frontal challenge to the status quo. If rock went from being a metaphor for modernity in the early 1960s, to a symbol of its excesses at the end of the decade, in the 1980s *los chavos banda*—lumpenproletariat punk rockers in the capital—embodied the utter collapse of Revolutionary promise altogether. A stark sociological emblem of *la crisis* (Mexico's "Lost Decade" of the 1980s), these punk rockers were now embraced by intellectuals as an authentic representation of popular culture. Viewed as an expression of cultural imperialism in the early 1970s, rock culture had come full circle as the redeemer of democratic practice and urban social protest.

As some of the language already employed in this introduction may suggest, this is a book about not only Mexico but also the larger questions of transnationalism and identity-formation strategies under late capitalism. A transnationalist perspective searches for cultural meaning amid the seeming rubble and chaos of late-twentieth-century modernity. Whereas earlier theories of cultural imperialism emphasized a monolithic conversion of cultural identity to the benefit of multinational capital, a transnationalist perspective offers a more nuanced reading of identity as social process. As Arjun Appadurai writes, the question is one not of cultural homogenization *versus* cultural heterogenization but of how the two are interactive: "What these arguments [that is, homogenization versus heterogenization] fail to consider is that at least as rapidly as forces from various metropolises are brought into new societies they tend to become indigenized in one or another way: this is true of music and housing styles as much as it is true of science and terrorism, spectacles and constitutions."[29] A fundamental contribution of transnationalism as a theoretical concept is that it allows us to widen our discussion of the nation-state to take into consideration what Appadurai labels "global cultural flow": the ongoing, patterned dispersion of people, media images, technology, finance capital, and ideology that interrupts the delineated coherency supposedly fixed by national boundaries. This flow dramatically accelerated during the 1960s as global economic conditions favored multinational capital and the mass media, on one hand, and the rise of middle-class consumerism and travel, on the other. The global circulation of goods, people, capital, and ideas was scarcely even: as the dominant economic and military power, the United States disproportionately influenced the tone and content of such flow. It was no surprise, therefore, that an ensuing backlash occurred in the 1970s in the form of a debate over cultural imperialism, which by then had become synonymous with Americanization. While ample evidence suggested that the media were indeed overwhelmingly American, in a more fundamental sense this debate reflected the loss of control by ruling regimes as well as intellectuals to arbitrate a discourse of national identity. The nation-state could no longer be addressed as a self-contained cultural entity holding nationalist guard against the outside world. There was increasingly a "global cultural economy"[30] in which local and global actors had a potential role to play, but the rules were no longer familiar.

In retrospect it seems reasonable to suggest that U.S.-influenced popular culture did in fact contribute to the processes of democratization that culminated in the fall of authoritarian as well as communist regimes throughout the world. When the Soviet Union accused North Atlantic Treaty Organization strategists of using Elvis Presley as a weapon in the cold war they were not being entirely paranoid.[31] Yet this raises the very difficult question of determining the line between cultural imperialism and cultural reappropriation. In the case of Mexico, where local bands performed in English for their audiences (who demanded as much) and were supported by national and transnational capitalism, this question is particularly relevant. The point of this study at one level, therefore, is to discern how global marketing strategies intersected with state apparatuses and audiences to shape and contest the terrain of mass popular culture. At the same time, this is also a study of Mexico during a period of rapid modernization that culminates in political crisis for the ruling party. Rock music becomes our pretext, our window into viewing this crisis of the Revolutionary Family. Some might argue that rock was mere coloring or perhaps background noise for the "more important" events of that period.[32] But rock mattered. It mattered both as an instigator of modern values and as a reflection of the modernization process itself.

The book is organized chronologically, taking the reader from the mid-1950s, when rock 'n' roll was first introduced into Mexican society, through to the early 1970s, in the aftermath of Avándaro and the collapse of the rock counterculture as a commercialized activity. Each chapter uses the thread of rock music as the basis for exploring rock's cultural ramifications on society at large, ranging from its initial association with *desmadre* (the collapse of social order) in the 1950s, to its reappropriation as "high culture" by the middle classes in the early 1960s, to the influence of countercultural values on the 1968 student movement and the emergence of jipitecas who refashioned an image of rebellion introduced by foreign hippies, to La Onda Chicana's culmination at Avándaro and the backlash that followed. Throughout each chapter, therefore, there is an effort to show how rock music and its countercultural spin-offs were shaped and contested at the levels of production and reception by capitalist interests, the state, and consumers. Where the narrative wanders into a discussion of transnational and local marketing strategies, it is meant to remind the reader that rock was a cultural commodity subject to the logic of capitalism, even while that logic was also shaped by local restraints and demands.[33]

One cannot separate Mexico's 1968 from the global context, which included not only the student revolts in Czechoslovakia, France, the United States, and elsewhere but also an emergent, globally shared repertoire of imagery, slogans, fashion statements, and music that now linked youth, psychically if not materially, to each other's struggles.[34] If Mexico's countercultural undertone does not come to mind when conjuring up an image of the 1968 student movement, this is due more to a lack of emphasis in the historiography than to the corresponding reality at the time. Today, the rock festival at Avándaro remains a mark of cultural shame unmentioned next to the martyred victims of Tlatelolco. But this historical amnesia is also due to the more material circumstances related to the movement's repression and cooptation in the years following Avándaro. In the wake of the festival, the commercialization of Mexico's counterculture was abruptly halted. Today there is scant commercialized evidence of the counterculture's very existence; little remains for nostalgic recycling. It is as if Woodstock existed for U.S. youth only in popular memory rather than a widely distributed double album and feature-length documentary film.[35]

But Mexico indeed had its "Avándaro generation": those marked by the defeatism of the 1968 movement; who experienced a cultural rebellion tied to rock music, Latin American protest song, and a rediscovery of indigenous roots; who challenged the values of their parents and in turn challenged the legitimacy of the PRI itself. Through La Onda and La Onda Chicana (its native rock counterpart) a critical discursive space was opened, producing an outlet for alternative articulations of self- and national identity among urban youth, male and female, from all classes whose impact is still felt today. This work is an attempt to begin the recovery of that story.

1 *Rebeldismo* in the Revolutionary Family

Rock 'n' Roll's Early Impact on Mexican State and Society

When rhythm and blues crossed over to become rock 'n' roll around 1955, white youth and their parents in the United States were put on a collision course of values that set in motion important transformations in the cultural landscape of this country. When that same rhythm was imported into Mexico on the wings of transnational capital and in the suitcases of individuals traveling abroad, something similarly profound transpired. Rock 'n' roll became a discursive prism through which filtered the hopes, fears, and anxieties of a society undergoing rapid modernization. For many adults, the new youth culture attached to rock music epitomized the cosmopolitan aspirations of a middle class in ascendancy. But at the same time, the sudden challenges to patriarchal authority in the home and society suggested the darker risks of rapid development and the need for greater control over the mass media. Ultimately, what these first years of rock 'n' roll in Mexico produced was a societal consensus that neither the impact of foreign cultural trends nor the tastes of youth could be halted. But at the same time, this consensus rendered that the state has the obligation to safeguard the nation from the unwarranted excesses of modernity.

ROCK 'N' ROLL'S ARRIVAL

The first taste of rock 'n' roll in Mexico had little to do with youth rebellion. Imported from abroad, rock 'n' roll swept the nation in the mid-1950s, along with the cha-cha-chá and the mambo, both introduced from Cuba. Rather than catering to youth, however, rock 'n' roll was popularized by orchestral "jazz bands" performing mostly for working and middle-class adults. With the exception of the young singer and actress Gloria Ríos, rock 'n' roll was initially "made by adults . . . who considered it just another [dance] style."[1] It had immediate appeal to a culture raised on dance. Significantly, two of the principal issues that catalyzed negative reaction by Anglo society in the United States—rock 'n' roll's "beat of sexual intercourse"[2] and its "jungle strains"[3]—were largely irrelevant in the Mexican context. This can be explained by the following: First, the representation of rock 'n' roll successfully marketed around the globe was overwhelmingly a white one, with its attendant associations of a modernizing aesthetic. By usurping the role of African American performers, Elvis Presley and Bill Haley, among others, had put a more palatable face on rhythm and blues, thus largely disassociating this music from its African American originators.

Second, the fear of "cultural miscegenation"[4] that largely characterized White America's reception of rock 'n' roll was something of a nonissue to Mexicans.[5] In fact, Mexicans identified rhythmically with the African roots of rock 'n' roll, precisely that element associated with savagery, exaggerated sexuality, and a breakdown of the moral code in the United States. Mexicans were raised on close cultural ties to the Caribbean and a passion for *música tropical*,[6] so exploring the rhythms of rock 'n' roll became at once a celebration of modernity and an addition to the lexicon of corporal expression enjoyed by all Mexicans. The important impact this new style had on dance audiences, not only in Mexico but throughout Latin America, is perhaps best conveyed in a song performed by the Cuban-born singer Celia Cruz. Set to the rhythms of a rumba cleverly fused with a back-beat, this dance song was titled simply, "Baila el rock and roll " (Come Dance the Rock and Roll):

The mambo created a rage in
    New York
	El mambo hizo furor en
	    Nueva York

But the cha-cha-chá pushed it aside.	pero el cha-cha-chá lo derrotó.
Now a new rhythm has appeared	Ahora un nuevo ritmo apareció
and it's the restless rock 'n' roll.	y es el inquietante rock and roll.
Come and dance rock 'n' roll	Venga a bailar, el rock and roll
Come and feel its richness.	venga a sentir, de su sabor.
With its beat, you will feel	Con su compás, tu sentirás
a real sensation.	una deliciosa sensación.
Such is the new rhythm,	El nuevo ritmo es
tell me if you want to know it, ah!	díme si lo quieres conocer, ¡ah!
Come so that you learn it,	Ven para que aprendas
rock 'n' roll.	el rock and roll.

It's the rage of New York	Es el furor de Nueva York
and now it's arrived even here. . . .	y hasta aquí llegó. . . .
I'll offer it up to you.[7]	Te lo brindo yo.

For a society already attuned to the mambo the gyrating hips of Elvis Presley were scarcely scandalous. Rather, what would ultimately matter to Mexicans was rock 'n' roll's affronts to patriarchal values. Even the valence of singing in English came to have dual meaning: on one hand English conveyed a notion of cosmopolitanism, yet on the other it underscored the dangers of foreign cultural influence on the Mexican family.

The first Mexican recording to feature a style incorporating elements of the new rhythm was made by the orchestral leader Pablo Beltrán Ruiz, who in 1956 recorded an instrumental single on the RCA-Victor label titled simply (in English), "Mexican Rock and Roll." Within months, the jazzy rhythms and "youthful" feel of the new style caught on, and scores of orchestras, large and small, jumped on the rock 'n' roll bandwagon, contributing to what one author has described as the "de-tropicalization" of dance bands.[8] In effect, as audiences came to expect variety even the mambo lost its novelty and "was played along with *danzones* [a slower dance rhythm from Cuba] and North American rhythms, becoming [just] one rhythm more."[9] These other dance styles by no means disappeared, though their popularity among the young went into decline during the 1960s and did not recover until the advent of the cumbia (a rapid dance rhythm that originated in Colombia), which took the country by storm in the early 1970s.[10]

Rock 'n' roll's early popularity among adults must be seen not only in the broader context of a cultural tradition of incorporating novel dance fashions to suit urban popular tastes but as a reflection of the transformation in the relationship with the United States as well. As a result of closer ties established during World War II, a discourse of economic and diplomatic cooperation had supplanted the previous rhetoric of revolutionary nationalism. Hence, the big-band sound of orchestral leaders like Glenn Miller and the new, "jazzy" rhythms of early rock 'n' roll came to symbolize the modernizing forces that were every day working to transform Mexico from a rural-based economy to an urban, industrial one.[11] In one example, the Mexican actress Silvia Pinal promoted a hybrid invention of her own called the "can-rock," which would fuse "the old with the modern" in a new dance step: "The Can-Rock, as its name indicates, is a combination of the veteran Can-Can and the ultramodern Rock'n Roll. From the first, she has taken its [sexual] boldness and from the second, its moments of extravagant craziness. The result . . . is a modern dance within the reach of youth."[12] Appealing to an older generation already seeped in the styles of música tropical, rock 'n' roll thus offered a visual and corporal language for negotiating the impact of rapid modernization and of closer ties with the United States.

But before delving more deeply into the impact of rock 'n' roll on Mexican society during the late 1950s, it is important to address the concrete questions of how this music arrived and what impact it had on local artistic production. It is a curious and telling fact, for instance, that with the rise in consumption of rock 'n' roll there was also a rise in exports of "traditional" Mexican music (such as *rancheras* and boleros). In other words, the musical representation of Mexico abroad continued to be characterized by a stereotypical folkloric image of the mariachi, at the same time that more and more urban Mexicans (especially youth) were rejecting that style in favor of *música moderna,* a wide-ranging category that included rock 'n' roll. The role of transnational culture industries was intrinsic to this process of global dissemination, though at the same time Mexico's own recording companies also came to play an important part. It is important, therefore, to describe a portrait of the recording industry's landscape in which local companies both benefited from and competed with transnational interests.

TRANSNATIONAL AND LOCAL MARKETING STRATEGIES

Mexico's earliest recording studios were established in 1936 not by a transnational corporation but through the investment of local capital. Discos Peerless[13] was founded by the investors Eduardo Baptista Covarrubias and Gustavo Klinckwort Noehrenberg during a time when "foreign records had monopolized all sales and one could [only] acquire Mexican artists recorded abroad,"[14] who were then reexported back to Mexico. The company dedicated itself to discovering and contracting Mexican talent. Meanwhile, distribution of the influential RCA-Victor label took place under the administrative direction of Emilio Azcárraga Vidaurreta, who, with his son Emilio Azcárraga Milmo, would go on to found Mexico's television and broadcasting conglomerate, Telesistema, in 1955. Emilio Azcárraga Sr. worked for RCA-Victor from the company's start in Mexico in the 1920s (when it was just Victor) until the 1940s, when he apparently turned over his duties to his nephew Rogelio; "don Emilio," as he was known, had his sights set on larger projects. In the mid-1950s RCA established its own recording facilities, a move that led Rogelio Azcárraga to separate from RCA's distribution network and form a separate recording label, Orfeón, in 1957. Rogelio took with him not only invaluable experience learned while working as a distributor for the RCA-Victor label but a good portion of its artistic catalog as well.[15] Earlier, in 1947, CBS had also established recording facilities. And around that time a second Mexican company, Musart, was founded as a result of a split between Baptista and Klinckwort, the founders of Peerless. Thus, by the mid-to-late 1950s, five major record companies—three owned by local capital (Peerless, Orfeón, Musart) and two transnationals (RCA, CBS)—dominated production and distribution in the Mexican market for music.

The move into Mexico by RCA and CBS, the two transnational companies with production facilities in place by the 1950s, was part of a broader strategy of market expansion by these companies not only in Mexico but also elsewhere in the world, and not only in the field of music but in entertainment and electronics generally. A steady increase in Department of Defense contracts subsidized development of technology in such areas as electrical wiring and magnetic tapes, while the advent of television and improvements in phonographic recordings and playback apparatuses generated an unprecedented demand for new consumer products. Such product diversity was aptly revealed on the cover of a 1957 *Annual Report* for the electronics firm, Audio Devices, Inc., a company with important contractual relations with both CBS and Capitol Records in the sale of magnetic recording tape.[16] The cover of the report displays an image of a record album with a rocket blasting across the inside label; superimposed on the album is a reel of magnetic recording tape and a computer adapter wire.[17] In another example, an advertisement for RCA reproduced in its *Annual Report* read: "If you sometimes fly . . . Enjoy music . . . Use a bank . . . Worry about the weather . . . Build missiles . . . Or send messages . . . RCA is part of your life."[18]

International sales and investments were central to the growth strategy of these transnationals. With the promotion of import-substitution strategies in Latin America, there was an overall reduction of manufactured consumer goods exports (household and consumer appliances) from the United States to the larger industrializing economies. But it also meant that new marketing niches could be exploited by companies that directly serviced developing economies' needs in the manufacture of these same products. RCA's 1957 *Annual Report*, for instance, noted that "tubes and transistors were widely chosen as multipurpose tools of electronic progress particularly in Italy, France, Sweden, Denmark, Brazil, Cuba and Mexico" and pointed out that sales were ahead of the previous year.[19] Import-substitution strategies also indirectly encouraged the location of subsidiary plant operations (often owned via joint-capital ventures) in industrializing centers of Latin America. As a 1958 CBS *Annual Report* noted, "A large part of the Free World is embarked upon a program of industrialization. This is especially true of Latin America, our most convenient market. . . . In the future, exporters must look toward foreign manufacturing and licensing for additional income. As the larger nations develop local industries, they will need to purchase components, machinery, and heavy equipment."[20] Thus CBS jointly operated a television picture-tube plant in Buenos Aires, while owning a minority interest in television assembly plants in Argentina and Peru, both of which produced television sets under the trademark label "CBS-Columbia."[21] RCA proudly acknowledged its role in marketing its products around the world: "Electronics has become a major unifying influence in the modern world, linking the continents by radio and fostering the exchange of knowledge and culture through the extension of broadcasting and recording services. RCA, through its world-wide network of commercial communications and its development of television and radio systems for service in many nations, has contributed importantly to this global pattern."[22] This global pattern of the transnationals' direct participation in the development and distribution of communications and entertainment technology—not to mention programming content—intensified throughout the 1960s.

Beginning in the mid-1950s, musical production and distribution became an increasingly significant part of overall corporate revenue. The boom in record sales generally during the 1950s can be attributed to several factors. For one, technological advances and economies of scale rendered increasingly more effective sound equipment at a lower price. Secondly, economic growth in the recovering European economies and in the modernizing Third World economies, coupled with a shift in demographics, also meant that more young people had available income to spend on leisure activities. Finally, the advent of rock 'n' roll, though initially anathema to the large record companies (with the important exception of RCA, where Elvis Presley recorded), quickly proved its earnings potential, and soon afterward it radically transformed the record industry itself. As Kenneth Shore writes, rock 'n' roll "was to become the dominant force in popular music not because of the plans of the major companies, but in spite of them."[23] Thus in its *Annual Report* for 1958, for example, CBS reported that "the [Columbia Records] Division has not attempted so far to meet the large demand for rock and roll recordings,"[24] a position that only began to change with Columbia's contracting of folk-rock and rock groups after the mid-1960s.

International sales of records nonetheless became an important component of overall corporate expansion. While, unfortunately, the corporate records that might reveal precise sales volume for specific artists are missing, by piecing together the available sources we can still glean a sense of music's increasing contribution to profits.[25] In 1957 RCA was reporting that record sales were 18 percent higher than the year before, with broadening markets in Australia, England, Germany, Sweden, Venezuela, and South Africa contributing to the increase in profits.[26] Likewise for CBS 1956 sales volume of records was up 50 percent from the previous year, a record high for the company: "Not only from Maine to California but from Sweden to South Africa, Brazil to Japan, record sales increased. Sales by Columbia's globe-girdling network of subsidiaries and affiliates increased 50% over the preceding year. In established markets such as Europe, record sales established new high levels."[27] A photograph of workers unloading crates of records appeared with the following caption to underscore the importance of Third World markets: "International record boom increases volume of Columbia's foreign subsidiaries, such as this one in Mexico."[28] In 1958 Columbia Records held its first Latin American Convention in New York City, out of which emerged a strategy to target even more aggressively the Caribbean and South American markets. By 1959 the company could report that "[f]or the first time, records from Columbia's Argentine subsidiary were sold in other South American markets," while new licensing arrangements had been established in Argentina, Uruguay and Peru.[29] Also, for the first time in the fall of 1960 a vice-president for Latin American operations was named. With recording studios now established in Argentina and Mexico, manufacturing facilities in many other countries, and licensing arrangements throughout the hemisphere, CBS claimed 30 percent of the Latin American market.[30]

Mexico was particularly suited for the commercialization of popular music. With its 240 radio stations Mexico ranked fourth in the world, behind the United States, China, and Brazil.[31] In terms of production quality, according to Mariano Rivera Conde, vice president of RCA-Víctor Mexicana, Mexican radio and television "far outstrip[ped] its competition in Latin America."[32] At the start of 1960 *Variety* was reporting that Mexico's outlook for the year ahead was one of optimism, "that it will be a new cycle of prosperity and advances in the commercial, technical and artistic branches" of the broadcasting industry.[33] The strength of radio and television was offset, however, by the fact that just over a quarter of a million homes actually owned record players and sales of albums ran in the single digits, not tens of thousands, much less millions.[34]

Though the number of integral subsidiary plant operations—those which combined recording studios and record-pressing facilities—was still limited to a select number of countries, the transnationals increasingly pushed to have their label distributed in a local market. This might even involve the pressing and distribution of one transnational's record label by another transnational, depending on the makeup of the market. In other cases, records were directly imported from a subsidiary operation in one country into another foreign market, a practice that became increasingly costly as nations began to erect protective tariff barriers to cultural products. Nevertheless, an emergent common strategy was to establish a base for subsidiary operations in one country that could reach across to a regional market.[35] For example, production facilities in Argentina readily served the Southern Cone and Andean markets, while a Mexican-based subsidiary could serve the Caribbean and Central American markets. This approach was copied by the Mexican company, Peerless. In teaming up with the transnational recording company Polydor (which itself later entered the Mexican market directly), the two companies sought to establish a joint-venture subsidiary operation in Argentina or Uruguay, "with the object being to elaborate and distribute Mexican and European music to the countries of the extreme south of the continent."[36]

RCA's strategic use of its Mexican subsidiaries during this period is particularly revealing. It demonstrated the coincidence of a low-wage subsidiary operation, on one hand, with the exploitation of a native product for global export on the other. Beginning in 1959, RCA began to manufacture records at its Mexico City plant for export to the United States. RCA was responding to the small yet still significant demand for what it called "international records"; that is, foreign-language hits and specific market niches, such as Mexican American communities in the Southwest. While the total volume of foreign-language music was steadily increasing, the per-unit sales of any particular record remained relatively small. This did not justify large-scale production at greater expense within the United States. However, "the smaller and more flexible Mexican factory [could] operate profitably with such low-unit sales."[37] Targeting the Mexican American population in the United States also affected CBS, which shifted its Columbia Records' catalog accordingly.[38] At the same time, RCA launched a major new initiative to market "the best of [Mexican] folklore music and interpreters" to markets throughout the United States, Latin America, Europe, and the Far East.[39]

In fact, according to *Variety*, 1959 was a "banner year" for the Mexican

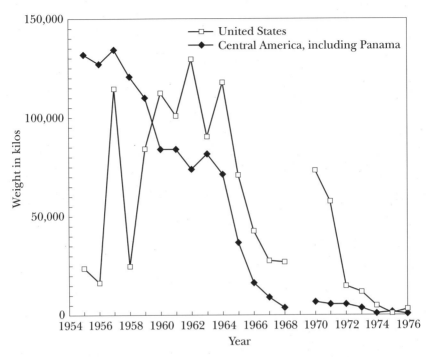

Graph 1.   Record exports from Mexico, 1955–1976. Source: *Anuario del Comercio Exterior* (Mexico City: Banco Nacional de Comercio Exterior, 1955–1976); data unavailable for 1969.

recording industry, with sales increases of 15–25 percent, topping the previous year's peak.[40] Led by what a government report termed "the sentimental richness of Mexican music,"[41] record exports soared, and a story in *Variety* noted the industry's "assault on foreign markets"[42] (see Graph 1). Orfeón was no onlooker to this global marketing strategy. In late 1958 the company could already boast of distribution pacts with Cuba, Puerto Rico, Colombia, Venezuela, Argentina, Brazil, Canada, Spain, France, the United States, and parts of Africa. Perhaps anticipating a protective tariff against imports, the company launched a major expansion of its Discos Mexicanos (DIMSA) facilities during 1959 with the goal of "mak[ing] its recording studios one of the most modern in Mexico."[43] In October of that year the company announced plans for its label to be introduced into Japan and other Far Eastern markets, thus approaching its goal "to achieve worldwide distribution" by the turn of the decade.[44] "In general," concluded the *Variety* report, "the Mexican industry as a whole looks forward to inauguration of new ideas in production, exploitation and distribution of disks—not only in Mexico but in the world market."[45]

This strategy of internationalizing Mexican artists continued through-out the 1960s and was duplicated by the other major record companies.[46] All Mexican performers under contract with CBS Records, for instance, were now considered for an "exploitation plan" to include "globe circling tours."[47] And in a reflection of the growing significance of the Mexican American population in the United States, in 1962 RCA also initiated an-other shift in tactics. No longer would distributors have to order directly from the RCA-Víctor Mexicana subsidiary. Recordings made in Mexico were now pressed directly in the United States, assuring both quicker dis-tribution in the U.S. market and greater promotion for the artists.[48]

If the record companies are to be credited with the promotion of Mexi-can music beyond the nation's borders, extending the nation's repertory of rancheras and romantic ballads to such disparate markets as Argentina, Ja-pan, and Holland, at the same time these same companies served as vehicles for the torrent of foreign tunes into the Mexican market. Between 1956 and 1959 record imports surged to a new high, leading to talk of a govern-ment ban on imports to protect local industry.[49] In early 1959, for example, *Variety* reported that a "flood of new disks bearing foreign labels and fea-turing internationally known singers and orchestras have appeared on the local market."[50] Rock 'n' roll was, of course, part of that torrent, though it was by no means alone. Moreover, access to imports, including rock 'n' roll, was restricted by economics, a fact adjusted somewhat as local press-ings accommodated and later displaced such demand. As Eréndira Rincón explains:

> The fact is that people who had access to that music were those with money. Of course, because it was difficult to get a hold of . . . everyone talked about it, and the collections were like treasuries. When someone found out about a recording of such and such and some friend lent it to him, or whatever, it was like a status boost. "I've got the original re-cording of whoever" and like that person became a total star for the next few days, until the rest of us got it as well.[51]

With those words, let us now return to our story of rock 'n' roll's impact and the transformation of urban culture during the late 1950s.

ROCK 'N' ROLL AS A METAPHOR OF DISORDER AND PROGRESS

The transformation of rock 'n' roll from an adult musical style to one adopted for and aimed at youth was not long in coming. In an important difference from rock 'n' roll's reception in the United States, where it was first experienced by working-class teenagers and was later appropriated by middle- and upper-class youth, in Mexico this process was essentially reversed. Rock 'n' roll began primarily as a middle- and upper-class phenomenon, not only for its associations with a modernizing aesthetic but especially because of its limited access. Most records were imported, and ownership of record and tape players was extremely limited. On the other hand, radio, jukeboxes, and films did offer an important mass cultural space that could be shared by a diverse audience. But on the whole, it seems that rock 'n' roll and its attendant youth paraphernalia largely excluded the lower classes until the late 1960s, when for other reasons this began to change.[52]

If in the United States the central tension encoded in rock 'n' roll during the 1950s was between Anglo and African American culture, in Mexico what came to matter in the public discourse was the association of rock 'n' roll (and later rock) with *desmadre*. An offensive, lower-class slang word, desmadre expresses a notion of social chaos introduced by the literal "unmothering" of a person or situation.[53] This stands in antithesis to that other Mexican phrase, buenas costumbres, which encapsulates all that is proper and correct—"family values," as we might say in the United States. In challenging the social rules contained in buenas costumbres, the irreverent, raucous spirit of the youth culture threatened to undermine the very patriarchal values of parental authority that permeated middle-class social values. As Rincón describes it, buenas costumbres meant: "[o]f course not saying bad words; or for example if guests arrived who were older than you, you had to show them the utmost courtesy: very clean clothes, treat them with the appropriate respect, give them a kiss on the cheek if they were close to the family, help your mother prepare everything necessary to receive them, and so on. The men did not have to do any of this; men simply didn't even enter into this category of thinking."[54] In these unwritten social rules, daughters were subordinate to sons, and sons to fathers. As a saintly figure, in her abnegation the mother acted as the moral fabric of the family unit.[55] Through her passed the social values necessary for proper upbringing. The father, on the other hand, instilled respect for authority via a stern benevolence backed by the threat of punishment. This was of course an idealization, but there was a great deal of truth in how such values were manifest in middle-class life. Reflecting on this, Rincón continued:

> My father was the ultimate authority; apparently everything worked and functioned according to what he said. But for that reason, my father had it quite well. He took charge of intervening in disputes when

he wanted to; and when he didn't want to, he didn't. He had that privilege. While in reality, the standard for everyday behavior was set by
my mother. She used the name of my father almost like a "monster";
he was like a god. If you were good, your father was going to be happy,
and if you were bad your father was going to hit you. Actually, my father never hit me. He was very different in that sense. He was very
sensitive and wise, but still very comfortable [in his role].[56]

These social values at the familial level reflected in microcosm the idealized
patriarchal state, in which the Virgin of Guadalupe (coopted by the PRI as
a patron image of national identity) played the role of the suffering mother,
and the president the commanding voice of the father. The very notion of
a "Revolutionary Family," a term originating in the late-1920s corporatist
arrangement of societal actors, directly reflected this patriarchal structure.
Respect for one's parents and elders—in a gendered, hierarchical manner—
was to be inculcated in the family and generalized for society. Thus, the "unmothering" of the social order—the literal interpretation of desmadre—
connoted the failure of parents and society as a whole to instill those
essential moral values (respect, suffering, discipline) embraced by buenas
costumbres. In particular, however, women bore a disproportionate responsibility for this cultural outlook. They were expected to retain their
"purity" (both as virgins until marriage and as suffering saints afterward),
while men were expected to demonstrate their virility. Hence, when societal alarms began ringing over the breakdown of buenas costumbres,
the "lax morality" of young women was a central target. Boys, too, were
blamed, not for dispensing of their role as machos (that will come later,
when they begin to let their hair down), but rather for turning their virile
energies against the sacrosanct values of patriarchal authority itself.

Clearly a number of factors relating to the modernization process had
begun to transform, if not undermine, the framework of buenas costumbres, such as the entry of women into the workforce, rural-urban migration patterns (which separated and placed new stresses on families), and the
rising incidence of divorce.[57] But perhaps no single factor was as dramatically significant as the irreverent, raucous spirit of the new youth culture,
embodied in such mass cultural male icons as Marlon Brando, James Dean,
and Elvis Presley. These figures not only offered new role models of confrontation in the home but immediately overshadowed the official heroes of
the Revolution, whose own exaggerated masculinities had become a direct
extension of the patriarchal state itself.[58] Arguably, a postrevolutionary nationalism that openly celebrated the virile revolutionary figure had ironically laid the groundwork for a different vision of heroic masculinity: the

youthful, gallant outcast who rode a motorcycle, raced cars, or strummed his electric guitar.

Yet, at the same time, rock 'n' roll also embodied a modern lifestyle that appealed to many adults' sense of progress and prosperity, especially the desire to be viewed by the outside world as advanced. Indeed, rather than fearing rock 'n' roll's associations with savagery, many middle- and upper-class adults eagerly latched onto rock 'n' roll as a status of modernity. From 1956 to 1959 the Mexican public was galvanized by the discussion of rock 'n' roll's transformative impact on society. But there was much more at stake in this debate than simply acceptance or nonacceptance of the new youth culture. Rock 'n' roll and its attendant youth culture had opened up an important discursive space not only for boys—who readily identified with the lonely male hero battling against the odds—but also for girls, who were challenged to break free of the traditional mold of proper behavior delineated by buenas costumbres. At risk was the cultural fabric of patriarchy deemed essential to social order in the family and, by extension, the nation itself.

Mexican advertisements for films imported from the United States often adopted a marketing strategy aimed at highlighting the notion of rock 'n' roll as an agent of modernity, while downplaying its associations with disorder. Many of these advertisements, for instance, underscored the notion that rock 'n' roll was an authentically modern movement sweeping the entire planet. Mexico, these advertisements explained, was caught up in a cosmopolitan wave that demanded the participation of all its citizenry. Bill Haley's *Rock around the Clock* (1957), for instance, was advertised as "the first American film with the authentic and provocative rhythm that is making the entire world crazy." Evoking the image of a nation unified on its march toward the same modern endpoint, the advertisement added: "Now all of Mexico dances rock 'n' roll!" Another advertisement for the film warned, "Try not to move . . . And see if you can!"[59] For adults perhaps already feeling outpaced by youth, advertisements for Haley's second film, *Don't Knock the Rock* (1957), offered the prospect of free dance lessons: Signed photographs of Bill Haley, "The King of 'Rock 'n Roll'," were to be given away, along with "certificates to learn how to dance 'Rock 'n Roll' courtesy of the Arthur Murray Dance Studio."[60] Significantly, these films did not target an exclusively youth audience. Rather, rock 'n' roll was promoted as a family affair. "A film and a rhythm for all ages!" read the announcement for *Rock around the Clock*. This language reflected an association in the public mind of rock 'n' roll with modern values and thus appealed to an image of the Mexican family as one attuned to modern times.

The Mexican film industry wasted no time in marketing native films with a rock 'n' roll content. Some of these simply dealt with the rhythm as a new dance style with little emphasis on youth per se. In this category, for instance, were musical-variety films such as *Música de siempre* (1956) and *Locura musical* (1956), films that took advantage of the "formula of much music and little argument." [61] These mostly showcased local performers interpreting hits from across a broad spectrum of styles, ranging from mambo to rock 'n' roll. But the industry also directly participated in the emergent debate over rock 'n' roll and the youth culture by producing a series of films throughout the 1960s that, while at times building on a long-standing genre of musical dramas and comedies, also sought to emulate the marketing success of rock 'n' roll-based dramas originating in the United States. These films largely fell into two categories: those that displayed an image of ebullient youth symbolic of the modernizing aspirations of the country itself and those that displayed an image of youth as delinquent and desmadre, disrespectful of authority and, at times quite literally, parentless. While the latter category always ended with a moral message, the image of rebellious youth that was presented had an important impact and often caused controversy.

The realization of these and other B films was regarded by critics as a distasteful collapse of the so-called Golden Age (Epoca de Oro) in Mexican cinema dating from the 1940s, and it is today regarded as a nadir in native cinematic production. Why the sudden decline of the highly regarded Mexican cinema came about is complex. According to the film historian Carl Mora, the collapse is ironically attributed at least in part to the very commercial success the industry once enjoyed. Buttressed by state subsidies and reined in by a closed actors' union, film production became increasingly reliant on the formulaic success of the "star system." Meanwhile, competition from imports (U.S. films shown in Mexico City between 1953 and 1958 averaged more than 200 per year, compared with fewer than 100 Mexican films for the same period) encouraged a crass commercialism "to make films more competitive on the international scene." [62] Mora continues, "The basic problem was that as films became costlier and had to be produced on an assembly-line basis, there was ever-greater reliance on 'formulas'—*comedias rancheras;* films based on dance fads—cha-cha [sic], charleston, rock and roll; comedies; lacrimogenic melodramas; horror vehicles à la Hollywood; American-style westerns; and 'super-hero' adventures in which masked cowboys or wrestlers took on a variety of evildoers and monsters. Quality plummeted but production increased." [63] What Mora misses, however, is an understanding that the new characters and themes—such as "El Santo" and the young rebel—served popular interests, especially among the growing youth population, in ways in which the older films could not. Though today these films are largely denied the prestige accorded to the classic cinema which predates them, that should not necessarily be a measure of their popularity and influence at the time.[64]

The films that focused on youth as a symbol of progress and modernity shared several themes. For one thing, they were all shot against the backdrop of the capital and, more specifically, the newly inaugurated (1954) National Autonomous University (Universidad Nacional Autónoma de México, or UNAM). This provided an opportunity to showcase the modern features of the capital and, hence, the nation's progress. Second, these films are virtually devoid of the politics of youth rebellion. In large part this is because parents are conveniently marginalized in the plots. Yet even the music itself is presented without the attendant controversy that began to surround it in real life. Rock 'n' roll was mostly treated as a new musical rhythm—now, directly associated with youth—in competition with, yet inevitably triumphing over, alternative musical styles. Members of an older generation who resist the rhythm are presented as stodgy and out of touch with the times, as in *Al compás del rock'n roll* (1956). Here a group working to thwart rock 'n' roll is represented as a clique of closed-minded older women called "The League of Virtue," a clear takeoff on the real-life conservative parents' organization, The Mexican League of Decency.

Third, not only do these films tend to avoid or trivialize generational conflicts, but social and class divisions are virtually ignored. As Emilio García Riera comments on the film *Viva la juventud* (1955), "[the students] live in a species of euphoric limbo and totally set apart from the social and political concerns of the student world."[65] The image of Mexico these films present is narrowly defined. A close association between rock 'n' roll, youth, and material progress is emphasized, and the young are presented as gleeful students without economic hardships. In fact, the films offer a completely flattering, but totally unrealistic, portrayal of university life: students all seem to have cars and live sheltered from economic (or political, for that matter) hardship. When Mexico's urban underside is depicted, such as briefly in a scene from *La locura del rock'n roll* (1956), this comes at night, with its associations of darkness and danger. In fact, if anything, rock 'n' roll becomes a means of mediating generational and class conflicts. For example, in *La locura del rock'n roll* latent class tensions between students at the working-class Polytechnic Institute and the more prestigious UNAM are displaced by the staging of a rock 'n' roll battle of bands from the two university systems. Against the backdrop of fights breaking out in the audience, the droll voice of an elderly narrator closes the film by explaining: "As you can see, the bonds of fraternity which unite students from the University and Polytechnical Institute are strong. Because everyone loves one another." In real life, rivalry between the two university systems was mediated in part by U.S.-style football games. But resentment and class antagonism also characterized students' political views of one another and largely kept the two systems from organizing jointly until the 1968 student movement.

In contrast to an earlier genre of cabaret films that centered on the "dark" side of urban nightlife and, for women especially, the attendant economic and moral hardships,[66] these films suggested the possibility of rock 'n' roll as a vehicle for social mobility. Forming a rock 'n' roll band was identified with "clean" business practices and staying within the boundaries of traditional respect for one's elders; youth, after all, only want to have fun. At the same time, the more modern notion of women exerting varying degrees of independence—and the implied challenges to machismo that this presents—is also explored in these films. For example, in *La locura del rock'n roll* a group of women students and their boyfriends decide collectively to form a dance band. But when the women are hired as an all-female group to perform música tropical in a nightclub, the men find themselves not only jobless but without an identity as *performers*. Meanwhile, the women quickly discover that their largely male audience is less interested in their music than in their bodies. Still, their performances afford them an economic security independent of their boyfriends, a fact that begins to rile the men. One night the girls, discovering that the boys are penniless, invite them to eat tacos. Considered a bold affront to traditional gender roles, one of the boyfriends angrily responds: "The problem with our times is that men have to feel like fools. Men are losing their quality as men. It makes me feel ashamed!" "But that's the good thing about our age!" his girlfriend retorts, clearly proud of her newfound economic and social independence, a reflection of real-life changes in middle-class gender roles. At this, the boyfriend stands up and challenges the rest of his friends to leave: "Whoever stays has no shame," he declares, before leading the boys away. Left alone, however, the women immediately become vulnerable to being accosted by several wandering men from the street. Their shouts bring the boys back running, thus offering the opportunity to redeem their manhood (and rectify the imbalanced gendered framework) by beating up the vagrants. Yet while this reminds the women of their proper place—their vulnerability in a man's world—it does not solve the conflicting structural reality of their mounting independence. Hence, the boys decide to battle the girls on their own terms, by forming a separate band—a rock 'n' roll band.

Here the boys have an important advantage. By 1956 the figure of Elvis Presley had transformed the performance style of rock 'n' roll away from a dance-orchestral emphasis toward the lone masculine interlocutor. Elvis, at least for Mexico, assured a specific role for men as interpreters of rebellion, making intrinsic the connection between musical performance and masculinity. Boys could emulate Presley's musical virility, and they did so as a means of testing and winning over girls, whose admiration for Elvis went beyond his dark, handsome features to his gutsy pride in the face of adult-laid obstacles.[67] Rehearsing relentlessly—"And we're playing pure rock and roll, man!" one of them shouts in English—the boys try to undercut their girlfriends' status, as the big competition of the bands approaches. Learning of their boyfriends' new strategy, the girls themselves now switch to rock 'n' roll but realize that without a male singer their image is doomed to failure. At this they secretly offer a job to one of the boys, "Richard," hiring him as their lead. Come the final competition the girls will win, but because of their new lead who looks, swaggers, and even sings—in English—just like Elvis (a fact not lost on movie advertisements):

> Give me rock 'n' roll
> Because I like it so much
> It's driving me insane.
> I really don't know what I'm doing!

With this, the females in the audience are sent into a frenzy, mobbing Richard on stage after the song.[68] "Elvis" has thus stolen the show, and, although he has won the contest for the otherwise all-female band, victory comes at the cost of reinscribing the boundaries of gendered performance: while Richard shakes and croons like a real rebel, the girls have acknowledged their subordinate role by changing into bunny suits for the performance.

The spurts of English-language dialogue and song also constituted an important aspect of these films. This reflected the explicit identification of rock 'n' roll culture with the United States, and Anglo society in particular. When one of the characters in *La locura del rock'n roll* asks in English, "Have you heard that rock 'n' roll? That new rhythm?" he is clearly identifying with an image of rock embodied in Elvis Presley and Bill Haley. The link between rock 'n' roll and modernity was thus grounded in the image of White performance. Secondly, English was fashionable among the upper classes, an indication not only of one's cosmopolitanism but also of one's social achievements in an economy increasingly tied to the United States. Most children of the upper classes had the opportunity to study and travel abroad; flaunting one's English became a recognized sign of wealth and privilege. For the middle classes, learning English was not only socially prestigious but also enhanced one's job prospects; this was reflected in the scores of English-language schools that proliferated during this period.[69] However, there was also a third interpretation, though one not invoked by this category of films. This was the association of rock 'n' roll sung in English with the *breakdown* of social order, exemplified in films such as *Blackboard Jungle*. Here English reflected not order and progress but an excessive modernity bordering on chaos.

Thus if rock 'n' roll had an implicit identification with modern values—underscored in Mexican films by the incorporation of the English language and trivialized gender conflicts—there was also an unruly underside associated with this imported rhythm. One reviewer of Bill Haley's *Don't Knock the Rock*, for instance, described it as "simultaneously complying with the two missions that the earlier [Haley film] fulfilled: arousing sympathy and taste for this musical rhythm . . . and provoking antipathy and repulsion." "If at times [the film] is enjoyable because of its music, at other moments it seems frankly provocative. One has the impression that the propaganda of this type of music has been making not a slowly convincing and delicate conquest, but [one] of violent shocks [and] bold challenges to the public, which at times reacts in energetic protest."[70]

A landmark film that established the association between the new youth culture and delinquency worldwide was *Blackboard Jungle* (1955), the first film to include a rock 'n' roll song (Bill Haley's "Rock around the Clock") as part of its sound track. Not only did inclusion of the song mark "the beginning of rock and roll's full breakthrough as a popular music form among the young," it "also laid the groundwork for a firm association of rock and roll and juvenile delinquency."[71] The film's title was translated as *Semilla de maldad* (Wicked Seed), and Mexican advertisements followed the pattern set by U.S. ads for the film in concentrating on the presumed licentiousness of Margaret Hayes, who plays an unwed schoolteacher in a rough city district. The Mexican translation, however, directly tied Hayes's loose morals to the unruly social order the film depicts. The two advertisements were distinct in other ways as well. In the U.S. promotion the crucial scene when Margaret Hayes is attacked and nearly raped in the school library is a central visual of the advertisement, her expression of sheer terror highlighted by the accompanying text: "The Scream in the Classroom!" Underneath this movie still is another shot of Hayes, this time provocatively adjusting a stocking. In the actual film, an ambiguous flirtation is established between Glenn Ford (who is newly married) and Hayes after he rescues her from the library attack and then takes it upon himself to crack open the psychology of the gangs that terrorize the school. This flirtation is then exploited by a young student seeking to avenge Ford's "tough-love" approach in his classroom. The U.S. version of the advertisement thus reads: "She was a teacher who was indiscreet enough to wear a tight skirt! What happened then could only happen in this big-city school where tough teenagers ran wild!"[72] The Mexican promotion also focused on Hayes's perceived sexual indiscretion but reconfigured the representations of physical danger as well as sexual flirtation. Instead of a movie still of Hayes in a short skirt, advertisements featured a drawing that depicted a voluptuous, "Latin-looking" Hayes—wearing a shoulderless blouse and a long skirt—parading in front of a school-yard fence. Several menacing and lust-driven youths reach out for her through the bars. Like the U.S. advertisement, her look is one of oblivion—or perhaps silent seduction—to the lascivious danger she has incited around her. The announcement reads: "The drama of youth led astray! The indiscreet [female] teacher provoked the students in a school where the youth let their malevolent instincts run wild. There the young [female] teachers are in danger and violence reins! You will not be able to forget what happened easily!" "For Adults Only," the advertisement warns.[73]

This focus on the "loose morals" of Margaret Hayes, the "indiscreet teacher" in question, exploited societal fears that associated rock 'n' roll culture with a flagrant disregard for buenas costumbres. In the film, Hayes's flirtatiousness directly challenged the parameters of social behavior, both as a daughter and as a potential mother. By acting unwomanly—by being economically independent and flirting with a married man—Hayes represented the transformation of feminine values that threatened to destabilize the system: without the firm commitment of a woman to her husband and home, the "malevolent instincts" of males are unleashed and the unmothering of the social order—desmadre—will follow. But the real issue was rock 'n' roll culture, which in the film presents an image of youth defying authority and thus, by definition, patriarchy. The moment the son (student) returns the gaze of the father (teacher) he rewrites the gestures of authority that have held the system in place.

Less than a year following *Blackboard Jungle*, a Mexican film that tied together the themes of delinquency, licentiousness, and rock 'n' roll shocked the capital. Indeed, it was scant coincidence that the sound track for *Juven-

tud desenfrenada (1956) was none other than Bill Haley's "Rock around the Clock," performed in English by Mexico's young star Gloria Ríos.[74] In *Juventud desenfrenada* the issue of motherhood as an integral concept of patriarchy and social order was driven home in explicit terms. Revolving around the complex lives of various youth, ranging from lower-middle-class to upper-class backgrounds, not one of the characters has a firm foundation of parental love. Here mothers are either self-absorbed or malicious, and fathers are literally missing (replaced by a drunken or absent stepfather as a result of divorce). Lacking moral guidance from mothers too self-interested to care for their children's fates, the male characters all turn to a life of crime and drugs, the females to a life of prostitution.[75] At one point the distortion of motherhood becomes so blatant that "Carlos" is forced to call his mother "aunt" in public, to avoid embarrassing her politically connected second husband by revealing a previous marriage. "All parents are the same," Carlos spits out at one point; "They're all fakes." What resolution the film provides comes when the same Carlos agrees to marry his girlfriend (whom he had once tried to force into prostitution) upon a doctor's certification that she is really a virgin; throughout, we had been led to believe that she was raped by her stepfather. From a priest we are told, "Only faith and love of God can save our youth."

Proclaiming the film's "basis in real events," newspaper advertisements provoked potential viewers with the questions: "Where are today's youth headed? Are parents to blame for juvenile delinquency?"[76] This was an indirect reference to the real escalation in numbers of divorces throughout the country[77] and an emphasis on a consumer culture that, as far as editorialists were concerned, undermined the stability of a stern authority figure in the home and led to pampering rather than discipline. Recalled today by the Mexican film historian Emilio García Riera "as one of the most repugnant pictures ever made [for its] loathsome display and vile moral hypocrisy,"[78] *Juventud desenfrenada* nonetheless was significant in that it openly exploited societal fears of changes in Mexican family structure and the concomitant impact of youth culture. "In this production there was nothing made-up, everything was true," wrote a reviewer in a promotional article shortly after the film's release; the plot "was taken from the archives of the youth Tribunal."[79] As in *Blackboard Jungle*, the connection between lax values and social unmothering (highlighted by rape) is clearly stated, only this time with the more explicit tie-in to rock 'n' roll. Thus in a promotional poster for the film a woman (whose skirt falls above the knees) is depicted being attacked on a couch by a young man, with the words "Rock 'n' Roll!" just underneath in boldface type.[80] Newspaper advertisements likewise stressed the links between wanton youth and the new music, proclaiming, "Rock 'n' Roll! The rhythm that maddens youth." And despite the pretense that this was a film about youth, as with *Semilla de maldad* the warning "Adults Only!" separated it from that other class of rock 'n' roll films promoted as "family oriented." For in *Juventud desenfrenada,* potential viewers were also enticed with the knowledge that the young actress, Aida Araceli, sheds her clothes: "The Youngest Nude in the World," one advertisement boasted.[81]

In an all-out effort to promote the film and deflect conservative criticism of its content, a contest was held in which participants answered the question, "What was it that most impressed you about 'Juventud Desenfrenada'?"[82] The winners were a male doctor and a female student. The latter's answer was published in full by the newspaper *Excélsior:*

> I was impressed by the intelligence of the format of the film, which captured all of the psychological moments which youth of our time are passing through and which, unfortunately, our parents cannot appreciate because theirs was another era. The problem of misled youth that the film presented interested me intensely. But how can youth follow the good path if society offers us so few examples? The excess of money in some homes and the lack of culture and comprehension in others is one of the causes of this problem. The only salvation is that youth turn their eyes toward morality and religion.[83]

Juventud desenfrenada encapsulated the association between delinquency, rock 'n' roll, and the undermining of buenas costumbres that had begun to enter into the public discourse. As Federico Arana writes in describing the mounting impact of this and other related films, "The press did not cease to point out the horrible plague of rebellious youth, driven by a diseased and money-making spirit."[84]

REBELDISMO SIN CAUSA

As in the United States, reports of juvenile delinquency leapt onto the front pages of Mexican newspapers, and critics lost no time in associating the apparent crime wave with rock 'n' roll and the degenerative moral values it introduced. For many, these new values reflected not progress but affronts to the traditional roles of men, women, and children in society. Rock 'n' roll fostered an attitude of confrontation and chaos, reflected especially in what one author has labeled the "rich iconography of delinquency" that accompanied the new youth culture in the United States but that seems pertinent in part to Mexico as well: "The styles we associate with it— leather jackets, blue jeans, the 'ducktail' haircut, the preference for the motorcycle—were all associated in the consciousness of the 1950s with rebellious, discontented, working-class teenagers who were always 'at risk' for delinquency."[85] One significant difference in Mexico, however, was the fact that this youth culture did not percolate from the working classes upward but, rather, the reverse. Curiously, when Marlon Brando introduced his working-class gestures and speech to Mexico City audiences in *The Wild One* (1953), his character at one level reflected the outlaw aura of Pancho Villa, whom O'Malley labels "the rebel without a cause."[86] Villa, in fact, was the one revolutionary hero deemed too caustic by the state to incorporate into the official Revolutionary pantheon.[87] For in Brando, as in Villa, a model of insubordination was nurtured explicitly from the rootlessness of the lower classes. Seeing *The Wild One*, "the imitators of Marlon Brando look[ed] for that equivalent language, that similar mode of speaking, prohibited and subversive, which commits an outrage against buenas costumbres," writes the novelist Parménides García Saldaña.[88] In emulating Brando, Mexican middle-class youth were, of course, pursuing an image of working-class culture taken from the United States. Yet their linguistic material, at least, came from closer at hand. For that "equivalent language" that García Saldaña writes about was to be found among inhabitants of the lower-class barrios in Mexico City, the only ones "who have the words which come closest to the image of the [rebel] hero and his mode of speaking. . . . There [in the barrio] is the language: greasy, untidy."[89] This transgression of the grammatical boundaries that delineated class differences not only challenged a notion of "proper culture" but introduced the prospect of plebeian disorder as well. As Johnny Laboriel, lead singer of the band Los Rebeldes del Rock, recalls:

> Coming out of the film, *The Wild One* with Marlon Brando, I knocked out some guy. Can you imagine? It's incredible how much of an influence that whole scene was. We rode around on motorcycles, with chains. I got kicked out of military school. We copied everything from the films, which we saw in the matinees. You know, you want to stand out so you adopt the pose of the winner. You see a film where everyone's drinking and singing, and you want to stand out in life too, so you do the same. It's incredible, rock 'n' roll was this wild thing. That's why it became a culture unto itself. Our parents didn't even have time to tell us not to do it; it hit like an avalanche. It was really incredible.[90]

Whereas Marlon Brando in *The Wild One* glorified the language, attitude, and fashion of the working-class hoodlum, James Dean in *Rebel without a Cause* (1955) offered an image of the alienation and defiance of privileged youth.[91] If imitators of Brando introduced a threatening image of the plebeian released, the influence of Dean became associated in the public eye with material excess and political corruption. Upper-class youth, whose wealth gave them access to luxury consumer items, such as cars and motorcycles, found that they could brandish their insolence with impunity because of political connections and class status; they became derisively referred to as *los juniors*. As García Saldaña writes:

> The rebellion of the admirer of James Dean (his violations of law and order) served to demonstrate to the rest that Papa was an important and influential person in Mexico City. Little Dean felt rebelliously content racing around in Dad's car, showing off at parties that he was The Son of His Dad, embellishing himself in the role that Daddy had Lots of Money and Daddy gave him all the money he asked for to get English cashmere suits, clothing from the United States, gold bracelets, etc. This Dude played the part of Don Juan well, his car attracting all the girls from private colleges for merry people to fall in love with him.[92]

Indeed, in the public mind-set the relationship between these films and juvenile delinquency was so close that the press appropriated the phrase *rebeldismo sin causa* (rebellion without a cause) as its standard description for youth disorder. At the same time, attacks on delinquency also opened up a populist but safe political space in which abuses of power by the rich were publicly condemned. Reporting the capture of two youths for check fraud, for example, a newspaper article described them as "two perfect examples of what have been called 'rebels without a cause'—20 and 24 years old, good seeming and well dressed, from wealthy families, superior education, and great desires to become professional delinquents."[93]

Debates about the rise in delinquency were complicated by the fact that it was linked to mass culture introduced from the United States. This raised the larger security question of a generation of youth that had chosen to adopt the rebellious posture introduced by a foreign culture. Attacks on the youth culture thus became part of a larger critique of the mass media in general and the foreign mass media in particular, which were collectively regarded by intellectuals, the press, and eventually the government authorities as directly undermining the social fabric of Mexican society. For some, this became a question of cultural imperialism. The fact that national filmmakers emulated a formula of youth rebellion only contributed to the material for this debate. Indeed, the mass media provided a new discursive lens through which arguments over national identity, social stability, and patriarchy could be buttressed as well as reexamined.

CULTURE WARS AND THE BACKLASH AGAINST ELVIS PRESLEY

The tension between accepting rock 'n' roll as a modernizing agent and viewing it as the embodiment of a threat to social stability was manifested in the press and the public mind-set during the mid-to-late 1950s. This conflict mirrored the profound changes present in everyday life: the increased cultural and economic ties with the United States, manifested especially in the rising consumer culture; the rapid transformation of the urban environment, reflected in both the development of new public works and increased rural migration to the capital; a political environment in which the rhetoric of the Revolutionary Family belied the reality of a closed political system. The official heroes of the Revolution had come to have less relevance for a new generation of urban youth who discovered a closer connection with James Dean and Elvis Presley than with Benito Juárez or Emiliano Zapata, much less Jorge Negrete or Javier Solís (both renowned ranchera singers). This fact was not lost on concerned editorialists and members of the government. "Foreign influence, that which is established by stronger countries over those which are economically weaker," one writer editorialized, "shines itself directly in the environment. . . . James Dean is the mirror where today's youth look."[94] "The struggle is an arduous one," another editorial stated, "because concepts and habits from other countries and races have filtered into Mexico which differ diametrically from the nature of our lives and ideology."[95] Signposts of cultural hybridization were everywhere. While some may have seen this as heralding a liberalization of authoritarian values, others viewed the changes with alarm. The clearest culprit was the influence of an increasingly globalized mass-media culture, which transformed figures such as Brando, Dean, and Presley into teenage idols, whose dress, gestures, and even language became incorporated into the lexicon of everyday rebellion:

> The majority of these young punks are dressed extravagantly, not only Texan style [that is, blue jeans and boots] but in clothing never before admitted under the criterion that we have for these things, and imitating the styles which appear in the cinema, foreign magazines and among some exotic visiting artists. Becoming lost is the unity within the family and respect for one's elders, in the belief that the norms and customs that structured the home are now "old fashioned" and don't match up to the demands of modern development.[96]

Nothing less than the future direction of society itself was at risk in these cultural transformations.

What was at stake in the triumph of one discourse over the other was a cultural framework through which the process of modernization could be negotiated. At one extreme, embracing a version of rock 'n' roll stripped of meaningful social conflict suggested the possibility of experiencing the pleasures of modernity without the pain of the social costs of adjustment. At the other extreme, demonizing the youth culture by linking it with social disorder served as a prop to resist the unsettling transformations of an economy that was undergoing rapid changes in social and cultural values. In this, there was a curious coincidence of criticism from both conservatives and leftists. For example, the famed muralist David Alfaro Siqueiros, a life-long communist who was later jailed for his support of striking workers, was quoted in 1957 as saying: "Pornographic films and rock 'n' roll and its derivatives have [brought] Mexican youth to the border of an irredeemable moral crisis."[97] Rock 'n' roll had emerged as a central fixture in the struggle over the terms of Mexican modernity.

By the start of 1957, the mania for rock 'n' roll had begun to reach new heights. In January it was announced that Mexico City would stage its first "'Rock 'n Roll Festival' . . . with the participation of the most important bands, jazz groups and interpreters of this new rhythm." The public was invited "to take part in the [radio and television] transmission [by] dancing and singing rock'n roll."[98] As Federico Arana observes, "The public was so enthusiastic for the new rhythm that no one was shocked by the news appearing in the press that Elvis would be coming to Mexico," an event strongly lobbied against by the Mexican League of Decency.[99] Though Presley was said to have declined an invitation to participate in the festival, he donated a guitar, "an exact replica of the one which he uses, so that it can be presented to the best jazz group which interprets rock'n roll."[100] Shortly thereafter, a Mexico City radio station carried an exclusive interview with Presley. Calling him "a consecrated artist," a newspaper reviewer noted that the interview "plainly confirms the prestige of 'Champion of Musical Hits' which the radio-listening public of Mexico has granted to [Radio Exitos],"[101] one of two stations (Radio Mil was the second) dedicated to serving a younger-generation listening audience during the late 1950s.

The emergent cultural wars over rock 'n' roll, however, took a dramatic turn shortly thereafter. On 19 February a comment gleaned from an alleged border interview with Elvis Presley appeared in a sidebar of the gossip columnist, Federico de León, in which the rock 'n' roll star was quoted as saying, "I'd rather kiss three black girls than a Mexican." Two days later, a Mexican woman was quoted in the same column as saying, "I'd rather kiss three dogs than one Elvis Presley." At first unnoticed by the public at large, this exchange soon unleashed a torrent of anti-Presley criticism that sustained a powerful backlash against Presley and the mass media itself. Most people now dismiss the remark as completely false, some even attributing it to an act of political vengeance against Presley. For instance, Herbe Pompeyo of Polygram Records in Mexico City claims that a "high-up Mexican political figure" wanted to contract Presley for a private party, for which he sent the performer a blank check to fill in as he wished. Presley, according to the story, returned the blank check, so the politico, extremely offended, invented the storyline about Elvis not liking Mexican women.[102] For Arana, who went to great lengths to investigate the credibility of de León's citation, the quotation amounted to nothing short of a conspiracy by "government officials [and] the newspapers in which they collaborate"[103] to "liquidate the rock and roll monster"[104] that had been unleashed by the mass media. In fact, even at the time different commentators questioned the authenticity of the quotation. In one case, a writer drew the connection to conservative opponents seeking to "indefinitely proscribe this rhythm,"[105] as had recently occurred in Cuba. There, during the waning days of Fulgencio Batista's dictatorship, rock 'n' roll was denounced as "immoral and profane and offensive to public morals and good customs."[106] In an effort to defend his own honor—and record sales—Presley responded to the charges by answering that he "has never used disrespectful terms for Mexican women." Moreover, "a certified copy of this declaration" would be immediately available in Mexico for his fans.[107]

Fallout from the alleged comment, true or false, nonetheless had an immediate impact on the direction of public discourse. What is especially interesting is the way in which this response was couched in gendered terms, rather than directly challenging the comment as racist.[108] Radio Exitos, which only a short time before had received accolades for its exclusive interview with Presley, announced that it was now leading a boycott of the "insolent artist" after having read de León's column over the air. The station, described as "enjoying the largest youth audience in the capital," reportedly received "thousands of telephone calls from all social strata supporting the decision to completely suppress [Presley's] records."[109] The reporter who filed this story made little effort to hide his bias: "Quite commendable is the action taken by this radio station, which spontaneously came out in defense of the dignity of Mexican women." Next to the article is a large photograph of Presley, mouth open and eyes angled downward, in an open-collared shirt and sports jacket. The caption reads, "He's very manly," an assertion mocked by the accompanying text: "Dressed in woman's clothing, nobody would say he's a man."[110]

That Presley had gone from the epitome of virility to being called a transvestite was actually a short leap in gendered logic. By challenging the traditional boundaries of dance performance—for a man, shaking hips and contorting lips were considered "feminine" gestures—Presley had actually made himself vulnerable to the charge of *maricón* (homosexual). Attacking Presley thus became linked to a reaffirmation of Mexican masculinity, which had been undermined not only by the popularity of this imported idol (who shook his hips and sneered) but also by the "modern values" he heralded. His emasculation by the press can best be described as a rhetorical strategy for the strengthening of a heroic nationalism subverted by the transnational mass media. The latter were blamed for having introduced competing male icons of authority and, thus, for displacing an image of youth as obedient and of women, in particular, as the bearers of "proper education and values." Presley had institutionalized a gaze of defiance and a gesture of chaos—the confrontational, unbounded territory introduced by rock 'n' roll—which challenged society by its direct appeal to youth. After all, it was Presley and his ilk who, by seducing the hearts of young Mexican women (and inducing Mexican men to mimic him), had cast a spell on countless youth, drawing them away from the traditional values and national heroes propagated by the PRI. Questioning Presley's manliness was one way of undermining his authority as a sex symbol and role model.

The uproar over Presley's alleged remark came just days before the release of a musical-spoof film entitled *Los chiflados del rock'n roll.* By examining the transformation in marketing of this film we capture a glimpse of the significance of the Presley uproar. Roughly translated as, "Crazed for Rock'n Roll," the film featured renowned ranchera performers Agustín Lara, Pedro Vargas, and Luis Aguilar and thus fell well within the boundaries of a discourse on rock 'n' roll as novel musical style rather than youth rebellion. A reviewer noted that the film "neither exalted Presley, nor had the slightest relationship with his excesses."[111] But the timing was such that the producer, Guillermo Calderón, faced pressures from groups organizing against Elvis Presley to prevent the film's release.[112] Overnight, advertisements for the movie changed dramatically to incorporate the dispute over Presley. Whereas earlier advertisements had featured caricatured drawings of the featured artists, now they juxtaposed a series of well-armed, male "revolutionary" fighters (in large sombreros) firing point blank at a feminized Elvis Presley—tight pants revealing hips distorted to exaggeration—under the heading, "Die Elvis Presley!" (see Figure 1). Cheering on these "revolutionaries" are drawings of full-busted women in bikinis, Playboy-bunny versions of the legendary *adelitas* (female followers of the revolutionary struggle).[113] During this same period, leaders of the Federación Estudiantil Universitaria (FEU), a powerful student group linked to conservative elements of the government, planned "a gigantic protest against the dancer and actor . . . during which there will be a 'burning' of [Presley's] records . . . who, in public declarations, sought to defile the Mexican Woman."[114] Playing on this theme of a public bonfire, a subsequent advertisement for *Los chiflados* announced that the film was in its "second 'burning' week!" The text continued:

> Burn his records!
> His forelock!
> His photos!
> His guitar!
> Burn everything that you wish, but . . .
> Put yourself in a good mood by coming to a 'burn'
> With the true kings of fun and of Rock'n Roll![115]

A different advertisement for the film played even more directly on the idea of Mexican machismo as the safeguard of patriarchal values, this time by linking it with rock 'n' roll itself: "Long live the authentic kings of rock 'n' roll, valiant and 'profligate' . . . but incapable of lacking respect for a woman!" Adding emphasis to the notion that Mexican men were in fact *superior* to their U.S. counterparts, the text continued: "Even if she's light-skinned [*güera*] and doesn't speak Spanish!"[116] Mexicans, in other words, did not need an outsider to teach them how to be "real men." Moreover, they had their own men capable of performing rock 'n' roll (e.g. Agustín Lara), but within the gendered boundaries of respect that delineated buenas costumbres. This respect presumably preserved the modernizing aspects of rock 'n' roll along with its machismo, while policing it from falling into desmadre.

Complicating the public's response to Presley's remark were the contradictions encoded in the youth culture itself. On one hand, rock 'n' roll symbolized the leveling of an older order. The rock 'n' roll gesture—characterized by rupture and defiance—directly challenged the steady gaze of parental authority, substituting rebellion for obedience. Such defiance,

Figure 1. Following the scandal over Elvis Presley's alleged comment, movie advertisements for *Los chiflados del rock'n roll* changed dramatically. Source: *Excélsior,* 9 March 1957, A21.

in turn, opened up a critical space for women, who began to question their own subordinate role. This relationship between policing the boundaries of respect for one's elders and upholding patriarchal authority over women was made explicit in the conflict over Presley. One writer, for example, made little effort to hide his antagonism toward rock 'n' roll, emphasizing the view that Mexican honor and virility were at stake in the protests against Presley: "Fortunately the Mexican [man] has a high sense of dignity, respect for women, virility and authentic probity that loathes anything that offends the Mexican woman. The sentiment of repulsion toward the wretched and unsettling rhythm has flown toward the four cardinal points since we learned about the infamous insult that was hurled at our women from one of [Presley's] television programs in the United States."[117] To be sure, the most reactionary elements rallied to the cause of rock's expulsion. Federico de León, responsible for publishing the alleged Presley remark, thus wrote triumphantly (though prematurely) that "Mexico is celebrating the funerals of 'rock 'n' roll.'"[118]

On the other hand, rock 'n' roll embodied a concept of modernity that coincided with the progressive, consumer-oriented platform of the Revolutionary Family itself. Rock 'n' roll's spirit of innovation and restless energy offered an image of youthful exuberance and progressive change that symbolized a nation on the move, one bounding out of the poverty and backwardness associated with the pre–World War II period toward a new Mexico, allied with the United States and confident to be host of the Olympics in the decade ahead. Suppressing the styles of youth was a reflection of closed-mindedness, for one must keep pace with the times. "Youth of today," argued one writer, "shake to modern rhythms just as others before them did to the rhythms of their era."[119] In fact, the student group that organized the burning of Presley records, the FEU, sought to isolate Presley from the rock 'n' roll trend in general by announcing that the "struggle is not exactly against rock and roll, but against Presley who offended our women with his public remarks."[120] For the "modernizers," therefore, ultimately the question was how to censor the noxious influences of the mass media while retaining the modernizing elements so basic to an image of progress. "The advantage" for Mexico, according to one editorialist, "is that in spite of the 'rock and rollers,' our youth, in the majority, have not lost their sense of responsibility toward their country, the family, and themselves."[121] Preserving these values within the framework of a modernizing ideology was the task at hand. Hence the battle against Presley became less a struggle against rock 'n' roll per se, except by the rhythm's most ardent detractors, than a struggle to protect the buenas costumbres that undergirded a patriarchal society and state.

THE *KING CREOLE* RIOT

A second incident involving Elvis Presley, this time a riot at the screening of his film *King Creole*, occurred in May 1959 at the Américas Cinema in Mexico City. Newspaper announcements for the film, whose title was translated as *Melodía siniestra* (Sinister Melody), had appeared only the day before. Moreover, these were sparse and lacked the graphics that usually accompanied films of the rock 'n' roll genre. One, for example, simply proclaimed: "Elvis Presley. The idol of the young in his first great dramatic performance." This was not to be a family affair: "Adults Only," the advertisement intoned.[122] According to newspaper accounts, the unrest began when more than 600 "rebels without a cause" entered the theater without paying. Taking to the balcony section, they "dedicated themselves to destroying the seats, which they threw onto the floor below them, along with bottles, lit papers and all class of projectiles." But the real raucousness erupted when a group of females tried to leave the theater and "were stripped of their clothing by the savages, whose pawing left them naked." The newspaper went on to describe the rioters as "in the majority, university students." However, this claim was contested by the student leader "Palillo," an organizer of the anti-Presley protest more than a year earlier, who responded that "hundreds of [nonuniversity] youth" were also involved, a point which, even if exaggerated, suggested a certain class diversity on the part of the audience.[123]

The sensationalist tone of the article was not entirely off base, though there were clear biases. The account, for example, fails to mention the fact that riot police (the feared *granaderos*) arrived on the scene and brutally accosted exiting youth at random, noting only that "there were no arrests."[124] The Mexican novelist Parménides García Saldaña, a cult figure of the later counterculture generation, afterward wrote a short story titled "El rey criollo," based on this event. The story gives us a feeling for the charged atmosphere of the theater, no doubt a reflection, in part, of youth efforts to "reclaim" Presley as a virile hero of the young, after the attacks he had faced a short time earlier. The cinema became an anarchic, masculine-defined public space that united teenagers from different neighborhoods and classes beyond the realm of parental or state authority. As opposed to the university, here was a setting policed *solely* by youth (an ironic mockery of the announcement's warning, "Adults Only"). Given the opportunity, the crowd unleashed its rebellious defiance, drunken with the pleasures of self-authority. As the lights went down, García Saldaña relates, a national news-service clip was shown, and "everyone [started] telling the asshole narrator to shut-the-fuck-up." The buenas costumbres that dictated proper language and etiquette (especially toward elders in authority) was gleefully put aside. The audience then burst into song: "Me voy pa' el pueblo, hoy es mi día, chingue su madre la policía," which roughly translates as, "I'm with the people, today's my day, screw the police."[125] The theater pulsated with the desmadre of rock 'n' roll.

Yet this disorder, which cast aside the buenas costumbres inculcated by one's parents and elders, reinscribed the commanding gaze of male over female. The nominal independence that some women experienced in relationship to traditional gender roles (that is, attending the theater without a male chaperone) was swept away by the male-controlled space of the movie house. As García Saldaña relates:

> [W]e entered the theater and went up to the balcony. Up there it was just for the guys, raucous and not a single gal. It was as if at the entrance they had put a sign saying that the men go up and the women down, or something to that effect. . . . Before the film began, it was pure chaos, a fuckin' riot as they say more vulgarly. The different gangs shouted: Here the Guerrero [neighborhood]! Here the Roma! . . . And then some chicks come in with leather jackets with swastikas painted on them, pony tails and bobby socks real rock and roller like, with their books and notebooks. And a group of guys gang up around them [and shout], "Dance!"[126]

In commanding the women to dance, the men here made explicit their control over women's bodies while emphasizing their own role as narrators of youth rebellion. According to García Saldaña, partway through the movie another group of girls entered the theater, looking for seats:

> And out of the silence game the shout, "Meat! Meat! Meeaat!" And a group of guys went flying at them. And they started to scream and the guys began to make fun of them, grabbing their asses, their breasts, everything. . . . Some guys tried to stand up for them, they began throwing fists and the girls managed to get out, half-dressed. It seemed that everything had calmed down, but then they started to tear up the seats and throw them and everyone ran like crazy in all directions, as if the theater were on fire.[127]

Unfortunately, we do not know more about the specifics of what actually happened in that theater: how class tensions may have played a part, to what extent the insults and grabbing were limited to one group of boys, rather than a cross-section of the audience, and so on. In any event, the scene quickly turned into a riot once the police arrived. Federico Arana recalls that as he was running out of the theater and into the street he was cornered by a group of granaderos. Without provocation, they "kicked us in the stomachs and beat us with their rifle butts, meanwhile making fun of our situation, in a perverted and cowardly way, until they managed to capture a few scapegoats." [128] In the public's mind the riot clearly signaled nothing less than the breakdown of social order under the degenerate influence of rock 'n' roll. That several women were practically raped in public only reinforced the belief that a loosening of feminine virtue was directly connected to youth's confrontational posture and thus the collapse of patriarchal authority.

Editorialists were quick to seize the opportunity to once more link an evident crisis in values with the influence of rock 'n' roll. In one example, the social caricaturist Abel Quezada used the occasion of "Teachers' Day" (15 May) to make a commentary on the idea that youth paid more respect to Elvis Presley than to their elders (see Figure 2). Titled "Maestro de la juventud," the cartoon played on the double meaning of *maestro* as denoting both *teacher* and, literally, *master*. The cartoon shows a humble-looking student, bowing slightly and offering a bouquet of flowers to a towering giant; only his legs and part of an arm fit into the frame. Labels indicate to us that the giant is none other than "Elvis Presley" and the humble student, "El rebelde sin causa." [129] In another cartoon, also by Quezada, rock 'n' roll is represented as a fascistic device manipulating the masses. Under the title, "Al son que le toquen" (To Whichever Tune They Play), a jukebox blaring the words "rock and roll" is directly compared with Hitler's and Mussolini's "entertainment" of the masses in their own times.[130]

Responding to what it described as "a rising and threatening sickness which is manifest in the so-called 'rebels without a cause'," *Excélsior* editorialized that the "primary cause is found in the breakdown and disunion of the Mexican family over the last years." [131] A rising consumer culture, coupled with a liberalization of attitudes toward divorce, directly contributed to the undermining of parental authority and thus the loss of respect of child toward adult, according to *Excélsior*. "This is beginning to be not a plague, but a luxury of modernity," the newspaper lamented shortly thereafter. "The young want to be free and sovereign men [*sic*], rich and adventuresome, owners of cars and participants in worldly pleasures, when they hardly have reached the age of fifteen." [132] For middle-class teenagers, however, as Federico Arana recalls, the reality was more that "we lived narrow,

Figure 2. Cartoonist Abel Quezada's critique of Elvis
Presley came on Teacher's Day 1959. Source: *Excélsior,*
15 May 1959, A7. Used by permission.

boring, almost provincial routines." He continued, "In general, the 'rebels'
weren't much besides shy and ordinary kids who put on red nylon jackets
like that of James Dean or leather ones like Marlon Brando . . . and annoyed
their family with their baneful mania of seizing the bathroom with the object of practicing the Elvis style raised-lip, popping a zit here or there and
maintaining the hair mop and ducktail in good form."[133] But for the authorities, highlighting the connection between delinquent youth and privilege served to distract from the larger question of mounting poverty in the

urban slums and the dictatorial nature of political society. Later the attorney general, Fernando Román Lugo, in seeking an explanation for delinquency by youth "who are not in poverty, who live in well-formed homes, who are not lacking in entertainment or stimulation," ascribed the problem to "the lack of a Mexican feeling in our homes" brought about by an absence of discipline.[134]

THE SOCIAL THREAT OF REBELDISMO

The perceived crisis in the family became directly linked to political unrest across the nation as strikes erupted during the transition from the administration of Adolfo Ruiz Cortines (1952–1958) to that of Adolfo López Mateos (1958–1964), former secretary of labor. During 1958–1959, union conflicts extending across a spectrum of workers—telegraph, teachers, railway, and petroleum—and centered in the capital "captured the imagination" of the nation and, according to one author, "caused the regime to totter visibly." [135] Significantly, these labor challenges reflected rebellion by dissident union members (catalyzed by Demetrio Vallejo of the railway workers) against their corrupt leadership. "The demands of the rank and file developed out of grievances which sprang from the realization that the party-union relationship [had] changed from union support of the party to party domination of the unions, by means of venal leaders." [136] The repudiation of the *charrismo* system—the political imposition of union bosses by the PRI—paralleled, if only symbolically, the questioning of authority reflected in the youth culture itself. Particularly disconcerting was a strike led by elementary school teachers, which lasted for nearly two months and was characterized by open confrontations with the police. "How is it possible to establish mental discipline in children when the teacher revolts and becomes a striker?" demanded an editorial in *Excélsior*. Discipline must start within the family, for the nation was a reflection of this basic social unit. The breakdown of institutional hierarchy must be checked at its roots: "Once the 'rebellion without a cause' has started, in that domestic error a new spirit shines in the heart of the child within the school; because here they do not instruct the students in the inviolable and absolute respect for private property, nor in the individual and reciprocal needs for order, nor in the deference owed to hierarchy and one's elders, nor in the moral obligations and social obligations between adults and minors." [137] As the family unit itself continued to show signs of greater liberalization, connections between workers' "lack of discipline" and the lack of parental control over children became more urgent. At one point the weekly newsmagazine *Jueves de Excélsior* editorialized:

> It's a shame to contemplate that in Mexico the principle of authority
> has been lost and that because of this problems are arising daily, rang-
> ing from the apparently insignificant rupture in the harmony of the
> family, due to [parents'] lack of influence over their children, to the na-
> tionally transcendent disturbances such as the wrongful stoppage led
> by railway workers, the recent strike by teachers, and the disorders at
> the National Polytechnic Institute. Youth vandalism, whose seed is
> found in the bosom of the Mexican family . . . is another nuance of this
> grave problem, in that its full branches touch all spheres of government,
> dangerously threatening the security of the country.[138]

The threat of university students' unrest was of particular concern, especially following earlier protests over transportation fare increases and efforts of solidarity with striking workers. This fear was reflected, for example, in an editorial entitled "Rights and Obligations" published in the progovernment magazine *Juventud,* edited by an organization called "Center for Civic Publicity":

> The first obligation of the student is to study. The effort made by the
> family and the nation to give the student a career must have as a com-
> pensation an attitude of personal responsibility on the part of the stu-
> dent. The time to study is sacred. To waste it in idleness, squander
> it in the skipping of classes, put it to poor use in fights and fruitless
> disturbances—quite distinct from the fight for a just cause—is to waste
> this collective effort and prejudice the individual, taking away oppor-
> tunities to prepare oneself for a remunerative job and [to be] socially
> useful.[139]

The problem of delinquency—*rebeldismo*—was thus seen as more profound in its implications than mere appearance. It suggested a frontal challenge to traditional social hierarchies not only of teacher to student and parent to child but also of union boss to worker, police to citizen. "If this amoral condition continues to penetrate our society," intoned *Excélsior,* "it is no exaggeration to say that the collapse of the family will lead to the collapse of society, the state, and the nation."[140] Capturing these fears was a drawing for the June 1959 cover of *Jueves de Excélsior,* featuring a semiclad woman startled out of bed by lurking shadows on the wall. On the bedspread are the initials, "D.F.," indicating that the woman represents the capital district. Projected on the wall are three red shadows with separate texts superimposed: "Rebel" (with a Presley-style hairdo and a dangling cigarette), "Assailant" (a man covered by a face scarf), and "Criminal" (a man in a gangster-style hat). At the bottom of the drawing appears the word "Insomnia."[141] Plainly, the alarming interconnections among youth rebellion, robberies, and "illegal" strikes were causing many sleepless nights for the capital's denizens.

REIMPOSING A CULTURE ORDER

Articulating a "crisis of values" as lying at the heart of other social ills conveniently deflected questions concerning the larger issue of Mexico's authoritarian regime. As was the case historically and would continue to be true in the decades ahead, the PRI manipulated conflicts over cultural issues as a means of absorbing criticism without directly threatening its hold on power.[142] The debate over "family values" in which rock 'n' roll played such a central role thus allowed the regime to focus on the issue of cultural content in the mass media, rather than the political content of elections and syndicate repression. More specifically, attention was raised by the growing trend away from traditional cultural values, reflected in the youth culture and linking this shift to the undermining of an older, more familiar cultural order. This was a transformation the incoming López Mateos administration, initially at least, sought to address. Having declared during his campaign for the presidency that he intended to govern "on the extreme left within the Constitution" (he later softened his rhetoric after some U.S. $250 million left the country from the private sector), López Mateos fomented a spirit of cultural and economic nationalism.[143] This bolstering of Mexico's folkloric heritage was balanced by efforts to project an image of Mexico domestically and abroad as a modern, cosmopolitan nation. Such a dual strategy was reflected, for example, in the twin completion during his administration of the Museum of Modern Art and the massive Museum of Anthropology, both located in Chapultepec Park in Mexico City. The president also extended support for the Ballet Folklórico, a dance troupe that had been transformed into a national symbol of Mexican cultural authenticity during the previous administration.[144]

Facing pressures from the League of Decency as well as the Mexican Society of Authors and Composers, which had seen its members' earnings drop dramatically as foreign artists dominated the airwaves, López Mateos highlighted his commitment to native song. As I noted above, ironically this decline in domestic interest was the flip side of an export boom in Mexican music throughout Latin America, the United States, and Europe. In early 1959 the secretary of communications announced that radio stations with less than 25 percent native content would be fined 5,000 pesos (U.S.

$400). To assist in their programming formats, a catalog of acceptable Mexican tunes prepared by the Instituto Nacional de Bellas Artes (INBA), the government performing arts bureaucracy, was "mailed to stations throughout the republic."[145] Shortly thereafter, *Variety* reported that government "inspectors are now busy making a day and night check of all music" in an effort to enforce the native-preference order.[146] In apparent conjunction with this policy, the Department of Music at the UNAM organized what was announced as the first "Song Fair," the aim of which was "to present tunes no longer popular from older composers." As *Variety* described the fair's organization: "All will be of the romantic ballad type and [the] festival will nix anything that smells of modern rhythms or commercial tunes, which would 'mutilate' [the] whole idea of [the] festival."[147] These actions coincided with the announcement that plans were under way to centralize a collection of "[a]ll of Mexico's folklore music . . . via records, text, choreography, still photos and motion pictures" in a new museum, a reflection of concerns that native music be forever preserved.[148] There was even a youth group, "Juventudes Musicales de México," formed most likely with government funding, that was dedicated exclusively to the "object of infusing and exalting a love for good music among the youth of Mexico." In a letter to López Mateos, the director of the organization asked that the Mexican leader accept the title of "Honorary President" and thus assume "aegis of this institution, not only because you are Mexico's first citizen but for your love of culture and of our youth."[149] In another example, the governor of the state of Aguascalientes petitioned to receive federal assistance for a campaign promoting native musical performances in the countryside, describing this tactic "as the best dike against the invasion of cha-cha-chás, 'rock'n roll' and other exotic rhythms that threaten to displace music that is authentically Mexican."[150]

These actions emerged in the context of a wider struggle by conservatives to root out "immoral" influences more generally and mass cultural influences in particular. In 1959 a sweep by the appointed mayor of the Federal District, Ernest P. Uruchurtu, led to the closing of numerous nightclubs and an imposition of a 1:00 A.M. curfew on night entertainment, in a move that *Jueves de Excélsior* claimed "has merited the most enthusiastic applause of society." Under a photograph of young couples dancing in a ballroom setting, the text read: "GREAT PART of the clientele of the more than 200 cabarets and metropolitan hovels are made up by youth from both sexes that hide away in the depravation and become converted into social pariahs, without occupation or benefit."[151] In the realm of mass culture, pornography, delinquency, gratuitous violence, and, significantly, "distortions of language" all became a central focus of the brewing backlash.

This moralization drive ironically coincided with an announcement by the National Chamber of Broadcasting Industries (a private industry group) that Mexican programming was "classified among the most moral and clean in the world, . . . far above the broadcasts of Cuba and the United States."[152] This statement no doubt reflected the association's efforts to deflect mounting criticism aimed at the mass media. In fact, as early as January 1957 the film section of the Department of Interior Affairs had notified the Association of Film Producers and the National Chamber of Cinematographic Industries that "all films which present nudism . . . [and] abuse themes dealing with immorality" in foreign, as well as in Mexican films, were henceforth prohibited.[153] Pressure to create such a censorship board had come from the Mexican League of Decency, which applauded the decision and was also directly represented on the board.[154] As one writer editorialized, foreign films had become a danger "by exploiting crime to such a detailed extent that they constitute a true school for all of the misled inclinations of an unsettled youth." At the same time, "native cinema had committed grave errors for the sin of profit" by exploiting an image of the Mexican character that glorified violence while distorting the "authentic" nature of local customs. At stake was an "accurate" representation of Mexico: "[A]s the majority of these national productions are exported and seen abroad, this has been creating a truly noxious propaganda, instead of presenting the real aspect of Mexico and the Mexicans, exalting its authentic traditions, its genuine virtues, the simpleness of its customs, and the multichromatic beauties of its folklore, with respect to regional characteristics, without hodgepodge or adulterations."[155] Local productions were thus pressured toward self-censorship while foreign films faced the prospect of being denied entry altogether.

In early 1958, for example, *Variety* noted that the U.S. film, *Runaway Daughters* (translated as "Lost Adolescence") was "the first to get gonged in the government's intensified cinematographic moralization drive."[156] After the outbreak of violence at *King Creole*, future Elvis Presley films faced a ban. Throughout the 1960s other films, including ones by Presley and the Beatles, also faced censorship or restrictions on their exhibition permits. In 1965, for instance, the Beatles' *A Hard Day's Night* was shown only after a ten-month wait imposed by the censorship board.[157] Films that depicted Mexico in a negative light, "reflecting real or imagined slights of national honor,"[158] were especially subject to closer scrutiny throughout this period as part of a broader campaign to contain an image of Mexican development. Banned, for instance, was Frank Sinatra's *Marriage on the Rocks* (1966), which the government found represented Mexico "as a primitive country without medical care, drinking water or municipal services and where the most important business was the divorce industry." [159] While on the whole it appears that these guidelines were subject to negotiation and the conflicting pressures from film distributors, by the end of 1959 the campaign against immoral themes and distortions of national character culminated in legislation aimed at radio and television as well, as we will see in a moment.

The moralization drive begun with film reflected a more profound sense that mass culture had become a pernicious vehicle misrepresenting Mexico, on one hand, and undermining the bedrock of traditional patriarchal values, on the other. The impact of this campaign is revealed in part by an examination of the records during this period for the Qualifying Commission of Magazines and Illustrated Publications, the official government censorship bureau for printed materials. While the commission was largely ineffectual, serving more as a lightning rod to deflect conservative criticism than to actually maintain policing powers, the debates and discussions found in its annals are an important reflection of the concerns raised about the damaging role of mass culture then being expressed. In writing a history of the commission, Anne Rubenstein has argued that the Mexican state, "by appearing to limit printed entertainment in Mexico without actually exercising control, opened up a space in the public discourse for conservative protest that would not lead to serious political challenges or violence." [160] Nevertheless, the commission's guidelines suggested a great deal about its rigid sensitivity to offensive material that had ramifications on the public debate at large. First written in 1944 when the commission began its work and updated in 1953, these guidelines stated: "It is immoral and contrary to Education [to] publish, distribute, circulate, present or sell in public" material which contained the following characteristics:

I.   Writings, drawings, etchings, paintings, printed matter, images, advertisements, emblems, photographs or other objects which stimulate the excitement of dangerous passions or sensuality, and

II.   Publications, magazines or comic books of any of the following types:

   a)   that adopt themes capable of destroying the devotion to work, the enthusiasm for studies . . . ;

b) that stimulate the excitement of dangerous passions or of sensuality which offends modesty and proper behavior;

c) that stimulate passivity, the tendency toward idleness or faith in fate as a regulator of conduct;

d) that contain any sort of adventure in which, eluding law and respect for established institutions, the protagonists obtain success in their undertakings . . . ;

f) that, with the intention of pursuing the story plot or due to the nature of the characters, directly or indirectly provoke disdain toward the Mexican people, their abilities, customs, traditions, history or democracy;

g) that utilize texts which systematically employ expressions that offend the correct use of the language; and

h) that insert articles, paragraphs, scenes, plates, paintings, photographs, drawings or etchings which, by themselves, contain the aforementioned objections.[161]

The concern with "expressions that offend the correct use of the language" (section IIg) is particularly relevant, for the popularization of barrio slang was associated with moral degeneracy and violence. Policing the boundaries of grammar was regarded as central to the maintenance of social order itself. In one example, the permit for an entertainment magazine, *Follies de América*, was denied by the commission for "offending good taste and the respect which we owe to the language." The committee member reviewing the solicitation argued that the magazine used "vocabulary that is frankly coarse and precocious" and that "falling into the hands of adolescents [will] incite them to drain their vital energies that are necessary not only for their physical development, but for the profundity and clutches of their minds." In sum, the reviewer argued, "the nation is passing through a cultural crisis which is accentuated with this type of publication."[162] Another magazine, *Diversiones*, "which is advertised as specializing in cinema, theater, radio and television," was also declared "illicit" because of the nature and tone of its contents: "The material which illustrates the magazine is constituted in great part by semi-nude movie personalities, or tourist nightclubs, what they now call the older cabarets. The rest of the illustrations correspond to scenes involving modern dances such as the cha-cha-chá, the yompy [*sic*], rock-and-roll, etc." Of particular concern to the reviewer was the repeated printing of common slang which, "besides its vulgar style, is an affront to syntax."[163] Despite its judicial ineffectiveness, the concerns of the commission are evidence of the persistence of doubts and hostilities expressed toward the youth culture and the pressures that helped shape its containment during first half of the 1960s. But if the commission ultimately lost the battle to restrict the popularization of rock 'n' roll, its moralization drive did have an impact on later fanzines' contents: in praising Presley (whose comeback was already at hand) and other youth idols, magazine editors made every effort to argue for the "clean intent" of rock 'n' roll artists and steered clear of sensationalizing their immoral excesses.

The most important feature of this moralization drive was the public debate over proposed legislation that would, for the first time, create specific legal guidelines for television and radio broadcasting. A special congressional commission was established in late summer of 1959 in the wake of the *King Creole* incident, with the aim of "prohibit[ing] the diffusion of songs and programs which are outspoken apologies for crime and which, *per se*, contribute to the growing wave of crime and homicides in Mexico."[164] Prior to such legislation, guidelines had been largely set by the National Chamber of Broadcasting Industries in cooperation with the secretary of communication. But with the new legislation the "ethical guidelines" supposedly followed by the chamber were expanded on and written into law, though with evident influence by the chamber itself (which publicly supported the legislation).[165] One voice that challenged the proposed law was the Asociación Interamericana de Radiodifusión (AIR), a nongovernmental organization which lobbied on behalf of broadcasters throughout Latin America. In a letter to President López Mateos the president of AIR urged that new legislation was unnecessary and could only result in the undermining of free expression, "that nourishing element of our times."[166] Unmoved, López Mateos voiced in a speech made before a meeting of AIR delegates in Mexico on the eve of the vote in Congress: "To be Mexican is to be free and the law that is being debated to control Mexican radio and television, thought over and discussed by Mexicans, will provide for the guarantee of expression in Mexico."[167] As the legislation came to a vote in the PRI-controlled Chamber of Deputies (where it passed without a single dissenting vote), one congresswoman summed up her support:

> [R]adio and television have permitted excesses in their programming that affect the morality of our homes and it is clear to think that if the child or young adult lacks a spiritual base, [one that is] doctrinaire and moral, they will adopt, without a doubt, the examples which they hear and pick up from transmitted programs lacking adequate orientation

and without precise goals. For this reason, the [proposed legislation] establishes maximum responsibility for the sponsors and organizers that allow transmission of programs which damage children and contribute to juvenile delinquency and the formation of men and women without moral scruples and lacking respect for society.[168]

As passed by the Congress in January 1960 the Federal Law of Radio and Television stated the following goals:

1. To affirm the respect for social morality, human dignity and family ties;
2. To avoid noxious or disturbing influences on the harmonious development of children and youth;
3. To contribute to the cultural elevation of the population and to conserve its national characteristics, customs, and traditions, the propriety of the language, and to exalt the values of Mexican nationality;
4. To strengthen democratic convictions, national unity, and international friendship and cooperation.

To achieve these goals in part, the state authorized for itself the right to free airtime lasting up to one-half hour daily, "dedicated to the diffusion of themes of educational, cultural, and social orientation."[169] (This followed the concession for the creation of an educational channel earlier in 1958.)[170] The bill sanctioned additional state programming for those "stations which, because of their power, frequency or location are likely to be captured abroad, in order to divulge cultural representations of Mexican life, increase commercial relations, intensify tourist propaganda, and transmit information about national events."[171]

The legislation, however, contained a mixed message concerning the question of free expression and censorship. On one hand, it stated that the "right to information, expression and reception by radio and television is free and consequently will not be the object of any judicial or administrative inquisition nor limitation by any prior censorship, and that it will be authorized under the terms of the Constitution and the law."[172] This, however, was directly contradicted in a following article, which established explicit boundaries on free expression. Not only were cultural and grammatical transgressions proscribed, but, significantly, so too were defamations of public heroes and, in apparent deference to the League of Decency, of religious beliefs. Article 63 thus stated: "Prohibited are all transmissions that cause the corruption of the language and are contrary to buenas costumbres, whether that be via malicious expressions, impudent words or images, phrases or scenes involving double meaning, apologies for crime or violence; also prohibited is all that denigrates or is offensive to the civic cult of the heroes and religious beliefs, or racially discriminates; furthermore, prohibited are the use of jokes in poor taste and offensive noises."[173] At the same time, the law stated that broadcasters "must take advantage of and promote local and national artistic values and expressions of Mexican art."[174] Expressions in a foreign language were also prohibited unless authorized by the secretary of interior affairs, and then only in cases where "a Spanish version, [either] exact or summarized" was used.[175] Foreigners were explicitly prohibited from becoming associates of or controlling the broadcasting medium in any shape or form.[176]

Enforcement of this extensive law (105 articles) was to be divided among three governmental bureaucracies: the Departments of Communications and Transportation; Interior Affairs; and Public Education. That these new legal guidelines were never scrupulously followed is indicative of the political influence which owners of the mass media, such as the Azcárraga family, exerted. Indeed, as *Variety* remarked, if followed to the letter the legislation would have meant "a death knell to the hundreds of ranchera ditties here which eulogize killers, drunks and general no-goods."[177] Like the Qualifying Commission for Magazines and Illustrated Publications, the legislation aimed at radio and television lacked judicial enforcement. However, its existence did have an important impact on the public discourse and would be used periodically to justify government harassment and occasional censorship of radio and television broadcasts. Even before the law was implemented, for example, a decree by the Office of Public Events of the Federal District "strictly prohibited comics and impersonators from using [offensive] mannerisms in their presentations," which included "appearing like homosexuals."[178] It would seem that homosexual behavior threatened patriarchal values by mocking the virility of all men and thus, by implication, subverting the protective role of man over woman.

With regard to the rhythm that in no small part energized the nationalist and patriarchal spirit behind the new legislation, *Excélsior* announced in a headline on the eve of the vote in Congress: "Young People Have Forgotten Rock'n Roll and Prefer the Oldies." According to a radio-station survey, Mexican youth had "turned their backs on the rabid 'rock-roll' [sic]" in favor of more "sentimental melodies."[179] But this appears to have been more self-congratulatory than accurate. That same week, for instance, *Variety* reported that disc jockeys from two Mexico City radio stations were being sent to the United States "to perfect their English and to brush up on modern radio broadcasting procedures."[180] And in numerous middle-class homes, boys were already tuning their electric guitars and honing their gestures in reverent emulation of their pop heroes. The real impact of the legislation was that it exerted pressures toward self-censorship. This self-containment of media representation affected all matters of entertainment, including the imminent explosion of a homegrown rock 'n' roll movement by youth, the subject of the next chapter.

2 Containing the Rock Gesture

Despite the backlash against rock 'n' roll, the moralization drive under way could banish neither the demand for the new rhythm nor the yearnings of youth, who sought to follow in the footsteps of their foreign teen idols. In fact, government efforts to blockade the arrival of foreign music indirectly contributed to the emergence of a native rock 'n' roll product that rapidly supplanted imports. What this debate over mass media did affect, however, was the content of an emergent Mexican youth culture. By placing clear boundaries on artistic expression, the recording companies, television, radio, film, and print media collectively promoted an image of Mexican rocanrol stripped of its immoral associations, thus rendering a form of "high" popular culture also suitable to the modernizing aspirations of the middle classes. Indeed, rocanrol served as an apt metaphor for the modernizing Revolutionary Family itself: cosmopolitan, consumerist, yet bounded. The new youth culture was literally contained by the cultural industries, which at the same time nurtured and marketed it.[1] Though its content was framed by production and marketing enterprises wary of provoking conservative reaction, Mexican rocanrol nevertheless had a profound impact on the transformation of everyday life for urban youth, above all from the middle classes, during this so-called Grand Era of Mexican rock 'n' roll.[2]

TRANSNATIONAL AND LOCAL MARKETING STRATEGIES

When youth from the middle classes began to form their own bands in the late 1950s, practicing as best they could versions of hit songs in English by their favorite foreign rock 'n' rollers, the recording companies initially took scant interest in their efforts. The market for music was still defined by imports, on one hand, and by Spanish-language ballads and música tropical, on the other. From the industry's perspective, competition for the youth market largely came down to which companies had access to foreign artists. Leading this pursuit was RCA, which distributed Elvis Presley, and Rogelio Azcárraga's company, Orfeón, which distributed The Platters as well as Bill Haley and The Comets. In fact, the latter two groups were actually brought to Mexico City by Orfeón in late 1959.[3] But by this date, Orfeón's own strategy had begun to change as it weighed the rising costs of imports against the lucrative potential of local bands recording Spanish-language cover versions for a wider market.

With the growing importance of foreign markets for recorded music during the late 1950s, one of the transnationals' strategies was to promote an artist by producing several versions of a hit sung in the local language, most often French, Italian, Spanish, or German. The idea was to preempt competition from a version of the same song performed by a local artist. In one case, for example, Elvis Presley sang two verses of his song "Wooden Heart" in (phonetic) German. Peter, Paul and Mary also later recorded in German and French as well as Italian.[4] Even the internationally renowned Mexican group Trío Los Panchos reportedly recorded in Japanese for Columbia Records.[5] The recording companies found "the procedure [of translation] highly economical since only the vocal has to be re-recorded, with the instrumental part being taken over from the original tape."[6] Ironically, this switch to local-language translations was a reversal of an earlier trend by European performers who had made English-language versions of their own hits "slanted to crash the American market."[7] Noting that "the growth of the international market . . . has opened up a vast new revenue potential," a vice president and head of artists and repertoire for Capitol Records pointed to a Spanish-language recording of Nat King Cole (which had sold 100,000 albums in Latin America) as an example of the direction that foreign marketing must take.[8] Likewise, the new vice president for Latin American operations at CBS recommended that "the American publishers should prepare Spanish lyric versions of their songs along with the English"[9] as a measure of countering the ease with which local cover versions of a popular song were being produced. Such covers threatened to dip directly into the profits of the transnationals. As one agent of the music industry noted, "The cover appears so quickly that in many cases the American company does not have the opportunity to get its record released."[10]

In Mexico, the recording company Orfeón can claim credit for first cultivating local talent as a response to demand for imports. Though a relatively small company, Orfeón had important connections to other mass media—the Azcárragas collectively owned a network of radio stations, published various music-oriented magazines, and monopolized the infant television industry—and thus the necessary motivation and flexibility to experiment with new ideas. As José Cruz Ayala, former artistic director for several companies, including Orfeón, during the 1960s, recalls:

> [Orfeón] had more advantages as a domestic operation at a given moment because they were less structured in terms of the use of studios, etc. . . . I'm not saying that CBS was totally different, but obviously there was a difference in policy. At Orfeón there was nearly unlimited access to the studios, compared with CBS, which had its headquarters in New York and thus dictated policy from there. Furthermore, CBS had an extensive catalog featuring all types of music, whereas Orfeón did not. So [Orfeón] could actually dedicate more time and money to that type of recording [rock 'n' roll].[11]

According to Federico Arana, sometime in late 1959 Rogelio Azcárraga of Orfeón pushed its artistic director, Paco de la Barrera, to contract a group that could perform rock 'n' roll covers of foreign hits in Spanish.[12] This was a strategy for maneuvering itself into a more competitive position vis-à-vis the transnationals. Naturally, because the latter had greater access to foreign recordings their attitude toward covers was more conservative. Johnny Laboriel, former singer with Los Rebeldes del Rock, one of the most important groups to emerge during this period, describes his experiences producing covers, first for RCA and later for Orfeón:

> Because it's a case of duplication [with a cover], you have to make it even more real for the people who receive it. It's like, for example, if I recite a lot of catechism for people whose native language is Náhuatl, I'm going to have to adopt it to their reality. That's what happened with rock 'n' roll taken from English. In the beginning, for instance, the director of RCA-Víctor, Rafael de la Paz, was totally against doing covers. He wanted us instead to sing rock 'n' roll versions of Mexican music. He tried to have us do a song called "La borrachita," a dreadful thing. . . . We said, "Forget it, this isn't going to work." So we went to Orfeón Records, where they accepted us, and the only Mexican song we ever played to the beat of rock 'n' roll was "La bamba."[13]

In an interesting tale, an artist-and-repertoire person at CBS reportedly risked his own savings to record a new group, Los Teen Tops, against the wishes of the general manager, André Toffel, when he "realized that rock 'n' roll in Spanish was going to cause a commotion in the market for records."[14] Within days, two of the group's songs—"La plaga" (a cover version of "Good Golly Miss Molly," by Little Richard) and "Rock de la cárcel" (a cover of Elvis Presley's "Jailhouse Rock")—shot to the top of the charts in Mexico and, shortly thereafter, in Spain and parts of South America as well.[15] As it became clear that Spanish-language covers had broad appeal, RCA did an about-face and quickly zeroed in on the burgeoning market throughout Latin America created by rocanrol. Thus in the fall of 1960 RCA transferred its artistic director, Ricardo Mejías, from its Mexico City subsidiary to Buenos Aires. In Argentina, Mejías "launched a 'new wave' of disk talent, with the accent on youth, in marked contrast to RCA's former policy of plugging the favorites of the past." Within a matter of months, record sales in the Southern Cone soared, and the subsidiary began "registering its biggest sales of any time in its close to 40 years in Argentina."[16]

By early 1961, the bandwagon effect caused by the sudden switch to Spanish-language rocanrol had completely transformed the industry. While literally scores of songs were performed in a rock 'n' roll style, *Variety* reported that around "25 clicked really big with [the] public and about 90 to 100 others just barely held their own."[17] It was overwhelmingly a movement started by and aimed at middle-class youth, who suffered most from the high cost of and limited access to imports. Forming a band was an economic challenge, but one that offered lucrative potential as the market for music suddenly opened up. As Manuel Ruiz, an ardent rock 'n' roll fan from the era, recalls:

> The first rock groups were formed around 1959–1960, when people first began to get hold of instruments imported into Mexico. There weren't any at first; here no one made them. . . . They were expensive and not just anyone could say, "I'm going to buy a guitar and drum set and form my own band." No, the instruments were expensive! You needed to have money and couldn't be too poor, although a lot of people bought them on layaway. But even this took a lot of sacrifice if you were from the middle or lower-middle class.[18]

Mexico's Grand Era of rocanrol (1959–1964) mostly centered in the nation's capital district, though its influence reached far beyond the district's borders. Largely performing covers—or *refritos*, as they were called—bands with such names as Los Loud Jets (Orfeón), Los Locos del Ritmo (Orfeón), Los Rebeldes del Rock (Orfeón), Los Teen Tops (CBS), Los Black Jeans (Peerless), Los Hitters (Orfeón), Los Hooligans (Orfeón), and many others became not only national stars but, in certain cases, international ones as well.[19] "The avalanche hit so hard," recalls Johnny Laboriel of Los Rebeldes del Rock, "that suddenly you heard only rocanrol on the radio. All of the jukeboxes played rocanrol. And then the *cafés cantantes* [music clubs] came into being."[20]

FROM ROCK 'N' ROLL TO *ROCANROL*

Virtually every song recorded during this period was a translation of a foreign hit imposed on the musicians by the recording companies themselves. When rock 'n' roll first arrived in the mid-1950s singers had naturally tried to imitate the English original. As Johnny Laboriel tells it, "The first time I heard rock 'n' roll was on the jukebox. We used to go to this ice-cream café, and it was there that we started to hear what it was all about. I remember the first word I heard was 'darling,' but shouted out like this! . . . So that was the first thing I did. I started to sing rock 'n' roll. But I didn't know any English . . . [so] I used to sing to the girls, making up the words as I went along."[21] Singing in guttural English undoubtedly came across as more authentic, but it was largely impractical for recording. (Gloria Ríos was an exception, with her masterful rendition of Haley's "Rock around the Clock.") Moreover, because of the close associations between rock 'n' roll and rebeldismo, copying the English original connoted a level of authenticity that record producers were at this point anxious to tone down. What was needed was a Spanish-language equivalent that maintained the essential rhythm and structure of the original (with perhaps some token English thrown in) but that provided greater control for producers who needed to deflect assaults by conservatives. For Orfeón, the process was simple: "We saw what was a hit in the United States . . . and then we brought in the record, in fact even before it was sold here [in Mexico], and we immediately made a cover version with one of our [contracted] groups. Then we promoted it on television and radio . . . and in twenty-four hours we had a record on the street for sale."[22] Marketing Spanish-language covers of foreign hits was a strategy that directly undercut the transnationals' inherent advantage, as José Cruz Ayala explained:

> In an album by Los Teen Tops, there exists the best of the best as a copy, so it already had a certain preestablished sales value. They were already covering a series of points—one already knew which songs were going to be hits. . . . You took the recordings by Elvis Presley and could choose not just one but lots—there were easily twenty to forty songs that one could make a cover out of—and this was the same with the recordings of whatever other person that occurred to us.[23]

Such was the popularity of rocanrol that despite a 1961 recession that affected record sales in other Latin American markets, *Billboard* reported that "[t]he significant and still increasing trend of 1961 in Mexican music has been the absolute predominance of rock in record sales and radio programs," performed by the "dozens of teen-age singers and 'wild' rock groups [that] have been and are still recording."[24]

Rocanrol was above all a middle-class phenomenon, which neither replaced the mass appeal of more traditional musical styles nor reached much beyond urban consumers of the capital and provincial cities. Nonetheless, its impact significantly realigned musical tastes and fashions, in the end redefining an image of Mexican modernity that had been overly dependent on the stereotyped mariachi performer. For example, in early 1961 an agreement was reached between Channel 5 of New York City and Telesistema to initiate an exchange of videotapes featuring how each country had influenced the other's musical styles. Not by coincidence, the first program was "devoted to [the] invasion of Mexico by rock-and-roll rhythms, with [the] top groups interpreting the frenzied music appearing in the segment."[25] According to a report in *Variety* in early 1961, rocanrol had "eclipsed all other melodies," leading to "one of the poorest years [for traditional music] because of the frenzied switch to rock and roll."[26] Government policy, which had aimed to influence popular tastes by threatening sanctions against radio stations dominated by foreign-language songs, now adopted the added position of a protective tariff. In mid-1961 the tariff on imports went from U.S. $0.005 per kilo on records with a 10 percent ad valorem to U.S. $1.20 per kilo and a 40 percent ad valorem. This meant that the average cost of an imported record increased around 50 percent, resulting in a notable drop in imports[27] (see Graph 2). While the tariff undoubtedly reflected the combined pressures of musicians' unions, nationalist government officials, and local media interests, its impact was twofold. First of all, it forced a shift toward local pressing from the masters which, where available, now replaced imports. *Billboard*, for instance, reported at the end of 1962 that "90 per cent of records formerly imported are now pressed locally."[28] This created a boon for local production. Secondly, however, the new tariff also induced record companies across the board to market a native rocanrol product as a more flexible substitute for costly imports.

Indeed, a 1962 report by the Banco Nacional de Comercio Exterior indicated that "modern rhythms" were "displacing the music that is authentically Mexican." The report argued that the popularity of such rhythms had created incentives for the recording industry to tailor domestic demand according to trends set by "those countries from which modern music originates."[29] Clearly, the marketing trends *were* being set by styles imported from abroad, and the record companies, both locally owned and transna-

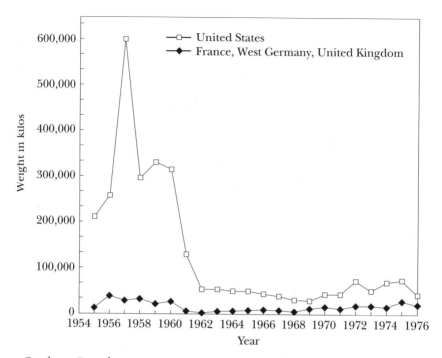

Graph 2.   Record imports into Mexico, 1955–1976. Source: *Anuario del Comercio Exterior* (Mexico City: Banco Nacional de Comercio Exterior, 1955–1976).

tional, were active participants in the process. Orfeón, for instance, in addition to promoting its own contracted artists, had signed an exclusive, two-year contract with Bill Haley "to handle r'n'r rhythms in Spanish, to [the] accompaniment of Mexican musicians."[30]

Best epitomizing this influence was the international sensation caused by the twist. At the start of 1962 *Variety* was reporting that "the [twist] dance craze has spread around the globe,"[31] and RCA's Mexican subsidiary was quick to promote the style locally, seeing it as an opportunity to "'rejuvenate' traditional Mexican songs."[32] As Rubén Fuentes, artistic director at RCA-Víctor Mexicana, said, "We will give a Latin twist to The Twist," pointing out that such standards as "Bésame mucho" would be "adapted to 'twisting.'"[33] In an effort to arrest this "exotic rhythms kick," the Mexican Society of Authors and Composers, in collaboration with the National Tourist Council and the major record companies, promoted a Mexican Song Festival as a way to "renew interests in national tunes."[34] Still, an artistic director at CBS argued that Mexican composers would benefit "if they would learn to keep up with the times and musical fashions, and create accordingly." This position was backed by a spokesperson at Orfeón, who urged that composers should pursue "new ways of expression" aimed at youth.[35]

Reaction to the popularity of rocanrol varied, with certain radio broadcasters eagerly promoting it while others viewed it as anathema and deemed it "vulgar, obnoxious and in bad taste."[36] One radio station, for example, flatly refused to program rocanrol calling it "a sample of bad taste that we must avoid at all cost."[37] Calling them "musical rebels without a cause," Alfredo Urdián, an executive with the powerful Mexico City Musicians' Union, announced a boycott in October 1960 of any establishment that allowed young rockers to perform, arguing that the measure was necessary to protect "legitimate musicians" from "unfair competition."[38] This campaign was underscored by a petition to the Office of Public Entertainment asking it to issue a decree prohibiting dance halls from hiring, in *Variety*'s words, the "youthful musical maniacs."[39] Yet two months later it was announced that an Association of Rocanrol Units was being formed as an ad hoc union for the musicians. According to the group's president, Antonio Figueroa, its purpose was to "'dignify' rock and roll in Mexico and to weed out questionable elements," such as "student or worker groups who 'think' they can interpret rock and roll rhythms."[40]

This reflected a fundamental ideological element of the movement, which was to be reinforced at all levels of the media during the 1960s: the containment of rock 'n' roll began with the musicians themselves but extended to all aspects of their media representation. Having vowed to "sweep the Mexican musical scene clean of the 'musical hoodlums,'"[41] even Venus Rey, head of the musicians' union, soon succumbed to the reality of rocanrol's popularity with the public. In a measure of the rhythm's inexorable march, now wholly backed by television and radio, by the fall of 1961 the musicians' syndicate had agreed to accept the rocanrol groups as "meritorious" members of the union but on the condition that for every rock 'n' roller hired, a "bona fide union musician" must also be contracted, a clause no doubt difficult for the union to enforce.[42] As a current director of sales at Orfeón, Carlos Beltrand Luján, now recalls, "Everyone had a friend in some [rocanrol] group. And they all performed in afternoon gigs. . . . [S]oon after their records came out, all of this pushed aside demand for the foreign groups. We all supported our [Mexican] groups and bought their records. Of the five or six radio stations that had supported foreign rock, only one remained. . . . The rest started to support rock in Spanish."[43] By the end of 1962 *Billboard* was reporting that the best-selling U.S. artists were "[o]ut of favor, and practically never played at radio stations." "No English lyrics . . . are accepted by the Mexican public," the trade magazine noted.[44]

As a result of Orfeón's all-out investment in rocanrol, the company saw its share of the total domestic market for all music increase from 2 percent in 1957 to 16 percent by 1962, still far short of RCA's 40 percent.[45] In fact, despite a climate of hostility and conflict with RCA and CBS, Orfeón's ties to other media placed the company at an important advantage over the transnationals, allowing Orfeón, according to Beltrand Luján, to capture around 80 percent of the rocanrol market by the end of this period.[46] Conflicts first emerged between Orfeón and RCA toward the end of 1961, when the latter sought to discredit Orfeón by claiming that it was headed toward bankruptcy, a charge far from true. In fact, the conflict in large part centered on Orfeón's undercutting the transnationals by developing "cutrate and bargain sale tactics," a strategy that had set off a price war in the industry.[47] But the price war was only one side of the picture that was emerging. The other concerned the transnationals' steady moves to compete with Orfeón for the rocanrol market. For example, CBS initiated an aggressive marketing strategy aimed at broadening its market share throughout Latin America, a company trend that accelerated throughout the decade. In an effort designed "to give [CBS] a stronger foothold in the international market," the company pursued a strategy "to have greater involvement in the local artists & repertoire production activities, creating [a] product for the specific country itself as well as [a] repertoire of value to the entire international area."[48] Thus, starting in 1961, new recording studios and expanded manufacturing facilities were built in Argentina, and the company announced that it had "launched long-range plans to broaden [its] distribution and recording operations in all major markets throughout the world."[49] During 1962, the company was reporting "excellent sales volumes . . . by wholly-owned records subsidiaries in Argentina, Australia, Brazil, Canada and Mexico."[50] In June 1962 CBS increased the capitalization of its Mexican subsidiary, which was now generating 352,000 records per month.[51]

Shortly thereafter, Orfeón began to accuse CBS of stealing its artists and dominating the newly formed Mexican Association of Record Producers, leading Orfeón to quit the association briefly in protest.[52] Meanwhile, CBS continued its advance into the Spanish-language markets, upgrading its facilities in Latin America and establishing a distribution contract with the Spanish recording company, Hispavox, through which Columbia Records' Latin American artists, such as Los Teen Tops, were now distributed in Spain.[53] In 1963, the transnational could report that the "Columbia Records U.S. repertoire is not only now packaged, distributed and promoted throughout the world by foreign subsidiaries and affiliates, but, in turn, these companies record native artists which are marketed on a world-wide basis by Columbia." [54] With their offers of lucrative contracts and the accompanying benefits of recording for a global company, RCA and CBS quickly cultivated their own roster of Mexican rocanrol performers, often aggressively luring artists away from contracts already established with other companies. In various instances, for example, contracts with Orfeón were broken as performers switched recording companies. [55] In one notable case, Los Locos del Ritmo switched from Orfeón to CBS, where they were promoted throughout South America as well as the southwestern United States. [56] Indeed, via their recordings and appearances in film, groups such as Los Teen Tops, Los Loud Jets, and Los Rebeldes del Rock came to be widely known not only throughout the republic but also in Latin America, Spain, parts of the United States, and even Europe and Asia. [57]

While the transnationals had tremendous advantages—their economies of scale, direct access to cataloged material, and global marketing networks—Mexican companies were also able to compete for the rising consumer demand created by what the industry was calling *la nueva ola*, or "new wave" of youth-oriented music. Orfeón was best positioned to take advantage of this opportunity because of the company's complex ties to other mass media, but other local companies also profited. [58] Thus in 1960 Orfeón launched its own television program as a front for its contracted artists. Initially called *Premier Orfeón*, in 1962 the name was changed to *Orfeón a go-go*, which reflected its strong youth-oriented catalog under the popular Orfeón label. Around the same time as the start of *Premier Orfeón* RCA announced that it was following suit with its own weekly program to "featur[e] one or more of the firm's recording artists, as well as dance routines." [59] A score of dance-oriented television programs cropped up around the country in rapid succession. In short, the rocanrol boom affected the entire industry, from the recording companies to the radio and television networks. While exports of "traditional" Mexican music continued to show modest signs of increase during this period, especially to the growing Mexican American communities in the United States, domestic demand was dramatically displaced by la nueva ola of music groups targeted at youth.

DOMESTICATING YOUTH REBELLION

If in the United States rock 'n' roll was under constant surveillance by conservatives in the media and in Congress—the containment of Elvis's rotating hips on the *Ed Sullivan Show* and the payola hearings in Congress being the best-known examples [60]—in Mexico musicians ceded a priori control over their recorded material to the record companies. Original compositions were strictly curtailed, although one rocanrol composition, "Yo no soy un rebelde" by Los Locos del Ritmo, in fact became an important hit (see below). With closely matched renditions of the original composition and Spanish lyrics that often had little to do with the original, these songs came to be known as *refritos,* from the verb *refreír* (to re-fry). Suggesting notions of reappropriation and making anew, the refrito in fact came to embody the containment of rock 'n' roll via its Spanish-language domestication. As Víctor Roura, a contemporary rock critic, has written:

> If with Elvis Presley the rock genre lost all of its roots (the song of blacks) to become another article of consumption, though with evident differences from traditional North American music . . . here the Hooligans or Teen Tops or Rebeldes del Rock or Locos del Ritmo were obligated by their artistic directors to introduce only the scenic [aspect of the] movement. Never the pelvis offensively displayed. Mexican rock and rollers were always under artistic quarters. Not one contestable act (nor was there a reason for it). Not one intention of changing the direction of the song, much less modifying a way of life with their music.[61]

Rock 'n' roll's gestures of defiance were circumscribed by the record companies, the film industry, and ultimately the musicians themselves, who above all realized that the key to success and stardom was conforming to a discourse of nonthreatening rebellion. Rocanrol was promoted as mere entertainment, as just "another branch of the market for music."[62] Carlos Beltrand Luján of Orfeón recalls how his company went to great lengths to promote an image of its contracted artists as studious and family oriented: "In sum, we made it clear [to the public] that this [musical] tendency was not doing anything to them, that they kept being good family children [*hijos de familia*] who paid attention to their parents; that the girls who sang rock 'n' roll were not getting pregnant or anything."[63]

By introducing the musical rhythms of foreign performers, but with "homegrown" lyrics and a clean-cut image more palatable to the concerns of adults, the companies discovered a formula for naturalizing a cultural phenomenon previously regarded as controversial and even subversive. Víctor Roura's cynical point that "[t]he bourgeoisie imposed the beat" on Mexican rock 'n' roll is not entirely off the mark.[64] The reappropriation of rock 'n' roll as rocanrol suited an image of the modernizing Revolutionary Family, both in an economic sense—as Mexico shifted from an agrarian economy to an industrial one—and in a social sense, embodied in the notion of greater communication between parents and children in an age of liberalizing values. Spanish-language rocanrol literally domesticated the imported rhythm by removing the stigma of rebeldismo that adults and the government had found threatening, while retaining the modernizing aspects that had such broad appeal. Symbolizing the commodity culture and technological achievements of a modern nation, the image of rocanrol promoted by the cultural industries steered clear of outright challenges to patriarchal authority. On the cover of a *Jueves de Excélsior* from early 1962, for example, we find a drawing of an entire family dancing to the new rhythm, from the hip-looking older son and daughter, to the parents, and even to the youngest children (see Figure 3). The text reads simply, "The family dances the Twist." [65] This image was not too distant from what may have really occurred, as one informant from a conservative Catholic family recalls. Noting that her mother learned to dance rocanrol "at the same time as we did," Conchita Cervantes explained: "She danced with us because she has always been outgoing, jovial. She even helped us out a lot. Like, she helped us to organize parties: she pushed back furniture, swept. She organized everything so that we could have a party." In this case her father was not a dancer in general, but even he "didn't mind parties, and he preferred that they took place in his own home rather than outside." [66] As a metaphor for modernity, Spanish-language rocanrol in fact conveyed an image of familial harmony, but always under the rubric of assent to parental guidance and restrictions.

The numerous youth-oriented films produced during the first half of the 1960s reflected this mounting containment of the youth culture, despite the fact that the reality was an increasingly uncontained attitude toward parental authority. While certain films dealt openly with themes of delinquency, these were linked directly with irresponsible fatherhood and the lack of discipline within the home. Unlike in *Juventud desenfrenada*, where absentee parents provided the premise for disorderly youth,[67] parenthood in these delinquency films is always redeemed; children and parents both repent and pay the price for their misdeeds. Moreover, mothers are never depicted in a negative light, whereas fathers are directly assailed for their failings. For example, in *Juventud sin ley (Rebeldes a go-go)* (Lawless Youth, 1965),[68] the arrest of two boys from rival gangs sets the stage for a drawn-out, didactic lesson in the meaning of fatherhood and the moral significance of motherhood. The background of one gang member reveals a working-class family in which a drunken father steals from his wife's earnings and blames her for their son's delinquency: "You're at fault for spoiling him!" he shouts at her early in the film. "Shut up, you're drunk,"

Figure 3.   "The Family Dances the Twist." Source: *Jueves de Excélsior,* 1 February 1962. Used by permission.

she responds in a challenge deemed acceptable because the father had re-linquished his patriarchal authority through irresponsibility. Meanwhile, the father lashes out at his son: "You're a bum with nothing to aspire to but being a delinquent!"

But it is the middle-class background of the second gang member that is more relevant (and it is he who becomes the focus of the film), since here the issues of delinquency were more troubling in their complexity. The mother is divorced and raising her son alone, though with the moral support of a symbolic father, a priest. Hiding the truth from her son that his father had left her for a younger woman, she allows him to grow up believing his father to be dead. In reality, the father is a politically connected judge who, with blatant hypocrisy, appears one night on television denouncing lax parenthood as the basis for *rebeldismo*. Learning of his father's true identity, the son assaults him one night in the hope of getting caught. His plan works, and the ensuing political scandal forces his father's resignation. But when the son accuses his mother of deception (for not telling him the truth about his father's identity), the father hits him: "Your mother is a saint. I was the bad parent." Scolded by the authorities with the words, "A good judge begins in his home," the father must now watch as his son is sent off to a juvenile penitentiary. There, to the rhythm of the band The Rockin' Devils, the locked-up boys sing:

Just leave me alone	Que me dejen en paz
Just let me be.	que me dejen vivir.
I can't speak no more	Ya no puedo ni hablar
I can't sing no more.	ya no puedo ni cantar.
Just leave me alone.	Que me dejen en paz.

Although the son languishes in jail, the incident has brought the parents back together. "Every day I admire and respect you more," the father says to his former wife, reinforcing her moral superiority. The film ends with mother, father, and son praying in church to the Virgin of Guadalupe (the ultimate symbol of motherhood) for her strength and guidance. As the priest approaches them, the father turns to his son and asks for his forgiveness. To this the son replies: "Forgive me father. Forgive me both of you."

In another film of this genre, *La edad de la violencia* (The Age of Violence, 1963),[69] again the relationship between delinquency and the redemption of fatherhood emerges as a central theme. Featuring the rising rocanrol star César Costa, here appearing (rather unconvincingly) as a Marlon Brando–inspired hoodlum, Daniel, a narrator opens the movie against the backdrop of a motorcycle gang roaming the streets of the Mexican capital late at night: "This is a true story to show youth that crime never pays," we are told somberly. Daniel's father was once an important doctor, but when he performed a failed abortion (leading to a patient's death) the mother fled in shame, and the father, having lost his license, turned to alcohol. Costa (Daniel) and his sister (Nancy), in turn, lose all respect for their father, and both fall into a life of crime. But when one of their robberies goes awry, a gang member is critically wounded, and Daniel compels his father to try and save him. Enforcing his own authority within the family of the gang, Daniel stages a mock assassination of a gang member blamed for the fouled robbery. But this too goes awry, and the member (in love with Nancy) is killed. Called in to try and save him nonetheless, the father for the first time stands up to his son and confronts his own irresponsibility: "All of us are guilty. Me above all." His final act of redemption, however, is to turn the gang over to the police, declaring to Daniel: "A long time ago I stopped being your father." He indicates to the police: "Here, we are all assassins." In the final scene father turns to son, beckoning now with renewed moral authority: "Come, my son. You can still return to living and become a good man."

After 1962 such films were themselves displaced by others featuring jubilant youth (often the same actors) against the backdrop of rocanrol as an expression not of delinquency but, rather, of upwardly mobile aspirations and frivolous consumption. In comparison with their counterparts produced in Hollywood, these films avoided the dichotomy of "the college versus the corner,"[70] a central narrative feature of many U.S. teenage films. What they shared, however, was a strategy of presenting an alternative image of youth, one that "was a carefully constructed ideal, part of a systematic attempt to make teenagers *nice.*"[71] Unlike films such as *Juventud sin ley* and *La edad de la violencia,* the mere implication of economic want itself was conveniently purged from these later films, a return to the style characteristic of youth cinema from the mid-1950s (*Juventud desenfrenada,* discussed in the previous chapter, being an important exception).

While reactionaries such as the League of Decency are outwardly mocked, buenas costumbres are explicitly interwoven into the plot structure. In the film, *Twist, la locura de la juventud* (Twist, The Craze of Youth, 1962),[72] for example, the protagonist, Enrique Guzmán of Los Teen Tops (playing himself) pays for his college education by running a soda-fountain café where his band performs. "It's a place," as one character exclaims, "with rhythm!" In an opening scene the "League of Spiritual Health" arrives to close the café down, forcing the band to switch hurriedly from a twist version of "La cucaracha" to a waltz. Though Guzmán's rocanrol group is denounced by the league all the same, a sympathetic judge throws out the case for "lack of evidence." Determined to entrap him, a young female ideologue from the league (Rita) sets out to film Enrique dancing the twist—considered immoral—but the plan backfires, and her spying is exposed. Later apologizing for her actions, Rita says to Enrique, "I had a different idea of you. I thought you were a bad student who just wanted to have fun." To which he replies, "And what's wrong with having fun?" Rita decides that Enrique is right and joins his cause. Declaring that "each generation has its rights . . . above all those regarding its own music," Rita renounces all ties to the League of Spiritual Health and joins the world of youth and diversion, exclaiming, "Long live the twist!" The film ends with everyone from all generations, including the conservative members of the league, dancing the twist.

In another film, *La juventud se impone (La nueva ola)* (Youth Take Over, 1964),[73] via rocanrol intergenerational differences are resolved, and the family unit itself is strengthened. In this film, the modern metropolis of Mexico City symbolizes a country caught in the throes of progress. Rocanrol has the city enveloped; there is no escape from it on the radio and television. The plot revolves around attempts by César Costa and Enrique Guzmán to match their single parents with one another. Meanwhile, the sons' own romantic pursuits benefit enormously from their status as rising rocanrol stars. Costa's father, a widower, is an opera lover with great hopes that his son "can only make it to the Fine Arts Palace" by becoming an opera singer. The father, however, is completely inept with women and openly receives advice from his son on how to date. Guzmán's mother is also widowed, but with more modern habits and tastes (such as dancing the twist) and with a morbid fear of aging. Her image as a "modern woman" directly challenges the traditional view that widows must shield themselves from immoral distractions, forever mourning the death of their husband.[74] Yet at the same time, each parent is single as a result not of divorce but of circumstance; there is modern-day tinkering but no major affront to buenas costumbres. In an effort to set their parents up with one another, the sons deceive them by claiming that each is interested in what the other enjoys, that is, opera and twist. On their first blind date the parents immediately clash over musical tastes (symbolic of their traditional versus modern lifestyles) but decide they like each other anyway. Meanwhile, Costa and Guzmán become embattled in a fierce musical competition, a fight that embroils the entire city. Rocanrol is ultimately presented as a modern dance style that an older generation—even ardent opera lovers—can learn to appreciate. In the end, the dueling sons reconcile their differences by performing a ballad duet at the wedding of their respective parents, reflecting not only the moderation of youth but also the place of modern values in society.

After 1964, a spate of films with names such as *Fiebre de juventud* (Youth Fever, 1965), *Amor a ritmo de go go* (Love to the Rhythm of Go Go, 1966), and *Los años verdes* (The Wonder Years, 1966) continued their "cult of the rock and roll youth style," as Emilio García Riera characterized one such film.[75] Casting aside all associations with the real-life conflicts then emerging, these films instead presented an image of youth in which generational and gender conflicts are resolved through mediation by the family and, where necessary, figures of higher authority.

In *Los años verdes*,[76] for example, the themes of sexuality, parental guidance, and benevolent authority are all tied together against the backdrop of rocanrol. The film takes place at an unnamed private university where men and women are kept from socializing, a situation that a young philosophy professor suggests to the school director needs changing. "There isn't a single reason [for the policy]," he tells the also young female director. "The kids get along in open comradeship without any other notion than healthy diversion. Sometimes I wonder if it isn't we the adults that, with our many prejudices, don't complicate the lives of adolescents, placing obstacles in their path when we should be removing them." The professor wins the director over to his side, leaving only an old woman administrator (dressed in black mourning) as a symbol of resistance to the new liberal order. Although the school brings together students from different social backgrounds by offering scholarships, the image of students presented is nevertheless one of luxury. None is truly destitute, and the line "a poor student, like me" uttered by one character suggests a notion of relative, rather than absolute, poverty as the main problem of society. When two students from different family backgrounds fall in love and are falsely accused by the old woman of having had sexual relations, they run away from the school out of shame. Finding them, the female director is forgiving and states that their real crime was not their feelings but their method of expression, that is, breaking the law by running away. Referring to the female student, Luisa, as "My child," the director instructs them both to "return without fear" to the symbolic family represented by the school. In a metaphor for the stern benevolence of the ruling regime, the director calls in Luisa's parents (her mother and stepfather who had "abandoned" her while they traveled the globe) and berates them for not being more attentive to the love and attention required by their daughter. The film ends with Los Hooligans performing a waltz in tribute to the benevolence of the director. Symbolizing the mediating role of music and the coherence of the larger societal family, the director accepts an invitation to dance with the philosophy teacher. The film closes with all couples, young and old, dancing a waltz together.

This image of a contained youth culture was promoted at all levels, from films, to radio, to the numerous fanzines of the period. The latter served a large teenage audience not only throughout the republic but, in the case of *México canta*, for instance, reaching Central and South American countries and parts of the United States as well. It is perhaps unsurprising to find that

Figure 4. *México Canta* featured the buttoned-down look of refrito groups like Los Locos del Ritmo during the mid-1960s. Source: *México Canta*, October, 1965, in the author's personal collection.

these magazines presented a clean-cut image of rock 'n' roll, both Mexican and Anglo, which, after all, matched the global teenybopper fad (see Figure 4). As was true more generally, for instance, the pages of these magazines served as a medium for juvenile communication about such concerns as finding opposite-sex pen pals, discovering tidbits about the private and public lives of local and Hollywood stars, and learning the lyrics of the latest songs (often translated into Spanish). *México canta* was, in sum, "a magazine dedicated to youth gossip,"[77] a statement (sent in by a reader) that was no doubt apt for all magazines of this genre. Still, there was almost an exaggerated effort by writers to present an image of rocanrol as non-threatening, healthy entertainment. In an article on the twist, for instance, one writer noted that while prohibited in certain places around the world, "every generation has its own craziness." He concludes by stating, "We are for the Twist because it is a healthy and fun dance."[78] In another example, a feature article on Los Locos del Ritmo opens by declaring, "They're not crazy! They're just four dynamic, happy, and enthusiastic young students in pursuit of a dignified career which provides them a clean and honest living."[79]

It is revealing, nonetheless, to witness efforts by the government's Qualifying Commission of Magazines and Illustrated Publications, which, at least in one case, sought to suppress the spread of magazines that openly exploited the public's taste for rocanrol. Dating from a licensing petition in January 1962, the magazine *La Historia del Rock 'n' Roll y el Twist*, was denounced for its very title which, according to the commission, "contains foreign words which have no grammatical significance whatsoever,"[80] a dubious attack, given that *rock 'n' roll* and *twist* were both part of the vernacular by that time. In fact, the magazine's title had mutated since its first issue. It started with the name *La Historia del Rock 'n' Roll* in November 1961; then *Es la Historia de la Juventud* was added in December; and it finally settled on *La Historia del Rock 'n' Roll y el Twist* for its fourth issue.[81] In a second petition for licensing, also denied, the commission noted that "this is a publication which directly exalts persons who have reached notoriety as singers of rock 'n' roll and twist . . . such as Elvis Presley, Bill Haley, Paul Anka, Bobby Darin, Chubby Checker, etc." The magazine therefore "promoted customs foreign to our own" and fell within the limits set by the commission guidelines on censorship: "In that which is referred to as its literary content, this publication is dedicated to promoting the life and successes of artists and pseudo-artists who interpret recently created melodies, known by the names of 'Rock 'n' rol' and 'twist' which in recent days have reached a surprising and ephemeral popularity and that, in sum, are nothing but musical turns which directly damage proper taste and propose to eradicate authentically Mexican popular music."[82] Moreover, the magazine "utilized texts which systematically employ expressions which offend the correct use of the language, as is the actual title of the publication . . . and, as is natural when dealing with foreign songs which, when translated employ vulgarized equivalents, the publication in question employs diverse words that are not Spanish."[83]

Although the commission's battle was ultimately a lost cause, the language and obstacles raised in these debates reveals the important presence of conservative influences that helped shape a contained discourse of youth rebellion. By the latter half of the decade, however, as the content and imagery of rock music became bolder (a point explored in the next chapter), the task of containment itself took new turns.

THE SOCIAL USES OF *ROCANROL*

While the image of youth presented on the screen and in magazines was overwhelmingly one of conformity, the reality of rocanrol's impact on everyday life was often more decisive. Though the majority of songs from this early period dealt with themes of teenage romance and leisure time, they were written in such a way as to not offend adult morals. Yet in a society where girls were still prohibited from attending social events unescorted, where teenage dating was regarded as a trajectory toward marriage, and where children lived with their parents until—and even after—marriage, such songs staked out an important space for youth apart from, and even at times against the sensibilities of, conservative parents. In the song "La chica alborotada" (The Wild Girl, a cover of Freddy Cannon's "Tallahassee Lassie") by Los Locos del Ritmo, for example, teenage flirting is intimately tied to the new youth culture:

That wild girl	Esa chica alborotada
is a little insane	es un poquito alocada
and if you look for her	y si acaso tú la buscas
she'll say you like her.	te dirá que tú le gustas,
She's my wild girl	es mi chica alborotada
and she'll never change.	nunca cambiará.
If you watch her walk	Si la miras caminar
you'll start to shake.	te pones a temblar,
Her skirt's at her knees, oh!	¡falda a las rodillas, ay!
what calves, ooh, ooh, ooh.	qué pantorrillas, ou, ou, ou.
If you take her out dancing	Si la llevas a bailar
she dances real cool.	baila a todo dar.
She dances rock 'n' roll	Baila rock 'n' roll
and the twist as well.	te baila twist también.[84]

In an examination of several songs from this period one finds various references to the connection between rock 'n' roll and youth liberation that, if sanitized by the media presentation of the groups themselves, undoubtedly created important "slippages" that were exploited by young consumers. For example, in the refrito of "Good Golly Miss Molly," originally performed by Little Richard, Los Teen Tops' version, "La plaga," becomes:

Here comes the gal, she sure likes to dance.	Ahí viene "La Plaga,"[85] le gusta bailar.

And when she's rockin' and a-rollin'	Y cuando está rocanroleando
she's the queen of this place.	es la reina del lugar.
My parents told me	Mis jefes me dijeron
to quit that rock and roll.	ya no bailes rock and roll.
If we see you with that girl	Si te vemos con "La Plaga"
your allowance is over.	tu domingo se acabó.
Let's go see the priest	Vamos con el cura,
'cause I want to get married.	que ya me quiero casar.
It's not that you're real good lookin'	No es que seas muy bonita,
but you sure know how to dance.	sino que sabes bailar.[86]

Knowing how to dance is thus directly associated with being wild and breaking the rules, even if the lyrics return to marriage as the endpoint of the relationship. Interestingly, in the original lyric by Armando Martínez *jefes* (literally, old men, as in "my old man") is as *padres*, (parents), while the line "Vamos con el cura" (Let's go see the priest) is as "Esto ya va en serio" (This is getting serious). On the one hand, therefore, we see a transformation of a respectful discourse into colloquialisms; on the other, we see the substitution of a nonreligious referent for one with explicit ties to Church-sanctioned marriage. Still, this was a far more wholesome version of the song than Little Richard's, which also centered on the theme of the wild girl. The first stanza, for instance, goes:

Good golly Miss Molly,
sure likes to ball.
And when she's rock'n and a-rolling,
can't hear your mama call.

In other refrito recordings many of these groups consciously mimicked the linguistic intonations of Elvis Presley (while refraining from his patented pelvic thrust), Chuck Berry and others; though performed in Spanish, guttural references to the original were obvious. Presley's influence, especially, was strongly evident. This was reflected, for example, in a refrito of his song "King Creole," the title of the film that was the setting of the 1959 riot in Mexico City. In recording the song, Los Teen Tops directly referenced the ill-fated showing of the film two years earlier. And while there are noticeable similarities between the original and the refrito lyrics, significant differences are also present. The original goes in part:

There's a man in New Orleans
who plays rock and roll.
He's a guitar man with a great big soul.

He lays down a beat like a ton of coal.
He goes by the name of King Creole.

You know he's gone, gone, gone,
Jumpin' like a catfish on a pole.
You know he's gone, gone, gone,
Hip-shaking King Creole.

When the king starts to do it,
it's as good as done.
He holds his guitar like a tommy gun.
He starts to growl from 'way down in his throat.
He bends a string and "that's all she wrote."

You know he's gone, gone, gone. . . .[87]

In the Spanish version, "King Creole" is not only a source of authenticity—
as he is in the original—but, moreover, a site of knowledge, suggesting that
those who have "seen him" (that is, in the film) really know what's going on:

There's a man in the city	Hay un hombre en la ciudad
who likes to play rock and roll.	al que le gusta el rock.
He's a guitar man	Toca la guitarra
with a great big soul.	y te sabe cantar.
The people who see him	La gente que lo ve
say he's the best.	dice que es el mejor.
And they all know him	Y todos lo conocen
as the King of Rock.	como el Rey del Rock.
They say, "Come, come, come"	Le dicen, "Ven, ven, ven."
'Cause I want to see you dance.	Que te quiero ver bailar.
They say, "Come, come, come."	Le dicen, "Ven, ven, ven."
Now's the time to kick back.	Ahora es tiempo de gozar.
When he starts to play	Cuando empieza a tocar
the people start to scream.	la gente empieza a gritar.
And he moves like you	Y tiene un movimiento
wouldn't believe.	que no puedes creer
When he plays the blues	Cuando toca el blues
Oh, I want to die!	¡Oh!, yo me siento morir.
And everybody begins to shake.	Y toda la gente se comienza a
	mover.
They say, "Come, come, come". . . .	Le dicen, "Ven, ven, ven". . . .[88]

What is notable about these songs is the fact that, despite a commercialized
image of rocanrol as intergenerational (or at least inoffensive to adults), the

lyrics make explicit the connection with youth. Despite parental guidance and even participation, ultimately this was music for and by youth.

Perhaps the most significant song from this period and one of the only original tunes actually recorded was "I'm No Rebel" (Yo no soy un rebelde) by Jesús ("Chucho") González of Los Locos del Ritmo. By directly referencing the public furor over rebeldismo, the song encapsulated the controversy over delinquency while promoting native rocanrol as a defining vehicle for youth:

I'm no "rebel without a cause"	Yo no soy un "rebelde sin causa"
Nor some wanton youth.	Ni tampoco un desenfrenado.
All I want to do is to	Lo único que quiero
dance rock 'n' roll,	es bailar rocanrol
so just let me hang out	Y que me dejen vacilar
without a hassle.	sin ton ni son.
Check out Los Locos and let's form	Mira a Los Locos y formemos en la
a fan club.	plana una afición.
Bring along any chicks you	Traigan chamacas que anden
see and get them to party	viendo y que nos den un buen
with us.	jalón.
Even without the rebel's records,	Sin los discos del rebelde habrán
we'll have a real good time.	un buen vacilón.
Let's shake our hair	Que se suelten las melenas,
and let our forelocks hang.	vengan abajo los copetes.
Hey, let's take off our ties	¡Ay!, que se quiten las corbatas
and put on our [leather] jackets,	Que se pongan las chamarras
our guitars are dangling	las guitarras en las rodillas sin
and we won't stop playing.	parar.
Here, we've got Italian switchblades	Aquí hay navajas italianas
and blue jeans,	pantalones que sean vaqueros,
and our legs are a-tremblin'	que nos tiemblen nuestras piernas
uncontrollably.	sin cesar.[89]

Not only did the song incorporate the imagery of rebellion, but its use of certain street slang—*jalón, melenas, vacilar*—directly commercialized a grammar of youth rebellion as well. The song, of course, was an exception, though an important one. As the novelist José Agustín would later comment, it became a "quasi-hymn among youth."[90]

In general, however, lyric content was largely devoid of generational conflict. All the same, the songs were belted out with the same rhythmic

Figure 5. Scores of Mexican bands emerged by the early 1960s to meet the demand for rocanrol, as in this unidentified photograph, probably taken at a private party. Source: "Concentrados: sobre 2206, 'Rock and Roll,' n.d.," Hermanos Mayo Photo Archive, Archivo General de la Nación. Used by permission.

ferocity of their imported originals (see Figure 5). It *was* rock 'n' roll, after all, and the emphasis was on playing it at the highest possible volume. Describing conflicts with her parents over playing the music at home, one informant recalls: "There always arrived a point when your parents told you to turn it off. Not for the lyrics, which were in Spanish, but because of the noise. That was the [only] problem we really had. It's not that your parents were shocked by the lyrics, like they are today, but more because of the scandal the noise created. For them it was something new, because none of the music from their era was so noisy as rock 'n' roll."[91] Of course, it was not just the noise that was problematic. Rocanrol, despite its domestication, still implied a disruption of social control for many adults. This was especially true, for example, when it was introduced into social spaces marked by traditional hierarchies. In one anecdote, an informant recalls what happened when a group of students brought a recording to their secondary school:

> Being a good girl from an intellectual and traditional family, I was a
> very good student, very well behaved. All of the teachers loved me.
> And one day I was with a group of girlfriends studying and they put on

a tape. I guess one of them had parents who had brought them a tape player from who knows where—that was quite extraordinary for a kid of that age to have a tape recorder—and she brought it to school and put on a cassette of Mexican rocanrol. Suddenly the director of the school chanced to pass by and it became a huge deal. She reacted so sharply, so irrationally, it was as if she had caught us taking drugs or something. She called our parents and made a big scandal. She even mentioned in at the school assembly.[92]

Nor were other socially sanctified spaces immune to the rocanrol invasion. For example, concerns of an older generation were also reflected in criticism of the transformation of the *posadas*, a traditional religious celebration held for nine days leading up to Christmas. A communal reenactment of the biblical story of Joseph and Mary's quest for shelter, the posadas had a long cultural heritage in Mexico and were a focal point for community celebration. Each night members of the community *piden posada* (ask for shelter) from their neighbors in a ritual of call-and-response singing. Gathering in numbers after being "turned away" by each household, the wandering choir finally receives posada, which culminates in the breaking of a piñata and a night of festivities. But these festivities were not isolated from the new youth culture, which began to introduce its own set of values to the event. One writer's reaction to this transformation provides a sense of the contradictions experienced by an older generation that both embraced the country's modernization process and yet felt threatened by the implications of such change. "We don't want to fall into the opinion that all that belongs to past epochs is better than the present," the author began. "The customs and systems are changing and we believe that today life is more practical and comfortable." He continued: "However, it is regrettable that certain customs, deeply rooted in tradition, are transforming, are changing radically and are losing their form and spirit unnecessarily.... Today the 'posadas' only retain a superfluous aspect—the adornments, wreaths, *Nochebuena* [poinsettia], colored lights—and are converted into carousals, with 'aggressive' dancing and swinging legs and hips in the 'twist,' without anyone recalling the original and genuine spirit of these traditional fiestas." In an accompanying photograph showing a young couple dancing together, contrabass and drumset in the background, the text reads: "The 'posadas' that are organized today by young people do not have any of the traditional characteristics and end in 'twist' exhibitions and other contortions of the modern dances."[93] The permeation of a religious festivity by rock 'n' roll thus suggested the ways in which the youth culture had begun to transform traditional cultural relations at an everyday level.

Another important social space for rocanrol were private parties at home, which acquired the name *tardeadas* from the word for *afternoon*. Following the midday meal, which in Mexico is an important family function, youth had the late-afternoon hours to dispose of their leisure time as they pleased, as long as parents approved (or were eluded). Hopefully, someone offered his or her home for the gathering. Even in the more conservative homes, youth discovered ways of being daring, such as one woman's description of tardeadas that took place in her own home: "My [older] sister formed a neighborhood 'club' and even made up club IDs. They organized various games centered around dancing. One was a 'strip game' [*juego de prendas*], where you throw the dice or spin a plate . . . and if you lose you throw in a watch or a ring, something. And then you danced what the group says. Like, "Imitate Elvis Presley," and so [the losers] had to do it."[94] Taking off one's clothes (as shown in a juego de prendas in the movie *Juventud desenfrenada*) would have passed the boundaries of respect; squirming around like Elvis was bold enough. Under the watchful eye of parents, these parties stayed far within the boundaries of excess. As another informant described the tardeada, "It was a youth get-together exclusively to listen to music and, of course, to dance. No one even considered drinking alcohol at that time. It was unheard of that a party got out of hand."[95] However, for women, especially, even these parties could be deemed off limits by anxious parents. As the first informant continued, "But my family was so traditional that I wasn't able to participate much in that either. I just didn't have permission to go to such things. Imagine, [these parties] brought men and women dancing together!"

Rocanrol as a musical style had infiltrated popular culture at various levels, appearing, for example, at birthday parties and even *quince años* (a coming-out-to-society celebration for girls turning fifteen). Yet while many parents may have accepted the rhythm itself, the fashion statements that accompanied it revealed the underlying conflicts between the generations. As Conchita Cervantes recalls,

> You know, for example, the way of dressing was very difficult for my parents to accept. That guys would arrive at a party without a tie or without a jacket, for instance. That was a big problem in my home: that the neighborhood kids arrived in pullover sweaters and tight pants, styles of the rock 'n' roll culture. . . . I remember my father even chasing boys from my home because they did not arrive in a tie at our birthday parties. If it was an informal party, they could come in a shirt and sweater, but if it was a more formal party then everyone had to come in a tie. No one entered in a regular jacket, none of that.[96]

Thus rocanrol may not have been subversive of buenas costumbres on the face of it, but in its usage it became a wedge against the dictates of parents and other voices of authority.

Actual performance spaces for live rocanrol ranged from organized concerts for the public, to private parties, hotel nightclubs, and the numerous cafés cantantes that began to dot the capital landscape. But other than Bill Haley at the start of the decade, few foreign performers actually appeared during this period. In 1962 reports again circulated that Elvis Presley would be coming to Mexico City, a rumor that proved to be untrue.[97] When Frankie Avalon appeared in 1965, the audience became so enthusiastic that *Variety* would afterward call the resulting chaos a "riot."[98] In fact, keeping the crowds away from local rocanroleros was sometimes trouble enough. At a performance in Puebla for César Costa, former leader of the Black Jeans, police reportedly resorted to throwing photographs of the artist into the crowd to avoid a melee.[99] Yet commercial sponsorship of bands led to tours throughout the republic (and in certain cases beyond), where artists performed in concert halls, cinemas, and even bullfighting rings. One of the more important sponsorship tours was organized by the Corona Beer Company, which joined together bands and solo artists from various record companies. Ranchera performers thus shared the stage with younger stars, although the rocanroleros were distinguished by their separate travel accommodations: the "Camión a go-go" (Go-Go Bus).[100] Record companies also organized musical competitions in conjunction with radio and television stations, which attracted listeners and viewers with trophies for contestants and giveaways for audiences.[101]

But the most significant social spaces that merged around rocanrol were the cafés cantantes, also identified as cafés existencialistas and cafés a go-go. These places served as focal points for youth reunions, and, both in practice and in representation on film, they came to have a mixed reputation. While they varied in size and category, ranging from fancier nightspots such as the Chamonix, which served upper-class youth in Polanco, to danker holes such as the Sótano (Basement), which catered more to the middle classes, all featured live music (frequently by the same bands) playing songs from the hit charts. These were not clubs in the traditional sense: no alcohol was served, and generally they were not for dancing. Rather, they provided an escape for youth from the watchful eyes and ears of adults, organized around the language of rock 'n' roll: "The atmosphere conformed somewhat to the notion of rock itself, in that there was a rejection of the established norms. For example, back then the seats and tables were really low. The lighting was very, very dim. . . . In general, basically one went to those places to get picked up, or to go there with your date and have a good time. There in the darkness nobody knew who was who and so it was really comfortable."[102] In films from this early period, the cafés are depicted variously as modern nightspots (in *La edad de la violencia* a Picasso painting hangs on the wall) or shady hangouts (as in *Juventud sin ley*) and were generally associated with malevolent deeds. Later films sought to adjust this image, as in *Twist, la locura de la juventud*, where the well-lit café doubles as an ice-cream parlor. Johnny Laboriel, who performed in numerous clubs with Los Rebeldes del Rock during this period, argues that prior to 1965 an atmosphere of "healthy entertainment" unmarred by drugs or alcohol prevailed.[103] If this was the atmosphere on the whole, it did not stop police harassment, and in 1963 many of the cafés were shut down on the pretext that they fomented criminal activities.[104] Moreover, parents looked with concern on such unsupervised social spaces, and with the shift from rock 'n' roll to the more irreverent style of rock performance around 1965, these clubs faced even greater repression.

A HEGEMONIC ARRANGEMENT

The containment of rock 'n' roll during the early 1960s was part of a broader movement of self-policing the boundaries of media representation. Such efforts to "clean up" the representation of modern Mexico did not originate with agents of the media, but, under the pressure of conservative watchdog groups and the 1960 law regulating broadcasting, every effort was made to demonstrate a willingness to conform rather than provoke. Thus in July 1963 the National Chamber of Broadcasting Industries addressed a letter to President López Mateos reaffirming its commitment to "elevate the cultural, civic, and social level of our transmissions in order to comply faithfully with the social function which the law requires."[105] The letter prefaced an agreement drawn up between the chamber and various advertising and commercial interest groups to "autolimit ourselves . . . in the production of radio and television soap operas, as well as other ethical and moral norms that should be observed by the people who directly or indirectly participate in the transmission of radio and television." The origins of the pact were an explicit response to what the letter alluded to as an "impending threat . . . derived from a definitive current" of conservative media watchdogs, such as the Mexican League of Decency. This "current" was continuing to accuse the radio and television industry of "transmitting themes which offend morality and family values" and thus not complying strictly with the Radio and Television Law of 1960.

The new pact in actuality simply reaffirmed many of the basic provisions established in the 1960 law (see chapter 1). For example, in terms of language any "impudent, obscene expressions [and] sentences using double-meaning" were to be eliminated. With regard to the image of "matrimony, family [and] home," it was agreed to "maintain a consistent practice with respect to matrimony as the fundamental [element] of the family, the home and society." Suicide would be "proscribed as a solution to any problem." Significantly, music and dance received special mention. To be eliminated were "transmissions of every musical selection whose lyrics might offend even the most open-minded persons." The censorship of music underscored the broadcasters' commitment "to orient the transmissions in a way that complies wholly with their social function as cooperating with the resolution of problems in Mexico, fortifying democratic convictions, national characteristics, cultures and traditions of the country, and combating the influence of ideologies which undermine and are contrary to our Institutions." Also covered by the pact was the self-censorship of "imprudent and lewd attitudes and scenes [on television] taking special care with dances," a reference to the often risqué shots in youth films of underage females' legs and undergarments when dancing. "All 'close ups' or 'takes' that concentrate attention in a way that is intentional and improper will be eliminated," the pact stated plainly.

This document suggests several things. For one, it reflected an attempt by commercial interests to fortify their position in the face of continued attacks against them by conservative interests. Second, it suggested the ineffectualness of the federal government in enforcing the 1960 law, since the pact largely repeated, though in greater detail, the same themes covered by the earlier law. Third, it underscored the importance the broadcasting industry placed on not wanting to create problems with the government over media content. By expressing directly to the president their intentions to "comply faithfully with the social function" assigned to them by law, broadcasting interests sought to preempt any excuse for broader censorship by the regime. The larger picture that thus emerges is a hegemonic arrangement between the ruling regime and the major figures of the mass media in which the latter operated under relative autonomy in exchange for a policy of self-censorship. It was under these conditions that a contained youth culture was successfully commercialized for the first half of the 1960s. However, as the logic of this movement later changed—as psychedelia emerged as the leit motif of the youth culture abroad—the cultural industries would find themselves constrained by a hegemonic arrangement that restricted commercializing new gestures of rebellion.

Nonetheless this was rocanrol's Grand Era, a term used to this day. While several of these bands continued to perform throughout much of the 1960s, around 1963 the record companies found that steering star performers away from group efforts and into the modern *baladista* (romantic soloists) style then emerging in vogue internationally (led by artists such as Paul Anka and Connie Francis) was both more manageable and equally, if not more, profitable. Johnny Laboriel was an exception to this (remaining faithful to his Rebeldes del Rock), but César Costa of the Black Jeans and Enrique Guzmán of Los Teen Tops joined the ranks of female performers Julissa and Angélica María to begin solo careers. "The end result," writes Roura, "was a ballad that was less perturbing, less committed, more tranquilizing"[106] than music with a backbeat.

Spanish-language rocanrol had been promoted by commercial interests and adopted by mainstream society as a metaphor for modernity: an exuberant, nonthreatening vehicle for the expression of liberalism and leisure consumption. Indeed, in the aftermath of the 1958 student and union conflicts, rocanrol appeared as a convenient distraction for youth, one purged of its direct ties and associations with rebeldismo. Repackaged as a product of the modernizing Revolution, Mexican rocanrol and the baladista style that followed were proffered by the cultural industries as the embodiment of familial harmony and social progress, a medium for improved communications between the generations and a moderator of youthful restlessness. Containing this image, however, proved increasingly precarious after mid-decade. With the arrival of the Beatles and the new wave of British (and in turn, U.S.) bands that they heralded, rock 'n' roll shed whatever lingering charm it once retained for adults and became simply rock. With the resultant change in musical expression came renewed fears of youth disorderliness and the coincident reality of political crisis.

The interests responsible for producing and distributing native rocanrol were keenly aware of conservative and xenophobic currents in Mexican society and thus sought to avoid provoking a possible backlash by presenting a contained version of the youth culture. This version glossed over themes of juvenile delinquency and social alienation to present an image of youth as the modernizing agents in a society of benign paternalism. Via the promotion of a native rocanrol movement a different self-image of Mexico, one that contrasted with the stereotyped vision of campesinos sleeping lazily under their sombreros, emerged. Thus bilingual liner notes from an album by Los Rebeldes del Rock not only indicated the group's marketing in the Anglo world but also highlighted the transformed image of Mexico that the industry and the band hoped to project: "Music is the and [*sic*] result of the animated status of the multitudes[.] Musically we have liverd [*sic*] several cycles, the Waltz, the Charleston, the Swing, the Fox-trot, the Boogie-boogie [*sic*], etc.; leading todays [*sic*] modern craze[,] the product of youths [*sic*] search for new horizons in music—Rock! Rock 'n' Roll, authentic symbol of modern youth, represents their anxieties in a new musical sense with which they have not only revolutionized rythm [*sic*] but also musical techniques. This current has also affected Mexico." [107] The global tours by groups such as Los Locos del Ritmo and Los Loud Jets (known as The Mexican Jets abroad) underscored for Mexican society, if perhaps less so for the world at large, the transformation of Mexico from a Third World nation targeted for consumption to an exporter of global popular culture. Appearing in a photograph at the 1964 World's Fair in New York City, the Mexican Jets came to represent the cosmopolitan aspirations of the country's elite and middle classes alike.[108] As long as the record companies and television producers had virtually complete control over the musicians' recorded performances, the transmitted image of rocanrol was closely cropped for any gestures of defiance that might violate the established norms—and laws—governing the representation of youth, family, and nation. Thus for Víctor Roura, this period was characterized by nothing less than a "simulated rebellion" [109] that served the interests of an older generation as much as it did the young. However, in spite of its circumscription by the media, the movement had a profound impact on society. Containing the strategies of consumption of this music—its relationship to the transformation of cultural values and its spatial conquests—was a less tenable proposition.

3 La Onda

Mexico's Counterculture and the Student Movement of 1968

Precisely at a moment when the baladista movement appeared to be draining rocanrol of its driving forces, the Beatles arrived and changed everything. As elsewhere in the world, the British invasion of Mexico signaled a definitive shift in the musical direction of rock 'n' roll toward what increasingly became known simply as *rock*. Musical composition and performance style changed dramatically, as a new level of competition swept across the Atlantic and raised the stakes of teenage tastes. Pushed aside were crooners and twisters alike, replaced with the more irreverent postures of the new rockers. In Mexico, once again the association of English with authenticity became inextricable from the new rock product. The containment of rock 'n' roll via its Spanish-language domestication now entered into crisis as audiences increasingly demanded "the real thing," anxiously emulating the new fashions and gestures of defiance by groups once more introduced by transnational capital. By 1968, as the cultural industries wrestled with the contradictions of containing the images and sounds of the psychedelic revolution, families and government alike discovered that the emergent counterculture had laid the basis for turning patriarchy on its head.

THE BRITISH INVASION AND *EL ARTE DE FUSIL*

If the British invaded North America via the Atlantic, in Mexico they came via the Rio Grande. Starting around late 1964, a new wave of bands literally versed in the emergent rock scene abroad descended on the capital from the northern provinces in search of record contracts and broader audiences. Accustomed to performing for tourists in nightclubs along the border, these bands bowled over Mexico City crowds with their adept English-language renditions of the latest rock sensations. Overnight, Spanish-language re-

93

fritos became trite, second-rate efforts compared with the "originals" that these new bands performed. In fact, as the novelist and rock musician Federico Arana recalls, these "frontier armies," as he labels them, created an economic crisis for other bands. In order to defend their commercial turf, the older bands found themselves in competition with musicians whose mastery of English was far superior. "In sum," Arana writes, "this was a crisis for us rockers, as we had quite a bit of work to catch up on. All of those middle-class consumers of records from the latest British superstars were dying to hear 'live' hits such as 'Twist and Shout,' 'Girl,' 'I Saw Her Standing There,' etcetera."[1] With names such as Los Dug Dugs, Los Yaki, Los Belmonts, Los Apson, Tijuana-5, and Javier Batiz and His Famous Finks, these new bands dramatically transformed the cultural scene emanating from the capital.

These exact English-language covers of the original became known as *fusiles* or *el arte de fusil*, literally "the art of projection" (from the verb *fusilar*, "to take aim"). As greater importance was placed on access to the originals, a concept of authenticity explicitly grounded in English-language performance and the imported album, the idea of the refrito was disparaged, and record companies were forced to shift their approach accordingly, though they still resisted breaking free of the formula of Spanish-language covers. On studio recordings, all groups were still pressured by the companies to sing Spanish refritos; this was the only way bands could expect airplay for their songs. But records pressed in Mexico now generally included both English and Spanish translations (as well as credits, something that had been neglected earlier) of the song titles. Moreover, liner notes addressed the significance of what lay inside, as with the 45 rpm single of the Rolling Stones' "Paint It Black": "The Rolling Stones hold the trump card among all of the other interpreters of modern music: their authenticity. They're authentic in how they play, sing, dress, speak, behave in public or any other situation; in how they select their repertoire, make their [musical] arrangements, and devote themselves wholly [to what they do], from their image of wanton abandon to the depths of their thinking."[2] Whereas earlier the lyric content had been less important than the musical rhythm—allowing for the wide success of the refritos, which often took liberties in their translations from the original—now *what* was said became as important as *how* it was said.

But in live performances, audiences increasingly demanded a more "authentic" version of the tunes they were hearing, which required singing in English. The novelist and critic José Agustín, in praising the quality of Los Dug Dugs—a band from Durango that built a reputation based on its precise interpretations of foreign rock, especially the Beatles—wrote that the band's performance of certain difficult songs in fact "exceeded the original versions."[3] This striving to perfection in English may be explained partially by the fact that while middle-class youth yearned to be a part of the global counterculture, their lived experiences were in fact defined by cultural marginalization. Magazines widely disseminated images, lyrics, and stories about the rock movement abroad, and radio stations began to play selected hits of the new music. Yet unconditional access on demand was out of the question, except perhaps for the upper classes: due to high tariffs, records were still exceedingly costly and difficult to come by. Moreover, the prospect of seeing a well-known artist perform live was virtually nil. Seen from this perspective, the mimicking of foreign rock styles and intonations was not only an attempt to *belong* to a global movement; it also became an act of defiance against a cultural and political structure that limited and denied access to rock as (world) popular culture.

The route by which Los Dug Dugs came to Mexico City and achieved fame is instructive of this process. Armando Nava, the band's lead guitarist, singer, and flautist, explained how he went to Tijuana with a group he had first formed in high school. On the border they found work playing at cabaret theaters catering to tourists. "We started off playing music in Spanish, but then played in English too," he said. As band leader, he immersed himself in Beatles songs and, despite his lack of English, managed to learn the lyrics. When he felt the group's repertoire was perfected, the band headed for Mexico City in the hopes of striking it big. In the capital they literally became agents for the introduction of music that was defined above all by its scarcity. Describing the market for rock in Mexico City, Nava recalls that it "was virgin in terms of the music we brought with us. . . . They hadn't heard this music before. For example, we started [our first concert] with the Beatles, 'You've Got to Hide Your Love Away,' and the crowd went nuts. Nobody played those things."[4] In fact, Los Dug Dugs' introduction of the Beatles' repertoire preceded the arrival of Capitol Records, the Beatles' label, which did not establish a subsidiary in Mexico City until 1965, after the Beatles were already a worldwide sensation.[5] Up to that point, the Beatles' catalog was distributed locally by Musart, a company not particularly known for its rock selection. As Nava explained, "Music in English became extremely popular in Mexico, but it took forever for what was known [abroad] to arrive. . . . For example, we already had the albums. We brought them directly from the United States and would learn the music before it even came here. Then when we played it we were the ones who made it popular, even before it was on the radio. . . . That was an important factor in why Los Dug Dugs became so well known."[6] It was precisely this lack of access to rock as a mass cultural phenomenon that reinforced a sense of cultural distancing and hence the urging by fans to "get closer" to the original.[7]

The problem of access was due above all to the high tariff barriers that discouraged mass distribution. One informant who grew up in Cuernavaca, an hour's drive south of Mexico City and where rock was even less available than it was in the capital, recalled how the limited availability of rock transformed the acquisition of a new album into a communally experienced event: "[Our music came] from people who went to the United States. We were always trying to track down those people who traveled back and forth to tape another record. . . . Buying [albums] wasn't very widespread. It wasn't very easy. So, [people's collections] were like treasuries. . . . If someone got a new record it was a question of getting together to listen to it at whichever house had the best record player and comment on it, admire it."[8] From the industry's perspective, the tariff walls meant that record sales required a lengthier process of reproduction from the original master. As Enrique Partida, who worked with Polydor Records (now Polygram) relates, "Music wasn't really imported [by record companies] then like it is today, with the compact disc. Everything was done in Mexico. The master tape was brought to Mexico, and the record was produced with art on the album cover and everything. Importation [by the companies] was rather limited [because of high tariffs]. So, the process [of producing an album from the master] took between six months and a year . . . That is, with the exception of the Beatles [after 1965]."[9] This process imposed a rationale of economic efficiency that inevitably compromised the integrity of the original album. A song's availability depended on the company's decision to acquire the master (determined by licensing agreements and presumptions of the local market for a particular artist), which in itself could mean up to a year's delay. Moreover, the record companies were quite content to reproduce composite albums or simply 45 rpm singles of an artist's hits—which could be exploited on an individual basis—without regard to the orientation of the original album's presentation.

The record companies understood the demand for rock clearly enough, but their marketing strategy closely followed the trajectory of an earlier musical product. What they failed to grasp was the longing of fans for greater access and the need to "get closer" to the authentic rock commodity. It was not only the song that now mattered but, ultimately, access to its authentic presentation as well.

Thus, album covers and even song titles were often deformed through

translation or simple misspelling, according to the whim or, more generally, ignorance of the local producer. In a period when the album cover itself would become increasingly integral to the concept of the record as art
commodity, access to a second-rate version reinforced a sense of cultural
marginalization. As Armando Blanco, later founder of Mexico City's first
rock-paraphernalia shop, Hip-70, dedicated in particular to the importation
of foreign rock, commented, "Many times [the record companies] changed
the tracks, or from two records they produced only one, thus wrecking what
was traditional and sacred concerning the album cover and the movement
itself—above all, the spirit that was under way." [10] Hence the massification
of a rock *concept* embodied in the images, discussions, and available sounds
linked to the rock phenomenon occurring abroad contradicted the limited
accessibility of rock as a *commodity* within the reach of the middle classes.
Moreover, the marketing of rock music occurred without regard to an authentic replication of the original rock commodity itself. Rock music's consumption was thus doubly fetishized: first because of the nature of rock as
a mass cultural commodity (that is, the masking of production that occurs
in the studio); and then because of the inherent distancing of Mexican rock
consumers from the original product (a situation that distorted the exchange value of the rock album still further). [11]

Though the public had only limited access to the actual recordings, the
impact of the British invasion was felt nonetheless, especially in the transformation of radio programming. Local bands continued to receive airplay
for their covers, now mostly ballads, but other stations dedicated time exclusively to the original, a change of vital significance for a younger generation coming of age. As Jaime Pontones, now an important rock disc jockey
in Mexico City, recalls:

> I remember listening to Radio Mil, where they played Los Teen Tops,
> Los Rebeldes del Rock—all of those groups—and one day, I changed
> the station and came upon Radio Capital . . . and I started to hear what
> was already being played on Radio Mil, only in English! And suddenly,
> after hearing "Jailhouse Rock" in Spanish, I now heard how it sounded
> in English. I was totally blown away! And I think that happened to a
> lot of people of my generation; that is, they passed from Los Teen Tops
> and whatnot to the first "English Wave" around 1964 or so. [12]

Being close enough to actually see the Beatles or the Rolling Stones in
person—or the countless other groups that heralded the rock revolution—
was highly unlikely. Mexican audiences instead would have to remain content with the simulacrum performances of local bands that, by necessity

and default, emerged as the interpreters of a countercultural consciousness exploding around the world.

THE *CAFES CANTANTES*

The most important performance spaces for rock were the numerous youth clubs that had mushroomed throughout the capital by 1965. As already noted, these clubs had a dubious image in the public mind-set, where they were connected with rebeldismo, despite their generally innocuous reality. Their existence remained dependent on the benevolence of the authorities. But if in the early 1960s the cafés had served as an alternative space set apart for youth, with the switch to rock performance in English their entire ambiance began to change. For it was here in the cafés that middle-class youth could truly experience the sensation of belonging to a universal rock movement that was denied to them at so many other levels. This sensation was conveyed, above all, in the performance style of the scores of bands that now filled the clubs' rosters. The clubs were still essentially juice bars, but those in attendance began to imagine themselves as part of a more cosmopolitan world.

Compared with Spanish-language rocanrol, whose restrained provincialism came to remind audiences of their Third World entrapment, live performance in English allowed musicians and audiences alike to project themselves onto a fantasy space of a universal rock movement. It allowed them to believe, at least momentarily, that they were indeed with the Doors, Cream, or some other world-famous band. As Manuel Ruiz explained, going to see a group perform at a café cantante was as close as one could be to the real thing: "[You went there] if you wanted to hear good rock, if you wanted to hear an identical copy of the hits in English, but live. Here [in Mexico] you would never dream of seeing the Beatles, the Animals, the Stones—never! But there [in the cafés] you could close your eyes and hear the exact same songs played live, only by bands generally from Tijuana."[13] Eréndira Rincón, who admits that she was not enamored with rock at that point, nevertheless describes hearing this music performed live:

> It was interesting, like it left you anxious to keep hearing more. You wanted to know what they were saying, and how what they were saying meshed with music that was so different from what you were used to hearing. I mean, you heard it [on the radio], but not much. At that time there was a lot of Mexican rocanrol, and everything was pretty homogeneous sounding. There weren't any original ideas, and everything was like a great mass of similar music. The other was different, let's say more stimulating.[14]

Mexican fusiles could replicate—indeed, *exceed,* in the words of José Agustín—the original. This was no small feat. It soon became a source of pride among musicians and some promoters, who viewed this as evidence of Mexicans' global integration. As Iván Zatz-Díaz sardonically recalled, "I remember this very solemn announcement on the radio talking about Los Dug Dugs and how they became the first group to be officially accepted as having mastered the sound of the Beatles. That Los Dug Dugs sounded like the Beatles. And that was a 'great moment of pride for Mexicans,' that this little Third World country could have a group that was recognized as sounding just like the pinnacle of what the civilized world had to offer."[15] For all but the most linguistically inclined, the poorly articulated lyrics were mostly indistinguishable and, at any rate, nonsensical to a Spanish-speaking audience. Still, English lyrics were routinely printed in rock magazines, and this undoubtedly made song content that much more accessible. More importantly, as in the first period of rock 'n' roll in Mexico, English was considered an inextricable part of the feeling produced by rock: shouts of "Hey," "Oh yeah," "Right on," and other cues might be heard in live performances, suggesting not only the popular accessibility of the new argot—like what "Darling" and "Baby" meant to a generation earlier—but also the significance of a fantasy space of vanguard participation. "When you discovered the song in the original it sounded much cooler when they said 'Oh, yeah!' instead of the Spanish, 'Oh, sí!' . . . It sounded younger, rebellious, cool," noted one informant.[16]

By 1965 the atmosphere of the cafés was changing, as a certain level of drugs and alcohol entered the environs and an atmosphere of desmadre edged aside an earlier emphasis on *diversión sana* (healthy diversion). Johnny Laboriel of Los Rebeldes del Rock describes these changes from the perspective of one who stayed with the style of rocanrol against the forces of the fusil:

> It wasn't the public itself that was changing, but the mentality of the people. Alcohol started to be introduced, and people began to get really wild, jumping up to dance on stage, throwing things and creating all sorts of chaos. That's when the government began to realize that [the clubs] were a hazard, that rock 'n' roll had gone from being something healthy to something unhealthy and noxious. People took advantage of [rock] as a pretext for their desmadres and sexual exploits—screwing in the bathroom and that whole scene.[17]

Laboriel's view that rock was returning to a state of desmadre reflected a sense that, as in the 1950s, an older generation was losing control over the direction of youth. His argument that drugs and sex infiltrated the ambiance of once-tranquil juice bars was no doubt partially true, though also reflective of his own biases. At any rate, this image of youth run amok was again exploited by the authorities. As Manuel Ruiz, an ardent patron of the clubs, argued:

> The president [Díaz Ordaz] didn't like the fact that rock had become the focus for kids . . . and they began to make up all sorts of bullshit and lies [about the clubs]. I mean, I went to a lot of cafés cantantes and it was just not true what they began to say about prostitutes going there and that drugs were sold and whatnot. . . . There was marijuana, but it wasn't yet in style. People barely knew about it, and no one had it. Nor had psychedelics arrived yet.[18]

In offering an unmonitored social space not only for middle-class youth but for upper-class and, one suspects, to a degree lower-class youth as well, the clubs posed a new threat to adult society. The cafés were distinct, for instance, from the adult-oriented cabarets (which also faced the constraints of a curfew after 1959).[19] "If you wanted an atmosphere where you could feel free, talk about what you wanted, do what you wanted, dress as you wanted, then you had to go to a place where you could hear rock," explained Ruiz. The noise of the cafés was youths' noise, not the shouts of parents or the admonitions of teachers and work supervisors. As one journalist described it:

> The music doesn't stop. Scarcely the last syllable fades away from "I Am a Believer" [sic] when already the first from "They Coming to Take Me Away" [sic] jumps out, reiterative, on top of one another with the throat of the singer accelerating from a trot to a gallop. Those present get excited. Some hum softly. Others mark the rhythm with their palms on top of the table or with their heel on the floor, or shake their hips in their seat or, if their enthusiasm really bursts forth, they raise their hands, roll their eyes and shout the consecrated cry, "ye-ye-ye-yeee!"[20]

The clubs thus served as a kind of transcultural performance space where the styles, gestures, and sounds of the youth culture from abroad were transposed for a Mexican audience, who relished their imagined shared identity with other youth from the First World. In the words of one editorialist, the clubs were "considered hotbeds of new values."[21]

Since the first clean-up sweeps by Mayor Uruchurtu in 1959, the cafés had always been an open target for arbitrary raids and closures by police. As one author has written, "the formula that reunited youth and live rock music was a direct ticket to incursions, closings, and police abuse."[22] Scattered throughout the city, the cafés suffered accordingly. Through political connections and bribes, some were able to operate despite harassment, but in general their existence was always precarious.[23] Then, in early 1965, the government launched a series of overnight raids on some twenty-five clubs throughout the capital, stating officially that "the only objective is to complete its fight against noise."[24] To this, however, was added the familiar claim that the clubs "foment 'rebellion without a cause' that leads to a heightened level of juvenile delinquency among us."[25] In an explicit acknowledgment of how English-language performance had once more become associated with rebellion, the cafés were also condemned for abetting "the loosening of customs by means of the perverted imitation of those negative aspects of foreign language usage which are totally in conflict with the idiosyncrasy of our population."[26] Not surprisingly, the raids were universally praised by the press, which tended to view all unsupervised, youth-oriented spaces with suspicion. Calling them "centers of perversion and activities by evil-doing groups," one newspaper editorialized: "It is not self-serving moralism to applaud the indefinite closure of these centers, as they are the readiest means for corruption and have enjoyed a certain impunity, sheltering themselves under the falsehood that they served as centers of 'healthy diversion' [diversión sana] for youth. Nothing is more false than that."[27] Several days later the newspaper continued its diatribe against the cafés, calling them "places where, each afternoon and every night, delinquent youth come together . . . in order to make their criminal plans." Calling the raids "an administrative act in the public interest," the article uncritically supported the government's position. "These closings are based on exhaustive investigations, effected by specialized inspectors; they are not arbitrarily dictated, as that would be a grievance against the constitutional guarantee of liberty of commerce and work."[28] Such editorializing indicated that the discourse of rebeldismo was never entirely discarded and, in fact, served as a convenient pillar of support for government actions. Perhaps it was not mere coincidence that the closures came at a moment when (as in 1958–1959) unauthorized strikes—this time by medical students—confronted the incoming administration of President Gustavo Díaz Ordaz. In any event, for both youth and the working classes, it was an ominous indication of the limits on expression that the new regime would tolerate.

COUNTERCULTURAL STIRRINGS

Closing the cafés was a stopgap measure at best, though it did have the immediate effect of limiting live rock to the elite nightclubs. Still, the real challenge to authority was already fermenting in the home. This challenge was incipient and still principally stylistic, though a few years later, when the right political conditions were met, it would have more profound implications. In short, fashion was becoming politicized, and rock music, in particular, was again becoming a wedge against traditional social values and a vehicle for free expression. While foreign rock provided the crucial reference points for this rebellion, local rockers successfully transcribed this music for a native audience, in turn grafting a hybrid sound and image that directly served the needs of the middle classes. "Rock," explains Manuel Ruiz, "was a tool." And Mexican rock was a handmade instrument: "It wasn't just some copy, but I'm telling you it sensitized us. All of that [foreign influence] was transferred to your national reality, and it made you rebel against whatever got to you. Like it got to you that you couldn't dress as you wanted, and you felt better because that's how you saw other people looking, like in the photographs of your idols."[29] In fact, the changing image of rock—the shaggy hair, psychedelia, and irreverent and aggressive posture of many of the new bands—had already become a rising concern for parents who feared the influence of foreign mass culture on their children. In an editorial entitled "Rights of Adolescence" parents were warned about the "idols of the 'New Wave,'" epitomized by the Beatles (appearing in an accompanying photograph with their patented weird expressions). "Your children will venerate these new groups, for which we cannot find the appropriate adjective," the editorial stated. Though the writer did add that "not everything about them must be censured and, when you do it, be constructive."[30] Shortly thereafter the cover of *Jueves de Excélsior* featured a caricature of a Mexican rock group, varying in skin tone from dark to light. Unstyled, matted hair, faces and bodies grossly twisted, the appearance of one even suggested that of a transvestite. The text succinctly explained: "The 'Mexican Beatles.'"[31] Once again, the emasculization of rock performers became a response to the threat of cultural subversion. "We live in an age of clay gods, of false values that arise from styles and whims," expressed another writer. "It is necessary to educate [youth] in spiritual, moral, and intellectual matters before it is too late."[32]

This new round of criticism underscored the difficulties that the cultural industries would have in promoting the new rock sound. On one hand, there was a need to accommodate the rapidly changing styles of youth. The market was changing, and so too must the companies in order to keep pace. On the other hand, however, encouraging bands to pursue an image of anguished rebellion was an invitation for censorship from parents' associations and perhaps even the government. By late 1965 various television programs—including *Hulaballoo* [*sic*], *Yeah yeah,* and *Discoteque a go-go*—were geared to lip-synched rock performance (some were even reportedly using English-language lyrics) that "rous[ed] the live studio audiences to a screaming, jerking fury."[33] To be safe, however, record producers insisted on continued control over record content, despite the activities of bands in live performance. With Los Yaki, for example, whose lead singer raved and swaggered on stage like Mick Jagger, Mexican bands were able to project a more aggressive posture in accordance with the changing times. As the liner notes from one of the group's albums read, "As soon as 'Los Yaki' enter the recording studio the atmosphere is transformed; Benny [the lead singer] begins the disorder, followed by [the rest of the band]. A drumbeat mixed with a joke [from the band] and a few guitar chords are sufficient to electrify the atmosphere, contaminating producers and recording technicians present in the studios. This same phenomenon is found everywhere they play, which is exactly the reason why 'the aggressive sound of Los Yaki' is so popular."[34] Others, however, kept to a clean-cut image to avoid police harassment and safeguard their careers. "Wherever we found ourselves," a member of the Los Desenfrenados (The Wanton Ones) said, "the authorities intervened and, on various occasions, even wanted to book us, thinking that we were 'rebels without a cause' and not artists."[35] While rebellion sold records, the mass media nevertheless sought to promote an image of rock as anything but disreputable.

Once more, a discourse of contained rebellion that stressed the *diversión sana* of rock returned. For example, in an article on the band, Los Sparks, they were quoted as saying: "We are not REBELS, but just want to enjoy ourselves without harming anyone." Referring to the group as one whose music was "distinctive, aggressive, and with great impact," the article also noted it was the first rock band to play at the Veranda Bar in the "elegant Hotel María Isabel," in the capital district.[36] In a review of another band, Los Apson, a writer called the group "five kids full of enthusiasm, anxious for glory, and already with a hefty bank account that allows for the meeting of certain whims, though always for the benefit of the group."[37] Moreover, in an effort to contain any doubt that Los Apson were *malinchistas* (cultural traitors), the writer added, "The culture of the North seeps from their pores, and although they're a little bit influenced by North American customs, they are more Mexican than pulque."[38] Finally, looking to counter an image of rock as increasingly disorderly and irreverent, an article on the famed Los Locos del Ritmo emphasized that "they are not crazy [but] just five dynamic, happy, and enthusiastic students in a dignified, clean, and honest career." Asked what his greatest ambition in life was, the lead performer, Rafael Acosta, replied: "To become a man in every respect."[39]

All the same, the politics of hair and the subversive influence of an emergent hippie movement abroad was becoming a central issue in Mexican society. At first the Mexican press treated the hippies as a strange yet fathomable "problem" facing industrialized nations alone. A June 1965 cover drawing for the magazine *Jueves de Excélsior*, for example, showed a long-haired couple walking a sheepdog; wearing sandals and smoking a pipe, the man has an expression of starry-eyed thoughtfulness, while the woman looks dazed, perhaps drugged. The context of the scene is identified by the text: "New York 1965." In a subtle play of language, however, the text continues: "'Existentialism' is no joke" (El 'existencialismo' no es una tomadura de pelo).[40] Using the equivalent expression for "pulling one's leg"—"tomando el pelo"—the text suggests that the fad of existentialism had traveled beyond the philosophers, instilling in youth their critical ideas of identity and existence. Indeed, the influence of such philosophers and novelists was apparent among a growing sector of university youth. As José Agustín writes, "In reality these youth were a hybrid of existentialists and beatniks, but in Mexico they became known as 'existentialists.' I imagine that's why they called the cafés by the same name, as well as any 'strange-looking' young person."[41]

While the setting was New York City and not Mexico City, already there were small groups of youth, mostly politically conscious students from the middle classes, who had openly begun to defy societal norms of fashion as a vehicle for self-expression and criticism. As Eréndira Rincón recalls about this period:

> I began to dress as I wanted to. For example, we used to go to school in huaraches, which was considered extraordinary. . . . On the buses people looked at you strangely, and they'd say things to you, aggressive things under their breath. But that only made you feel like you had an identity. . . . It allowed you to identify yourself with a culture that you considered more authentic, not a copy of something else . . . Because people in the countryside still use huaraches. So it was like wearing your credo and going against the majority of people in the city, who were imitating the gringos.[42]

But imitating the gringos was itself becoming an issue of concern for adults, as the proliferation of commodities and images from the counter-culture abroad steadily redefined the reference points for being "cool" versus "square" in youth's search for new identities and self-expression.

For boys, being cool meant breaking free of the mold of the societal father, whose values were inscribed not only in his manicured appearance but also in his proper language and the music he listened to: "You had to dress 'like this' and have your hair 'like this' because if not, you were going to look like a bureaucrat, a manager, anything but a young person. You would look like a señor. In fact, it was pretty common back then if you saw someone who wore short hair, conventional clothing, and listened to baladas románticas to say, 'Oh man, that guy looks like a señor.'"[43] The disheveled look of the new rock bands introduced a fashion rage for long hair on boys that, despite its relative tameness in 1965–1966, rapidly became a litmus test for familial confrontations. As Manuel Ruiz continues:

> When I was twelve or thirteen years old, every week my father went to the barber, and so every week he took me along with him for a haircut too. But I started to rebel. Around 1965 I saw photos of the Rolling Stones, and I looked in the mirror and said, "No way." The hair on the Stones at that time wasn't even that long, really, but compared with mine it was like I had a crewcut. . . . So I said to my dad, "Dad, I don't want to get my hair cut like that," and my dad said, "It doesn't matter if you like it or not, because you're going to get it cut." And that happened in most middle- and lower middle-class homes.

For many middle-class girls, the need to be free by defying traditional stereotypes of what it meant to be a lady were equally pressing: "You would feel really down if, for example, someone compared you with 'your cousin Lupita,' like by saying, 'Wow, you and your cousin Lupita are so alike.' That was horrible, because you had to be you, and nobody else. . . . That was the idea of individualism: being original, rejecting what was expected."[44] When another article on the transformation of the posadas appeared in late 1966, the issue had gone beyond mere irreverence for tradition, as suggested by the headline "Posadas a go go."[45] Now the line that had formally divided the sexes was itself dissolving. At the root of this threatening transformation was rock music: "Boys and girls are barely distinguished by their dress, since both wear pants and long hair, amusing themselves by making grotesque contortions to a background 'noise' of drums, electric guitars and bass, which they call music." In an interesting detail, the author noted that couples did not follow one another's steps or a male lead, as in the past. Rather, "[e]ach one jumps and moves in his own way until exhausted."[46] Thus even the fundamental structure of dance was disappearing, in which girls no longer had to wait for a boy's invitation and individualism prevailed over partnership.

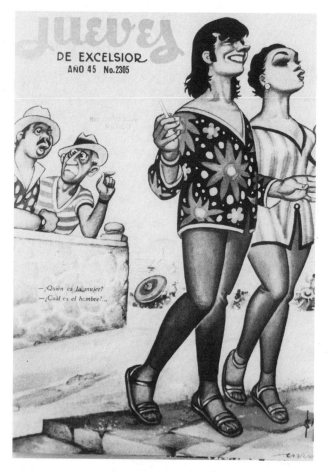

Figure 6.   "Which One Is the Woman? Which One Is the Man?" Source: *Jueves de Excélsior,* 22 September 1966. Used by permission.

THE ARRIVAL OF THE HIPPIES

By mid-1967 an additional factor was causing alarm among adults: the steady influx of young foreigners who identified themselves as hippies. This was reflected, for example, in a 1966 cover of *Jueves de Excélsior* that depicted a young couple as foreign tourists at the beach (see Figure 6). The man is decked out in green tights, a flowered shirt, and sandals. The woman is wearing red tights and a striped shirt. Their gender is discerned only by our privileged frontal view: breasts are the immediate sign of difference between them. From behind, however, the opposite would seem to be true; his hair is long, while hers is short. Leaning on the wall facing their backs are two older men, with mustaches and hats (though not sombreros). The accompanying text reveals their dialogue: "Which is the woman? Which is the man?" Gender confusion is further highlighted by the couple's exaggerated hand and body motions; both are also shown smoking.[47] If the drawing suggested a trivializing of countercultural fashion, the issue was becoming anything but so for Mexican society.

Mexico had in fact long been a country of attraction for bohemian travelers, dating back to the postrevolutionary fervor of the 1920s and providing new appeal for beatniks in the 1950s.[48] In 1955 a New York banker and amateur mycologist named R. Gordon Wasson, along with his wife, Valentina, and a photographer, Alan Richardson, visited the Mazatec Indian village of Huautla de Jiménez in the highlands of Oaxaca. Under the guidance of a local shaman, Wasson and the others encountered the powerfully hallucinogenic mushrooms known locally as *los niños santos* or *teonancatl*.[49] Whereas for the Mazatec the mushroom's power was highly respected and sought only under conditions of infection—physical or spiritual illness—and guided by a *curandero* (medicine man), beginning with Wasson outsiders began to seek out this powerful natural drug for purely experiential reasons. As María Sabina, the renowned curandera who gained fame as a result of Huautla's sudden exposure, related, "Wasson and his friends were the first foreigners who came to our village in search of the niños santos . . . [but] they didn't take them because they suffered from some bad element. Their reason was that they came to find God. Before Wasson, nobody took los niños simply to find God. They were always taken to cure the sick."[50] Spores from the fungus, newly identified by Wasson as *Psilocybe mexicana*, were brought to Paris, where they were artificially cultivated. Then in 1958 the Swiss chemist Albert Hoffman created a synthetic of the active hallucinogenic ingredient contained in the mushroom, naming it psilocybin. The future basis for LSD had been discovered.[51] Huautla de Jiménez was placed on the psychedelic road map and forever changed.

The first youth from the United States filtered into Huautla as early as 1962, but their numbers increased and their origins diversified after 1964.[52] By the summer of 1967 more than seventy were living there, mostly from the United States but also from Canada and parts of Western Europe. Some had been directly influenced by the article Wasson wrote for *Life Magazine*. They came in search of an indigenous experience, despite the fact that they did not generally speak Spanish, much less the indigenous Mazateco language spoken by most of the local people. They rented cabins in the surrounding villages for weeks and even months at a time, living meagerly, at times reduced to bartering for food, and always in pursuit of the mushrooms. "Never, as far as I can remember, were the niños santos eaten with such lack of respect,"[53] recalled María Sabina in describing the abuse of ritualistic mushroom consumption. She continued: "It made no difference to them [the hippies] if they chewed on them in the shade of the coffee trees, on top of a boulder, or on a mountain trail."[54] Living frugally, the hippies contributed little to the local economy; once they discovered how to find the mushrooms themselves, even local vendors lost out.[55] This was not the class of tourists the government aimed to attract with the approaching Olympics, though, ironically, the romanticized folkloric image used in tourist advertising and cultural promotion had fashioned an appealing image of an exotic, "lost" Mexico waiting for rediscovery.[56] As one writer noted, "At the same time that Mexico increases its importance and attractiveness as a center for tourism, it suffers along with the majority of other great cities of the world from the invasion of undesirable visitors, of foreigners who abuse the traditional hospitality of our country and the tolerance of our laws."[57] Huautla, especially, had become a "magnet for 'tourists'" who "in reality are disoriented, eccentric, ridiculously dressed, shaggy-haired, bearded, malodorous youth, who aren't interested in the natural beauty of the Sierra Mazateca, nor are they really students, attracted in the interest of scientific investigation, as they claim."[58] A few Mexicans also showed up during this period, mostly it appears, from the upper classes. Alfredo Díaz Ordaz, son of the president, was reportedly one of them.[59] By 1969 scores of Mexican youth would also be found amid the hippie population.

If from the locals' viewpoint the hippies contributed little to the economy and showed utter disrespect for indigenous beliefs, from the hippies' perspective their indigenous experience was transformative. Through their selective appropriation of different aspects of local culture—food, dress, rituals—the hippies literally reinvented themselves by repudiating, at least ideologically, the capitalist culture of their native metropolises. "All forms of modernist art and thought," Marshall Berman tells us, "have a dual character: they are at once expressions of and protests against the process of modernization."[60] On one hand, we must locate our understanding of the hippies in this light, for the flight away from modern capitalist culture would ultimately, inevitably lead these individuals back to that same modern culture, only on different terms. On the other hand, travels by the hippies also occurred in the historical context of a profound shift toward a postmodern consciousness. This involved rejection of the "codifications of modernism . . . based on a teleological view of progress and modernization."[61] The hippies reflected a radical critique of everyday life that drew on new aesthetic strategies and techniques to explore the "contradictions and contingencies [of the modern world], its tensions and internal resistances to its own 'forward movement.'"[62] The entire modern notion of bounded wholes and delineated identities was thus directly challenged by the hippies, in a process that involved the techniques of reappropriation and cultural fusion. In their superficial emulation of native dress and ritual, the hippies became a living bricollage of cultural meanings, incorporating styles and philosophies of native peoples in ways that ultimately served to enhance their own modern selves.

Describing the central market of Huautla as resembling "Greenwich Village of New York or Piccadilly Circus of London," one writer expressed his bafflement at the seeming contradictions in hippie fashion: "The strangest part about their ostentatious colors and designs is that they've added the shirt and trousers made of coarse cloth used by the aborigines. The girls, in general, wear 'shorts,' miniskirts, or pants in the plaza but, according to what we've been told, there hasn't passed a day that some don't show up practically in their underwear."[63] Appearing in the early fall of 1967 on the front page of the widely-read newspaper *Excélsior*, the article catalyzed government action. Less than two weeks later the Department of Interior Affairs forcibly ejected thirty-six *hongadictos* (mushroom addicts) from the Huautla area. "All of these pernicious foreigners were 'hippies,' dirty and long-haired, some of whom appeared nearly insane because of drug abuse."[64]

The hippies, however, did not disappear readily, and by the spring of 1968 renewed reports of long-haired, unkempt, drug-taking youth appearing not only in Huautla but Acapulco and Mexico City as well led to cries of a veritable invasion.[65] Mexico's largely conservative press reacted strongly to the negative influence of "so-called 'hippies'" which one writer summedup as, "unkempt, unproductive, shaggy, [and] queerly dressed." He continued, "[W]ith those outrageous displays, [their] indolence, slovenliness, overgrown beards, and absurd garments, they pretend to live peacefully, being exotic to conceal their vagrancy and rebellion against work [and] wholesome values."[66] In the streets of the nation's capital the rising tide of foreign hippies was causing a special sensation. "The 'hippies' are multiplying," exclaimed the text under a photograph of a psychedelia-donned couple in Mexico City: "We find them in the streets, the main avenues, the Alameda [a downtown park], the 'zona rosa.'"[67]

The Zona Rosa was a multiblock shopping and café district frequented especially by tourists and the upper class. Reportedly baptized the "Pink Zone" by the iconoclast artist José Luis Cuevas, the district prided itself on its cosmopolitan atmosphere, and local businesses actively cultivated an aura of the avant-garde. Drawing on Marshall Berman's description of the Nevsky Prospect of nineteenth-century Saint Petersburg, the Zona Rosa also became "a kind of free zone in which social and psychic forces could spontaneously unfold," presenting the denizens of Mexico City with "a prospect of all the dazzling promises of the modern world."[68] Here tourists and Mexicans with spending money could shop for imported fashions and records, experience the sounds of native rock bands, attend gallery openings featuring performance "happenings," converse at the numerous outdoor cafés, and purchase authentic "folk art" by indigenous street vendors. In June 1967 Cuevas used the Zona Rosa to unveil his "ephemeral mural," which he meant as an implicit critique not only of the muralist movement itself (whose longevity Cuevas openly rebuked) but also of the monopolization of wall space used by the PRI for political propaganda.[69]

The Zona Rosa soon gained a reputation for its countercultural air as well as for being a haven for long-haired, drug-smoking, foreign hippies whose "example is pernicious,"[70] as one editorialist admonished. Beginning in February 1968 the *judiciales* (federal Judicial Police), notorious for their brutality and corruption, began a "campaign to clean up the [capital] city of dangerous 'hippies,' marijuana smokers, drug traffickers, and LSD addicts." Foreigners caught by police in what *Jueves de Excélsior* viewed as "laudable raid[s]," mostly carried out in the Zona Rosa, were transported to the airport, "where they are placed on the first available flight so that they can live a life of indifference and vice in some other place."[71] Meanwhile, efforts to contain the influx at the source led to "precise instructions" given to border officials and airport immigration agents not to allow into the country "dirty, long-haired North American youth."[72]

The "pernicious example" that hippies set for Mexican youth was an even more serious problem. It was bad enough that "the fads and music of the hippies [are] exported," as one editorialist commented with obvious reference to the burgeoning rock movement, "but [now] also hippies of flesh and blood" were flooding the country.[73] In fact, while foreign hippies were living representatives of the countercultural avant-garde, their stylistic emulation of indigenous cultures introduced an image of modernity that reflected a composite of "modern" and "folkloric" traditions. As middle-class Mexican youth copied this image of the avant-garde as it emerged abroad, they unwittingly reabsorbed elements drawn from their own cultural traditions. One might see this process as an ethnically complex double mirror: mestizo youth began to copy Anglo hippies who were copying indigenous Mexicans. By traversing the Mexican countryside and making a fashion statement out of using huaraches, long hair, indigenous dress, and hand-crafted jewelry, the hippies were inadvertently revalorizing Mexico's indigenous population in the eyes of urban middle-class youth. As one editorialist astutely noted, "If one argues that long hair has become a 'national' issue, there's already the locks of [Aztec chiefs] Cuauhtémoc and Cuitláhuac to persuade [youth] to let their own grow."[74] Yet when the leftist cultural critic Carlos Monsiváis first took note of this "Mexicanization of the hippies," as he put it in early 1968, he harshly criticized them as imitative and inauthentic: "Of what great [material] abundance can the Mexican hippies [claim to] deny? Against which high technology do they protest in the name of love?"[75] Lost in this critique was an understanding that a revalorization of indigenous culture had opened up an important psychic space for dissent. This opening offered Mexican youth a vehicle that was both modern and culturally relevant. It allowed youth to invent new ways of *being* Mexican, ways that ran counter to the dominant ideology of state-sponsored nationalism.

MEXICO'S RISING COUNTERCULTURE

By early 1968 the fashion of social protest among a growing population of youth from the middle classes had become a matter of public debate and concern. The fact that the outward manifestation of this protest was located in fashion and a new jargon—rather than traditional street protests, as activists and intellectuals on the left would have preferred—made such youth an easy target for criticism. One author, for instance, offered a critique of the cafés cantantes—where "the strident music stuns, the prolonged enclosure bloats, the stunned state deviates, the bloatedness debilitates"—while urging: "It is not for robust youth to enter into a cave but to come out into the open air, to march into the sun."[76] The view that rock culture not only distracted political energies but also reinforced subservience to foreign values became more pronounced as Mexico's rock movement spread. In an article entitled "The New Generation," Carlos Monsiváis denounced what he considered "an imported generation that is more or less measured by the speed at which it reproduces fashions." He continued: "[I]t is a Derived Generation, which shouldn't surprise us given the semicolonial conditions of the country. It doesn't possess its own idols or engender its own autonomous lifestyles. . . . Everything is imported: the fashions, songs, protest buttons, ties, dance styles, wide belts, miniskirts, heroes, radicalisms, rejections and approvals."[77] There was truth to this, of course. A countercultural fashion imported on the wings of transnational capital had become widely commercialized by early 1968.

Indeed, the business of appealing to the demands of the youth market were dramatically affecting the attitudes of media executives and record agents, who themselves began to "change their image from staid business stalwarts to hip modern trend-makers."[78] At about this point an important split began to emerge between the local and transnational companies, with the former adopting a more cautious strategy and the latter aggressively pursuing new musical styles. For instance, while Orfeón stuck with its consecrated baladista artists, Capitol Records was actively engaged in cultivating "new talent and new trends" as part of a coordinated effort "to find [musical] voices to express Mexican youth's frustrations, fears and restlessness."[79] As André Midani, president of Capitol Records of Mexico, was quoted as saying in the summer of 1967: "We are not interested in the Mexico of yesterday nor the Mexico of today. We are interested in the Mexico of tomorrow. We are creating an image of [a] youthful company in tune with the now generation. The young in Mexico are fighting off the old traditions. They belong to the new wave sweeping the world. Mexican kids are just as hip as kids anywhere in the world. And Capitol wants to be as hip as the kids."[80] In fact, the company reportedly went so far as to hire two psychologists whose job it was "to study and analyze talent, to appraise whether it has the necessary spark to project to the youth of today."[81] Pursuing this more radical image of youth directly contradicted the terms of an earlier hegemonic arrangement, which had strictly delimited the boundaries of rebellion presented by the cultural industries. With their often direct connections to television and radio (where payola was often the norm), the record companies were principal leaders in this movement. As one report noted, record-company executives could "be seen in the go-go cafes, rock clubs and 'in' neighborhoods, dressed in mod outfits at debuts, talking to the kids, picking up preferences and carrying them back to the office."[82]

As elsewhere in the world, youth readily identified with the new feeling of rock music. Groups such as the Doors, Jimi Hendrix, Janis Joplin, the Rolling Stones, and the Beatles captured the sentiments of a generation in revolt against tradition. As Todd Gitlin writes from the U.S. perspective, "Coupled-up love had long been a staple of pop music. Now, for the first time, the normal culture of teenagers was becoming infiltrated by grander ideals: freedom, license, religiosity, loving community. Blurry as the pop images were, they added up to intimations of a different way of life."[83] Listening to this music, participating in private and (more likely) group experiences, and discussing the meaning of the translated lyrics and how one felt about the changing times, war, violence, the repression of governments and the movements for liberation all refashioned the cultural setting of leisure for youth universally. Having reached into numerous corners of the globe, rock now belonged to everyone, and nationality was no prerequisite for participation. "Rock," noted José Agustín in his 1968 book, *La nueva música clásica*, "cannot be limited by borders but develops in every country, acclimating itself to [local] characteristics. Rock is not the patrimony of the United States, even though it first surfaced there."[84]

The changing cultural sensibilities of Mexican middle-class youth were marked not only by what kind of music they listened to but also by how they wore their hair, what kind of clothes they put on, what language they used, what they read, and in general what their attitude toward authority was. By late 1967 this new style and attitude of rebellion had acquired a societal label: La Onda. Literally meaning "the wave," La Onda in fact connoted a modern sense of movement and communication, as in radio or television "wavelength."[85] As the young novelist José Agustín, whose iconoclastic novels *La tumba* (1964) and *De perfil* (1966) launched a new generation of writers, wrote, "Above all, an onda is movement, and as such, is change. . . . la onda is also energy, or is associated with it, as in the electric, electromagnetic, or hertzian waves; and as we know, these electric waves allow for communication (telegraph, telephone and/or television)."[86] The word itself apparently first surfaced in the early to mid-1960s, when it was used to refer to "a plan, a party, an ambiance"[87] offering the possibility of diversion, communication, and, especially, rock music. The term stuck, while its meanings expanded. For example, it evolved into a pronoun for "thing," as in "pass me that onda." By the late 1960s, variations on the term formed the foundations of a new hip jargon among youth, as in "Qué mala onda" (What a bad trip, deal, person, etc.) or "Qué buena onda" (What a cool trip, deal, person, etc.), language that was widely circulated among the middle classes, especially, and that served as boundary markers between the generations. In fact, Monsiváis compared the *ondero* to Norman Mailer's hipster in the United States, arguing that La Onda represented "a new spirit, the repudiation of convention and prejudice, the creation of a new morality, the challenging of proper morals, the expansion of consciousness, the systematic revision and critique of the values offered by the West as sacred and perfect."[88] Monsiváis preferred to use the label sparingly, arguing that La Onda described only a handful of "radical, vanguard" rebels; Sor Juana Inés de la Cruz (the seventeenth-century dissident nun) and Demetrio Vallejo (leader of the 1958–1959 railway workers' strike), Monsiváis indicated, had also been onderos in their own right. But this definition was too parsimonious, on one hand, and yet too overreaching, on the other, to properly suggest what La Onda was coming to mean. For La Onda was rapidly emerging as Mexico's own countercultural movement, grounded in a fusion of native and foreign rock music, literature, language, and fashion. If this was indeed a colonized generation of youth, stupefied by the rhythms imposed from abroad, La Onda held out the possibility of a critical cultural consciousness. For this was a new transnational and transcultural era, as Monsiváis himself noted, in which "Che Guevara, Malcolm X, Allen Ginsberg, Fidel Castro, and Mick Jagger"[89] all rested on like pedestals of significance.

As the signs, images, and commodities associated with an increasingly radical youth counterculture abroad proliferated, the line between rock as fashion and rock as social protest was becoming blurred. Certainly La Onda's outward manifestations readily lent themselves to commodification, as in a 1968 advertisement for the Valiant car featured in the rock magazine *POP*. The advertisement features a woman with long, blond hair in a minidress playing a guitar with the text of her "song" placed within a psychedelic-stylized bubble: "Valiant has the same fire as my heart. . . . Valiant is the boldness of youth. . . . Valiant is a thrill!"[90] In fact, *POP*—which first appeared in February 1968—epitomized La Onda's accelerated commercialization and the exploitation of youth's yearning to feel part of a universal movement. With its psychedelic covers, advertisements for paraphernalia of the rock generation (stylized guitars and mod outfits, for example), feature articles on local and foreign bands (arranged in a pastiche from hard rock to romantic baladistas), and an advice column for distraught youth, *POP* openly proclaimed itself the vehicle for a new generation: "This isn't just 'another magazine,' because POP is like you . . . POP is young, happy, and enthusiastic. POP is 'in' and *en la onda*. POP is psychedelic. POP is crazy about the Beatles, the Monkeys, and the Rollin' Stones. But POP also likes Los Yaki, Los Belmonts, and the Rockin' Devils. . . . Angélica María, Enrique Guzmán, Julissa, César Costa . . . POP is fascinated by the new youth styles of both girls and guys. POP knows all about the latest rock 'n' roll records."[91] If La Onda was conditioning sectors of middle-class youth to social protest, *POP* promoted itself as the standard-bearer of the counterculture as style. When one reader, for instance, complained that his parents did not understand why he liked "to dress in the latest fashions . . . let my hair grow and dress like a hippie," the magazine's advice columnist responded: "Dear Hippie: You should try to understand that your parents come from another era. On the other hand, if you like how the hippies look, don't try to imitate their dirty aspects, but only the folkloric parts. I advise you to make a deal with your parents: if you get good grades in school, then they should allow you to let your hair grow a little. If you put it to them this way, you'll see it will work." [92]

The argument that imitating the "folkloric parts" of the hippies was somehow more appropriate is indeed interesting, for it was precisely this aspect that ultimately offered the most radical critique of Mexican society. At the time, however, this turn to indigenous culture (ironically, in an attempt to be seen as modern) could still be trivialized, and at one point it was literally caricatured by *POP.* In a later cartoon featured in the magazine, for instance, an Indian woman draped in a rebozo is depicted selling huaraches: "Specially priced for hippies." [93] As one female informant from an upper-middle-class conservative family relates:

> The new fashions were very tempting. It was a change that liberated you from being "properly dressed," with your clothes always being ironed, a handbag, a ribbon in your hair. The hippie was totally carefree in appearance, and you tried to adopt that aspect to a certain point. . . . But I was never an authentic hippie. I mean, I had my hippie symbols, the long, straight hair, even the headband at times. I used makeup sometimes, bracelets, a shoulder bag. . . . [My parents] let me dress like that, but within limits. If they needed you present in their society, you had to arrive properly dressed. And they'd say, "You can't wear that, save it for when you go out with your friends." . . . So you had to go dressed up like some doll.[94]

But in other households the fashion of rebellion, especially for men, became a vehicle for challenging one's parents, in particular the authoritative voice of one's father. As Manuel Ruiz explained, "Your parents asked you why you wanted to wear your hair like a girl. They asked you: 'Are you a girl or a homosexual?' They couldn't believe that you'd wear the same jeans all week long. And if your father told you your pants looked greasy or smelled, then it was like he did you a favor by telling you that. Because that's want you wanted to achieve." [95] Thus if La Onda was about keeping pace with the styles of youth abroad, it also introduced fashion as a vehicle for breaking free of traditional roles and challenging buenas costumbres, the "proper family values" of respectable society.

THE BREAKDOWN OF CONTAINMENT

As rocanrol had served the modernizing aspirations of the middle classes a generation earlier, so La Onda coincided at one level with Mexico's self-promotion as a modernizing nation, in tune with the transformation of attitudes and fashion throughout the world. This was reflected, for instance, in a widely quoted interview in which President Díaz Ordaz stated his defense of long hair, the miniskirt, and other youth fashion statements as falling within the boundaries of free expression. In April 1968, in a three-paragraph article in the *New York Times* under the heading, "Mexican Leader Sees No Harm in Hippies," Díaz Ordaz is quoted as saying: "Everyone is free to let his beard, hair or sideburns grow if he wants to, to dress well or badly as he sees fit, so long as he does not harm others' rights or break the law."[96] If the president was looking to bolster an image of Mexico as a tolerant, open society on the eve of world attention focusing on the Olympics, his words may have had an impact. This was reflected, for example, in a letter to the president written, strangely enough, by a U.S. serviceman stationed at Fort Bragg: "It was a great pleasure for my friends and me to read the comments attributed to you in the *New York Times*. . . . We feel that your thinking is in perfect harmony with the finest traditions of democracy, and this is especially heart-warming today when so much of the world is controlled by facist [*sic*] and communist dictators."[97] In fact, the association between rock and modernity was so intertwined that while most of the cafés cantantes remained closed, other clubs geared toward tourists and the elite continued to do a healthy business. As one report on the capital noted, "Nightclubs are not for the poor or [the] peso counter."[98] Many of these clubs were located in the Zona Rosa, while elite hotels, such as the newly opened Aristos or the Hilton Belvedere also offered steady work for select bands. As a reporter described one such performance: "[A] good rock group, clean-cut in red blazers, blasts away to a floor full of well-dressed young people and a couple in formal wear."[99] Thus, while for the middle classes La Onda came to be defined in terms of struggle—for access to rock performance, for the right to dress up in the latest fashions, against the threat of police harassment because of long hair—for los juniors of the elite, La Onda became a badge of privileged access, a passport to being "in" without fear of reprisals.

If circumscribing the rock gesture was central to the hegemonic arrangement between the cultural industries and the state, this arrangement was rapidly coming undone as La Onda pushed against the logic of containment. "Naturalizing" Elvis Presley in the guise of Enrique Guzmán had once been possible, but accomplishing the same for Jimi Hendrix would not be easy. For in contradistinction to the highlighting of pubescent angst reflected in early rock 'n' roll, by 1968 rock had been "converted into a dignified, complex and revolutionary musical quest," as José Agustín described it.[100] Though younger artistic directors at the transnationals pushed to stay on top of the rapidly transforming youth market, producers at Telesistema were less anxious to accommodate the psychedelic revolution. According to Luis de Llano Jr., who, in 1969, as director of promotion at Telesistema, launched a video-rock program, "La Onda de Woodstock," the old guard at Telesistema "was not interested in longhaired people."[101] This conservative stance was eroding, however, as the logic of rock demanded a relaxation of strict controls over image and performance. Perhaps the most vivid example of this broadening of market sensibilities was the avant-garde rock-performance television program *¡1, 2, 3, 4, 5 a Go-Go!* shown live weekly for a brief time on Telesistema. Launched in early 1968 by Alfonso Arau and afterward continued by the Chilean filmmaker, Alexander Jodorowsky, the program integrated rock music and theater to produce spontaneous television performance.[102] As one witness-participant described an episode, "Los Dug Dugs explode with Magical Mystery Tour, and we start to paint without any idea of what's going on. . . . [D]ogs are barking into the amplifiers, [and] a zapatista . . . transforms his face while singing in English. . . . [A]t the guitarists' feet and wearing a tambourine for a halo, some dude is playing the flute while simultaneously beating a pre-Hispanic drum. . . . Next Thursday at 7 P.M. on Channel 5 maybe we'll again enter the electronic, ephemeral, panicked euphoria."[103]

With the closing of the cafés, middle-class access to live rock performance became more irregular. Not until 1968 did live rock for the masses find a new commercial outlet, an ice-skating rink at the southern end of Insurgentes Boulevard, a commercialized strip not far from the UNAM. This seemingly odd location to showcase rock makes better sense, at least ideologically, if we view ice skating as associated with an inversion of the underdeveloped tropics. The rink, in fact, became a weekly meeting ground for displaying the accouterments of modernity.[104] Every Sunday "the authentic youth," as one writer described them, would gather to listen to live rock by groups like Los Dug Dugs. "Boys and girls in Beatles and Hindu fashions [and] huge mustaches" gathered around, we are told. "Groups with miniskirts and necklaces" made up the crowd, as youth with "skates tossed over the shoulder [wore] a look of intense suaveness on their faces."[105] If these youth pursued La Onda as a fashion statement, they did so increasingly at the risk of enraging their parents and testing the boundaries of buenas costumbres that still defined societal values.

Many university students regarded this fashion with cynical scorn, if not distrust. Foreign rock itself was generally held in high esteem—part of the universal vanguard culture with which students around the world now identified—but Mexican rock was mostly derided or ignored altogether. In part this was because of rocanrol's close affiliation with elitist pretensions. Mexican imitators, especially the more recent bands that performed in English, seemed to many a pathetic attempt at copying gringos. Moreover, the PRI-financed *porras* (pseudo-student groups that often functioned as infiltrators and agents provocateurs) were known to support rock concerts on school campuses, making the Mexican bands (if not the music itself) somewhat suspect. Meanwhile, the Cuban Revolution had reawakened interest in Latin American culture and an outward posture of ideological distinctions drawn along the lines of musical taste. "Everyone, all of us began to be interested in music from Latin America and Mexico, in what was happening in Latin America," recounts Oscar Chávez, a Mexican folk singer who came to prominence during this period.[106] Radio UNAM, the official university station, devoted a quarter of its musical programming to Latin American folk music; the rest was classical music.[107]

The UNAM's newly opened Popular Culture Center, which united students from different universities in the city and around the country, stayed away from rock despite sponsorship during the center's first year in existence of "bossa nova, jazz, corral poetry, [and] social and protest music."[108] Eréndira Rincón, later a participant in the student movement, spoke about the relationship between rock and folk on the UNAM campus: "In general, you'd find both Latin American music and rock, but not at the same event. Never. That's because, supposedly, the publics were different, though in reality they were the same. We were always the same people, but the idea was [that the music] was directed at one group or the other."[109] Indeed, the tone of a lone rock review—of Cream's *Disraeli Gears* album—featured in the official student newsletter suggested that rock music *was* taken seriously by many students.[110] Ironically, the sheer inaccessibility of the original rock album had helped to elevate foreign rock to the plane of high culture. This was also reflected, for instance, in an avant-garde dance performance sponsored by the General Office of Cultural Diffusion of the UNAM in the summer of 1968 titled "Beatlemima" and set to "the most selective of modern popular music," including the Beatles and the Rolling Stones.[111] Thus, on the eve of the student movement of 1968 a grammar of youth rebellion that incorporated discourses of a Latin American folk revival, rock music, and revolutionary struggle was widely disseminated. Though class and ideological differences still characterized youth in general, such a grammar had nonetheless laid the foundation for the transcendence of such differences in the name of a common movement.

THE STUDENT MOVEMENT OF 1968

The formation of a student strike committee—Comité Nacional de Huelga (CNH)—formed the structural backbone of the student movement that erupted at the end of July 1968. Like the movement itself, the formation of the CNH was essentially a spontaneous event, unrelated in any direct manner with other political groups or activities.[112] This is not to say that the student movement came together in a vacuum: despite the overall appearance of political tranquillity, confrontations between university administrators, government security forces, and students at numerous campuses had escalated around the country since student participation in the massive union strikes of 1958–1959.[113] Indeed, the convocation of a national student conference in 1963 had led to the formation of the Central Nacional de Estudiantes Democráticos, a broad-based movement for university and political reform. At the same time, the impact of the Cuban Revolution catalyzed a more radical wing of student activism advocating a guerrilla strategy of revolutionary insurrection. Yet during the 1960s these two distinct, if at times complementary, wings of student activism neither anticipated nor directed the massive protests that rocked the nation's capital during the summer and fall of 1968.[114] In fact, the CNH ideologically repudiated any affiliation with formal political organizations (either student or opposition political parties), a position that ultimately contributed to the movement's strengths as well as weaknesses.[115]

As Charles de Gaulle had famously discounted the possibility of student unrest in France, so too did Díaz Ordaz reject the likelihood of protests in Mexico, even as capital cities around the world began to feel the reverberations of the Paris uprising and the "Prague Spring." The approaching Olympics were heralded by the PRI-dominated mass media as evidence of the nation's transformation from a bandit-ridden, agrarian economy into a modern, industrialized nation. But the Olympics also placed into sharper relief the dictatorial nature of decision making and the distorted economic priorities of the regime. For many students and labor activists, a well-known history of police repression against those who openly questioned the political status quo belied Mexico's proud international image as a progressive, democratic nation. As world attention began to intensify in the context of the approaching Olympic games, the stakes of protest and response increased exponentially. Perhaps that explains why a series of relatively inconsequential events among disparate student groups in the capital at the end of July—a rumble between rival school gangs; a march celebrating the Cuban Revolution; a protest against earlier police incursion of a vocational school—triggered the massive unrest that unfolded.[116]

Police repression related to the above incidents catalyzed an immediate response by student representatives from the UNAM and the Polytechnical Institute, who together drew up a preliminary list of demands and discussed the notion of organizing a general student strike. As word of the meeting spread, students at university-affiliated high schools and vocational schools around the capital spontaneously declared their solidarity, capturing several city buses (a familiar tactic of student activists), which were used to blockade streets. Police and army infantry pursued the protesters, firing tear gas and clubbing heads with rifle butts. Just after midnight the following day (30 July), the government responded with a disproportionate use of force: bazooka blasts forced open the baroque wooden doors of the San Ildefonso High School, located in the downtown district where numerous students and teachers, many of whom were wounded, had taken refuge. The invasion of the UNAM-affiliated high school not only violated the constitutional protection of school autonomy but also led to dozens of injuries and arrests, including of neighborhood residents, some of whom had poured boiling water onto soldiers in an attempt to prevent them from entering the school. On 1 August, the president appealed for reasoned submission in his famous "extended hand" speech: "Public peace and tranquillity must be restored. A hand is stretched out; Mexicans will say whether that hand will find a response. I have been deeply grieved by these deplorable and shameful events. Let us not further accentuate our differences." [117] At the same moment, however, Javier Barros Sierra, the widely respected rector of the UNAM, led a march of some 80,000 students down a principal avenue of the city. Signs reading "The outstretched hand has a pistol in it" signaled the students' cynicism toward dialogue; a coffin marked "Dead Government" was paraded about. Within a week, a formal strike committee was formed to represent more than 150 public and private high schools, colleges, vocational schools, and universities throughout not only the capital but with links to schools in the provinces as well. If the strike had begun as a movement of solidarity by students in the capital who were fed up with arbitrary repression, with the formation of the CNH the movement now looked to broaden its constituency to incorporate other sectors around the country.[118]

Formalized in the CNH, the student movement actually pushed for limited, reformist goals. Unlike student movements in the United States or France, for instance, the Mexican movement did not advocate a distinctively radical social or political agenda.[119] Rather, student demands and discourse were carefully structured in terms of respect for the 1917 Constitution, which contained guarantees of free speech, democratic process, and economic redistribution. Yet the sheer audacity of students to invoke these rights implied that the regime—the *Institutionalized* Revolutionary Party—had shortchanged the population in fulfilling the goals of revolutionary upheaval some fifty years earlier. As one student leader remarked, "Our arms were the Constitution; our ideas; our peaceful, legal demonstrations; our handbills and our newspapers. Were these the arms of hard-liners? Of course they were. Here in our country anything that represents a spontaneous movement on the part of the people and of students, an independent popular organization that forthrightly criticizes the despotic regime that unfortunately rules our lives, is considered dangerously militant."[120]

Six demands formed the actual framework of the students' official petition:

1. Freedom for political prisoners
2. Elimination of Article 145 of the Penal Code
3. Abolition of the riot police (granaderos)
4. Dismissal of the Mexico City chiefs of police
5. Indemnification for victims of repression
6. Justice against those responsible for repression

If we assess these demands, we note that they encompass both local concerns (dismissal of the police chiefs) and national ones (freedom for political prisoners). Nowhere did they call for the resignation of the president, much less cancellation of the Olympics. But in their directness and simplicity, they challenged the very legitimacy of the ruling party to govern justly and democratically.

The six demands constituted a series of petitions that embodied the students' rage at the authoritarian nature of Mexican politics. One category of petitions concerned the material and legal basis for years of government repression. Thus the first three demands called for a freeing of political prisoners (with particular emphasis on the jailed railway leader Demetrio Vallejo, whose image was often displayed by protesters), dismantling of the hated granaderos, and the annulment of antiquated legislation that provided a quasi-legal basis for government repression. The latter referred to Article 145 of the federal Penal Code, the so-called social-dissolution clause

that dated back to World War II efforts to fight internal subversion instigated by the Axis powers. The article provided for harsh penalties against
those who "in word, writing, or by whatever other means propagate ideas,
programs, or conduct that tend to produce rebellion, sedition, riots, disor-
ders, and the obstruction of the functioning of legal institutions."[121] This
category of demands underscored the absence of guarantees for public dissent and the utter lack of due process. A second category addressed the legal accountability of public officials tied to recent repression and justice for
families and victims of government violence. This amounted to an implicit
critique of a political and judicial system that, monopolized by the PRI, negated the possibility of democratic representation and legal oversight.

Finally, the movement insisted that all political dialogue regarding these
demands be made public; that is, within full view of the mass media. This
was a tactical decision meant to avoid the mistakes of other groups in the
past which, in settling for closed-door negotiations, had discovered the government's agility at dividing and conquering. But if the demand was tactical in that it aimed at avoiding cooptation, it also had strategic implications.
For by settling on nothing less than a public dialogue with the president,
the students meant to underscore the utter absence of legislative recourse,
despite the formal dressings of a competitive party system. Furthermore,
such implicit attacks on the centralization of power called into question the
moral authority not only of the ruling party but also of the president himself, a position that directly violated the unwritten rules of protest politics in postrevolutionary Mexico. As a recent work on the subject argues,
what gave the student movement its historical significance was the protesters' irreverence for a political system that negated the existence of a
civil polity.[122]

In actuality, the tone of the movement resembled a cross between the
early civil-rights marches in the United States and the more contempora-
neous marches in Paris, Prague, Berkeley, and elsewhere, in which solem-
nity mixed with festivity and a shared protest culture was evident.[123] Men
marching in short hair and suits were accompanied by those in long hair
and jeans; women in dresses accompanied those in pants and miniskirts. In
part, this diversity reflected generational differences. But it also reflected
the eclectic cultural sensibilities of the student population, influenced on
one hand by the history of student activism and on the other by the rock
revolution. Evelyn Stevens's description of the UNAM campus in the midst
of the movement as a "discreet and decorous version of the Woodstock
spirit"[124] is thus revealing. At the UNAM, gatherings organized around
folk-music performances, political theater, poetry readings, and collective

mural paintings all formed an integral aspect of student-movement culture.[125] The raising of political consciousness associated with the student movement reinforced the place of Latin American folk music over rock, which was still more strongly identified with youthful diversion than with serious political struggle. But foreign rock's close associations with the avant-garde and ties to student-movement culture elsewhere in the world kept it from being condemned as imperialist, except perhaps by the most radical elements. Even in the midst of the struggle rock found its place on the UNAM, as one participant recalled: "When the university had been taken over by the students and you were there for two straight days, well sure, you played music over the loudspeakers to make the time go by, and that's when you heard a lot of rock."[126] Yet if rock music was not central to the Mexican student movement in the way it was in the United States during antiwar protests, it nonetheless had an important contributing role. Mexican performers may have been derided as would-be rockers by student leaders, but the fomenting of a rock counterculture by these local bands was an inextricable aspect of La Onda's broader development. And it was through La Onda that so many young people were sensitized, in the language of one informant, to be outspoken against arbitrary, patriarchal authority.[127] Jaime Pontones, in his early teens at the time of the student movement, recalls his attitude:

> I was very young and didn't have any clear sense of political reality, but I supported the youth, the students. This was because Díaz Ordaz was a shithead, as were all the police; because they persecuted people with long hair; they repressed those who smoked pot; because they didn't allow rock; because they were a bunch of shithead moralists. I didn't understand much about the movement except that they were from the UNAM, that they were students and youth, and that they listened to rock.[128]

In fact, though many middle-class households forbade or pressured their children not to get involved, the influence of La Onda was clearly present in appeals to join the movement. As Manuel Ruiz, who ultimately stayed clear of the movement, recalls:

> One of the student leaders or someone would come by and push you and your group of friends, saying, "Isn't it true they don't let you walk around with long hair? Isn't it true they don't let you listen to rock? Isn't it true they don't let you dress like you want to? Isn't it true there aren't any places to listen to rock? Isn't it true the education system is rotten and all the teachers are bad? Well, come on and join the strike! We're going to unite and take over the streets!" And in my opinion,

that's how the student movement got started. . . . But I knew it was a waste and wasn't going to change anything, except get a bunch of students killed.[129]

At the same time, the movement further entrenched brewing conflicts in the home, as many students were forced to choose between following their conscience and obeying the directives of their parents.

This was especially true for women.[130] Female participants in the student movement found themselves confronted not only by the obstacle of overcoming the privileged male terrain of political organizing but also by the much stricter demands of parents prohibiting their involvement. If La Onda had begun to open up a new realm of personal freedom, experienced in the shortening of skirts and the wearing of pants, the student movement radicalized that experience by placing women on an equal footing with men. While more traditional divisions of labor occurred—women generally were responsible for organizing meals for returning brigades—women also found themselves on the front lines, having their voices heard and sharing the dangers of repression with their male cohorts. For these women, participating in the movement was nothing short of a totally transformative experience, which instilled self-respect and led to the questioning of traditional gender values. One woman, for example, broke up with her boyfriend, who had stayed clear of the movement and criticized her participation. The notion that women were to be protected by men was cast aside not only by the realities of social protest but by the ideology of a democratic movement as well: "We fought shoulder to shoulder [with the men] and we couldn't see any difference between what were our roles and battles and what were theirs. . . . In this period we were all androgynous. We were brave fighters, the same as any man. . . . We didn't see any difference in what we needed as women and what men needed."[131] If women were successful at carving out a respected role as participants and even leaders, conflicts at home were often more traumatic. Numerous parents could not relate to the fact that their daughters were involved in a public protest, that they returned home after dark and even spent the night in strangers' homes, that they had found a voice which would not be readily silenced. In some cases, women found themselves thrown out of the house by parents who "refused to permit their homes to be considered 'like a hotel.'"[132]

Despite such challenges, the class, generational, and gender diversity of the student movement was its strongest asset. This diversity reflected the more profound impact of student strategizing, which sent upper- and middle-class activists into working-class neighborhoods and in turn forced a transformation of cultural values in an effort to create a unified front. Class boundaries were transcended not only in spatial terms but linguistically and stylistically as well. Where La Onda had been defined by its hip but still essentially tasteful jargon, the process of reaching out to youth from other social classes not only distributed this jargon more widely but also, at the same time, broadened its vocabulary as it incorporated slang from the lower classes. As one student at the Polytechnical Institute remarked, "At Poli I never heard expressions like 'mummies,' 'squares,' people 'on the right wave length' [onderos], and so on. . . . Maybe they use that kind of language at the UNAM, but it seems more like the jargon of intellectuals or small groups hankering to be part of the Movement, to be 'in.' When we talk among ourselves at Poli, we use the crudest sort of language, bricklayers' language."[133] Words such as *cabrón, desmadre,* and *chingar* entered into student vocabulary, a shift that Evelyn Stevens noted when she pointed out that "the 'filthy speech' revolution . . . had apparently spread to Mexican campuses." "Profanity and obscenity emerged in the discourse of the protesters," Stevens described, "with the expected effect on their elders."[134]

At the same time that La Onda was radicalized by direct contact with working-class culture, its constituency was expanded to include lower-class youth, who were made to feel a part of this universalizing rock movement. Indeed, even some of the social barriers that had once kept upper- and middle-class youth from fraternizing were overcome, as students from different class backgrounds found they shared a common language in La Onda. Thus the pretense of youth solidarity had the important impact of rupturing the rigid class lines that had traditionally separated one group from another (geographically and socially), in turn temporarily masking the realities of economic difference.

Perhaps the strongest indication that rock could no longer be contained within the boundaries of mere entertainment and that La Onda had moved beyond a fashion statement was an editorial in *POP* that exhorted its readers not to partake in the "cowardly" demonstrations then being carried out by students:

> NOW YOU'RE A CITIZEN! . . . The days of being a "rebel" are past. Now you're a MAN. . . . And men are RESPONSIBLE for their acts. . . . Don't listen to demagogic agitators because YOU ARE NOT SHEEP, BUT MEN. Don't take to the streets and commit crimes against your Country; that will be left to the half-wit "rebels." [N]ow you are MEN for real and must concern yourselves with CONSTRUCTION, never with destruction.[135]

Urging readers that "the days of being a 'rebel' are past" revealed the underlying conservative ideology of the magazine, despite its proudly psychedelic orientation. Yet containing La Onda as a symbol of modernity was no longer possible; it had now become a source of empowerment.

STUDENT STRATEGY AND TACTICS

The organizational strategy of the movement took various forms, which reflected both the centrality of student energies and the need to overcome the preponderance of government propaganda disseminated by the mass media against them. Student activists worked hard to cast the movement as fundamentally democratic in its goals, especially to counter government claims that "subversive elements" were underwriting the unrest. With institutional channels for reform—elective office, state bureaucracies, large sectors of the press—monopolized by the direct influence of the ruling party, protest politics necessarily shifted onto the terrain of the everyday and became a battle for the hearts and minds of the citizenry. This was done, for instance, by forming numerous "people-to-people brigades" that took their message directly to the bureaucrats, workers, housewives, and others they met on the streets, in marketplaces, at the entrances to factories, on public transportation, wherever they might be heard. The students handed out leaflets listing their demands and appealed to a language of constitutionality. They also collected donations; contributions helped to fund the cause and counter accusations of foreign support. With the participation of students from the Fine Arts Theater, street theater modeled on the "happenings" staged in Berkeley and elsewhere also became part of the tactical repertoire. Such students formed groups that role-modeled different sectors of the population in staged street confrontations designed to draw an unsuspecting public into a debate over student activism.[136] When the government utilized a discourse of rebeldismo in an attempt to identify student actions (such as painting graffiti and commandeering buses) with wanton violence, the movement responded with a poignant display of discipline: During the so-called Silent March on 13 September, tens of thousands of people paraded mutely down a principal avenue in the capital, many with adhesive tape over their mouths. As one placard stated: "To The People of Mexico: You can see that we're not vandals or rebels without a cause—the label that's constantly been pinned on us. Our silence proves it."[137]

A second strategy employed by the students was to "poach" on government-ritualized domains in an effort to reappropriate their meanings.[138] Such spaces included, for instance, the Angel of Independence statue and, most importantly, the Zócalo (central plaza), "the neurological point of monopolized ritual space."[139] The temporal transformation of the Zócalo from a regimented parade ground reserved for ceremonial design into a festive, declamatory, public meeting ground was profoundly symbolic in its implications. "We had to take over the Zócalo; we had to deconsecrate the Zócalo—and we did, three times," explained one student protester.[140] At the same time that "taking command of the streets" aimed to disrupt the parameters of meaning assigned to public places, students also reappropriated national heroes long incorporated into the official pantheon. This gesture of reappropriation, however, did not come instinctively. Initially, in fact, the faces of Zapata and Villa were discarded in favor of Che Guevara and Mao Zedong, who served as symbols of revolutionary utopianism around the world. As one participant commented, "I never thought of Zapata as a student symbol, an emblem. Zapata has become part of the bourgeois ideology; the PRI has appropriated him. Maybe that's why we chose Che as our symbol at demonstrations from the very first. Che was our link with student movements all over the world! We never thought of Pancho Villa either. His name never even crossed our minds!"[141] But when the press used such references to international revolution as a pretext for slandering the movement (the red-and-black strike flag was raised in place of the Mexican flag in the Zócalo after one demonstration), student leaders pushed for a purging of such symbols and instead urged the adoption of Mexican symbols and heroes. New orders from the strike committee now implored: "Let's have no more vituperative slogans, no more insults, no more violence. Don't carry red flags. Don't carry placards of Che or Mao! From now on we're going to carry placards with the portraits of Hidalgo, Morelos, Zapata, to shut them up. They're our Heroes. *Viva Zapata! Viva!*"[142] This decision was profoundly significant, for it reflected a direct challenge to the PRI's monopoly of the symbolism of Mexico's revolutionary heritage. By parading images of Villa, Zapata, Juárez, and others the students implicitly questioned the government's right to speak in their name, while suggesting that they instead had the right to do so. If earlier commentators had feared the replacement of such national heroes by the likes of James Dean and Elvis Presley, this reappropriation suggested an ironic inversion of their concerns. Now the nation's revolutionary heroes were being used against the government itself.

Finally, student strategy confronted the legitimacy of the Revolutionary Family by directly mocking the president's moral authority to speak for all Mexicans. This irreverence took various forms, including the rewriting of revolutionary corridos, the biting sarcasm of lithographs that cleverly drew on familiar public images, and the liberal use of graffiti, which often incorporated language and slogans drawn from other student movements worldwide.[143] In fact, many students openly expressed their feelings of solidarity with other such movements, as articulated in one CNH document: "We are conscious of our historical vision: to transform reality, to transform society. And in this task we are not alone. For the first time youth from around the world are identifying with one another in this common task."[144] In one example of this irreverence of taking on the old order, a poster displayed a superimposition of the president's profile (whose jutting jaw and protruding upper teeth lent themselves easily to caricature) over that of a gorilla donning a riot helmet, thus suggesting the barbarity of state force. And in a remake of a commercial ditty, the students chanted:

> Tell me, tell me, Gustavo,
> Tell me why you're a coward,
> Tell me why you've no mother,
> Tell me, Gustavo, please tell me.[145]

Still another banner read: "Free tuition for granaderos enrolling in literacy classes."[146] "Suddenly the old rules no longer applied," writes Evelyn Stevens. "I saw buses speeding down the avenues, their sides painted with the slogan 'Death to Díaz Ordaz.'"[147] But despite the seriousness of the students' cause, or perhaps because of it, protest was often characterized by a "carnivalesque spectacle,"[148] a sight common in the inversion of any hierarchical order. Observing a moment in which the police chief and a granadero were burned in effigy while others paraded around a coffin labeled "dead government," Stevens noted that "[i]n spite of the raucousness, there was no violence; the crowd was in excellent humor, in a mood to find each incident hilariously funny, as at a circus."[149]

THE MASSACRE AT TLATELOLCO

With the approaching Olympics, the stakes were raised for both sides to resolve the deepening crisis. Contrary to the government's claims that the students sought a disruption of the Olympics, the movement in fact aimed to leverage world attention to address its calls for greater democratization. Nonetheless, as the students' sense of empowerment grew, the regime feared the mounting embarrassment and disruption of public order. Then, in mid-September, the army directly occupied the main UNAM campus and, several days later, the Polytechnical Institute as well, thus once more violating the constitutional protection of university autonomy. Scores of students were rounded up and imprisoned; many others were forced to go underground.[150] At the Polytechnical Institute, pitched battles took place between the army and students. The heightened repression was taking its toll on the movement; meetings drew fewer participants, and the leadership hoped for a solution prior to the Olympics.[151] On 1 October the army withdrew from the UNAM (though remaining at the Polytechnical Institute). The next day representatives of the CNH met with government officials to discuss a resolution to the conflicts, but the meeting went nowhere and, if anything, proved to be a government tactic to divide the leadership.[152] Already there were signs of a radicalization of strategy by some members, who now carried weapons and advocated armed revolt; several of these members, it was later revealed, turned out to be government-paid provocateurs. By this point, the movement was heavily infiltrated by federal security agents. A march had been planned for that afternoon (2 October) to protest the continued occupation of the Polytechnical Institute, but at the last moment the leadership decided to cancel the march—word had spread that the army was massing its forces along the planned protest route—and to hold a meeting at the Plaza of the Three Cultures instead. The change in tactics meant that the demonstrators became sitting ducks for the military.[153]

The plaza where the scheduled meeting was to be held was set in the midst of a massive public housing project called Tlatelolco. The plaza itself acquired its name because of the juxtaposition of pre-Conquest Aztec ruins with colonial and postrevolutionary architecture. Located just north of Mexico City's center, the site was a compromise meeting ground for student participants from the various schools and universities. It was also home to scores of middle-class workers, housewives, and children, including students. The meeting that evening drew between 5,000 and 10,000 people, many of whom were simply residents of the apartment complex. But as the meeting began it became increasingly obvious to the leadership that something was wrong. Unidentified people tried to enter the balcony where the main speakers were staged. Notes were passed to the speakers that the crowd was full of judiciales posing as spectators; in fact, members of the Olympic Battalion (trained for security at the Olympics) were placed throughout the crowd. Later it was discovered that journalists, who were given privileged access to the balcony, were also infiltrated by government forces. Suddenly a helicopter began to circle overhead, and two flares were dropped. Within moments shouts rang out from the crowd as army troops filed into the plaza from the street, blocking off the only route of escape. Soldiers began to fire point-blank at the crowd, killing and wounding men, women, and children at random. To this day, the events of that evening have remained etched in the memory of all Mexicans as the Massacre of Tlatelolco.

Accounts of the massacre itself are still largely dependent on oral histories, as the official story remains shrouded in secrecy and denial. It remains unclear, for instance, who gave the orders to send in the army, though it was widely assumed that Secretary of Interior Affairs Luis Echeverría was directly responsible. Subsequent interviews, however, have suggested that orders may actually have come from Defense Secretary General Marcelino García Barragán, who was determined to clear up the "political mess" produced under civilian watch.[154] For its part, the government maintains that student sharpshooters targeted army troops, provoking a response. In fact, armed provocateurs *had* infiltrated the movement by that point and may, indeed, have fired on either the army or the crowd. Some members of the CNH also carried weapons for defensive purposes, but at Tlatelolco the balance of forces made armed resistance folly; weapons were quickly discarded to avoid discovery by the army.[155] Foreign journalists present for the pending Olympics put the number of dead at more than 200, while official figures admitted only to 49 (including an army captain).[156] Hundreds were wounded. To prevent an accurate count, the military cordoned off hospitals and morgues, and many people were simply "disappeared." In the subsequent hours soldiers continued their offensive by conducting apartment-by-apartment searches throughout the Tlatelolco complex for people in hiding. Those who were arrested were taken first to a military base and then to the Lecumberri prison, filling its cells far beyond capacity. Those who were not captured went farther underground or into exile.[157]

The students had generated a considerable amount of support for their struggle, reaching into broad sectors of the middle and working classes in the capital.[158] For their supporters, the students acted as the moral conscience of the nation, assuming the risks of confrontation in pursuit of a goal of social justice and democracy. But in their efforts to forge a common front with unions and the peasantry they also discovered the depth of state corporatist control and the impact of official propaganda used against them. In fact, while many Mexicans supported the students many others viewed their actions with alarm and undoubtedly agreed with newspaper and television reports of agitators, communists, and, especially, wanton youth. For a broad segment of the population, the empowerment of youth had come at the expense of adults' own sense of disempowerment and humiliation. "This is about a challenge of adults' capacity for comprehension, a defiance of their imagination and of their experience at governing," one editorialist wrote on the eve of the massacre in an article appropriately titled: "Youth

Power: The Parricides."[159] Indeed, while many parents (especially those from the lower middle classes) supported their children's participation, for many others the students' brazen assault on public authority only mirrored outrage at challenges to patriarchal control in the home. One public employee's comment that "It's the miniskirt that's to blame"[160] no doubt summed up the attitude of many adults. "If they ask me what the student movement of 1968 was all about," one participant wrote two decades later, "I could tell them that it was the history of how a son rebelled against his government because he could not confront his father, while a president who felt impotent against his own son's rocker lifestyle took revenge against hundreds of students."[161]

One day after the massacre the PRI-controlled Congress voted on a resolution approving the use of force to quell the students. Outside the Congress more than 500 mothers protested against the army's continued occupation of the plaza at Tlatelolco. Blame for the "disturbances" was quickly placed on communists and other foreign "agitators." The state, writes César Gilabert, "made sure there were no victims, only culprits."[162] Two weeks later the Olympic games opened, with a conservative and compliant press praising the advances of Mexico's modernization. As more arrests assured the effective dissolution of the movement, it became clear that the government would permit no further organizing against it. With no hope of continuing, on 4 December the CNH officially disbanded. But tanks and guns could not easily erase the memory of what had transpired or contain the spirit of free speech and democratic values the student movement had embodied. The regime might recapture the *places* where its institutions and public figures had been mocked and challenged, but it could not as easily contain the continued symbolic resistance to its authority. For the students' activism and the massacre that put an end to it had affected "the consciousness of a generation and [signaled] the beginnings of the demystification of the country."[163]

4 *La Onda* in the Wake of Tlatelolco

After the massacre there was, in a fundamental sense, nowhere for youth to turn to but La Onda. As the student movement had been creatively informed by the changing sensibilities of youth, in turn La Onda was itself transformed from a fashion statement and middle-class struggle within the home into a more broadly based expression of protest unavoidably grounded in the political events of that summer and fall. Despite the increasingly commercialized aspects of the counterculture (marketing a countercultural aesthetic was still profitable), for many La Onda was given new meaning after 1968. In the aftermath of Tlatelolco, the counterculture became an important vehicle for channeling the rage and cynicism felt toward a political system that denied democratic expression and toward a family structure that seemed to emulate it. "You see now why I'm a hippie," commented one youth after the massacre.[1] La Onda became a pretext for desmadre, for openly defying the buenas costumbres of family and society through drug consumption, liberated sexual relations, and in general replacing familial dependency with independent living. Where the student movement had politically empowered broad sectors of youth—and influenced by example others who stayed away—La Onda offered the possibility for continued protest, only now by repudiating rather than engaging society as a strategy for change. In the words of the noted Mexican critic Gastón García Cantú, a "hippismo of the left" characterized many of those who had once been a part of a now-disintegrated movement.[2]

JIPIS, XIPITECAS, AND JIPISMO

The massacre succeeded in dismembering a political and social movement at its moment of greatest strength. In the aftermath one element of the student population became further radicalized, while the majority was consumed with a sense of impotence and failure.[3] To be sure, ongoing contact between friends, family members, and others with those imprisoned kept alive a spirit of political activism, often at great personal risk. Within the prison itself a culture of resistance and of solidarity prevailed, despite often tremendous hardships.[4] Those who could fled abroad to avoid persecution for their involvement. A minority took to organizing armed revolutionary struggle. But for the majority, the massacre produced feelings of "a terrible sense of frustrated impotence," in the words of one participant. "After the massacre, each person was left to confront their own individual demons, because each had lived it in their own particular way."[5] As Carlos Monsiváis would write several years later, "there [was] no Vietnam war" for Mexican youth to confront; instead there were "the institutions of the Mexican Revolution and [the ideology of] National Unity."[6] As a twenty-five-year-old reader of the magazine *POP* wrote in the spring of 1969, "We want to do what our souls tell us, given that we don't want to be a copy [of foreigners] and we don't want another revolution where a million Mexicans are slaughtered; we want peace and understanding. Our position is not meant to bother anyone, because we already know that incomprehension brings on the granaderos, as well as many more sad nights [like Tlatelolco]."[7] With the massacre the PRI had revealed its commitment to one-party rule, but many adults had concurred with the view that youth had lost respect for authority, beginning in the family and extending to the presidency. "We didn't have to fight [against] a war," one woman explained. "We fought against a corrupt society, [one] that was suffocating us, that was deceiving us." She continued, "That was our war, and rock [music] helped us to scream; rock for me is about that scream, a universal scream."[8]

In the days and months following the massacre, renewed reports of the emergence of a Mexican hippie movement filled the pages of the press, and editorialists from the right and left found equal cause to criticize them. Alternately referred to as "hippies" (in quotation marks), *jipis*, and later *jipitecas* (or *xipitecas*), the appearance of these youth in larger numbers reflected the continuation of a trend that predated the 1968 movement but that had been given new impetus by the repression. Mexican *jipismo* was overwhelmingly a middle-class movement, for it was among the middle classes that the values of patriarchy and religion were most strongly reflected. The more pressing questions of everyday survival influenced the actions of the lower classes, and the elite flaunted rebellion as a sign of their privileged access to fashions and trends abroad, but the middle classes used jipismo to escape familial and societal pressures. For some on the left, the spread of jipismo took on proportions of a government conspiracy. (One author has even suggested that the government distributed drugs among the students to encourage this apolitical alternative.)[9] "Dropping out," however, involved a complex process of simultaneously emulating the modernizing aspects of foreign hippies—whose psychedelia, music, and attitudes toward authority revealed their "advanced" thinking—and reappropriating as their own the hippies' turn to indigenous spiritual and cultural traditions.

Once more the confusion of gender roles, satirized by numerous cover drawings for the conservative weekly *Jueves de Excélsior,* evoked a common fear among conservatives that the bedrock values which had kept men masculine and women feminine were at risk. As one author described the situation, "The men do everything possible to look like women: their long hair, their tight pants, and even their way of walking. The women, in contrast, cut their hair short, wear trousers, use sweaters, and really, really do look like men."[10] The implications of such brazen cross-dressing seemed perfectly clear: The jipis were a direct threat to a hegemonic value system grounded in patriarchy and heroic nationalism. Mexican youth, ran a familiar refrain among conservatives, had "lost its vision of true heroism" by succumbing to the "false heroes" brought in largely on the wings of transnational capital.[11] So threatening was the prospect of a man looking like a woman that when forced to choose between the "manly" acts of student protest—uniformly denounced by the conservative press—and the "feminine" approach of passivism, one author concluded: "It's preferable to see youth discontent in an open and virile manifestation, in a vigorous, bold protest, [which is] much more [Mexican], much more comprehensible than the absurd attitude of 'passivism,' which is only a pretext for vagrancy and corruption. . . . Mexico needs men, not hippies."[12] "Dropping out" of society was thus as threatening a posture of defiance as was openly confronting the government by marching in the streets. Indeed, in that the former implied a restructuring of everyday values one could argue that its significance as a counterhegemonic force was even greater in the long run than was confronting the government on strictly political terms, terms that later proved readily cooptable.

But for many on the left, the jipi movement was too overtly depoliticized and, at any rate, still a second-hand copy of the "authentic" revolt against technocratic life that was embodied in the hippie movement abroad. When Carlos Monsiváis asked, "Against which high technology do [the jipis] protest in the name of love?"[13] he articulated the left's paradoxical sense of bitterness toward Mexico's jipi movement and simultaneous admiration for hippie culture elsewhere. This basic argument would be echoed many times over in later years. For much of the "new" Mexican left—supportive of the student movement, critical of authoritarian culture (including the Communist Party) and patriarchal value systems—the nation's problems were not linked to abundance but to poverty; not to overdevelopment, but to underdevelopment. Mexican jipis, no matter how hard they "tried to be like real hippies," in the end amounted to nothing more than a cheap imitation of a Western countercultural ideal that, ironically, most intellectuals respected.

THE ZONA ROSA

For those living in the capital, the Zona Rosa offered a learning environment and mirror for the inchoate jipi movement. Yet if the Zona Rosa offered a countercultural free zone for disillusioned middle-class youth, it was first and foremost an upper-class shopping district where the elite junior set came to display their cars and "in" fashions, while tourists—including visiting hippies from abroad—marveled at Mexico's cosmopolitan achievements. Epitomizing this appeal to cosmpolitanism was the brief publication of the self-promotional magazine, *Zona Rosa*. Filled on one hand with cultural criticism by writers and artists such as Carlos Monsiváis, Alejandro Jodorowsky, José Luis Cuevas, and others, on the other hand the magazine's editorial position revealed the self-conscious need to project an image of the Zona Rosa as a controlled countercultural environment, where the intermixing of foreign and local jipis created an ideal touristic space. The fact that the district was designed precisely to promote an avant-garde aesthetic, but one closely regimented by the confines of commerce, drew the support of many conservative writers and investors. Thus, the Zona Rosa's Business Council worked closely with city administrators and the Department of Tourism to provide a clean, attractive, and, above all, impressionable image of Mexico for foreign visitors. Promotional plans included the creation of a "Zona Rosa Passport" filled with store coupons for visitors, along with organized folkloric presentations, beauty contests, art competitions, and even the creation of an FM radio station.[14] As one writer noted, "The 'Zona Rosa' has constituted itself as an outstanding tourist center in Mexico." The fact that here "one runs into strange types, some shaggy-haired, others meditative, bearded or wildly dressed" is precisely what gave the Zona Rosa its "exotic character . . . [its] cosmopolitan touch." "Its fame," the writer proudly concluded, "has moved beyond the country's borders."[15]

This debate over cosmopolitanism was at the heart of discussion concerning the Zona Rosa. Some saw in the fact that the district was capable of bringing together so many different types of personalities—from street vendors to noted intellectuals to hippies—a testimony to its progressivism; among its cafés and restaurants, its boutiques and art galleries reigned "the style of the avant-garde [and] the liberation of prejudices,"[16] exclaimed one writer. The Zona Rosa, wrote another, is "one of the most accomplished [social] environments in the country . . . a cosmopolitan point" of reference that must be defended at all costs: "[It is] an innate living together among people, emotional freedom, open comprehension, a pleasing appreciation that renews our senses; the lights, the sounds, their images, everything goes in the magnificent Pink collage that emits freshness and freedom."[17] Others were less enthusiastic and understood the Zona Rosa not as a liberated zone but as a contrived oasis. As one writer noted, while the Zona Rosa provided "the possibility of living for a few moments with symbols of freedom or protest," it did so within the confines of "several square blocks of privilege that allow us to deny the realities of our city." In the end, he concluded, the counterculture reflected in the Zona Rosa amounted to a trivialized, superficial version of "evolutionary social movements" with validity elsewhere but "out of context" in Mexico, where the styles and rhythm of the counterculture "are used like a great carnivalesque game of negation."[18] Carlos Monsiváis viewed the Zona Rosa as symbolizing the urge to belong to a "sphere of Mexico where underdevelopment does not reign, to belong to the non-Mexico . . . to exterminate all difference between Fifth Avenue [in New York City] and Génova and Hamburgo [the principal streets of the Zona Rosa]."[19]

For those living in Mexico City, however, the Zona Rosa still served as a locus of a countercultural rebellion. "That is where I came to know about rock, where I really came to know about what they were calling the jipi movement," explained one female informant. Recalling her first encounter with drugs, rock music, and the contradictory feelings they brought with respect to her strict Catholic upbringing, she described a party near the Zona Rosa: "[They brought me] to a house that was practically abandoned, where they were playing rock music: it was Janis Joplin, and it was the first time I had ever heard her. And it seemed so strange! Lots of shouting and noise, and I didn't understand anything! . . . And these weirdos were taking out cigarettes and everyone was smoking them backwards. . . . It was the first time I tried marijuana. . . . I left thoroughly terrorized and I went home and then to church. I had to confess."[20] It was also in the Zona Rosa that the avant-garde styles of foreign hippies—especially their fusion of pop culture with indigenous clothing and jewelry—would be (re)appropriated by aspiring Mexican jipitecas. An important example of this process of reappropriation was the use of huaraches. For foreign hippies, wearing huaraches was symbolic of a Third World rite of passage. The counter-cultural travel book, *The People's Guide to Mexico*, for example, devoted two pages to shopping for sandals and Indian clothing in its section on what to buy. "Almost every tourist will purchase at least one pair of *huaraches* (sandals)," the guidebook instructs.[21] The cynical comment by a Mexican rock musician two years later on the adoption of this "indigenous style" by Mexican youth is therefore particularly revealing:

> Look, what I view as false about Mexicans is that they're all stupid. . . . Before, no one used *guaraches,* and if someone put them on people would say: "Oh no, you look like an Indian!" Now, everyone uses them because someone who isn't even of our race, some *gringo,* started to walk with them in the Zona Rosa. The same thing happened with shirts from Oaxaca: before no one went near them; now they're every-where. It's one thing to copy the *gringos,* but another to copy what's already ours![22]

The comment was relevant not only to sandals and dress but also to a whole style of indigenous revival pursued by the hippies and in turn influential in Mexico's own jipi movement. It was widely rumored, for instance, that famous rock stars such as John Lennon and Jim Morrison had traveled to Huautla in search of María Sabina and the acclaimed mushrooms. One informant emphasized the influence such ideas had on local style:

> There was even a photo of Jim Morrison wearing a necklace called the *yaxhqui,* which is made up of tiny stones typical of Huautla. A lot of [Mexican] kids who went to Huautla wore the same necklace, and those of us who didn't go to Huautla but went somewhere else in Oaxaca to try mushrooms, well we wore that necklace at one time too. In fact, if you knew someone going to Huautla you'd ask them to pick one up for you. But all of that came about because we saw Jim Morrison or Brian Jones [wearing one]. . . . I mean, here [the necklaces] are from our own country, and we didn't even have one![23]

According to Alvaro Estrada, the *yaxhqui* was actually a string of light, wooden beads held together by a piece of red cord and used by the Mazatec as rosary beads in the church. As early as the mid-1960s hippies from the United States reportedly purchased these beads "by the fistful and combined them with the brightly colored string bracelets that were used as a headband, Apache style."[24] Thus while this rediscovery of Mexico's indigenous present was central to the ideology of jipismo, it ironically exposed the jipis to accusations of reflective imitation.

REENCOUNTERING THE COUNTRYSIDE

The same modern impulse that led North American youth to seek the "primitive" in Mexico, and through such encounters to reconstruct their own postmodern identities, deeply affected Mexican youth in the wake of Tlatelolco. In rejecting their own middle-class lifestyles, Mexican youth were simultaneously embracing its transnational manifestation, literally embodied in the countercultural practices of foreign hippies. This embracement, in turn, stimulated a nationalist gesture reflected in a return to the land and the revalorization of indigenous cultures.[25] It was in this way that Mexican youth adopted the gestures of a postmodern cultural politics guided toward a counterhegemonic strategy of popular (versus "official") nationalism. While foreign hippies certainly did not cause this jipismo movement, they were guilty—as elements of the press claimed in a distorted way—of directly influencing the direction the movement took. Thus at the heart of this "Mexicanization of the hippies"[26] was the ironic double-mirror effect I have already noted: the reabsorption of styles that youth from abroad had already appropriated in their mutual yet quite distinct flights from and expressions of modernity.

Numerous Mexican jipis during this period followed the example set by foreigners and set off to discover the Mexican countryside. During the late 1960s, scores of youth from Mexico's middle classes, many from the provinces and in large majority men, left their homes to crisscross the country. Hitchhiking—*pedir aventón* or *pedir un* ride—was popularized throughout the country, also suggesting the direct influence of the hippies. For most who did so, this meant voluntarily leaving one's home and being on one's own for the first time. It became known as *andar en el rol* and meant, in the words of one male informant, "traveling, getting to know Mexico."[27] For Joaquín López, his travels around the country "hitchhiking with my guitar" brought him the invaluable experience of an "Other" Mexico, an indigenous Mexico he had known about largely through the static discourse of an official nationalism. Traveling was about "discovering music, people [and] other distinctive worlds."[28] The experience of andar en el rol meant the possibility of reclaiming national territory and an official ideology of *indigenismo* through personal transformation. At the same time, it rebuked a myth of national harmony, in which the contradictions of ethnic, class, and cultural differences were ceremoniously masked by an official discourse that sought to define one's "place" in the progress of the nation. "There was a certain valorization," he recalled in describing his experience. "Maybe it was your first cup of coffee made by an Indian. I was a middle-class kid, and that was cool. It made you reflect on class and other relationships. . . . It was something very special that happened to our generation."[29]

At the same time, leaving home also represented an act of defiance against rigid familial and institutional structures. For Jasmín Solís Gómez, who disobeyed her family's wishes and ran away to Huautla, where she stayed for several weeks, the trip was "the first time that I could feel [free]." Indeed, she had made the trip not consciously seeking out an indigenous experience but rather to feel accepted by a group of several "liberated [high school] friends" with whom she had spent time in the Zona Rosa. En route to the sierra of Oaxaca, she recalled finding herself on a bus with Canadians and about thirty people from the UNAM, all "pure jipis" and all men; her "liberated friends" had chickened out. In Huautla she was introduced to mushrooms by a few of the Canadians: "Someone had a radio. I was listening to Janis Joplin, and the musical notes began to dance in front of my eyes. . . . The forest was full of colors and everything filled with music." The naturalness of listening to rock music while in the Mazatec Sierra tripping on hallucinogenic mushrooms reflected the fusion of modern and indigenous cultural experiences that informed the hippie and jipiteca movements. It was discovering the possibilities of such fusion that opened up new spaces of meaning for a generation of Mexicans raised on a modernizing ideology that separated the "folkloric" from the "cosmopolitan" spheres of everyday life. Choosing to explore this fusion implied making difficult choices about one's identity and outlook on life, choices that in turn directly affected the cultural terrain of hegemony. "The jipi and feminist liberation movements gave me a different possibility for growth," she told me.[30]

Processes of transculturation occurring in what Mary Louise Pratt has described as the "contact zone"[31] incited what I term a *nationalist gesture* in Mexican youth. This gesture involved the reparticularization of self- and national identity on terms that sought to sever the link between personal identity and the hegemonic project of nationalism inculcated by the political regime.[32] Through the influence of transnational images, music, and actors Mexican youth came to challenge a totalizing discourse of national identity, one that stressed the stasis of an indigenous present and the "correctness" of patriarchally defined hierarchies. Transnationalism introduced the possibility of selecting among multiple reference points in the reconstruction of one's national as well as individual identity. In this way, transnationalism becomes intimately linked with postmodern identity-formation strategies and the forging of a popular nationalism from below.

I use the term *postmodern* here in the sense of repudiating the ideological constraints imposed by an Enlightenment-based concept of the nation, which assumes fixed and bounded signs of a collective national identity. As Néstor García Canclini writes, "In several cases, cultural modernism, instead of being denationalizing, has given impulse to, and the repertory of symbols for, the construction of national identity."[33]

By pursuing a postmodernist impulse that critiqued modern society, Mexican youth acted out gestures of national and self-reimaginings. Such gestures inevitably involved the casting aside of fixed stereotypes of national identity and conforming to buenas costumbres in the search for new personal freedoms and new collective identities. Enrique Marroquín would later coin the Náhuatl-inspired term *xipiteca* (also written *jipiteca*) as a means of describing this phenomenon of cultural reappropriation and fusion. In his book *La contracultura como protesta*, perhaps the only serious attempt at the time to explicate the Mexican counterculture on its own terms, Marroquín uses the term *xipiteca* to denote the "creation of a genuine [Mexican hippie] subculture with original nuances."[34] I would argue that this subculture was in fact part of a broader countercultural movement (La Onda) with widespread impact. Jipismo involved a reimagining of national community that was reflected in the search for what Marroquín called "a lost Mexico."[35] Ironically, this search for indigenous cultural heritage was directly related to the experience of modernity. As one participant describes what took place: "it was a very strange combination [incorporating] selected elements from rock [music culture], but worked on, harvested in a very different context."[36]

Though much of the press and writers on the left and right alike sought to portray the jipi movement as a farcical imitation of the hippies or, worse yet, the direct result of imperialism, Mexican jipismo rapidly evolved into a countercultural force of its own. This possibility, as I have argued, was in large part due to the direct presence of foreign hippies, who served as avantgarde role models for the revalorization of ethnic difference and a recuperation of national histor(ies). Travels by countercultural agents from the metropolis and the imagery associated with the counterculture abroad offered a direct and tangible example of *how* to rebel: most dramatically, perhaps, by leaving one's home to travel the Mexican countryside. In turn, Mexicans reinscribed national territory with individualized and newly collective histories. By reinventing themselves as xipitecas, Mexican youth thus discovered new ways of being Mexican, ways that ran counter to the dominant ideology of state-sponsored nationalism.

Figure 7. Military authorities search a guitar case for hallucinogenic mushrooms and other possible drugs during a bust in Huautla de Jiménez, Oaxaca, in July 1969. Source: "Concentrados: sobre 1303, 'Hippies [mugrosos gringos de la época],' July 1969," Hermanos Mayo Photo Archive, Archivo General de la Nación. Used by permission.

THE REGIME CRACKS DOWN

In July 1969 judiciales, combined with agents from the Department of Interior Affairs, the Defense Department, and local officials, launched the "first combined hunt" for what *El Universal* headlined as "Vicious 'Hippies.'" Sixty-four Mexicans belonging to the Tribe of Christ commune, along with twenty-two foreigners caught in the raid, were arrested; all were officially charged with trafficking drugs. The foreigners—seventeen from the United States, four from Canada, and one from England—were promptly deported (see Figures 7 and 8).[37] Two days later *El Universal*

Figure 8.   Foreign hippies (probably from the United States) face the prospect of arrest and deportation following a raid on Huautla de Jiménez, Oaxaca, in July 1969. Source: "Concentrados: sobre 1303, 'Hippies [mugrosos gringos de la época],' July 1969," Hermanos Mayo Photo Archive, Archivo General de la Nación. Used by permission.

warned of the "grave dangers" facing Mexico because of the "contamination of our youth" by North American hippies.[38] The arrests were just one aspect of a wider crackdown. Jasmín Solís Gómez, the informant cited above, was in Huautla when she too was caught up in a raid: "I heard shots, shouts, and beatings and didn't know what to do. . . . They marched [the three Canadians and me] back to Huautla."[39] While police actions against foreign and Mexican hippies were well known prior to this, the federal orchestration of the arrests suggested the utility of highlighting the jipismo "threat" in the wake of Tlatelolco (see Figure 9).

Focusing government attention on the rise of jipismo not only distracted from the larger issues of reform and repression but, moreover, facilitated a strategy of conflating antigovernment protest with jipi radicalism.[40] By implementing a repressive policy against native and foreign hippies, the government sought to bolster support among conservative social groups such as small shop owners, middle-class parents, and, especially, rural and

Figure 9. Caught with hallucinogenic mushrooms, a Mexican jipi faces the prospect of arrest during a bust in Huautla de Jiménez, Oaxaca, in July 1969. Source: "Concentrados: sobre 1303, 'Hippies [mugrosos gringos de la época],' July 1969," Hermanos Mayo Photo Archive, Archivo General de la Nación. Used by permission.

provincial populations who felt threatened by the challenge to traditional family values—work discipline, respect for authority, gender distinction— embodied in jipismo. A central feature of the government's strategy was thus to rally sentiments of xenophobia and nationalist pride, a tactic which also overlapped with the official position that the student protesters were backed by "foreign agitators." Capturing this sentiment of support for the federal offensive against the "contamination" of Mexico by North American hippies is the August 1969 cover drawing for *Jueves de Excélsior:* a man with his shirtsleeves rolled up, broom in hand, sweeping a contingent of (male) hippies back across the border (see Figure 10).[41]

Mexico was not alone in its struggle to combat its "hippie problem." Many governments were forced to confront the influence of a U.S.-led counterculture on a generation of young people who refused to conform to their nation's ideological project of development, whether oriented toward capitalism or socialism. In Singapore, for example, entry was prohibited to tourists who wore "ornaments and clothes which leave one with the unmistakable impression that this is part of the contemporary aberrations found in the highly developed and affluent societies and imitated by not so

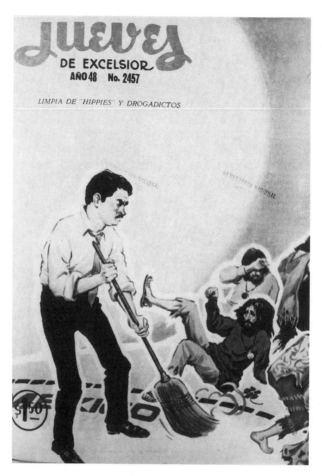

Figure 10.   "Cleanup of 'Hippies' and Drug Addicts." Source:
Jueves de Excélsior, 21 August 1969. Used by permission.

highly developed and affluent societies." [42] In the Soviet Union, the state
was obliged to declare the "legality" of long hair, a tacit recognition of its
inability to pursue a totalizing socialist project. [43] For governments the
world over, the "hippie problem" suggested a fundamental crisis of representation: "dropping out" of society, reflected through one's dress, language, and attitude openly challenged the ideological premise of the heroic
nationalism that characterized most post–World War II states. While in reality the hippie presence in most countries was never more than a minority, for an entire generation of modern, urban-raised youth throughout
many parts of the world the power of the hippies' appeal—to "do one's own

thing"—presented an unforeseen and complex new threat to national-developmentalist projects.

Despite drastic efforts by the Mexican regime, however, the flow of foreign hippie travelers into the country seemed unabated. An editorial that appeared one year after the Huautla raid cited the "need for a new, even more energetic intervention by the army and federal police" to stop the continued influx of hippies: "If the Secretary of Interior Affairs doesn't put a stop to the immigration of undesirables, soon we will have to support spectacles of homosexuality, massive drug addiction, and street violence, similar to what citizens of San Francisco, New York, London, and other large urban centers face."[44] These fears directly contributed to a public backlash against jipismo and led to heightened efforts by border guards to keep foreign hippies out. Judging from a report in *Rolling Stone* magazine, the problems facing hippies traveling to Mexico were taking their toll. "They don't like longhairs in Mexico," the travelogue opens. "If you are a man and your hair falls below your collar, expect to be—at least—stared at as if you were a civil rights worker in Mississippi, and—at worst—robbed or beaten by policía as well as bandidos."[45] Indeed, *The People's Guide* contained a special section dedicated to "Border Hassles," which stated in part: "If you do not look like the average tourist (and you long-haired, bearded, beaded and braless people have already guessed that there was a catch somewhere), you may not get average treatment when entering Mexico. . . . Mexican border officials have a straightforward attitude: people without money are hippies and therefore less desirable as tourists. . . . People with money are not hippies, even though they may affect hippie styles."[46] To beat the system, Carl Franz, the book's author, suggested a temporary fix of dress and presentation: "We look like small town teachers or college students from the early Sixties [when we cross]." He added, "The border officials love it."[47]

Though official sources that treat this theme are difficult to come by, one record found in the archive of the Department of Foreign Relations reveals the extent to which antihippie policy had reached the highest levels of power. The Mexican consul in San Diego came across an article in a local newspaper that described the difficulties facing U.S. hippies in Mexico. He forwarded a copy of the article to Mexico's secretary of foreign relations, who, in turn, forwarded the report to the appropriate authorities at the Department of Interior Affairs, with the accompanying message: "For whatever importance it might mean for this Dependency of the Executive [that is, Interior Affairs], with the present note is remitted a newspaper clipping from the 'San Diego Union,' which was sent to us by our Consul in San

Diego, California [regarding] the publishing of an extensive article warning North American drug-addicted youth about the obstacles they will come across [when] penetrating our country to dedicate themselves to their cravings."[48] Whether or not this message went into a larger file at the department is uncertain, though probable; access to its archives is still restricted. At any rate, Mexican officials were by no means alone in their fight against foreign hippie influence. When later "banned" from Lamu Island, Kenya, for disrupting village life, for example, Jerry Hopkins, writing in *Rolling Stone* magazine, blithely concluded: "The search for paradise continues."[49]

Some U.S. citizens even expressed their support for the stepped-up repression against hippie youth by the Mexican government. In a letter to President Díaz Ordaz, one writer stated: "May I offer my sincere congratulations on the stand you have takened [sic] regarding the long haired, hippie type, individual or so called? [sic] citizen, of our side of the border. Speaking for myself I am ashamed of their appearance."[50] Another person wrote, "I wish our government had the backbone to take a stand against such un-Godly, trashy mess as you have."[51] These letters suggest a projection of frustrations with the "hippie problem" in the United States onto the more "efficient" regime in Mexico. Moreover, they follow a pattern of support for Mexico's policy of repression against dissidents in general. Thus the author of the last letter concurred with the harsh approach to protesters, saying in conclusion: "I believe we could put a stop to riots here, as you did when they tried to prevent the Olympics from being held in Mexico. I have never [heard] of any more riots in Mexico."[52]

NORTH AMERICA'S NEPAL

By the late 1960s, travel by North American and West European youth to the Third World had become a rite of passage for the countercultural generation. Embracing the "underdeveloped world" became not only a sign of one's repudiation of materialist values but proof of one's humanism as well. And for U.S. and Canadian hippies Mexico, it might be said, became the poor person's Nepal. As Carl Franz remembers, "It was the closest warm, exotic place that you could go to—and the cheapest."[53] Or, as another former traveler from the United States succinctly put it, there was "more fantasy per dollar."[54] These comments match an analysis made by Marroquín in *La contracultura como protesta*: "There was an urge to travel, like the beatniks. But now, the goal is further away: India is paradise. Hippie communities are formed in the Orient. But it is difficult to go all the way over there. Mexico turns out to be tempting: close, cheap, exotic, savage, and legendarily hallucinogenic."[55] By 1969, "after the Summer of Love turned sour," Carl Franz recalls "a big migration South."[56] Or, as another writer summed it up: "political dissents or draft dodgers, potheads or college flunkouts, born again hippies or red light runners, rebel artists or just curious wanderers—anyone or everyone on the run [headed] for Mexico at some time or other at the turn of a turbulent decade."[57]

What is important for us to understand, however, is that the promotion by the Mexican state of native "color"—the living presence of indigenous cultures, the exotic adventure offered by visits to pre-Columbian ruins, the appeal of semideveloped tropical beaches—all directly contributed to the perception that premodern society was alive and well just south of the border. This folkloric representation of Mexico—an integral flip side of a cosmopolitan discourse linked to the promotion of the Olympics—was directly taken up by the hippies in their pursuit of native cultures, not to mention the quest for hallucinogenic mushrooms and the promise of cheap marijuana. Such a quest took them not to the Ballet Folklórico but directly in search of "the real thing": The reality of Mexico's largely indigenous countryside and the experience of direct contact with native cultures— about which, ironically, most urbanized Mexicans knew little. Carl Franz was particularly revealing about this relationship. "One of the reasons we used to go to the Museum [of Anthropology]," he told me, "was to get clues about the areas we wanted to visit." The Ballet Folklórico was skipped altogether: "I thought it was completely hokey."[58]

The stream of countercultural travelers to Mexico increased in tangent with the steady rise of tourist travel generally throughout the 1960s.[59] By the early 1970s, travel to Mexico had become an established tradition among the North American countercultural population. One important indication of this travel relationship was the tremendous popularity of *The People's Guide*, in the words of its author, "the first underground, countercultural travel guide to a foreign country" (see Figure 11).[60] First published in 1972, by 1979 it was in its fourth edition and seventh printing. Throughout the 1970s it sold between 10,000 and 15,000 copies a year, peaking in the late 1970s with sales of more than 20,000 a year.[61] Through *The People's Guide* and on their own, countercultural tourists developed a repertory of tourist sites to explore, places "off the beaten track," including favorite mountain villages and isolated beaches.

While many Mexican intellectuals regarded the jipis as a "cheap imitation" of the real thing, for at least some jipis it was the foreigners who fell short of the mark. Mexican youth immersed themselves in the reexperi-

Figure 11.   Cover of *The People's Guide to Mexico* (1972), a guidebook for countercultural travelers. Used by permission.

ence of native culture and traditions. Foreign youth, on the other hand, seemed "to come more for the drugs and the sun," as Joaquín López put it; "They weren't really part of our 'rol.'" "Some," he added, "adapted . . . and in that sense there was a valorization" of Mexican ways of life. But ultimately *understanding* Mexican culture was beyond the grasp or even the purpose of most hippies' travel experiences. For Mexicans, that experience was intrinsically different. "You went looking for the countryside," continued López, "and in looking for the country you meet up with campesinos, with Indians. And you're thinking about them, and they're seeing you with long hair. It was great."[62]

Foreigners, on the other hand, mostly used Mexico as a backdrop for their transformative escapes from the metropolis. "The exciting thing for Americans," recalled Carl Franz, "was to go to some Indian village and pretend you were Carlos Castañeda."[63] In fact, the level of actual contact between hippies and jipis often revolved around exchanges of money or food from the former for insider knowledge of local customs and drug connections from the latter. As Steve Rogers recalls, "I remember once thinking, 'Oh god, here come those Mexican hippies,' and they'd come and hit you up for food and dope, and they never even had a nickel. . . . You'd be down camping on the beach, and some Mexican hippies would sometimes come over with a guitar. They were pretty adept at scoring pot, and since the Americans had the money but no connections, the Mexicans would usually find something."[64] But it was the distinctive nature of their respective backgrounds that probably kept Mexican and foreign hippies away from one another. "I felt that usually Mexicans wanted to talk radical politics, whereas Americans were there just to have a good time," Rogers commented.[65] Indeed, this disjuncture between their conflicting worldviews is neatly encapsulated in a comment made by a self-proclaimed "die-hard" U.S. hippie coming to Mexico for the first time: "I love this country," he said. "Everyone lives like hippies down here!"[66] This romanticization of poverty could often reach extremes and, rather than bridge cultural differences, only served to underscore them. As the historian Catherine LeGrande recalls of her experiences as a student in Mexico, "I remember this one blond-haired gringa who went barefoot in Mexico City. Everywhere she went. I remember being angry at her, not only because it was dangerous but because it was really embarrassing. Once, we went into a market and this vendor cries out, 'Oh look at the poor gringa, she doesn't even have shoes!' It was incredible ethnocentrism on her part."[67] Thus for many foreign travelers, Mexico offered the fantasy of escape from the trappings of bourgeois life, an escape they could literally *afford* to make and that, by definition, was only transitory.

For U.S. hippies a degree of cynicism toward the Mexican jipiteca also played a role. Carl Franz, for example, remembers Mexican jipis as "a pale imitation of the real thing." He continued: "It's as though they never really got it. Most of them are from the upper class, as opposed to Americans who are from all over. They struck us as more like Weekend Hippies. And a lot of them did it to just to get next to American hippie girls. . . . You didn't have to scratch a Mexican hippie very deep to find a macho Mexican man [underneath]."[68] For U.S. hippies the ideal was to avoid people, to "dig" the natural landscape, and, when it became unavoidable, to learn to navigate one's way through local customs and idiosyncrasies. "Your arrival in a remote area will not go unnoticed," cautions *The People's Guide:* "People—curious, questioning, staring—are everywhere."[69] To its credit, one of the central values of Franz's guidebook is that it strives for what Dean MacCannell refers to in *The Tourist* as a "utopia of difference": "the possibility of recognizing and attempting to enter into a dialogue, on an equal footing, with forms of intelligence absolutely different from my own."[70] Thus Franz offers a way out of MacCannell's "prison house of signs"[71] suggested in the uncomfortable scenario of curious, staring natives:

> Once you've accepted the fact that there are going to be people around, you can take advantage of their curiosity to satisfy your own curiosity about them. I've found that there's no better way to get into an area than to select some likely looking person and suggest that I'd like to do something: go fishing, hunting, exploring, collect water or gather firewood. The response is almost automatically enthusiastic and quickly changes the relationship from frustrated curiosity about you to a desire to demonstrate something that they can do, whether it's climb a coco palm or lead you to an interesting ruin.[72]

This somewhat benign view of intercultural relations, however, is challenged by another reality of abuse and conflict. In an autobiographical short story, the writer Robert Richter captures the development of relationships between locals and foreigners at a seaside hippie haven in Baja California:

> Friction in relations developed early and naturally with simple cultural differences and attitudes. The young gringos wanted the isolation and the privacy of their own newly created world. They wanted only to hide out from a far away war and hassles at home—on their own—catching waves, living high, mellow and easy. . . . So the natives were intrusive and nosey to the gringos. The gringos were rude and crazy to them. Gringos had time and leisure and luxury, and the villagers had poverty and jungle-scrounging labor in a deceptive paradise.[73]

Richter's perception of inequality and unease beneath the allure of harmony is instructive. For even as they often abused and misunderstood their relationship with locals, U.S. hippies still viewed themselves as "the real thing," capable of full communion with Others as they navigated between modern and "pre-modern" worlds. Describing his experiences in Huautla, one hippie thus told a *New York Times* reporter, "There is a close bond of friendship and spirit of survival between the mushroom eaters and the local people."[74]

If La Onda belonged first and foremost to the middle classes during the mid-1960s (with los juniors flaunting their "in" fashions), after the student movement the lower classes staked out a claim on the rock counterculture as well. Why and how this occurred is no doubt complex. In part it is explained by the fact that rock is a mass medium—disseminated by radio, television, and film—and thus increasingly accessible even to those who could not afford to purchase albums or fanzines directly. Since the late 1950s, there had always been an element of the lower classes that sought participation in the youth rock culture (recall the *King Creole* riot in 1959), and it seems reasonable to imagine that this element grew during the 1960s.

A second factor was the experience and imagery of youth solidarity conveyed by the student movement, which contributed in an immense way to the transcendence—if perhaps often transitory—of class prejudice. Many students from private universities joined with those studying at the UNAM, the Polytechnical Institute, and the myriad affiliated schools throughout the capital to create a shared bond of struggle, despite often glaring class differences. This bond no doubt found expression in the common language of rock and the universalizing lexicon of La Onda, which now drew heavily on terms before seen as vulgar and crude. English words and phrases also became an integral part of this Onda lexicon and thus arguably became dissassociated from elitist pretensions, as they were reworked by youth in a broadening class context. This reappropriation even led to the creation of new words and phrases transliterated from the English, such as, for example, the word *simón*—slang for *right on*—which one U.S. journalist writing at the time suggested was the likely result of combining *sí* (yes) with *man*.[75] English had long been associated with upward mobility, though a parallel usage also existed. This was the value of English as a mechanism of *burlarse*, to mock the social habits—and the presumed "monopoly" of foreign cultural knowledge—of the upper classes, dating to the border *pachuco* slang popularized by the actor Germán ("Tin Tan") Valdés in 1950s Mexican cinema.[76] This latter usage was now popularized by the rock revolution as youth from the middle and lower classes strove for an identity beyond the straits of a repressive nationalism. "Like the *pochos*," writes García Saldaña, "Mexican youth were tired of speaking in Spanish. They found themselves pissed off at all of those words that signified a reality which existed thanks to the Mexican Revolution, which, of course, meant nothing to them."[77]

Figure 12. A roundup of Mexican jipis following a raid on a home in the wealthy Mexico City neighborhood of Las Lomas in early 1971. Source: "Concentrados: sobre 1303, 'redada de "hipis" en una casa de las Lomas,' 12 February 1971," Hermanos Mayo Photo Archive, Archivo General de la Nación. Used by permission.

Perhaps the most important factor underlying the incorporation of the lower classes into La Onda was that, as local rock bands proliferated, the limited venues for live performance clashed with increasing demand for them. This led to the formation of alternative performance outlets: on one hand, at schools and in the homes of the elite, and on the other, in improvised outdoor spaces toward the margins of the capital. Called *tocadas* from the verb *tocar* (to play an instrument), these concerts by local bands (singing in English) played an essential role not only in disseminating La Onda but in reinforcing its spirit of underground, semiclandestine culture as well. It was not surprising that the elite "junior set"—known colloquially as *los fresas*, which connoted either an acclamatory or derogatory label, depending on one's perspective—opened their homes to rock parties after 1968.[78] With money and political protection, los juniors could quite literally afford to wear their hipness generally without fear of the police. Such immunity was not always guaranteed, however, as suggested by a police bust at a home in the exclusive Las Lomas neighborhood of Mexico City (see Figure 12).

Participating in La Onda was an obvious sign of the elite's social connectedness with U.S. and European culture. "They *belong,*" Monsiváis wrote of los fresas; "they have friends, groups, situations predisposed in their favor."[79] The present-day rock group, the TRI, then known as the Three Souls in My Mind, in fact began by playing at tocadas in the mansions of Las Lomas de Pedregal, another wealthy neighborhood in Mexico City.[80] "It was a way of making money," described Manuel Ruiz, who went frequently to the tocadas. "You contracted some known band and sold rum and cokes. . . . But it was mellow. People were hired to keep an eye out for problems, but no one trashed the house, and everyone was happy. Besides, the organizer of the party made a nice bundle."[81]

While the elite sponsored open house parties, in the barrios and middle-class housing complexes (such as Tlatelolco), weekend tocadas drew thousands of people. Later named *hoyos fonquis* (literally, funky holes) by the novelist and rock critic Parménides García Saldaña, they had a spontaneous, often transitory, urban character. Though several of these performance spaces acquired actual names (for example, Chicago, Revolución, and Mandril), mostly they were noted for their semiunderground, often tenuous existence. Organized locally, all-day concerts featured numerous bands, often contracted to play at several sites around the city on the same day. According to Joaquín López, roadie and later member of the band La Revolución de Emiliano Zapata, "The hoyos fonquis were huge spaces in the urban parts of the city, warehouses that held 20,000 people. A stage was put up at one end and another at the other end. Bands were hired to play for an hour, and so you'd come for one set and then head off to another hoyo fonqui. . . . In the same day, you'd play at five different hoyos fonquis."[82] These spaces provided the key linkage between rock and urban lower-class youth after 1968.

While fresa denoted a person with wealth, *naco* (Monsiváis would later coin the term *la naquiza*) was reserved for the lower classes. Today, *naco* has come to mean someone who literally "lacks culture" or "proper etiquette," and it was in this sense that the lower classes were looked down on by the rest of society. As Monsiváis wrote at the time, "*Naco,* within this discriminatory language so characteristic of Mexico, equals proletariat, lumpenproletariat, poor, sweaty, greasy ducktailed hair, the profile of a head at Palenque, outdated in fashion by six months, out of fashion, or simply wearing crosses around the neck."[83] As rock music became directly integrated into barrio culture its containment as a sign of status in a modernizing society was irrevocably transformed. The lower classes increasingly claimed rock as their own, imposing their own voice on a medium which up to that point was still characterized by its privileged sense of access. Rock events became a pretext for desmadre and *reventón* (slang for partying), terms that conveyed a sense of anarchic festivity where social hierarchies were overturned and "respect" was located in a transient, unstable logic.

La Onda was becoming a bridge between the classes, superficial, perhaps, but real nonetheless. While part of the genius of Mexican nationalism has been the dissemination of mass cultural reference points that are shared by different classes (this is especially true for film),[84] in rock youth encountered an alternative set of references that identified them as a group in opposition to parents and society. While the upper and lower classes rarely interacted directly, youth from the middle classes took advantage of both social realms and might be called on to act as go-between for the elite, as Manuel Ruiz explains:

> Those of us from the middle class were close enough to those from the upper class so that we could relate to them and, from time to time, invite them into our scene. But we were also so close to those from the lowest class, those who were right there with the drug trade, that it was easier for us to buy marijuana and all sorts of other drugs. So a lot of times los juniors came up to us to see if we'd sell or give away a joint, or maybe just a hit of something.[85]

But if los juniors "belonged," as Monsiváis argues, their acceptance within La Onda was not guaranteed. Rather, their overstated efforts to belong often marked them as outsiders, impostors in a movement that prided itself on authenticity. Ruiz explained: "There were some funny moments, like los juniors who were so obviously juniors, so false. They'd come up to you and say [in English], 'Peace and love, brothers,' but in a tone so false and hollow that rather than [you] saying, 'Yeah, let's hang out,' instead they bummed you out. You felt like they were even making fun of you." Yet as this informant also pointed out, "rock at the end of the 1960s was [a] magic [that] . . . allowed the different classes to interact." Speaking of his experiences at private parties in the wealthy suburbs, he recalled that "A lot of times you'd leave a party really late and the buses and everything had already stopped, and suddenly some junior in his car would come up and say, 'where you headed, maestros.' You identified each other by the long hair and whatnot. And so they'd give us a ride. You'd go with them and be really appreciative of it. Without a doubt rock united us [in that way]."[86] Yet despite this mounting overlap between the middle and upper classes, there was an entrenched distrust by both the middle and upper classes of the nacos and of the element of total desmadre associated with the lower classes.

ROCK FOR THE MASSES

The first real opportunity for the classes to come together around rock was a stadium concert that featured a joint performance by the Union Gap and the Byrds in March 1969. Held at the Olympic Stadium, on the grounds of the UNAM, it was the first truly interclass, massive rock event in Mexico. The permit, in fact, had been in doubt until the last moment. Organized by the Hermanos Castro, themselves an internationally recognized ballad combo who had appeared on ABC's *Hollywood Palace* (alongside Big Brother and the Holding Co.),[87] profits were maximized by carving out differently priced sections from the enormous stadium. With the upper-tier priced at a mere 5 pesos (less than U.S. $0.50), the middle-tier priced at 10 pesos (around U.S. $0.75), and lawn chairs at 20 pesos (less than U.S. $2.00), the notion was to attract as broad an audience as possible. But not only was little effort made to maintain a separation between the differently ticketed sections, no one was assigned to police the floor of the stadium. "When the people saw that no one was watching over them, they pushed forward and invaded the lawn area without a second thought. In a few moments it was impossible even for the opening act, 'The Tijuana Five,' to arrive at the stage."[88] As those in the back continued to press dangerously forward, the Castro Brothers pleaded with the crowd to "show your level of culture and . . . degree of civilization so that we may confirm that the youth of Mexico are indeed ready for this type of event."[89] Concerned for the safety of the group, the Union Gap backed out of the concert altogether, leaving a string of Mexican groups to kill time until the Byrds, delayed at the airport, belatedly arrived.

When the Byrds finally took the stage and the first chords of "Turn, Turn, Turn" drifted over the inadequate sound system, sheer mayhem erupted, as the pent-up energies of waiting provoked a mad rush forward, dissolving any pretext of which seat belonged to whom.[90] In the impressionistic style that became his trademark, Carlos Monsiváis eloquently related afterward:

> And the seats go flying and the people scatter and the masses are the same on all sides, and the pitched battle begins, the riot, the general breakdown, the end. Seen from the summit of the stadium, the spectacle is at once formidable and convulsive. Those of La Onda get fed up and flee, convinced that the scene smells ripe for the granaderos of Baskerville, whose presence is thought to be imminent. The fresas try to keep listening, apprehensively protecting their girlfriends and their siblings

and their diploma which is only a few years off. . . . And the nacos, they take it all in (the generalization is coarse, but not untrue), at once experiencing the total burden of that classist substantive grounded in an aesthetic labeling, which in an instant of physical "kidding around" becomes the Other of the bourgeoisie . . . the thousand-headed monster of prerevolutionary mythology that threatened every proper Porfirian lady hidden in the basement of her hacienda.[91]

The implications of such a total breakdown in control over social space were profound. For state authorities, the concert clearly pointed to the limitations of control over mass popular culture.[92] Rock music had ceased to be the exclusive domain of the middle and upper classes. In the hands of the poor, it was even less containable. Yet for intellectuals and political activists who were still recovering from the blow to the student movement barely six months earlier, the prospect of mass rock concerts drew cynicism and despair. Monsiváis, for instance, later criticized those who attributed a political element to the riot (suggested by photos of youth waving a "V" sign, which was closely identified with the student movement), arguing that fans were only mimicking the performers without any clear sense of the symbol's meaning.[93] At that moment, the desmadre of rock seemed to be the antithesis of all the students had struggled and died for, a vulgar mocking of their martyrdom. For commercial interests, however, the concert (despite its fiasco) revealed the depth of pent-up demand for foreign rock.

Three months later the Doors also came to Mexico City. From the perspective of the entertainment media, the group was a hot commodity with tremendous commercial possibilities. A popular radio station known for its English-language programming, Radio Exitos, reportedly prepared for the group's arrival by playing their hit song, "Light My Fire," fifty times a week. Suggestive of the Doors' popularity was the observation that a jukebox version of their hit "The End" was said to be "so worn the words were indiscernible."[94] Telesistema, in fact, offered U.S. $20,000 in back-room negotiating for the right to a two-hour televised special on the band. The Doors, a Telesistema negotiator explained, represented "a life style that would be good for Mexico."[95] At that point, the group's reputation as a raucous and provocative musical act was already widely established; only a short while earlier Jim Morrison had been arrested on charges of public indecency while performing in Miami. On the one hand, it would be appropriate to interpret the above comment as indicative of a push from within the television giant—most likely by a younger generation of producers—to shed the restrictive terms of an earlier containment in favor of the direct marketing of youth rebellion. This trend grew stronger over the next couple of years (epitomized by the role of Luis de Llano Jr.). On the other hand, however, the proposed deal between the Doors and Telesistema never materialized, apparently canceled by the latter. The most plausible scenario is that Emilio Azcárraga Milmo, owner and director of Telesistema, vetoed the proposal. Despite Telesistema's early promotion of rocanrol, Azcárraga remained highly conservative in his values. This basic conservatism was revealed by the earlier cancellation of *¡1, 2, 3, 4, 5 a Go-Go!* (see chapter 3) and Azcárraga's single-handed decision to shelve Luis de Llano Jr.'s footage from the 1971 Avándaro rock festival (see chapter 6).[96]

The Doors' initial intentions were to take Mexico by storm. They had agreed to perform at least three concerts, each targeted at a different audience (in itself, a novel concept for a rock band of their reputation): at the 48,000-seat Plaza de México bullring at popular prices; a benefit at the Camino Real Hotel for the Red Cross; and finally, at an exclusive Mexico City nightclub. "The idea being that in one visit the Doors could perform to all levels of Mexican society."[97] While the idea of performing in a bullring, with its fixed-priced seating, would have resolved some of the logistical problems that contributed to the riot at the Union Gap / Byrds event, the image of 48,000 youth massed together (and under the leadership of a known rock provocateur) was beyond acceptance for the city government. Alfonso Corona del Rosal, the capital city's appointed mayor (1966–1970), essentially vetoed the performance by making himself absent from the capital when the necessary papers were to be signed. Without his signature there could be no concert. Mario Olmos, a thirty-one-year-old interior decorator who had brought the Doors to Mexico with assurances to the band of at least one mass concert, then bribed his way into the office of the president himself, "who reportedly gave his verbal okay," according to Jerry Hopkins, a rock journalist who was traveling with the band. If this is true, it may have suggested Díaz Ordaz's readiness to open the channels of rock as a means of siphoning off youth discontent; or perhaps it reflected the president's unawareness of what the Doors' act was all about. Maybe the president simply caved in to pressure from his rebellious son, Alfredo. At any rate, as Hopkins relates, the plan again fell through: "When the Regent [Corona del Rosal] returned, however, the president's verbal go-ahead disappeared in a swirl of polemic dust (and unanswered calls) and apparently the buck was passed back to the Regent, who just never got around to saying yes or no."[98]

In the face of bureaucratic intransigence, the original notion of reaching the broadest segment of Mexican society was extremely scaled back: the canceled bullring concert and suggested alternative performances at the

National Auditorium (where local rock bands had performed in 1966 and where leftist Latin American folksingers would appear with the government's blessing several years later) or at the Alameda Park (an outdoor park near the Zócalo) were all sidelined by city officials. In the end, the Doors were relegated to three performances for an upper-class audience in an exclusive nightclub, the Forum, run by Javier Castro, coproducer of the ill-fated Union Gap / Byrds event.

Restricting the Doors' performances to the Forum, where an obligatory dinner further upped the ticket price, reflected the regime's indirect efforts—short of forcing the tour's cancellation—to contain this vanguard rhythm.[99] At the Forum it would not be rock for the masses but rather rock, once again, for los juniors. Ironically, Jim Morrison's bearded face (and mounting potbelly) so utterly failed to fit the superstar's studly commodified image—reproduced in a fifteen-by-fifteen-foot mural on an outside wall of the club—that his own fans initially did not recognize him; the first night, they reportedly elbowed him aside at the door in an effort to get a better look at the band.[100] Whether he was self-consciously mocking his upper-class audience or simply making a half-gesture at communication, Morrison later introduced himself as "Fidel Castro."[101] In a review of one night's performance, Raúl Velasco, creator of the entertainment variety show "Siempre en Domingo" (later accused by the Guatemalan government of corrupting Guatemala's national values!),[102] derided Jim Morrison as a "red-bearded pirate crossed with Fidel Castro and the Hunchback of Notre Dame."[103] Outside the club, thousands of *chavos de onda* (hipsters) stood in the rain, straining to hear the music of their heroes. Inside, young couples in tuxedos and evening dresses sat politely at their dinner tables. Raúl Velasco continued: "The golden youth of Mexico came out in full to render homage to the myth of the Doors. . . . And they demonstrated their capacity of judgment in not surrendering (there was applause but not, we make clear, surrender) to the nightmarish world of Mr. Morrison."[104] Further emphasizing the "resistance of Mexican youth" to the disease of Morrison, a photograph of a woman drinking a soda carried the following caption: "A pretty young lady is surprised while drinking a Coca-Cola. Such was the wholesomeness of the atmosphere."[105]

Keeping the Doors away from the masses—at least in concert—while reviewing their performance in terms that glorified the aesthetic good taste of Mexico's (upper-class) youth could not, however, halt the impact of rock music on the middle and lower classes. Instead, efforts to contain rock's performance simply reaffirmed the significance of this music for those who were shut out. "Who is the Doors music for?" asked Parménides García

Saldaña in a review of one of the performances. "Obviously, but very obviously, it is not for the golden youth who drank lemonades and Coca-Colas at the Doors 'show.' And still more obviously, the Doors' songs don't speak about nor are they directed toward that [category of] youth."[106] Imported rock music could no longer be contained as a modernizing metaphor of a nuclear Revolutionary Family rejuvenated, as an earlier discourse of rocanrol had imparted. Rock music increasingly belonged to the masses, who in the particular context of U.S.–Mexican relations believed that it was indeed *their* music to experience and understand.

LA ONDA AS LITERATURE

By 1968, La Onda was experienced not only in rock music but through a new genre "of literature by youth and for youth"[107] as well. This genre was baptized *literatura de La Onda* by the literary critic Margo Glantz, and the label has remained despite criticism from some of the very authors she deemed to categorize.[108] Launched by the progressively independent publishing house, Joaquín Mortiz, the literature of La Onda offered youth, in the words of Elena Poniatowska, "for the first time a reading material that was very accessible and immediate [to their experiences], and as such [which] began to generate a new reading public."[109] The writing style of these young, iconoclastic authors also widely influenced a whole generation of writers and journalists, much as Hunter Thompson and Tom Wolfe had established a style of "new journalism" in the United States. Though most of these writers identified at one level or another with the counterculture, José Agustín and Parménides García Saldaña were especially visible.

Agustín, whose novels *La tumba* (1964) and *De perfil* (1966) first heralded this new style of writing with its countercultural sensibility, later delved into the realm of television, theater, and film. An ardent fan of rock music, Agustín's book *La nueva música clásica* (1968) helped establish rock as an avant-garde art form beyond mere pop, arguing that by the late 1960s rock "offer[ed] a new aesthetic order that no other musical current or artistic discipline could deliver."[110] Though critical of Mexican rock's lack of originality, Agustín nonetheless helped elevate the status of certain groups whose quality he respected (such as Los Dug Dugs), incorporating them into his film and television projects. His collaboration, for instance, on the screenplay of the cult film *Cinco de chocolate y uno de fresa* (1967) featured the Mexican pop singer Angélica María (with whom he was briefly romantically involved) in the role of a cloistered Catholic girl turned psychedelic ondera, as well as the music of Los Dug Dugs and Javier Batiz. Arrested at the end of 1970 on trumped-up drug charges, Agustín spent seven months in Lecumberri prison. Though his autobiography, *El rock de la cárcel* (1986), provides numerous detailed excursions into his drug experiences, at the same time Agustín denies feeling "part of the psychedelic movement or [a] spokesperson for the chavos de la onda,"[111] a role first attributed to him by the critic Margo Glantz. Indeed, his short stories and novels often approached La Onda from a distanced, at times cynical, perspective, even though he used the themes of youth culture and identity as building blocks for his work. Though not outspokenly political, Agustín belonged to the group called Artists and Intellectuals in Support of the Student Movement and attempted to introduce student politics into his creative projects. At least one of his writings, *Abolición de la propiedad* (1969), a short play framed by rock music, directly referenced the student movement.[112] He would later comment that the written word became for Mexican youth their own contribution to the rock revolution.[113]

If Agustín was wary of being pigeonholed as a spokesperson for La Onda, his cohort and close friend Parménides García Saldaña leapt at the opportunity. Though both Agustín and García Saldaña ridiculed the elitist pretensions of La Onda (in his short story "¿Cuál es La Onda?" Agustín perceptively mocks the moral hypocrisy of his upper-middle-class characters), García Saldaña was the one who recognized and identified with rock's growing proletarian edge. Having spent part of his youth taking classes in Louisiana, where he soaked up the rich blues heritage of contemporary rock, García Saldaña intuited the shifting location of rock away from the middle classes toward the barrios that had begun to occur in the late 1960s. In this, he was irredeemably negative toward native rock groups, which he considered—with the exception of the hard blues sound of Three Souls in My Mind—a second-rate imitation and alien to the needs of Mexicans. In a 1973 article, for example, he wrote that "the majority of [Mexican] bands . . . turn me off." "I want it to be clear," he continued, "that I like the scene of Chuck Berry, the Rolling Stones, [and] Santana, so that my harsh and not optimistic opinion regarding Mexican rockers is somewhat understood."[114] Yet more so than Agustín, García Saldaña identified with the element of desmadre that the lower classes introduced, and he carried this attitude over into his writing style. He was also famously irreverent of the intellectual, artistic, and political establishment, to the point of mocking noted intellectuals and refusing literary awards. Tragically, he died of a drug overdose in 1982.[115]

As chaotically hip explorations of (mostly) middle-class youth identity, the literature of La Onda captured the cultural attitudes and lifestyles of a segment of youth from this period, and especially the colloquial argot which separated the new generation from the old.[116] Rock music culture and an irreverence for established norms defined the characters and contexts of many of these writings. As Octavio Paz noted at the time, "[L]iterature written by youth is beginning to be critical, and this is occurring at two levels: as social criticism and as verbal creation."[117] Later, in describing his novel *De perfil*, Agustín wrote, "It's true, *De perfil* wasn't really literature, at least not as it was conceived of back then. Rather, it was a new proposition: as with rock, it sought to fuse high and popular culture, to legitimate artistically once and for all a colloquial language."[118] These authors' often radical approach to literary structure explicitly challenged the established canon composed of such luminaries as Juan Rulfo, Carlos Fuentes, Octavio Paz, and others. This radicalism was embodied not only in their selection of subject matter but also in their flaunting the rules of proper grammar and punctuation. In particular, the writings of Agustín and García Saldaña are filled with the celebration of youth slang, the direct incorporation of rock lyrics, words, and phrases in English, and, most blasphemously, the introduction of linguistic inventions in Spanish. Commenting on his publisher's criticisms of *La tumba*, for instance, José Agustín writes, "It bothered [him] that I would come out with wordsmadeupofvariouswords, that I Put Capital Letters Where They Did Not Belong, that I didn't highlight phrases and words in other languages, and other such details. I asked him not to apply supposedly general principles [of writing] to a work which, for better or worse, established its own laws, its own wavelength."[119] This contempt of established literary traditions mirrored the broader challenges to authority that were transpiring in society at large. At the same time, the liberal incorporation of excerpts from rock lyrics and expressions in English reflected a longed-for identification with the "universal" rock counterculture abroad.

Rock lyrics indicated a shared sense of hipness and offered a direct link to the avant-garde in other countries. For example, a passage from García Saldaña's *Pasto verde* (1968) epitomizes the inextricable location of foreign rock in his work (only the italicized parts indicate translation from the Spanish):

> *And I'm listening to* Lady Jane *by the* Rolling Stones *and in my calmness, I don't understand the lyrics but I begin to play around a little with the inspiration of the song* . . . Come on babe Come on come on COME ON! Help! Let's spend the night together not fade away not fade

away babe *I'm totally fucked-up.* . . . Yeah babe too much monkey business around n' around i need your love tonight get off of my cloud lady
jane just like a thumb tom blues queen jane approximately loveminus-
zeronolimit everybody must get stoned! [120]

Rock-inspired language thus provided this literature with a sense of organized chaos. This manifests itself as a frenzied quest for meaning in García
Saldaña's work, for example, or as the backdrop for youth exploration in
an uncertain age in José Agustín's writings. "Since I was a kid," Agustín explains, "the United States has been very close to me. I enjoyed rock, good
literature, and counterculture." [121] Ironically, the prevalence of youth slang
makes this literature largely inaccessible to anyone *other than* Mexican
youth. At the same time, English-language slang—expressed, for example,
in phrases such as "You know what I mean"—referenced the authors' cosmopolitanism, while also reflecting the mounting degree of English used in
everyday expression. Sometimes a Spanish equivalent drawn from colloquial language was used, while at other times an English word was simply
substituted for an idea or term not readily expressed in Spanish, such as
"underground."

Such incorporation of English spoke to the dual process of an erosion of
privileged cultural access by the elite and the simultaneous reappropriation
of foreign youth culture by the middle and lower classes. This interpretation of the use of English directly challenges a basic assumption of an
earlier literature on cultural imperialism: that the widespread use of English was "an indicator of class or at least a 'status symbol' for advanced
sectors" that symbolized the "seal[ing] of an alliance between the local 'advanced' bourgeoisie and North American interests." [122] While English did
remain a symbol of status among the elite, by the late 1960s it could no
longer be claimed as their private domain. As it spread to the masses, the
rock counterculture broadly disseminated English as a vehicle for challenging the very triumphalism of the bourgeoisie. The lower classes, especially,
may not have understood the precise meaning of rock lyrics and widely circulated phrases, but it was enough to have them in their own possession to
challenge the presumed monopoly on "high" culture to which the elite had
once been able to lay claim. This restructuring of the relationship between
access to foreign culture and class was directly linked to the massification
of foreign youth culture that mounted through the 1960s. The literature of
La Onda reflected and contributed to this demystification of English as an
elitist code. Thus if a dominant fact of this literary genre was the search for
new truths—personal, social, cultural—the presence of English not only
was an indicator of the problematic historical relationship between Mexico

and the United States but also served as an inextricable vehicle for unraveling the mystery of that relationship.

THE TWILIGHT OF DÍAZ ORDAZ

Under Díaz Ordaz La Onda prospered commercially, at the same time enduring a fierce repression. This contradiction had in essence always been apparent, but in the wake of Tlatelolco it became all the more blatant. By the late 1960s, La Onda clearly influenced the marketing spirit of the times (as the counterculture did for marketing in the United States), and a psychedelic tinge was incorporated into many aspects of sales aimed at youth. For example, even the conservative newspaper *Excélsior* carried an advertisement announcing the opening of a new boutique by the clothing-store chain, Palacio de Hierro: "Movement . . . action . . . youth . . . a boutique without comparison where we have brought together the latest of IN fashions . . . superwide pants made from the most outrageous cloth . . . transparent blouses . . . all of the most daring . . . all of the most innovative you'll find at Paraphernalia, the hip boutique for hip people."[123] In the music fanzines there was also an important shift in editorial direction, as younger writers were recruited and older editors were replaced. *México Canta*, for instance, went from being a narrowly based entertainment magazine to one increasingly attuned to the rhythms and needs of the counterculture.[124]

Yet, at the same time, access to imported rock—the "real thing"—remained limited for most Mexicans. Youth who liked rock had access to the images, even to the lyrics (often translated) of the emergent rock stars via fanzines such as *México Canta, Idolos del Rock, POP,* and others. But literal access to the music on one hand—especially the "original" record album—and diffusion by radio stations of what was actually available, on the another, continued to restrict the full repertoire of foreign rock to those with purchasing power. This gap in terms of access to an original rock product was bridged by personal connections to people who traveled abroad and, more significantly, to individual capitalists who recognized the profundity of local demand. For example, in Mexico City several music stores specializing in imported rock soon opened. One, Discoteca Yoko, offered a stock of well-known foreign groups plus "shipment of orders to any part of the republic." In an advertisement, a voice bubble reads: "Wow! What cool records! And where can they be had?"[125] Armando Blanco, founder of Hip-70 (which opened in 1969), later commented: "Those who were part of the underground scene, who didn't listen much to the radio, who didn't watch television, they were the ones buying records at Hip-70. . . . It was a true treasury to have the great American [*sic*] rock albums. They even smelled different." [126] The record companies understood the demand for rock, but their marketing strategy still closely followed the trajectory of an earlier musical product. What they failed to grasp was the longing by fans for greater access and the need to "get closer" to the authentic rock commodity. It was not only the song that now mattered, but ultimately access to its authentic presentation as well. By the turn of the decade, however, the marketing approach taken by the transnationals shifted dramatically, as we will explore in the next chapter.

After Tlatelolco rock became an intrinsic part of a political, social, and cultural conquest by youth in an environment conditioned by the threat of repression. "Before an act of protest or of rebellion, both unequivocal signs, think about rock," wrote Carlos Monsiváis at the start of 1970; it is "an over-powering language, whose speech is an inescapable part of youth." [127] Marching in the streets and making public demands had failed to budge the regime toward greater democratization. This provoked a greater radicalization by some students, on one hand, and a retreat from politics by the vast majority on the other. Seen from this perspective, the burgeoning of jipismo and the class expansion of La Onda is understood in direct relationship to youth's disillusionment and cynicism about the likelihood of political change. The channeling of this cynicism toward the rock counterculture is captured in a review of the group, Los Dug Dugs, from early 1969: "From the purist essence of rebeldismo, from the most obscure hippie roots, from the most profound corners of Underground Rock, have come the Los Dug Dugs . . . a dirty and disheveled look on the face of youth, [with] insolent gestures that offend. Like all their generation, they protest against everything and everyone. They break contracts, they don't want to record albums in Spanish, they're defiant, unpunctual, and apathetic." [128] Immersing oneself in La Onda meant the transformation of individual lifestyles—wearing long hair, taking drugs, demanding sexual and personal freedoms—which grated harshly against the predominantly conservative Mexican household. In the United States most youth had the option of attending college away from home, but in Mexico (unless one studied abroad) this was not the case. The economic and social ramifications of revolt, hence, were more severe, and many youth faced the prospect of either conforming to family standards or being ejected from their home. Such conflicts were exploited by the regime, which conveniently sought to conflate in the public mind-set the rebellion of students with a breakdown of patriarchal order more generally. Ongoing repression after 1968 thus became justified for large sectors of the public, which also experienced the new insolence of youth directly.

In fact, the escapism of the jipi movement was no guarantee against police brutality, which targeted such youth with a vengeance. Stories of *greñudos* (longhairs) being harassed in the streets, denied service on public transportation and in restaurants, picked up by the police for no reason and then dumped off with a forced haircut, became legion. "We were the weirdos, los greñudos," recalls Ramón García, an informant from the lower classes. "They harassed us wherever we went. . . . Perhaps like what happened in other countries with racism, only here it was directed toward the *roquero* [ardent fan of rock, also written *rockero*]. Like they wouldn't let you on the bus, ridiculous things like that. Wherever you went, there were the cops. The cops came after you, they beat you, they robbed you."[129] The communicative spaces offered by rock, therefore, were an essential focal point for the expression of anger, fear, and distrust toward authority in general, at the same time revealing the organizing impact of rock itself. "Here in Mexico, there are a ton of things that as youth we have to fix," wrote Carlos Baca in his weekly column, "Rock Subterráneo," in the magazine *México Canta*. "And to do so we have to be united, because they're closing down all of the places where we hang out and well, whatever, we've got to find other places then." One public space recently affected by police repression was the Parque Hundido (Sunken Park), where "now every Saturday the place is full of paddy wagons and whatnot so that 'not a single greñudo' is allowed to congregate."[130] One infamous occasion that highlighted the regime's obsession with youth protesters occurred toward the end of the Díaz Ordaz administration. A group of Mexican jipis bold enough to traverse the capital along a main thoroughfare handed out flowers and sang songs. Parading down La Reforma, they shortly arrived at the Monument to Independence, where they were met by granaderos who "beat them up, all the while they were handing out flowers and saying 'Peace, brother.'"[131]

In the twilight of Díaz Ordaz's rule his hand-picked successor, Luis Echeverría, sought a new political tone during his campaign for the presidency, one that would distance him from the very policies he helped implement during the previous administration. As secretary of interior affairs, Echeverría was widely held responsible for the orchestrated attacks on students and other protesters, culminating in the massacre at Tlatelolco. In choosing him as his successor, Díaz Ordaz most likely believed that the economic-development strategy of fiscal conservatism and political stability would be maintained. Such a strategy dated to the post–World War II period and was marked by restrictive labor and political conditions, which were deemed necessary for the stability of the peso and the continued influx of foreign and native capital investment. Mexico's economic "miracle" had been based on this approach, which not only rendered impressive annual growth rates but was rewarded with the prize of Olympic recognition. It was not clear yet what Echeverría's plans might be, but following his official nomination by the PRI there were indications that in the wake of 1968 a new strategy was in the making. Already he had raised parallels with the 1930s populist presidency of Lázaro Cárdenas, whom he emulated in his discourse and countryside campaigning. Echeverría recognized, above all, the need to reach out to youth, an approach that was reflected in his numerous visits to universities (but not the UNAM) around the country in the course of his presidential campaign. As one editorialist noted: "In his oratory remarks, some of which have been spontaneous and open, he has directed himself [to the students] and to youth in general, asking that their nonconformity be directed toward the common task of acting in the best interests of the country, above all breaking away from those elements that are conducive to the fragmentation of common interests and that deepen our divisions."[132] But Echeverría's campaign faced an uphill battle against despair and disillusionment, not to mention the mark of culpability assigned by students for his presumed role in the massacre. He was often rebuffed, at times violently, from the schools he visited. Slogans such as "To Vote in 1970 Is to Forget 1968" underscored the open wounds that had been created by the massacre.[133]

5 *La Onda Chicana*
The Reinvention of Mexico's Countercultural Community

As Echeverría's campaign for the presidency began, an important shift was already transpiring in Mexican rock toward the creation of original music, but still written and performed in English. This time, however, bands encountered the full support of the recording industry, especially the transnationals that had come to embrace the rapidly growing market for rock. Disparaging of refritos and fusiles alike, these original recordings reflected a fusion of rhythmic and visual sensibilities that combined elements of Mexican and Latin American culture interpreted through the lens of the counterculture abroad. Such a fusion, which heralded the musical liberation of La Onda from rote interpretation, dramatically shifted the tone and scope of the Mexican counterculture. With names such as La Revolución de Emiliano Zapata, La Decena Trágica, División del Norte, Reforma Agraria—and others in English, such as Peace and Love, Love Army, Three Souls in My Mind—native rock bands now became a vehicle for the reappropriation of a nationalist discourse, as well as a movement linked to the search for identity in the shadow of U.S. cultural domination. Calling itself La Onda Chicana, this native rock movement came to embrace a broad class spectrum of urban youth at the very moment that Luis Echeverría was about to take his oath of office. The specter of a broad-based countercultural movement posed a unique challenge to the incoming administration, which also faced widespread cynicism and incipient guerrilla movements in different parts of the country.

STRATEGIES OF THE TRANSNATIONAL RECORDING INDUSTRY

Since 1965, when Capitol Records arrived as a joint-venture operation with members of the Azcárraga dynasty, the music scene in Mexico had been dramatically transformed by the heightened level of competition among the transnationals. This competition reflected a more general expansion of the transnationals' global reach, especially in Latin America, but also the rising profits from rock music. For example, citing the popularity of several noted U.S. rock groups, along with the Broadway musical recording of "Hair," RCA reported that in 1969 its Records Division recorded its largest sales volume to date. During that year, a new corporate headquarters had also been established in Mexico City.[1] In 1970 the company reported that "popular music now accounts for more than half of all industry sales." Despite the weakness of the U.S. economy, the report continued, "both export sales and revenue derived from royalty payments [of records] from foreign countries increased" during the year.[2]

For CBS, the growing market for rock and other music also had an important impact on corporate profits. Continuing its expansion into Latin America, in 1965 a new subsidiary was established in Colombia, and in 1966 the company reported on the phenomenal impact international record sales in general had had on the company: "1966 was the most successful year to date for CBS in the international record market. Offshore record sales were the highest ever achieved, climaxing a five-year period in which sales of CBS-produced records abroad nearly tripled. . . . The [Records] Division now has a subsidiary in every major European market. Acquisition of a wholly-owned subsidiary in San José, Costa Rica gave CBS a record pressing plant in that country and a record distribution organization throughout the Central American countries."[3] By the end of the decade, CBS was fully immersed in promoting the rock revolution. "Our orientation at CBS is now, and always has been, directed toward the creative elements of business and art," stated the company's *Annual Report* for 1968. "Therefore, it is safe to say that when there are musical and cultural revolutions, we will be in the forefront."[4] In 1970 CBS reported that "[r]ock and other music now especially popular among young people constituted over 50 per cent of the Division's sales."[5] By 1971 CBS reported that its International Records Division was the company's fastest-growing segment, with operations in more than one hundred countries. Compared with average annual growth rates of 20 percent for domestic records sales since 1966, growth in international sales averaged 24 percent. In 1971 new recording studios were opened in Mexico, and a factory-office-warehouse complex was built in Argentina.[6]

In Mexico, this global marketing strategy by the transnationals edged aside the role of local companies, especially in the production and distribution of pop music aimed at the youth market. In 1966 a local company operating under the name Discos Universales (DUSA) was established in Mexico City. Shortly thereafter the company underwent a complete reorganization designed to position itself for "a cautious, careful preparation for the competition coming up."[7] By the end of the year DUSA was advertising itself as a company characterized by "youth, optimism, dynamism, aggressiveness [and] enthusiasm,"[8] exemplified by a wide-ranging rock-music catalog that included such groups as Cream, Jimi Hendrix, Eric Burden and the Animals, and the Doors. These groups all appeared on labels controlled by the transnational recording company, Polydor.[9] (Polydor was at the time controlled by the German company Deutsche Grammophon, which shortly thereafter fully merged with its sister company, Philips of the Netherlands, to form the transnational known today as Polygram.) DUSA, explains Herbe Pompeyo, who worked as an artistic director, "was a minor company . . . with the objective of becoming a strong company."[10] With the arrival of Polydor as a major share owner of DUSA in 1970, the company was indeed transformed into an transnational player with marketing linkages around the world.

Thus, by the end of the decade, the majority of foreign pop-rock bands were already represented through the four transnationals that now predominated: CBS, RCA, Capitol-EMI, and Polydor. Several local companies still acted as distributors for foreign labels, especially from Spain and Latin America, and certain companies, such as Musart, Peerless, and Gamma (a joint venture with Hispavox of Spain), in fact managed to distribute a limited number of foreign rock recordings via contracts with independent labels. Peerless, for example, distributed the Rolling Stones on the London record label as late as 1969. In another example, Musart (which had distributed the Capitol-EMI label up to 1965) still had the rights to the Liberty label, which produced such bands as Creedence Clearwater Revival and Canned Heat. And via Gamma, several U.S. labels, including Warner Brothers, United Artists, and Reprise, were all represented. Yet the transnationals, armed with greater resources and their wide-ranging rock catalog, clearly dominated the market for foreign rock. As far as Mexican rock was concerned, with the exception of Orfeón's earlier linkages with rocanrol, virtually all of the newer bands established contracts with the transnationals.

After 1968, the increasing demand for rock music was felt throughout the music industry, which intensified its efforts to promote and market a sellable rock product. This occurred at two levels. The first was an acknowledgment that the middle classes, whose buying power largely defined the pop market, wanted greater access to rock music produced abroad. Up to this point, record companies largely contented themselves with compilation albums of selected hits by groups drawn from a master. Yet as the focus of rock shifted from hit singles to a rock-art concept embodied in album-cover design and song order, record companies came to recognize the need to accommodate changing consumer demand. As Enrique Partida recalls from his days with Polydor, "Well, the rebel cry of youth begins to resonate, and so you view it . . . more from a market perspective: 'I've got to do something to keep this market from disappearing!' And sure, it was a rich mine [to tap]. I think that Woodstock had a lot to do with this. . . . Young people didn't want to watch a TV program anymore where they could see the same twenty hits they heard on the radio. They wanted their music. So, what did the companies do about it?"[11] Direct importation was still too costly, though it would continue to provide a niche for private dealers. Instead, the option chosen by the companies was a strategy based on replication of the original album. This involved an exact copy of the contents taken from the master tape and a faithful reproduction of the album cover itself. Though pressed in Mexico, the album appeared virtually identical to its imported original.

Polydor was the first company to make this shift to in-country pressing with its introduction of the series *Rock Power* (written in English) in 1970. Each release in the series was dedicated to the presentation of a rock album in its entirety (no more composite albums of hits), with a replica of the original album cover. Superimposed on each cover, a reminder that this was a re-presentation and not the original, was the series' logo: a raised fist in the peace sign on one side and a frontal view of an electric guitar on the other, which together framed the text: "Serie rock power: La nueva generación eléctrica" (The Rock Power Series: The New Electric Generation). Polydor advertised "Rock Power" as "The conspiracy of sound": "Polydor presents the advance guard of a great musical movement. A series destined to be converted into the vanguard of rock in Mexico. [Featuring] only current great artists and groups, [with] their best creations."[12] Recognizing the significance of this marketing move, the other major companies followed in direct suit: CBS with "Rock Revolution," Capitol with "Convivencia sagrada," RCA with "Heavy Blood," and Gamma with "All Sounds of Rock." As their music catalogs expanded, so did the perspective of personnel responsible for introducing the new music. Indeed, if the companies had initially been outpaced by individuals in their role as agents for foreign culture, this was rapidly changing. As Herbe Pompeyo explained:

We [at Polydor] knew that, hey, if we're watching [foreign films], then we also have to be listening to Jimi Hendrix. Why? Because Mexico is part of the world, and that was a part of world culture. So if important books are coming into Mexico, and important movies are coming into Mexico, and there are also people like Simon and Garfunkel, the Mamas and the Papas, Crosby, Stills, Nash, and Young . . . they also had to be distributed in Mexico. Because we couldn't be separated from what was happening in the world. . . . This was world culture. I believe there are things that are not specific to one's nationality.[13]

This marketing shift also had important repercussions within the communications media as a whole. At the time, at least three radio stations in the capital featured English-language rock, but programming was based overwhelmingly on passing hits rather than a more in-depth exploration of new rock groups and trends. With the change in attitude at the record companies, however, came an abrupt shift in commercial radio programming. As one writer recounted his discovery of the rock-specialty program "Proyección 590," "Cool, great, at last we were listening to short-wave radio! We anxiously waited for the song to end so we could find out what the transmission was and figure out what feat we had achieved. . . . Whaaat? It was radio 590! We hadn't left Mexico City! We kept listening, where it was explained to us that this was a new program that only transmitted the best music from the U.S. and Britain, the music which created and applauded La Onda."[14] Another rock station, Radio Exitos, likewise began to promote a new format. In an advertisement from the newly founded magazine *Piedra Rodante* (based on material drawn from *Rolling Stone*), the hip language of La Onda was adapted in a play on words: "Radio Exitos agarra el patín." Here *patín* referred to *patinar* (to skate: a roller skate constitutes the visual image of the advertisement), and *agarrar el patín* meant "to be with it." The advertisement continued: "Jim Morrison. Rolling Stones. Jimi Hendrix. Janis Joplin. . . . Each week Radio Exitos dedicates itself to praising the contribution of the great creators of rock. Their life and their music is commented on and presented throughout the course of the day in the first attempt to introduce seriously and rigorously the most important movement of our time, the music of rock."[15] At Radio Educación, the university station that prided itself on its high cultural programming, the first of what later developed into a wide range of weekly shows dedicated to rock culture also appeared.[16]

The massification of rock at the end of the decade via the transformation of the marketing structure—the promotion of native bands, the expansion of music catalogs, the shift in programming on local radio stations—

accelerated the accessibility of rock to urban youth. The initial contradiction of rock's intrinsic characteristic as a mass cultural commodity but with limited distribution was being overcome. Increasingly rock as a *commodity* was becoming accessible to larger segments of society. Commenting on the shift in strategy at Capitol Records, one critic noted that "the list of consumers will expand to reach the marginalized and popular sectors [of society], as a result of this correct projection [of rock music] toward the general public."[17] Together with the continuing proliferation of scores of native rock groups, not only was a more ambitious marketing strategy emerging—one that sought eventually to internationalize native bands—but the very fabric of the Mexican counterculture was developing in a complex and contradictory direction.

While the wider distribution of foreign rock reflected one level of shifting strategy to accommodate heightened demand, a second level involved the wider latitude afforded local musicians. Pressed into performing Spanish-language covers, native bands since the late 1950s had continually been frustrated by the conservative position of the cultural industries. Around 1968, however, this conservatism had begun to give way to greater experimentation. As one young producer with Capitol Records stated toward the end of 1968, "We're waiting for the important language of youth. The doors are open. . . . It's possible that rock is foreign to our culture, because we do not have the influence of blacks, but we do have a musical language that has been totally influenced by rock 'n' roll."[18] This call from the recording industry was widely heeded by musicians, who now openly rejected the fusiles that had defined the vanguard of rock in Mexico since the mid-1960s. Participation in the "universal rock movement" meant more than simply consuming direct copies of others' hits; it also meant producing hits of one's own making. "[A]ny mental retard can put together a cheesy band that dedicates itself to copying and [making] ridiculous translations of the gringos,"[19] wrote one rock critic. On the other hand, being truly modern, participating in the global movement of rock's transformation of modern society, required the dialectical construction of new musical sounds, as well as new rock gestures. (Indeed, the success of Mexican-born Carlos Santana proved that a role existed for Latin rhythms, if not for Mexico especially, in this global cultural-revolutionary process).[20]

Measuring a group's dedication to this dialectic increasingly became the norm for critical acceptance by rock critics and fans. Writing about a Chihuahuan band, Los Químicos, one critic noted, for example: "They prefer UNDERGROUND (subterranean) music to any other kind, which is to say they love the blues, acid rock and hard rock, although they also dig pure rock. . . .

[B]ut they also have original compositions, because for them ORIGINALITY is very important, something that is lacking in the rest of Mexico's [rock] groups."[21] No longer content with either refritos or fusiles, Mexican bands after 1968 began to write original compositions, but overwhelmingly in English. The influence of foreign rock on a native idiom had come full circle; many bands would soon cultivate an image aimed at an international audience.[22] Whereas before Mexican bands found their efforts at originality blocked by the recording companies, suddenly their music was embraced at all levels of the cultural industries. This shift reflected the more aggressive pursuit of local talent, especially by the transnationals, in the context of a transformation in industry strategy more generally. For at the same time, the very success of the fusiles had acted as a "launching pad," in the words of Enrique Partida of Polydor, for the mass marketing of foreign rock throughout the country.[23]

A clear example of this transition from fusiles to original compositions comes from the group La Máquina del Sonido. Contracted through CBS Records, they encountered fame through a cover version (in Spanish) of the Iron Butterfly song "In-a-gadda-da-vida," which was played on local radio. Then, in a dramatic marketing shift, CBS allowed them to produce an album of original music (with songs in both English and Spanish).[24] Jose G. Ayala, artistic director for CBS at the time, wrote for the album's liner notes: "The moment has arrived: Mexican rock groups (or at least, those here at CBS) are forgetting about copies. All of the groovy sounds that are heard on this album are totally their own." Víctor Blanco Labra, founding editor of *POP* magazine, was also quoted on the liner notes: "La Máquina del Sonido [is] an original anti-fresa, *underground* group that rejuvenates our faith in the productivity and creativity of Mexican rockers."[25]

Generally speaking, the transnationals were not only more eager but better equipped to record original music. This was true for a number of reasons. For one, the transnational subsidiaries generally featured newer equipment and better production expertise. Continued capital investments by the transnationals—for instance, to upgrade plant and technical facilities— were a steady feature during this period.[26] Second, common knowledge had it that recording with a transnational improved one's chances of reaching a broader public, likely even beyond the nation's borders. The "attendant advantage" of "[m]embership in a transnational system," as one author has put it, is that marketing and promotional campaigns are likely coordinated at a regional and international level simultaneously. "In other words, the transnational corporate system facilitates the recognition and seizure of opportunities in several markets at once while other firms are more narrowly

174 / Refried Elvis

intent on pursuing opportunities in only one."[27] In adopting an English-language performance style, these groups now aimed directly for the U.S. and European markets.[28]

A third reason was that the major local competitors either largely stood clear of this *nueva onda* of rock music or were dramatically overshadowed by the corporate reach of the transnationals. Orfeón, a major player during the refritos phase of rocanrol, had just a few new contracts of note, most of which were unstable. Lacking a definitive association with the distribution of foreign rock and having earlier dedicated itself to promoting Spanish-language covers, Orfeón did not actively pursue the new market for Mexican rock. Responding to the question of why the company was not more aggressive, Carlos Beltrand Luján, a former marketing agent with Orfeón, recalls: "Yes, there was a market, [and] perhaps we lost our compass a little bit there. We didn't have much economic success with what we used to carry [refritos], and we dedicated ourselves to other [musical] tendencies such as balada and promoting other new artists. The [rocanrol] groups that we had launched, well, the public was losing interest in them and that ended. . . . We moved away from rock; they were selling the original much more than the covers, that was the reason."[29]

In fact, the decision by Orfeón and other local companies not to invest heavily in the new wave of bands turned out to be economically astute: for a number of reasons, their popularity and promotion were short-lived, as we will see. While the transnationals ultimately could afford to incur certain investment losses, for other companies the shift in resources probably would have been financially more significant. One important exception to this development was the small recording label Cisne, which emerged around 1966. Joining forces in the 1970s with a second small label, Raff, the Cisne-Raff studios not only recorded some of the most important native rock in the early 1970s but, in continuing to produce albums after this period (especially by Three Souls in My Mind), directly sustained the native rock movement after the transnationals had broken or otherwise abandoned their existing recording contracts.[30]

A MEXICAN ROCK FUSION

Rejecting the translated refritos of an earlier generation and the *fusilado* copies of their own, a new wave of Mexican rock musicians emerged between 1969 and 1971 seeking to forge an original style of rock music that would be recognized as distinctively Mexican.[31] Moreover, if Mexican rock had once been associated largely with Mexico City, other provincial capitals now became known for their rock scenes as well.[32] The capital still continued to be the logical place of convergence, however, since the major record companies were located there. But at the same time, most bands continually toured the provinces. In this way a national public, projected from the capital yet nurtured by the provinces, was directly constructed. The logical culmination of these developments would generate both the musical festival at Avándaro in 1971 and the societal backlash and government crackdown on Mexican rock shortly thereafter.

What is central for us to understand about this new movement is that it was referred to as *La Onda Chicana*.[33] The term *Chicana* described a shift in attitude and musical creativity away from the dependence on copying and toward a new fusion of Mexican and foreign—especially U.S.—rhythms and protest images. "It was at the end of 1970 when the creative desire began to awake among our musicians, a desire that had not been totally present earlier, and an eagerness among our groups to advance at last and begin to CREATE music," wrote Armando Molina of La Máquina del Sonido.[34] The term also reflected the fact that English had now been adopted as the language of choice for recordings as well as performances. Thus to many outsiders—Mexican and foreign alike—La Onda Chicana seemed even more of a copy of foreign rock culture than before. But for Mexican youth who identified with La Onda Chicana, the label signaled the reality of recognition. The Mexican rock movement had been *named,* and this was regarded by fans and some in the recording industry as the crucial step needed for representation in the universal rock movement.

There is significant irony to the fact that while in the United States the Chicano Movement referred to a struggle for political power and cultural self-determination, in Mexico this term was being applied to a countercultural scene characterized by foreign rock influences and performance in English. Indeed, at one level these separate appropriations of the same term were completely contradictory: *Chicano* for Mexican Americans largely meant a repudiation of colonized values and the search for an "authentic" collective identity based on the notion of *la raza* (literally, race, a politicized notion of a collective self-identity based on racial, linguistic, and cultural attributes). As Carlos Muñoz Jr. writes:

> Whereas white youth radicalism contributed to the making of a counter-culture stressing humanistic values, Chicano youth radicalism represented a return to the humanistic cultural values of the Mexican working class. This in turn led to the shaping of a nationalist ideology, which

although antiracist in nature, stressed the nonwhite indigenous aspects of Mexican working-class culture. This nationalism defined Mexican Americans as *mestizos,* a mixed race people, and rejected identification with the white European/Hispanic roots of Mexican culture. It further called for the rejection of assimilation into the dominant, white Anglo-Saxon Protestant culture of the United States.[35]

While Muñoz's depiction of the Chicano movement underscores its romanticism, he no doubt misses some of the countercultural nuances that also filtered into Chicano identity (including the role of Mexican American rock bands from East Los Angeles and elsewhere).[36] Nonetheless, his interpretation rightly emphasizes Chicano youth's search for a nationalist identity apart from the United States. In Mexico, however, Chicano now referred to a *repudiation* of sacrosanct nationalisms. The term reflected a search for new collective identities based on a fusion of Mexican indigenous and mestizo culture with the rock counterculture that emanated, above all, from the United States. Thus, while one group scorned "modernity" in the search for Mexican "authenticity," the other rejected presumptions of nationalist authenticity in the search for new meanings to be found in that very same expression of "modern culture." Both Chicano groups, however, shared a similar fate: they were wrestling with the historic and more contemporary legacies of U.S. imperialism in their respective, and at times overlapping, searches for new collective identities.[37]

Yet if for Chicanos in the United States the struggle for liberation was spearheaded by political action, in Mexico this option had been squelched by the government massacre of 1968, a position reaffirmed by a paramilitarist attack on protesting students in the capital in June 1971 (see below). For many on the Mexican left, the emergence of a Mexican rock movement indicated the depoliticization of youth after 1968 and the transference of political action to cultural rebellion characterized by desmadre. For others, rock and politics failed to align with one another in Mexico during this period, unlike what occurred in other Latin American countries later in the decade, especially in Brazil and Argentina.[38] This latter position reflects a certain nostalgia for a "lost opportunity" common among critics in the United States as well: if rock had addressed political issues more explicitly, the energy of youth rebellion might have been harnessed in the direction of radical political change. Thus Víctor Roura, who has written extensively on rock, simplistically argues that Mexican rock was totally disengaged from politics during this period.[39]

Yet La Onda Chicana was not so much a shift *away* from a political discourse as the development of a trajectory intrinsic to the 1968 student movement itself: the rupturing of the state's monopoly over symbolic capital.[40] The significance of the Mexican counterculture (La Onda) lay precisely in its capacity to resist authority by reconstituting an imaginary community apart from the state yet tied to the nation. A countercultural discourse grounded in the political developments of 1968 was sustained after the massacre on account of the continued transnationalization of rock culture. It was through this resemanticization of foreign rock and the emergence of a native rock idiom (La Onda Chicana) that the discourse of an imagined Mexican community was wrested from state control.[41] Despite the centrality of foreign rock, it was largely through the development of La Onda Chicana that such a rewriting of national identity could in fact transpire. For if foreign rock provided the signposts of rebellion, native rock offered the possibility of transforming that rebellion into something constructive. The political impact of the Mexican counterculture was thus at the level of the everyday which, precisely because the state sought to organize everyday life around a coherent, containable discourse of national identity and ritualized practices, posed a challenge to the logic of social relations. As an active site of resistance, rock music culture (like the 1968 student movement) worked toward the delegitimization of state authority.

While the student movement represented a short-lived social movement for political reform centered in Mexico City, La Onda had become an "antisocial" social movement that extended throughout the country. Its membership was vast and loosely connected, yet bound together by a common (if abstractly defined) set of ideas and values. José Agustín later defined La Onda as a "common, youthful, universal, authentic and spontaneous spirit that allows kids to converge around rock music in order to organize for a qualitative change of society." [42] As a countercultural movement, its political acts were found in its mode of expression; its "politics" were an antipolitics. At the same time, however, La Onda's raison d'être was grounded in a mass-culture commodity, rock music, which was linked to national and transnational capitalist structures. This link suggested not only a level of dependency on such structures but also, and more important, the ramifications of commercialization. As long as foreign rock was kept at a distance its commercial implications could be downplayed by intellectuals, who heralded rock's vanguard contributions. But as foreign rock came closer to Mexico—so close that an emulative, native rock movement developed—the dangers of commercialization were loudly denounced. Furthermore, marketing of La Onda Chicana involved the commodification of images and symbols held sacred not only by the state but by the left as well. This double bind—dependency and commodification—formed the basis of a powerful, if in retrospect overly simplistic, cultural-imperialist critique of La Onda Chicana that still exists in some quarters.

While a number of Mexican rock groups had emerged by 1971, it is perhaps appropriate that the most commercially successful band to head this movement took the name La Revolución de Emiliano Zapata. "La Revolución," as they became known, first appeared out of Guadalajara in 1971 after they cut a record with Polydor.[43] In a unprecedented move, their original single, "Nasty Sex" (sung in English), was heard on Guadalajaran commercial radio. While the song's title suggests something erotic, the lyrics actually convey a more ambiguous message about the value of relationships in an age of sexual liberalization:

> Oh, my baby forgot
> That the rocks can also
> Sing a song of love.
>
> Oh somebody told me
> That she was sleeping
> With a tricky guy.
>
> Hey babe, change your manners
> And go by the way of the sun.
> Can't you see that this kind of sex
> Is gonna let you down?
>
> Let you down.
>
> Oh, take it so easy when I tell you
> Not to run away.
> Babe, try to understand
> And don't turn your face to reality.[44]

Is the song suggesting that the woman alluded to should not sleep with "a tricky guy" because he is someone who does not really care for her? Is there an implicit message not to "run away" from the "reality" of one's home? Ultimately, one doubts that it mattered much what the lyrics actually might have meant. The medium was the message. Within a brief period, La Revolución was heard on commercial radio stations in Mexico City as well. "With the inclusion of 'Nasty Sex' on Radio 590, La Revolución de Emiliano Zapata struck down a decade of intolerance and incomprehension: the taboo against programming songs by Mexican rock groups,"[45] wrote Parménides García Saldaña for the rock magazine *Piedra Rodante*. Although all of their songs on this first album were in English, they were hailed, somewhat exaggeratedly, by another rock critic as the "the most popular Mexican group of the last 355 years, exclusively with original ma-

Figure 13. By 1971 the impact of La Onda Chicana had completely transformed the image of *México Canta*, here featuring the groups La Revolución de Emiliano Zapata and La Inducción. Source: *México Canta*, August 1971, in the author's personal collection.

terial."[46] Even the normally cynical García Saldaña acknowledged that, "despite being a mediocre song, 'Nasty Sex' is danceable."[47]

In appropriating the name and symbolism of the nation's most revered peasant revolutionary, the musical group La Revolución de Emiliano Zapata had proved that via rock the state could be mocked while national identity was reinvented on new terms (see Figure 13). In fact, the most significant aspect of La Onda Chicana in general was that its rock performance could not avoid being an implicit critique of official nationalism. Under Mexico's authoritarian regime, any act of reappropriation suggested direct defiance of state-sponsored nationalism. In this respect, Mexican rock contributed to the creation of a countercultural community that outwardly criticized the official discourse of national community as it strove to reinvent that community on different terms.

In the case of La Revolución de Emiliano Zapata, this reimagining of community found a parallel in the student movement, where images of Zapata were also displayed by protesters. In both cases, Zapata was revered at the expense of state authority and legitimacy. However, in 1968 Zapata symbolized the unrecognized demands of the peasantry for land and liberty. Students battled with the government over which group most authentically represented Zapata's unfulfilled goals. By contrast, in 1971 the figure of Zapata appearing on record covers and music reviews suggested the *liberation from* a static, mythologized interpretation of the national warrior. As he appears, for example, on the cover of *Piedra Rodante*, eyes fixed on the viewer from atop his mounted horse—the long hair and bell-bottoms of band members posing in the foreground loosely hanging down—his meanings are now multiple: Which is the "real" Zapata? Who are the "real" Zapatistas? Indeed, how has his struggle been redefined? Who will represent that struggle? As the caption below the photograph sardonically suggests, we can no longer imagine Zapata only as a peasant revolutionary: "Who might have imagined that the Zapatistas would take the capital? Not even Don Venustiano [Carranza] would have believed it."[48] The reference is to the temporary capture and voluntary retreat from the capital by the Zapatistas during the early phase of the revolution; later crushed by the triumphant Carrancistas, Zapata's guerrilla forces never regained their strength. But it is also a reference to the fear of desmadre which capital residents presumed that the rural, poorly educated guerrilla army would bring upon their city. With the triumph of La Revolución (the band), once again the threat of social disordering lurked.

While the band's first album featured a classic photograph of a posing Emiliano Zapata printed over a metate-textured background (symbolic of the campesino), the cover for their second album was a photomontage of leftist and countercultural images and text: Salvador Allende, Che Guevara, César Chávez, "La imaginación al poder" (Imagination is power), "La libertad es hija de la libertad" (Liberty is the daughter of freedom), and other like materials are all found on the cover. The use of collage—of mixing images and references from foreign as well as national origins—reflected a strategy aimed at forging an original fusion that set Zapata (and the band) within the broader historical context of countercultural and revolutionary revolt. On the inside—although a single album, the cover opens up—

a grainy, black-and-white photograph shows band members sitting around an open campfire, recalling perhaps an image of the original Zapatistas, a well-recognized notion of Mexico's folkloric past—and its jipiteca present.

Other bands also sought to match the boldness of La Revolución in creating names drawn from the national consciousness. And like La Revolución, many emerged from the northern provinces, though they descended on the capital in search of record contracts and commercial opportunities. In creating names and images that specifically made reference to the Mexican experience, these groups forged an essential psychic space for youth in which they could reimagine themselves as social actors among the changing, newly constituted reference points of national identity. As the long-haired, countercultural look sported by band members of La Revolución suggested an identification of individual liberty with Emiliano Zapata, the group Bandido, for instance, recalled a nostalgia for the outlaw, beyond the reach of the state. Another band, División del Norte, was an obvious reference to the defeated popular army led by Pancho Villa. Finally, a group named Nuevo México underscored everything the movement stood for: the yearnings for a new nation constructed from the old. Still, not every band sought explicitly to appropriate imagery and symbolism from the national repertoire. Some of the best-known bands took names such as Love Army, Peace and Love, and Three Souls in My Mind.[49]

If images and band names could play an important role in the reimagining and thus reinvention of national community, it was, of course, in the music itself that the search for identity was centrally located. The music invested youth with a shared sense of collective power that was of their own making. As the lyrics from the song "Tenemos el poder" (We've Got the Power), by Peace and Love, expressed it:

> When we're on stage and making music,
> there's something that you can't take away.
> 'Cause our feeling's our own creation.
> It's awfully groovy to play together,
> and that's why I say:
> We've got the power.
>
> You've got the power.
> It's within you
> and somewhere you can feel it,
> communicate it.
>
> With our music we feel the power
> and all we want for all of you
> is to feel the same.

Say it proud:
We've got the power.[50]

Yet how does one reconcile the fact that certain bands, such as Peace and Love, sought an explicitly "Latin rock" sound—already pioneered by Santana—while other groups like the Spiders (Guadalajara) or 39.4 (Guadalajara) pursued a sound more closely modeled on Anglo rock?[51] Falling in between these two groupings, one locates bands that sought a greater fusion of rock, Latino, and indigenous rhythms, such as La Revolución de Emiliano Zapata, La Máquina del Sonido, Nuevo México, and Toncho Pilatos. Moreover, there was not necessarily any direct association between a band's name and its musical style: Love Army created a Latin-rock sound (and performed many songs in Spanish), while Bandido stylized themselves as a hard-rock group with an all-English repertoire. The first album by La Revolución, with their hit "Nasty Sex," showed little trace of Latin rhythmic influences (the influence of Creedence Clearwater Revival, however, was clearly evident) and was entirely in English. And while their second album reflected a shift toward greater inclusion of Latin American instruments and influences, virtually every song was still in English.[52] Perhaps the one common denominator among these bands, however, was an image of Mexican jipismo: long hair, indigenous necklaces and clothing; a posture of "dropping out" to form one's own communal society. Thus, where do we locate the fine line between popular culture—as an aesthetic as well as political effort at self-representation—and cultural imperialism, as the imposition of a dominant, foreign worldview and the simultaneous confinement of opportunities (in economic as well as cultural terms) for local representation?

This contradictory image can be explained in part by the competing demands of aiming simultaneously for a national audience and an international one. On the one hand, La Onda Chicana reflected an effort to reach out to a broad Mexican market attuned to international trends but now demanding greater originality. For some groups, therefore, the search for new compositions led them to experiment with different musical genres, ranging from the blues to indigenous folk music. As Joaquín López of La Revolución de Emiliano Zapata later explained, "[W]e loved to play the blues, but how far could we take it? How much did we really know about the blues? What we heard or what we made up, but that road ended quickly. You didn't have the base, a framework. So, there comes a moment when without such a base you begin the search. And so you begin to hear Andean music and whatnot, and you go from there, no?"[53] The group Love Army perhaps best articulated what the impact of this rock fusion meant for creating an original style of rock music: "We don't play anything that's copied. We play our own music, that's all. Of course it's influenced, but you can't label it as rock, soul, blues, mariachi, or anything else because it's none of that. It's our music 100 percent, with the name Love Army. . . . If one takes into consideration all of those influences, including Aztec music such as Náhuatl rhythms and musical ideas from everyone [in the group], from all of that emerges the music of Love Army, 100 percent made in Mexico."[54] In another example, the first album by Nuevo México was appropriately titled *Hecho en casa* (Homemade). Víctor Roura later commented: "The majority of their songs being instrumentals, *Hecho en casa* is a presentation of and testimony to a dignified coalescence of rock made precisely at home."[55]

Not surprisingly, many bands found inspiration in the success of Santana's Latin-rock music, which had triumphed on the world stage at Woodstock.[56] Carlos Santana had proved that rock could be an open-ended genre, capable of absorbing other musical sounds and rhythms. Indeed, Santana was the prodigal son for Mexican rock critics: he had made it in *gabacholandia*,[57] and his fans in Mexico hoped he would someday return. Describing a concert of his in Chicago, a critic for *México Canta* wrote:

> The kids follow the rhythm of Santana's incredible tunes, singing along with him; on all sides you see long-haired youth dancing to the rhythm of his music; their happy faces reflect the music's acceptance. . . . [T]otally amplified, the music reaches all the way to the marrow of your bones and makes your blood boil, igniting a supercharged energy; the feeling is general, and people dance with their feet, their legs, their arms, their hands, their head: getting off is easy if you follow the magic rhythm which these guys can play.[58]

Santana, in other words, had succeeded at what every Mexican band aspired to do. He had created a national as well as international audience and had done so by inventing a new rock fusion "that blended the acid-rock of the Haight-Ashbury era with blues and New York salsa."[59] Peace and Love was one band that reflected the influence of Santana. Their song "Latin Sentiment" (performed in English and Spanish) gives a sense of the music which accompanied it:

> We're getting all excited just
> By playing-hearing Latin music
> Congas, cowbells all the
> Rhythm section

All we want for everyone
Is to get in the groove and
Express yourself and
Do your thing anyway you
Want it

Clap your hands, kick your feet
Move your body all around
Feel the beat, you will see

Latin feeling, it's out of sight yeah!
Latin feeling, Latin feeling.[60]

For other Mexican groups, however, the strategy consisted of creating an "international" sound that reproduced the success of foreign idols such as Creedence Clearwater Revival, Chicago, and the Rolling Stones. For instance, the Spiders produced a sound quality that received favorable commentary from critics but that displayed virtually no Latino influences.[61] In a fundamental sense, therefore, we should recognize how the dual pressures of "nationalizing" and "internationalizing" simultaneously rendered two, in important respects distinctive, native rock styles: Latin-rock fusion and Anglocentric rock (derived from African American blues). In both cases, however, the notion of collage applied: the conscious effort to create, through the manipulation of band images as well as musical quotations, a native rock concept that spliced together international and native references.

The constant criticism by rock reviewers and the badgering by interviewers regarding a band's "originality" suggested that the rock aesthetic pursued by La Onda Chicana was considered by many to be inchoate at best and a colonialized copy at worst. In understanding the movement's apparent contradictions, we must avoid falling into the doctrinaire cultural-imperialist argument that presumes a mass of passive consumers of foreign culture, absorbing the aesthetic and ideological implications of a foreign rock "invasion." While the presence of foreign rock and the images that accompanied it were widely circulated, the musicians and their Mexican audiences became increasingly self-conscious about the need to create an original rock sound as well as an "original" countercultural movement. Mexican rock was not necessarily displacing foreign rock, but as new bands emerged and succeeded in commercializing their art form a new assortment of images and sounds began to complement and build on a foreign rock repertoire which already existed. Through this commercialization process, members of La Onda Chicana could feel increasingly connected to one

another and, perhaps more significantly, to a global countercultural movement in a way never before experienced. As one participant recalled:

> I believe there were pioneers who were capable of doing the same thing
> being done in the United States, making music that we enjoyed. True,
> it was music influenced [by foreign rock] in large part . . . but it was our
> own music. It unified us and while similar [to foreign rock], it was also
> different. It was uniquely Mexican. I remember quite well the band La
> Revolución de Emiliano Zapata; the name alone assured you of a sense
> of nationalist credibility. But they played rock in English and were
> Mexican. I don't know if they had any impact [in the U.S]. I doubt it.[62]

Thus, we must try to understand La Onda Chicana not only as a consequence of imperialism but fundamentally as a *response* to imperialism
as well.

How, then, do we account for the fact that all bands composed overwhelmingly in English? I would suggest there are four ways to understand
this phenomenon. First, there were clear pressures to record in English in
order to internationalize oneself, to seek success in foreign markets. Despite
Santana's success with the Tito Puente tune "Oye como va" (sung in Spanish), English was still the dominant language for rock, in itself an indication of the cultural hegemony exerted by the United States and Britain
over the rock movement globally. There was an overriding assumption by
most bands that the "real market" for rock was a U.S. and European one,
and thus in order to "make it" one would have to appeal to that market.
Armando Nava of Los Dug Dugs revealed in a 1979 interview that he
recorded in English "because my intention is to get my songs sent [to the
United States]."[63] Ironically, however, with the brief exception of Polydor,
Mexican recording companies gave scant marketing consideration to the
mounting Latino (Chicano) population in the United States.[64] "So, rock
can't be global?" asked the rock critic Víctor Roura prophetically in 1973.
"Will it always be self-enclosed within the same circle? Is English the only
medium for rock? Just because rock was born sung in English, one can't
sing in Spanish, German, French, etc.?"[65] Indeed, some bands produced
identical versions of their songs in English and Spanish in an apparent effort to appeal to a national and international market simultaneously. This
was also a necessary factor shaped by the commercial radio industry: stations dedicated wholly to imported foreign rock demanded rock in English,
and vice versa for Spanish-only music stations. Thus it became a common
strategy among bands to produce more than one version of their material.[66]

Second, the use of English, especially in live performances, was intrinsically linked to notions of the avant-garde and thus a more "authentic" rebellious sound. Even the refritos had incorporated English exclamations, guttural grunts, and drawn-out vowels in imitation of their Anglo counterparts. English connected the audience with an imaginary vision of vanguard participation, even when many if not most fans found the lyrics inaccessible. As Ramón García, a working-class fan of rock, later remarked:

> If in general, you didn't understand what was being sung in English, you at least knew they were saying something to you. It was somebody who reflected your ideas, who represented your people. Even when the [U.S. and British bands] were saying something, and they have nothing to do with your people, at any rate you're a human being, and so you capture something [of the feeling]. But to see someone play from a band [that you know], you really felt it. Immediately, you went wild for them; you felt that they were saying something [to you].[67]

Lyrics were often so poorly enunciated that even an English-language speaker no doubt had difficulty deciphering their meaning. Still, English was considered at the time to be an inextricable part of the "feeling" produced by rock, whether you were from the upper or lower classes.

A third explanation is suggested by the fact that performing in English allowed musicians greater latitude of expression in order to avoid direct censorship of their songs. As Víctor Roura writes, bands "began to incorporate political questions into their compositions, but they concealed them by singing in English."[68] Herbe Pompeyo concurred, noting, "It would have been difficult to get much diffusion for a song in Spanish" that contained controversial themes.[69] This would have been particularly true for the 1971 hit, "Viva Zapata," recorded in English by Los Locos:

> I'm gonna talk to you about Zapata
> He fought for the land
> He was Zapata.
> He died a long time ago
> But he's still on the road.
> Follow his teaching.
> Follow Zapata.
>
> I'm digging on the earth
> Until I'm exhausted.
> When seeds are growing up
> It makes me feel fine.
> I fight the way he did
> And that is how I feel.

Viva Zapata.
Viva Zapata.[70]

Other songs, such as the hard-hitting "Caminata cerebral" (Walk within My Brain) by Love Army, were written in English and in Spanish, with the hope that one might receive airplay:

Oh, what about what he said,
Already forgotten.
What happened with the thirty coins
That he gave you?

Because I don't believe what you're telling me,
I know it's not the truth.
What is certain is that I prefer
To walk within my brain.
I have to go.

Unions and bosses have
Lowered my morality.
If I keep my underwear on,
They'll lower that as well.

Because justice takes time,
I don't think I'll wait.
I prefer to walk within my brain.
I have to go.

Hey Christ, don't return
Don't let them shave your head!
No one will understand your Age of Aquarius.

Because I know that if you return,
You won't be preaching.
Just seeing your long hair,
People are going to freak.
Yeah, they'll make you cry.[71]

Roura argues that in the English version, written to enhance the chances of airplay, the song "lost all of its message. It was reduced to nothing."[72] This is debatable, as most listeners were probably also aware of the Spanish translation. In the case of Three Souls in My Mind, his biographer writes that Lora's "irreverent lyrics . . . were disguised" not only because of the English but also because the song titles were shortened on the album cover (for example, "Let Me Swim in Your Bed" became simply "Let Me Swim").[73]

Last, we can interpret the reliance on English as integral to an aesthetic notion of rock as poetry. The literary impact of performers such as the Beatles, the Rolling Stones, and Bob Dylan—in fact, all of the respected groups from that era—was considerable. Rock magazines devoted increasing amounts of space to publishing foreign lyrics with their accompanying translation. Fans regarded rock lyrics as part of a larger vanguard cultural movement; demand for such translations was high. As one reader wrote to the editors of *POP:*

> The articles on philosophy, psychology, theology, metaphysics . . . are in fact widely read and discussed. As youth, we're very interested in that material. . . . Oh yeah, I almost forgot! [Add] another section with lyrics to the songs from the best albums by: BOB DYLAN, DONOVAN, JOAN BAES [sic] JOHN MAYALL, GEORGE HARRISON . . . songs with a message, but of course translated into Spanish, as there are a lot of us who don't know English and so don't learn about the important message these songs are sending us.[74]

As we have seen, literary figures of La Onda lavishly incorporated rock lyrics, often left untranslated, into their writings. In general, rock lyrics were even more respected as poetry in Mexico than in the United States. This may have reflected a more deeply entrenched tradition of poetry and literature in Latin American thought. But there was another factor, too. The distancing intrinsic to all acts of translation generated a more profound aura surrounding rock lyrics: English created—and continues to generate—a sense of mystery to be unraveled, even more so when it involves popular culture.[75]

COMMERCIALIZATION OF *LA ONDA CHICANA*

The commercialization of Mexico's Onda Chicana lasted little more than a year, from the end of 1970 to early 1972. It was during this brief but intense period that Mexican bands tasted the reality of national fame as well as the possibility of international recognition. Supported by young artistic directors devoted wholeheartedly to the cause of rock—such as José G. Cruz Ayala at CBS and Herbe Pompeyo at Polydor—native rock music all at once was launched onto the national stage by the record companies and with the crucial support of radio and television. Ironically, the virtual prohibition of foreign rock performances provided a windfall promotional opportunity for native bands. From the companies' perspective, supporting native rock offered the opportunity to exploit further the rapidly expanding demand for rock music generally. "At that point the great majority of Mexican rock fans wanted national rock," recalls Enrique Partida of Polydor. "And so they [got] it. And the [record] companies [went] 'boom.'"[76]

Most Mexican rock artists hoped to produce rock for an international market as well as a national one. The transnationals (CBS, RCA, Capitol, and Polydor) seemed to offer a direct path to international fame. As Herbe Pompeyo explained, Mexican rock right away suggested its potential profitability, and this had an immediate impact on the recording industry generally: "At Polygram [*sic*], I believe we were a vital part in the record industry at that time. . . . We set a lot of standards. . . . Concerning Mexican rock, when [the other companies] saw what we had with 'Nasty Sex' and that we had signed on eight or ten groups, they also signed on groups."[77] For example, in a promotional advertisement for its *Ofensiva pop, '71* album, featuring songs by ten Mexican bands contracted with the transnational, CBS proposed "[c]reating the emergence of a Mexican rock without additives, authentic rock that revolutionizes the musical current of our country and communicates to everyone its enthusiasm for the musical movement that has been born, by ten of its groups."[78]

There was some limited success in exporting Mexican rock to other Latin American markets, but only Polydor was able—or committed enough—to export Mexican rock to a European or U.S. audience. In the most significant case, the company introduced the band La Revolución de Emiliano Zapata into the European market with their song, "Nasty Sex," which made the hit charts in West Germany. Moreover, for an indication of how a U.S. marketing strategy was emerging, we can look to Polydor's promotion of its contracted rock bands in a festival held in the Los Angeles Sports Arena in October 1971. The idea of the festival, an organizer remarked, was "to open doors in the U.S. for Mexican and Chicano pop music."[79] Singled out for special promotional treatment, La Revolución de Emiliano Zapata performed more than twelve concerts at high schools and universities throughout the state. As a writer for *Excélsior* commented, "In California, there is much interest [in the group] owing to the fact that all of the Mexican student organizations, or children of Mexican parents resident in North America, are part of different associations that have the Caudillo of the South, Emiliano Zapata, as their symbol, which is why the group of youth who have taken the name 'Revolución' have [met with success] in their efforts to integrate into the United States [market]."[80] Not all transnationals were as active as Polydor, however. Armando Nava of Los Dug Dugs later commented with regard to his experience at RCA: "They were a transnational, and to a certain point that worked in our favor. But they never did anything [for us]. They never introduced our material into the United States, even when we recorded in English. Nothing."[81]

What is important for us to consider here is the fact that, contrary to the general assumption that transnationals were solely conduits for cultural imperialism, in the case of Mexican rock the transnational recording companies offered the best, if not only, hope for the internationalization of the native rock movement. If we view La Onda Chicana as an attempt to rupture the restrictive boundaries of authoritarianism by inventing a new countercultural discourse, then we must also accept the fact that capitalist interests, especially transnational ones, became an integral factor in La Onda's rapid development on a national scale. Through the vehicle of national rock, the transnational recording industry offered the possibility of representing an image of Mexico—nationally and, more importantly, internationally—that was not directly shaped by the parameters of an "imagined community" [82] forged by the ruling regime after the revolution.

ECHEVERRÍA'S PROMISE

As president-elect, Echeverría's rhetoric and actions were specifically aimed at reincorporating the left and, especially, youth into his political program. Immediately on entering office, he announced a policy of *apertura democrática* (democratic opening) that heralded a liberalization of the press and a shift to the left in official actions and discourse. One of his first acts in office was to begin the release of political prisoners held since the 1968 crackdown.[83] Former participants in the student movement were then recruited for government and university positions. In a tradition well entrenched in the PRI, intellectuals were given subsidized public platforms to express their viewpoints. Out of its commercialized doldrums, a renaissance in theater and film occurred with the blessings (but also influence) of the new regime.[84] Indeed, in this context of an apertura democrática the language of "cultural and economic imperialism" became a useful polemical tool for the PRI. Attacks on the government, emanating above all from the left, for the PRI's past failures to redistribute income and defend "authentic cultural values" in the face of—especially U.S.—imperialism now enervated the very discourse and directly shaped the political strategy of the Echeverría regime in the coming years.

Under Echeverría official language and public policy shifted away from the foreign-investment, "modernizing" orientation of Díaz Ordaz toward a renewed economic nationalism, coupled with the language of Third World struggle. Where Díaz Ordaz had pursued a strategy of "stabilizing development," Luis Echeverría shifted to a strategy of "shared development," language that harked back to the populist period of Lázaro Cárdenas during the late 1930s. Its hegemonic grasp severely weakened by the ramifications of the 1968 student movement, the regime's populist strategy combined an image of the president as leader of the Third World in a struggle against imperialism, a commitment to rural development for Mexico's peasantry and price subsidies for the urban poor, the "Mexicanization" of foreign investment, and a commitment to cultural nationalism both at the national and, later, at UNESCO, international levels.[85] Once more the regime drew on the rich idiom of revolutionary nationalism to inform its direction and discourse. This was politically necessary, for election results indicated widespread cynicism and voter apathy.[86]

At the strictly symbolic level, for example, Echeverría frequently donned the campesino *guayabera* garment (a loose-fitting, rough cotton shirt), while his wife "appeared at parties dressed up in [indigenous] Tehuanan dresses, in the purest tradition from the 1930s." For official dinners and receptions, native fruit drinks substituted for the usual custom of serving wine and imported liquors.[87] These and other symbolic changes had their counterparts in the international arena. One important example was Mexico's leadership position at the United Nations, which became a confrontational arena between the developed North and the underdeveloped South. Epitomizing Mexico's renewed radicalism was Echeverría's warm embrace of Salvador Allende, who visited Mexico at the end of 1972 and at the height of U.S. aggression toward Chile's socialist regime. Echeverría also became Mexico's most widely traveled head of state, visiting numerous countries around the world in an effort to shore up symbolically, if less so in actuality, the nation's independence from the United States.

Under Echeverría, tensions between left and right-wing elements escalated, and for the first time since the 1920s political consensus within the PRI was sorely tested. This was most dramatically revealed on 10 June 1971, Corpus Christi Day. On this date in the capital, some 30,000 students marched in an act of solidarity with students who were protesting repression at the University of Monterrey. In actuality, conflicts at that university had recently been resolved, but a splinter group of radical students from the UNAM decided to go forward with the unauthorized march nonetheless: "More than anything, [the march] was an act whose principal sentiment was about *self-affirmation;* the movement desired, first of all, to demonstrate its existence to itself, its very being, its not being dead, and in turn, to proclaim this to the world. Taking over the streets was the appropriate way to achieve this."[88] Though the march's goals were muddled, the sheer fact that thousands of students had joined reflected the pent-up need to vent one's rage at the political system.

But Echeverría's political enemies extended beyond the student population. His early attempts to reform the old political and union guard, combined with pledges to redistribute wealth, had incurred the wrath of right-wing elements in society and in the PRI itself. Powerful industrialists, such as the Monterrey Group, were determined to discredit Echeverría, if not unseat him. While Echeverría may have viewed the protest march as an opportunity to further curry favor with the student population, his political enemies saw a chance to embarrass him. On the day of the march, as scores of policemen stood idly by, members of a known paramilitary group, the *halcones* (falcons), attacked the unarmed protesters with spiked boards, baseball bats, and guns, killing fifty students (many of high-school age), wounding hundreds more, and leading to numerous "disappearances." The halcones had direct links with the Monterrey industrialists, but they were also supplied and shielded from arrest by Mexico City's recently appointed mayor, Alfonso Martínez Domínguez, who had become a political enemy of Echeverría. Promises of a full investigation ensued, but they were buried shortly thereafter. In the political fallout Martínez Domínguez was dismissed, but Echeverría was also weakened.[89] From the perspective of the student population, no one doubted the political message. Student politics became even further polarized, to the point that open discussion on campuses was often suffocated. New urban terrorist groups emerged.[90] But most youth simply retreated from politics altogether, joining the growing numbers who adhered to the counterculture.

MEXICAN ROCK'S RECEPTION

With the heightened commercialization of La Onda came a deepening of its class makeup and a diversification of its audience along gender lines. In this respect, it demonstrated that mass culture was a powerful organizing tool that transcended class boundaries; rock was inclusionary.[91] The broadening appeal of rock coincided with a relaxation of restrictions on native concert performances as part of Echeverría's outreach to youth. More women joined the counterculture as well, influenced by the rising feminist discourse against machismo and the discovery in La Onda of new participatory spaces freed of the conservative social strictures of family and state. In a fundamental sense La Onda was proving itself capable of transcending class and gender boundaries to incorporate a diversified audience bound together by shared reference points in music, speech, and dress. Yet if this was the ideal, there were also important class and gender contradictions that defined this imagined community.

An indication of the underlying conflicts that characterized the inter-class nature of La Onda can be gleaned from a concert review of an outdoor

Figure 14.   Javier Batiz performs in the Alameda Park in Mexico City, c. 1971. Source: Federico Arana, *Guaraches de ante azul: Historia del rock mexicano* (Mexico City: Posada, 1985), vol. 3, 146. (Reproduced courtesy of Federico Arana)

festival that took place in Chapultepec Park—a gigantic public park in Mexico City known for its diverse class attendance—in the spring of 1971. Interestingly, the concert was organized as part of a government program to provide free Sunday entertainment, "or the official effort to get close to rock," as one reviewer cynically put it.[92] Indeed, other outdoor rock concerts were officially sanctioned under the apertura democrática (see Figure 14). Polydor threw its support behind the Chapultepec festival by offering a prize of 6,000 pesos (around U.S. $500), instruments, and a recording contract to the best band. The festival, however, turned tense when the audience, composed in large part of lower-class youth, created "an atmosphere of *chiflidos* [a loud whistling used to convey disapproval] and *naranjazos* [literally, throwing oranges]," apparently in response to the mediocre quality of the music. A woman, "good looking (but a bimbo)" and associated with the festival came on stage to try and calm down the crowd. But her false posture of hipness "contradicted the cultural intent of the event" (that is, an authentic countercultural gathering), in the words of the reviewer, and unleashed a torrent of derision and laughter from the crowd.[93] While the reviewer (a male) harshly criticized the woman's superficial understanding of La Onda, both the female stage announcer and the male reviewer revealed a fundamental misunderstanding of the audience's reaction. By seeing the chiflidos and naranjazos as an inappropriate response to rock—"modern music [that] is incomprehensible by the popular majority"[94]—the reviewer unwittingly revealed his own elitism, and a deeper appreciation of rock's relatedness to barrio culture was lost. If the middle and upper classes assumed that rock was meant to be revered, the aggressiveness reflected in the response of the festival's audience reflected the alternative perspective that, for the lower classes, *their voice* was to be heard as well.

For the lower classes, rock was (and continues to be) not just about listening but also, and fundamentally, about *participating* in the musical space organized by live performance. The opportunity to participate was provided especially by the hoyos fonquis, which introduced a reorganization of urban social space by situating rock performance as an inextricable aspect of barrio life. As Joaquín López recalled, "With the hoyos fonquis we're talking about a marginalized barrio made up of marginalized people who are attending these rock events. Not so much to dance—these weren't dances, exactly. They were more like auditions. . . . Sure, people danced, but you didn't get the feeling it was like a formal dance hall, you know? But rather, a mass concert."[95] Unlike the more regulated concert spaces, such as those at the National Auditorium and private music clubs, the hoyos fonquis were open-ended performance spaces that allowed for—indeed, endorsed—the kind of aggressive give and take central to rock's appreciation by the lower classes. The concert in Chapultepec Park seemed to mirror the conditions of the hoyos fonquis in terms of audience and also in the breakdown of respect for the performers and organizers.

Addressing the latent class tensions that were building, the reviewer described how the woman exacerbated an already tense situation by "communicating in jipi slang," whereas much of the audience "uses such slang in a more authentic way." She could not transcend her own class position simply by appealing to the language of the youth culture. This recalls earlier comments by Manuel Ruiz that the juniors used the vehicle of La Onda as a way to be seen as "with it," but this often came across as forced and artificial. The class conflict experienced along cultural lines at the festival led to "small outbreaks of violence, objects thrown through the air, and a generalized tension."[96] For the reviewer, the concert's disastrous outcome pointed to the "deficiencies" of rock's "projection and diffusion" in Mexico: "One can begin with the fact that the audience . . . [is] in its majority made up of people who don't understand rock for obvious reasons of customs, a culture deeply rooted in folklore, and the lack of appreciation for any modern expression with artistic intention. . . . Being fair about it, the Mexican masses are not yet ready for a rock festival, which doesn't mean they're not ready for rock."[97] What was really at stake, however, was not whether or not the "masses" were "ready" for rock; the assumption of rock as high culture reflected the obvious biases of middle-class critics. Rather, the criticism (repeated on other occasions) pointed to profound cultural differences between the classes in their consumption patterns and thus in the *usage* of rock music in their lives.

For the middle and upper classes, rock music offered a vehicle for rebellion, but one closely patterned on the ideal of the U.S. model. The relationship between audience and performer was interactive yet clearly bounded. For the lower classes, on the other hand, rock provided a vehicle for mass participation and the spatial reorganization of everyday life. Performers had to gain the respect of their audience precisely by breaking down the imaginary boundaries that kept the two apart. As Víctor Roura would later comment about the hoyos fonquis, "It's curious, but in order for a group to be respected it has to show a lack of respect."[98] Rock offered a fundamental shift in perspective and way of being, a shift marked by the possibility of participation and the articulation of needs. As Ramón García eloquently expressed it:

> I think that [rock] is about the support for reaffirming who you are. I believe that rock was born from restlessness in order to reaffirm that restlessness. Being from a country like Mexico, you can't keep from noticing so many things, so much injustice and all that. So if rock gave you some support or something that made you feel better. . . . I think that definitely rock is an essence, a way of life. It's a form of life. It's not about the moment, a momentary euphoria. It's a way of life, and as such its rhythm helps you to reaffirm who you are.[99]

These class-based values were not in fundamental conflict. Rock served as a common denominator for youth generally. However, because rock had different meanings according to one's class position, the ideal of a rock community was fundamentally flawed. Mass culture might indeed transcend class, but it does so neither uniformly nor with predictable outcomes.

THE LIMITS TO FEMALE LIBERATION

The parameters of female participation in La Onda were defined by parental conservatism from without and machismo from within the movement. Much more so than men, women experienced tight surveillance by parents of their dress, manners, and leisure activities. Adopting positions that involved more than a mere fashion statement—the decision to go unescorted, to engage in sex before marriage, to challenge the authority of one's parents—were infinitely more difficult for women. Moreover, where parents lectured daughters on the social importance of buenas costumbres, in the male-dominated culture of La Onda they encountered a double standard toward sexual relations that similarly defined their position. On one hand, La Onda stressed the idea of sexual liberation and the value of experimentation prior to marriage. On the other hand, women were expected to adhere to a higher standard of morality than were men. In reality, women who rebelled by seeking a liberated lifestyle outside marriage were denigrated not only by society at large but even within the countercultural community, which labeled them whores. As one female participant explained, "There were two terms for women: those who were 'decent' and those who were 'for fun.' Those women who wanted to enjoy themselves were condemned to follow a path toward 'decadence'; there were good women and bad women. 'I can have fun with my neighbor, but my family—my sisters, my mother—they're sacred, untouchable. I can have a sexual relationship with another woman, but I wouldn't marry her. My woman has to be a virgin.'"[100] This differed from the United States, where sexual experience came to be valued by men and women as a sign of openness to new ideas and changing social mores. Virginity was "out," and multiple relationships leading up to marriage were "in." By contrast, in Mexico women were expected to be "clean," while men were assumed to be "experienced." In a fundamental sense, therefore, not much had changed.

But everyday acts of defiance, ranging from wearing pants to participating in the anarchic youth spaces offered by the weekend tocadas, allowed women to discover new roles for themselves, in relation both to their familial settings and to the men who surrounded them, despite the inherent sexism of much of male rock performance at that time. In fact, Mexico would produce no renowned female recorded rocker (though there were several female baladistas). Perhaps this accounts for why Janis Joplin held a particular fascination for many women. She was commonly referred to as La bruja (the Sorceress).

Around 1970 a Mexican feminist movement, rooted in important ways to women's participation in the 1968 student movement, also began to take shape. The movement's coherence was marred by ideological and class divisions, which led to numerous splinterings. All the same, the relatively small but dedicated number of feminist activists worked to influence public discourse. In this they succeeded in calling attention to the issues of women's participation in the workforce, sexual stereotyping, harassment, machismo, and sexual freedom (including access to birth control and abortion).[101] As Jasmín Solís Gómez later reflected, "For me, the circumstances of the period gave me a lot. The jipi movement and feminist liberation all provided me with an opportunity for growth I wouldn't have had otherwise. . . . I wouldn't be who I am today. And I'm very happy with who I am. It cost me a number of confrontations [with my family], but it would never have happened had it not been for that influence."[102] The counterculture thus provided a context in which women could take new risks, often changing their lives permanently. But at the same time, the cost of those risks tended to be much higher than in the United States, where most middle-class children lived away from home permanently after high school. In Mexico, by contrast, most women continued to live restrained by the economic limitations and social taboos of living independently.

Marriage, for instance, was still considered a ticket to freedom from the restrictions of parental rule for many women. But marriage often offered the prospect of freedom from one's family at the cost of subservience to one's husband. As one female informant (divorced, and with a child) reflected, "the majority of my friends from that period are divorced." In marrying a Mexican jipi, she had hoped "for what all women wish for: to marry someone different, someone who will work hard, who will spend time with you, who dresses distinctively." But her husband continued to take drugs and live the lifestyle of an ondero, sleeping around with other women while she struggled to raise the family they had jointly created:

> What did we do? I don't even remember what I did. I was the one who was always working. . . . I was the one who bought the furniture for our home. I was the one who carried our child. I raised her and bought her everything—her clothing, everything. . . . I ask myself, "What did I do for all those years?" We were *novios* [going out] for five years, and married for four. . . . Once married, you have to sleep with him, be with him, attend to him, wash for him, iron for him, cook his meals. You say to yourself, "Now what do I do?" Although you already know the answer to that, as if you're living in a dream—or a nightmare— and you don't know what's happening to your life. Because for me, that was like a nightmare.[103]

While rock had challenged older hierarchies and in doing so had invented new participatory spaces for women, patriarchy was not destroyed by the rock counterculture (despite rhetoric to the contrary), simply reinvented.

The theme of an oppressive family structure contrasted with the liberated social values of La Onda is conveyed in the countercultural cult film, *La verdadera vocación de Magdalena* (The True Profession of Magdalena), which featured La Revolución de Emiliano Zapata.[104] In the film the female protagonist, Magdalena (Angélica María), is a shy, proper girl who works as a bilingual secretary and lives alone with her middle-class mother. Symbolic of her purity is a charm necklace containing the inscription: "Enemies halt. The heart of Jesus is with me." But at social events Magdalena is clearly the odd woman out. When she attends a party at the urging of a girlfriend, she feels foolish in the company of her more liberal cohorts; at one point, a female friend openly introduces Magdalena to her male "lover." As the party winds down, Magdalena is left without a ride home and so accepts an offer from Emetrio ("Eme"), a member of the rock group that had been performing. Apparently peer pressures overwhelm her, because she brings Eme home to bed with her. (It is never made clear whether they actually have sex, though the implication is that they do.) In the morning, Magdalena's mother assumes the man in her bed is really a girlfriend because of his long hair. But when she discovers the truth, she forces Magdalena and Eme to have a civil wedding. The three live together under one roof, but they have not changed their outlook on life: Magdalena refuses to have sex until she and Eme have a proper religious wedding; the mother treats Eme as a perverted, jipi freak; and Eme becomes increasingly exasperated out about the bind he is in (though he does care for Magdalena). Recording a new song, "Petra y sus camaradas," Eme vents his frustrations (in English), while revealing his underlying machismo:

> I'm going to tell you all about it,
> 'bout the girl that I met.
> She's always hanging on me,
> so I gotta treat her bad.
> Gotta treat her bad.
>
> Lord, I will.
> The next time that I see her,
> I gotta take her to bed.
> Gotta take her to bed.[105]

Among his band-member friends, the jokes revolve around Eme's sexually deprived "marriage." "It seems to me that what your Magdalena needs is for us all to screw her," offers one friend. "I go first," shouts one; "I'll go second," says another. Eme offers no defense of Magdalena, but he is still convinced that there must be a way of making her see the (liberated) light.

Meanwhile Magdalena's mother, driven to frenzy by Eme's lifestyle, attempts to electrocute him by rewiring his guitar and then flooding the hallway where his amplifier is connected. Nearly killed, Eme understands the message and leaves. With his apparent exit from the scene, Magdalena's mother now schemes to have her divorce Eme so she can marry a former boyfriend, Armando, who has miraculously reappeared as a successful businessman. Allegedly in the banana-export business, Armando invents various tales of wealth, including an apartment in New York City and a chateau in Switzerland. In fact, he is no better off than he was the last time he dated Magdalena, and he is secretly scheming himself so that he and his invalid mother can move out of their cramped apartment and into Magdalena's more spacious home. (When Magdalena cries to her mother that Armando will never marry her, now that she is no longer a virgin, her mother replies: "Of course you're a virgin. That pighead [Emetrio] isn't capable even of that. I'm sure you're still a virgin.")

The mother's plan is for Magdalena to entrap Eme by posing as her liberated twin sister, "Irene," who is visiting from Los Angeles. The idea is that Eme will fall for the sexier Irene and thus demand a divorce from Magdalena. The plan backfires, however, when Magdalena's experience as a liberated woman in disguise—at one point she lures Eme and his friends with the line, "I like to live life to its fullest, in all of its glory"—opens her to the realm of La Onda. She not only sings for the band—in English—at a massive rock festival (meant to be Avándaro) but has sex with Eme as well as another band member. By this point, Eme has figured out her disguise. In the end she decides to live out the Onda lifestyle for real (hence, her "true profession"), and this propels her to a life of stardom as a rock singer. To cover up for Magdalena while trying to enrich herself in the process, Magdalena's mother sobs to Armando that her daughter has "discovered her true profession—as a nun in a convent!" Armando, who had viewed marriage as a vehicle for his own upward mobility anyhow, does not miss a beat when he responds, "It's you I've always loved." To this the mother also eagerly obliges, still believing Armando to be a wealthy businessman. The movie ends with Magdalena's mother bitterly denouncing her situation—her own dreams of social mobility through marriage revealed as a sham—as Armando and his mother content themselves watching television in their new living quarters. In the final scene Magdalena appears in an interview on television, professing her love for her husband (Eme) and her life as a rock star. We also discover that she has changed her stage name to Irene, her true profession now fully realized.

The class and gender contradictions that characterized La Onda were masked in part by the image of a unified rock counterculture under the banner of La Onda Chicana. But as this counterculture broadened to incorporate new social actors, the unifying experience tied to a middle-class notion of rebellion was tested and reconfigured. By 1971 La Onda was no longer limited to a narrow notion of vanguard cultural rebels, as Monsiváis had once identified the movement, but had been transformed by the political repercussions of repression and the widespread incorporation of the lower classes. While an image of the liberated woman shorn of her obligations of upholding the moral fiber of society now existed, underlying this ideology of communal love were deeply entrenched views opposing equal responsibilities for men and women. Women's sexual liberation certainly scandalized society's buenas costumbres, but many men continued to regard a woman's proper role through the lens of machista assumptions regarding work, family, and leisure. Nonetheless, the ideology of a countercultural community at the heart of La Onda Chicana was broadly disseminated after 1970. This ideology was linked especially to a network of cultural industries that viewed the profits coming from the sale and marketing of a native rock product with particular interest. Where this marketing logic would lead and how a society under duress would respond are subjects for the next chapter.

6 The Avándaro Rock Festival

In September 1971, just three months after the deadly paramilitarist attack by the halcones on protesters in Mexico City and nearly three years to the day after the government-orchestrated massacre of students and workers at Tlatelolco, Mexico became the first Latin American country to present its own rock-music festival, popularly known as Avándaro. The concert drew more than 200,000 participants from across the country, and it clearly marked the commercial apex of La Onda Chicana.[1] But if the cultural industries hoped to emulate the marketing success of Woodstock, a societal backlash in the aftermath of Avándaro all but halted continued exploitation of the Mexican rock market. Attacks came from the left and the right as blame was assessed for the "lost souls" of Mexican youth. The Echeverría regime used this backlash as the basis for a frontal attack on La Onda Chicana. The regime's discourse of Third World nationalism was expanded to include public support for a Latin American counterpart to rock: the *nueva canción* (New Song) and folk-protest movement associated especially with left-wing regimes in Cuba, Chile, Peru, and now Mexico. Even though the cultural industries' support quickly withered, Mexican rock did not disappear. Native rock retreated to the hoyos fonquis, where it was fully reclaimed by the lower classes. At the same time, foreign rock retained its status as vanguard culture and coexisted with the new Latin American song movement, despite overt ideological battles waged in more radical corners against all manifestations of yanqui cultural designs.

VALLE DE BRAVO, AVÁNDARO

The concept of holding a rock festival as a showcase for native talent emerged as a logical consequence of the probing for commercial opportunities of La

Onda Chicana. At the same time, like Woodstock, there was little notion beforehand that the festival would take on the proportions it did. In fact, the concert itself—promoted as a "festival de rock y ruedas" (festival of rock and wheels)—was originally scheduled as only a sideshow to an annual road derby held each year at the Valle de Bravo, Avándaro, site, about two hours' drive northwest of Mexico City. Still, unlike the tocadas, this concert involved the participation of powerful commercial and political interests. Initiated by Justino Compean of the advertising firm McCann-Erickson Stampton, which managed the Coca-Cola account in Mexico, Avándaro offered a high-profile promotion of native bands and thus represented a key moment in the commercialization of the Mexican counter culture.[2] As one person involved in organizing the festival put it, "We've definitely looked to not bring in foreign bands, because we're trying to promote Mexicans in every sense. . . . Specifically speaking, well the British have very popular bands, as do the Americans, the Germans, the whole world, and very few Mexican [bands] have attained success. So we believe that by promoting this kind of festival, any number of Mexican bands can become an international hit. Certainly many of them deserve it, no?"[3]

Clearly the commercial success of the Woodstock festival demonstrated a potential for records and films.[4] Herbe Pompeyo, former artistic director with Polydor Records (now Polygram), revealed that Polydor hoped Avándaro would generate a "great popular explosion [of native rock] . . . with all the accompanying paraphernalia [of the rock counterculture] that already existed in the United States."[5] The festival was even carried live over Radio Juventud, a Mexico City station, until transmission was abruptly cut off by government censors because of foul language. This occurred when the band Peace and Love shouted: "¡Chinga su madre quien no canta!" (Screw your mother, whoever doesn't sing!) in response to lines from the Chicano song, "Marihuana boogie."[6] The television giant Telesistema was also there in force, preparing for television possibilities.[7] Meanwhile CBS, anticipating record spin-offs to follow, hired a helicopter to circle the concert grounds and drop leaflets announcing: "La Ofensiva Pop 71 de CBS está presente en Avándaro con Los Tequila," one of the featured groups.[8] In the center of the town hung a welcome banner: "Paz y amor. Coca-Cola."[9]

Still, in scheduling the festival as a side-show to a road derby rather than as the central attraction (as in the case of Woodstock), the organizers seemed to be probing the commercial potential of native rock rather than cashing in on it explicitly. This fact was reflected in the extremely poor sound system and inadequate organization that characterized the festival from start to finish. It was also reflected in the paltry sums paid to the bands, which received 3,000 pesos each, around U.S. $250.[10] As news of the festival spread, moreover, any practical notion of creating a controlled rock environment, suitable for commercial purposes or otherwise, quickly vanished.

The immediate danger from the organizers' perspective, as well as from that of the Echeverría regime, was that such a mass gathering of youth would turn into a political rally, in itself a clear misreading of the movement's tactics and goals.[11] For rock represented a turning away from traditional political organizing. The ideology of rock as it was practiced in Mexico was captured more by the concept of desmadre and the re-creation of community out of chaos than by a notion of struggle embodied in a socialist-inspired discourse of "unity through discipline." Avándaro, commented the writer Parménides García Saldaña afterward, was "a demonstration without speeches, or leaders, which showed that the only thing we want is music and marijuana."[12] Fearing that student organizers might be present among the crowd, precautions were taken nonetheless: "There are students present, and some will want to take control of the microphones in order to make a statement; this will not be permitted. Access to the microphones is under watch by four armed guards. It is necessary to identify yourself in order to pass [onto the stage]. The army is nearby. The presence of uniformed police and agents is a show of support [for the concert]."[13] With the exception of a "religious survey" passed out by the newspaper *Novedades*, the distribution of all literature was prohibited.[14] Federal, state, and local armed forces made the government's presence ominously apparent: up to 1,000 soldiers with machine guns milled around the perimeter of the concert grounds, though no violent incidents were reported.[15]

As it turned out, at least two efforts linking rock to politics did occur. The first was an announcement of a "minute of silence for 'those who died,'" which initially appeared to some in the audience as a political reference. "I thought that it was for what happened at Tlatelolco or [the halcones attack] of June 10th," commented one participant. "But it was for Jim Morrison, Janis Joplin, and Jimmy [*sic*] Hendrix."[16] The second, this time more direct, came in a song dedication by Alejandro Lora of Three Souls in My Mind: "In this festival a lot has been said about peace and love, and those things are really cool, but that is not rock. To show that we're concerned about things such as the tenth of June we're going to play a song by the [Rolling] Stones called, 'Street Fighting Man.'"[17] In the end, tens of thousands of youth, mostly from Mexico City but also making pilgrimages from all parts of the country, descended on the Valle de Bravo site for a long, cold, and wet night of music and revelry.

The festival itself officially began at 12 noon on Saturday, 11 September, with a yoga session, though large numbers of youth had begun to arrive several days earlier. While a number of lesser-known bands warmed up, the first scheduled act, Los Dug Dugs, did not begin until around 10:00 P.M. on Saturday. The music continued until 8:00 A.M. Sunday, when the last band to perform, Three Souls in My Mind, "had to end only a half-hour after they started: the sound system conked out altogether, and there was little option but to declare the festival over at that point."[18] In the aftermath of the concert, the road derby would be canceled. So too were plans for any future commercial exploitation of native rock. Orphaned by the mass cultural structure that had at various times sought to contain and then to cultivate it, Mexican rock—and the cultural memory integral to La Onda Chicana—would all but disappear from the national landscape.

THE PARTICIPANTS

At Avándaro, the increasingly diverse class makeup of La Onda showed its forces. Above all, it was the striking presence of so many lower-class youth, the nacos, as they were derogatorily called by the middle and upper classes, sharing a common space and musical culture with other youth that caught the attention of many writers. "Only a small minority is made up of the [upper-class] 'fresas,'" noted one writer. "The immense majority is formed by the [dark-skinned] 'raza.' It seems as if the entire youth population of Ciudad Netzahualcóyotl [a lumpen-class district] had descended on Avándaro."[19] The exact numbers of participants from each class are, of course, unclear. While some reports cited a majority working / lumpen-class element, the following is more likely an accurate description: "The majority . . . belong to the middle class; they are sons of bureaucrats, small merchants, small industrialists, professionals. . . . There are two minority groups: the first are sons of specialized workers, inhabitants of the proletarian *colonias* [neighborhoods] of the Federal District. . . . The second are the sons of financiers, industrialists, and [government] functionaries. They have arrived by car. . . . They are inhabitants of [the elite neighborhoods] Las Lomas, Polanco, San Angel, Florida, El Pedregal."[20]

In any event, it was clear that the class makeup of La Onda had diversified considerably since its pre-1968 origins. While at one level this cross-class alliance in support of a native rock movement was impressive, its real depth was less certain. Upper-class youth could boast of their easy access to foreign rock; for them, native rock would never be more than second rate. Middle-class youth were more likely to long for the success of a native movement, but their cynicism toward the quality of the music and the "education" of the rock audience made their abandonment of support after Avándaro predictable; it was via the middle classes especially that foreign rock was sustained throughout the 1970s as "high" popular culture. For barrio youth, meanwhile, rock had worked its way into an integral aspect of everyday life, where live performance offered the possibility of self-representation in a society which mocked and marginalized them.

All reports also remarked on the dearth of women at the festival.[21] While this was not necessarily an accurate reflection of female participation in La Onda in general, it does remind us that Mexican women faced much greater restrictions on their mobility and freedom of expression than did men. For the women who did attend the Avándaro festival, their motives, in part, suggested the impact of a countercultural discourse that stressed notions of community and defiance toward patriarchal subservience. For example, one twenty-two-year-old woman who attended the festival—"I went because I get along well with my mom"—remarked: "I felt for the first time a total independence, the absence of property. All of Avándaro was the absence of property; in terms of belonging to people, nothing belonged to anyone, except for myself—I belonged to myself."[22] For Lila Orta, a recent marriage meant the opportunity to attend Avándaro: "If I hadn't been married, most likely my parents would never have let me go. . . . So for me, it was an important personal challenge. I told myself: 'I'm married, I don't live with my parents any longer.'"[23] While at one level the concert was a "personal challenge" made possible by the fact of her marriage, after further reflection she remembered her experiences at Avándaro in more nightmarish terms. For in reality she found herself bound to the wishes of her husband and his friends:

> Well, when we went to Avándaro I had no desire to go. I had no idea what to expect. I knew that it was going to be in the countryside, [and] I said to myself, "What am I going to do in the open country if there are no houses, or bathrooms?" . . . The fact was, I was afraid of something happening [since I was pregnant]—that I might slip and fall. I fell like three times, [and] I told myself, "From here, I'm headed right for the hospital, because something is going to happen [to the baby]." I went because they dragged me there. In reality, I didn't have much of a choice except to try to enjoy myself, because although I was annoyed,

angry, cursing right and left—they weren't going to bring me home, right? My husband said to me, "You're coming with me, because you're coming with me." And so, I didn't say anything. I just went. I wasn't very happy.[24]

Curiously, because nudism was a central feature of the counterculture philosophy—and due to the dearth of women generally—photographs and film footage of Avándaro show a large number of nude men: standing around, bathing in the river, even dancing. Yet a reminder of the double standard borne by women was the scandal created when a sixteen-year-old girl initiated a "strip-tease" on top of a lighting platform. *Piedra Rodante,* the Mexican version of *Rolling Stone,* published six photographs in sequence of the act, accompanied by the text: "Wow, that chick really caught the vibes!"[25] Meanwhile, the mainstream press focused on the exhibitionist act as a means of highlighting the degenerate moral state of Mexico's rock culture generally. Later investigated by the attorney general's office, the woman was diagnosed as "suffering a severe problem of adaptation occasioned by the absence of her parents, who live in Monterrey."[26]

Nonetheless, the ideology of rock stressed the myth of a renewed community, and it was this idea that transformed Avándaro, like Woodstock, into a symbol of La Onda's possibilities. In fact, while no deaths were directly linked to the concert (traffic accidents took several lives, however), desmadre clearly triumphed. Footage from the event shows tightly pressed crowds passing bodies through the air, and reviews mention the rowdiness of those present. In one incident a drummer was hit on the head with an empty bottle hurled from the audience. In the battle over space that rock spearheaded—the need to capture space, to reorganize its symbolic infrastructure, if only temporarily—Avándaro represented a "liberated zone," albeit a contradictory one and under the watchful guard of the soldiers present. As one participant described, "one talked about [Avándaro] as being a part of Mexico that was free. In 1968 the [UNAM] was also declared a liberated territory, and I think that Avándaro was a little like a parody of that: a place where you could do what you wanted."[27] It was in this liberated space that Mexicans from all classes took stock of their numbers, exchanged histories, encountered other histories similar and dissimilar to their own. A chance participant from the United States later described the mood in the days after the event: "I remember the next day or so wandering around Mexico City flashing the peace sign at others who were coated in mud—'Avan-daró' you said, like it was a secret signal that you had been there. Like it was something really important. Somehow, because of the mud, you could just tell who had been there [to the concert]."[28] A commemorative volume of photographs called *Nosotros* (Us), published by Humberto Rubalcaba of the rock band Tinta Blanca, took pains to emphasize the magic and harmony of the event. "We went to see what we are like and how we act," reads a part of the text. "We went to get to know ourselves better, to know ourselves as being a part of the others, as well as [to support] the others. . . . [At Avándaro], [w]e mutually discovered that we exist."[29] Perhaps also, youth mutually discovered that profound differences divided the rock community along lines of class and gender.

AVÁNDARO'S REIMAGINING OF COMMUNITY

Virtually all of the music performed at Avándaro was in English. This reflected the trajectory of the Mexican rock movement at the time and captured the element of fusion that was central to La Onda Chicana. This fusion was also widely present in the importance attached to symbolic acts of reappropriation at the festival. Through a free association of symbols and signs of the nation—and of a universalized countercultural movement, generally—the youth culture actively sought to forge a new collective identity that rejected a static nationalism while inventing a new national consciousness on its own terms. As I have argued, this new consciousness was rooted in the notion of a Chicano identity: the fusion of a Mexican nationalist discourse with a countercultural discourse emanating from the United States and elsewhere. Such a shift in consciousness allowed for the simultaneous reembracement of national culture within the framework of an ideological distancing from an official nationalism linked to the state. The sense of participating in a global rock movement heralded by Avándaro thus offered the possibility of transcending nationalist ideology even as one reinvented it. As José Enrique Pérez Cruz, a participant, related, "I think, in a certain sense, we could say that [rock] fit the communist slogan, 'Workers of the world unite!' That is, 'Rockers of the world unite!' . . . Above all, [rock represented] a repudiation of borders. That was the real function of the music, for even when you didn't understand the lyrics, you still enjoyed the music. And that linked us [as Mexicans] to England, Spain, Latin America. Yes, that's the function I see in the music."[30] This separation of nation from state implied a threat to the legitimacy of the ruling party, which had always claimed for itself a privileged relationship to the national patrimony.

Perhaps most representative of this reappropriation at Avándaro was the transformation of the national flag. Reinventions of one's national flag and the discovery of new symbolic value through such reappropriation were

Figure 15.   The peace sign replaced the eagle and serpent emblem on numerous Mexican flags at Avándaro, here seen being waved. Source: Film still, *Concierto de Avándaro* (Dir. Candiani, 1971), Filmoteca de la UNAM. Used by permission.

common in countercultural movements worldwide. For example, incorporating the flag as an article of clothing became a statement of freedom *from* the state or the official meanings assigned to the flag (such as militarism in the United States). In Mexico, as in certain parts of the United States during this same time, strict laws prohibited defilement of the flag and other national symbols.[31] Yet the presence of flags—national and international—was pervasive at Avándaro.[32] This in itself was scandalous: the Mexican flag was hung from makeshift tents and wooden flagpoles against the backdrop of a mud-soaked multitude flouting national values. But photographs of a transfiguration of the national flag shocked not only conservatives but leftist intellectuals as well: several flags had replaced the eagle and serpent emblem with the peace sign (see Figure 15). Not only did this act represent a subversive affront to a primordial national icon, but, in that the ruling regime had long since identified the PRI with the colors and symbolism of the flag itself, the act suggested an attack on the political system as well. The peace symbol, referred both to the student movement of 1968 and to "peace and love" (also the name of a Mexican band), also appeared by itself on several homemade banners at Avándaro.[33]

But if the regime and conservatives were shocked by the reappropriation of the Mexican flag, intellectuals were even more disturbed by the widespread presence of the U.S. flag at Avándaro. This symbolized for many on the left La Onda's apparent reverence for imperialist culture, epitomized by the use of English as a dominant rock idiom. For intellectuals and other leftist critics, many of whom had participated firsthand in the student movement of 1968, the prominence given to the U.S. flag at Avándaro reflected their worst fears of cultural imperialism. Whereas in 1968 the "core" hegemonic powers, especially the United States, had been the direct object of hostility and frustrated rage by youth, the rock counterculture seemed to have swung that influence in the opposite direction. What this leftist criticism failed to take into consideration, however, were the multiple uses of rock music and thus the alternative interpretations that embracing "imperialist culture" might have had. Thus, while the U.S. flag stood for imperialism at protests in 1968, at Avándaro in 1971 it symbolized solidarity with youth abroad and especially the Chicano fusion at the heart of the Mexican rock counterculture. At one point, a large U.S. flag was integrated into a frenzied group dance, where it was shaken and waved about (see Figure 16).[34]

The evident centrality of a foreign discourse and symbols to La Onda Chicana did not reflect a simplistic subservience by the movement to colonial values, or even necessarily to foreign capital. After all, local capitalist interests both large and small were also involved in rock's diffusion. Even the fact that much of the music was performed in English did not necessarily reflect a homogenization of global culture at the hands of transnational cultural industries emanating from the metropolises. The trend toward experimentation in Spanish was evident at the time, and, while a global marketing structure clearly gave preference to English-language material, it was inevitable that a market for Spanish-language rock would sooner or later appear. This optimism for the future direction of La Onda Chicana was expressed by Armando Molina of La Máquina del Sonido: "The musical revolution [known as] 'Rock Chicano' is in full ebullience; each day the quality improves and chances for success are enhanced. To date, all of the groups are creating and providing us with different sensations; the diverse [musical] tendencies are proliferating and making manifest their initial impact."[35] For those who attended the festival, Avándaro therefore represented the *triumph* of a Mexican rock culture, its insertion into a global

Figure 16. During the Avándaro music festival the U.S. flag is held up and danced around, symbolizing the cultural fusion at the heart of La Onda Chicana. Source: Film still, *Concierto de Avándaro* (Dir. Candiani, 1971), Filmoteca de la UNAM. Used by permission.

rock ecumene from which it was previously marginalized. Displaying symbols otherwise regarded as imperialist—that is, the U.S. and British flags—must be understood in the context of La Onda Chicana's pursuance of direct representation in the universal rock movement. "We've done it," came a voice from the platform. "We don't need *gabacho* [U.S.] or European groups. Now we have our own music." As one participant afterward wrote: "At Avándaro, a feeling of 'raza' was awakened. We understood that we are Mexicans, not gabachos. It's our counterculture [onda]."[36]

This is not to deny the impact that a foreign model had on the ideology of the festival. The legend of Woodstock, in fact, weighed heavily on the minds of many participants, even influencing their actions and gestures. This was reflected in the promotional material for Avándaro, which drew on imagery and language from Woodstock. "I know a place high up in the mountains where it rains, the sun shines, and there's music, beautiful music," reads one promotional announcement in apparent emulation of the Woodstock literature. There was also a Spanish translation of a statement made at Woodstock (and footnoted in a citation on the pamphlet): "The person at your side is your brother. If you hurt him you're the one who bleeds."[37] And when the rains began at Avándaro, a rhythmic chorus reportedly rang out in English: "No rain, no rain," exactly mimicking the famous chant at Woodstock, which by this point had been commodified.[38] For the organizers of Avándaro the idea was nothing less than to "achieve the feat of bringing modern culture, already found throughout the world, here too."[39] Quoting a pamphlet handed out at the concert, the goal was "to experience the reality that we have wished for so much."[40]

While Avándaro represented the appropriation of a vanguard image of modernity borrowed from Woodstock and fused with local cultural practice, the ideology of the Woodstock festival itself likewise centered on the appropriation and romanticization of folkloric culture in part borrowed from Mexico, and from "authentic" cultural practices more generally. "We're setting an example for the world," announced one performer from the stage at Woodstock.[41] It was in part an example of how rock (as "modern" culture) and folk (as "authentic" culture) were not only compatible but also interdependent. More fundamentally, it was an example of how rock was an organizer of community. And if Avándaro was heavily indebted to the model of Woodstock, the latter was also at least indirectly indebted to Mexico. Indeed, Santana's performance at Woodstock epitomized the material as well as symbolic impact of these transcultural exchange processes. His success launched the possibility that Mexican rock could establish itself within a world market, while the "Latin rock" sound and image he cultivated contributed to the practices of Third Worldism that were intrinsic to the ideology of the U.S. counterculture more generally. Woodstock and the entire U.S. countercultural movement, for that matter, depended on the usurpation and appropriation of a universalizing metaphor of indigenous authenticity that the proximity of Mexico to the United States in part provided. Other repertoires, such as Native American, Afro-American, Indian, and Asian, existed, of course. But Mexico, especially for those living in the Southwest, offered a close and tangible experience of an exoticized Other.[42]

ASSESSING BLAME

The backlash against Avándaro was swift and had immediate repercussions on the entire rock movement. News and images related the event as harboring a community of drug addicts, nudists, and corrupters of national symbols. This struck at the moral conscience of conservatives, but it equally horrified those on the left. A consensus of culprits in fact emerged in which the finger was pointed at compliant government officials, profit-hungry cultural industries, lax parenthood, and U.S. imperialism. Practically no one stood up for the festival in the days and weeks afterward. As *Jueves de Excélsior* editorialized:

> It was the business deal of the century for drug dealers on the "Sabbath" at Avándaro that justifies society's great alarm. A mayor signs a permit authorizing a car race, and for one Mexican night (?) [*sic:* a reference to the organizers' original plans], a small village is converted by a businessman into a nudist camp and a refuge for drug addicts where, at the very least, marijuana, mushrooms from Oaxaca, LSD, and perhaps even opium and alcohol are consumed. . . . This, what happens every eight days in the United States, has unfortunately occurred for the first time now in Mexico.[43]

The newspaper *Excélsior* decried the "numerous violations, including the illegal use of the national flag, all of which are a consequence of the possessed imitation of patterns present in other societies."[44] This point was reiterated by the secretary of interior affairs, who stressed the "illicit use of the national flag, to the point of its deformation."[45] In the conservative provincial capital of Puebla, a group calling itself "New Youth" organized an anti-Avándaro rally. Protest leaflets declared: "In Mexico there is only one flag: the national one. In Mexico there is only one true youth: that which is patriotic. Youth have only one ideal to live up to: Mexico."[46] Seeking to stem fallout from the festival, the attorney general's office announced the launching of an investigation into the legality of the concert and a search for those "responsible."[47]

Indeed, the issue of responsibility dominated much of the sensationalist reportage of the festival. Under a series of color photographs displaying scenes from Avándaro, the news magazine *Siempre* headed one article: "Government, Church, Parents: We're All Responsible for This!"[48] One letter to the editor accused the government of "spoiling [youth] instead of giving them a good smack,"[49] which reflected the assumption that such an event could only have occurred with the PRI's blessing. There was truth to this, since Carlos Hank González, governor of the state of Mexico, had in fact signed the necessary permits for the festival; he later took much of the heat for its scandalous impact.[50] "The authorities of the state of Mexico have been very benevolent and farsighted," commented Alfonso López Negrete, a coorganizer. "They've given us everything: press permits and ample cooperation on the part of the army, as well as from those inside the government who are in charge of maintaining order."[51] Luis de Llano Jr., of Telesistema, who was in charge of filming the festival, attempted to deflect criticism of the media's role by pointing out that the Department of Tourism had helped promote the event (indirectly, one should add) by printing "a large number of wonderfully illustrated pamphlets . . . inviting people to visit Avándaro," which continues to be known as a mountain resort for the elite.[52] The complicity of certain government officials, if not at the national level then certainly at a local one, was clear. But did this in fact indicate a sanctioning of the festival by the Echeverría regime for political reasons of its own? Or did it simply reflect the opportunism of local officials influenced by likely profits from the festival?

There was good reason to suspect that Echeverría knew in advance about the festival and had permitted it to go forward. Only with permission from high up, most observers reasoned, could an event of such magnitude have taken place. With the memory of 1968 and the more recent attack of 10 June on the minds of all youth, many in fact feared the possibility of a government setup at Avándaro. As one participant recalled, "In planning to go to the festival, I was quite dubious and suspicious. Many were saying that once we arrived there the army was going to be waiting for us, and sure enough they were waiting, though not to repress us but supposedly to guarantee order."[53] The army's pacific stance throughout the festival—for example, refusing to make arrests for drugs (many later attested that the army itself was actively distributing marijuana)[54]—signaled that orders had been given to desist from provocations. This foresight was also reflected in the guidelines of the official pamphlet distributed by organizers: "The presence of the military forces and police is to ensure that a specialized body exists that is available to assist in giving help to those who require it. . . . Those in uniform should be identified as one who gives his help as if he were a brother."[55] Furthermore, when it became evident that many of those in attendance were stranded for lack of return transportation, President Echeverría ordered 300 school buses sent. This announcement produced both cheers and chiflidos from the crowd; at any rate, it seems that only a smaller number actually arrived. But combined with the bizarre omnipresence of armed soldiers refusing to intervene, these actions seemed to confirm the belief by many that the central government had indeed authorized the festival as a way to monitor, if not explicitly coopt, the youth counterculture.[56]

THE LEFTIST CRITIQUE

While the press and conservatives expressed outrage against the "satanic festival"[57] and the denigration of buenas costumbres by the counterculture generally, voices from the left also used Avándaro as a pretext for condemning the rock movement. Conservatives and leftists coincided in their identification of the mass media as the leading culprit in the corruption of youth. One writer for *Jueves de Excélsior,* for instance, argued: "We know that the mass media invent false idols which are fed to youth at their expense."[58] An emergent polemic, moreover, viewed rock as imperialist not only because it originated in the metropolises but also because many intellectuals regarded rock music as antithetical to political organizing. Thus a recently released leader of the student movement denounced Avándaro as amounting to a government plot to anesthetize youth: "As long as we lose ourselves in this kind of gathering, the most reactionary forces, the government, will be happy. They promote and make [such gatherings] possible, looking to drown out the just and valid voices of rebellion and dissatisfaction among youth, hoping that with a few pesos spent on drugs, the repression of 1968, the massacre of Tlatelolco, the assassins of last June 10th, in sum all of the injustices committed against the people, will be erased."[59] As Carlos Monsiváis later summed it up: "The left [saw] in Avándaro a plot to depoliticize youth, a licentious step against the memory of June 10th. The right was terrorized by the violation of Hispanic tradition."[60] One could not imagine a clearer manifestation of cultural imperialism than the phenomenon of Mexican rock groups modeling themselves after their foreign counterparts and performing in English. "At Avándaro," concludes a commemorative book of photographs and text, "one saw between green smoke [an apparent reference to marijuana] a small but synthetic image of Mexican society in its absolute state of dependency."[61]

To be sure, this position was not unanimous. The writer José Emilio Pacheco, for example, argued in an editorial in *Excélsior* that "Woodstock-tlán"—as he called the festival—allowed youth to express themselves freely, to be "liberated from tensions that are becoming more unbearable every day." "After Tlatelolco," he wrote, "every party became a funeral. Having fun has ceased to be spontaneous, [and has] unconsciously become an object of determination." Avándaro had offered youth "not only the possibility to hear music and avoid being beaten up by halcones and porras but also an opportunity to be in the open country . . . knowing that for two days straight, el relajo [going wild] was an order and obligation" for all present.[62] The well-known television news reporter Jacobo Zabludovsky accurately argued in the introduction to *Nosotros* that Avándaro must be understood within the unfolding logic of repression in Mexico: "One cannot understand Avándaro without [considering the massacre of] 1968, without [considering the paramilitarist attack of] June 10th [1971]. One cannot understand the youth of 1971 without [recognizing] the passion of those three years and without [understanding] the experience we [*sic*] have gained." [63] The radical priest Enrique Marroquín, who was outspoken in his defense of La Onda, perhaps best articulated a nonimperialist interpretation of Avándaro: "One criticizes precisely those of us who are trying to reconquer a genuine experience of our identity [raza], sure that 'rock will speak for our people.' We want to find our music, make it an expression of what we carry inside of ourselves; make it truly 'folklore,' this understood in its original form and not simply as an attraction for tourists. In this sense, the rock at Avándaro was a rebirth of our raza." [64] At a conference organized shortly afterward titled "Who Was at Avándaro?" held in the Israeli-Mexican Cultural Institute, the writer and critic Ricardo Garibay concluded:

> Youth, those who were at Avándaro and those who weren't, are living Avándaro as if Avándaro were still occurring or had just ended. They are living it as something they themselves created without knowing with exact science how or why, or what for. They live it still—for how long will they live it?—as if something had stayed within a parenthesis, like a product of the atrocities that stayed between parenthesis, like the measure of a society without a foundation, without firm ground, from which they feel detached, apart, enemies, a society that doesn't consider them, and that they don't want to consider. Yes, they are like foreigners in their own nation, in their own land. [65]

Thus for most intellectuals, Avándaro quickly came to symbolize a vision of youth cut adrift from the system, or worse yet: colonized "foreigners in their own land," a phrase suggested by Carlos Monsiváis (writing from abroad) in an editorial to *Excélsior* in the days after the festival. [66] Monsiváis was, in fact, one of the few intellectuals who changed his position on Avándaro. Having initially described the festival as "one of the great moments of mental colonialism," he shortly afterward characterized the event as a "powerful, vital affirmation" of civilian participation. At the same time, however, he argued that Avándaro "signifies fundamentally a confused and inarticulate rejection of a concept of Mexico" which the PRI "confiscated, codified and incarnates." [67]

Yet for its participants, the native rock movement held out the hope of a rebirth at the symbolic as well as organizational level: a rejuvenation of symbols, language, and meaning, and a reorganization of class relations within society. As the liner notes from a Three Souls in My Mind album read, "For those who dig what's 'really happening' in rock, Three Souls in My Mind has much to offer. Their music is acid, heavy, aggressive. To listen to it live is to feel oneself transported into another cosmic dimension. . . . They've said it before in another way: 'Rock isn't about peace and love; rock is about revolution.' Because rock is about rebirth."[68] Mexican rock directly challenged the state's capacity to monopolize cultural meaning and national identity. The rebirth referred to by Three Souls in My Mind was precisely a rebirth of youth consciousness in the demoralized and repressive context following the Tlatelolco massacre. Avándaro, for all of its shortcomings as a musical festival (which were many), had stood for something positive and reaffirming: the triumph of youth's participation on its own terms. This suggested a fundamental subversion of a hegemonic discourse that emphasized unity under a Revolutionary patriarchy.

Nonetheless, it was extremely difficult for the left to resist drawing a relationship between rock and imperialism. La Onda Chicana seemed to reflect the culmination of economic and cultural policies that subjected Mexico to U.S. domination. As an editorial in *Excélsior* entitled "Cultural Colonialism" read, "[I]f it is quite sad that a nation's soul is carried off—which amounts to a cultural conquest—it is sadder still, indeed shameful and abominable, that such a nation, of itself and for itself, gives up willingly, indeed joyously sells and turns over its soul. . . . Honestly, how far have we fallen into a colonialist situation, where we are but an appendage to a foreign culture?"[69] Or, as Luis Cervantes Cabeza de Vaca, a former student leader, proclaimed, "Imperialism is to be congratulated, for now it exports not only technology, industrial inflation, and our finished primary goods but also its breakdown, its own crises of a decadent consumer society."[70] The combination of rage against the previous political regime of Díaz Ordaz, along with the success of anti-imperialist movements in many parts of the world—especially Cuba and Chile—energized the search for a meaningful discourse among Mexican intellectuals. "Cultural imperialism" and "economic dependency" emerged as polemical terms in developing a critique of society and of international relations more broadly speaking. Moreover, this critique served as a means of legitimizing the very role the intellectual continued to play in Mexican political life. Thus in one extreme manifestation, a writer for the leftist magazine *¿Por qué?* (which was later shut down by the government for its support of leftist guerrillas), described Avándaro as "a plan put into place by U.S. imperialism in a clearly evil alliance with the national oligarchy."[71] At the same time, the Echeverría regime directly embraced this critique as a strategy for co-opting it. "Without doubt," writes José Agustín, "Echeverría understood that in the new post-68 context the artistic, philosophical, and academic intelligentsia would suit his government very well, and he cultivated it."[72] Indeed, backlash against the rock counterculture served a crucial role in Echeverría's efforts to reclaim the state's symbolic role as cultural arbiter and defender of national borders.

The backlash catalyzed by the Avándaro music festival generated an intense debate in Mexico over what it meant to be "Mexican" in an age of increasingly transnationalized—"Americanized"—media representations. President Echeverría encouraged this polemic as central to a strategy of renewed nationalism and thus his regime's efforts to repossess control of a public discourse of national identity. A 1972 cover from the magazine *Jueves de Excélsior* captured this nationalist spirit. It showed a Mexican charro purchasing a Mexican flag from a vendor whose display included the swastika (symbolizing attacks by right-wing groups on his policies), the communist hammer and sickle (symbolizing attacks by left-wing groups), and a peace sign (symbolizing the cynicism toward all politics by the counterculture). The text reads: "I'm only interested in my own."[73]

THE CRACKDOWN

Whether Echeverría in fact authorized Avándaro or not, in the aftermath of the festival the state turned its administrative and repressive forces against the native rock movement at the levels of production, distribution, and consumption. While leftist critics had suggested the regime's cynical use of rock as a means for placating youth, Avándaro had revealed the political dangers of rock as well. From the regime's perspective, the sheer numbers that rock managed to organize must have made a deep impression; nobody had predicted the turnout at Avándaro. The possibility that the festival would turn into a political rally—whatever that might have looked like—were, for the most part, contained by the organizers' precautions. Yet rock music, at least in its live performance, clearly presented a situation for government forces where order could not be guaranteed. Rock "organized" people—or at least presented the opportunity for organizing—and proved it could do so, however tenuously, across class lines.

But the government's fear of rock as an organizing tool—rock's demonstrated capacity to bring together large groups of people from diverse social backgrounds—was only part of the story explaining the repression that soon followed. For a fuller understanding, we would also have to consider the ideological component: rock was no longer simply a metaphor of modernity but had become a metaphor for community as well. Rock music, especially native rock music, suggested the possibility of reorganizing national consciousness among youth in such a way that the state was not only mocked but left out of the picture altogether.

The production and distribution of La Onda Chicana were immediately targeted by the regime. In effect, any song or image related to Avándaro was prohibited by the government. According to Herbe Pompeyo, a government memorandum was circulated to all radio stations in the capital "saying, or rather *suggesting*, that they don't make any reference to Avándaro, or play anything to do with Mexican rock."[74] This was reflected, for example, in the prohibition of a ballad entitled "Avándaro," recorded in anticipation of the festival's outcome. By direct order of the secretary of interior affairs, the song—which deals with the themes of community central to La Onda—was removed from radio stations, in spite of its popularity:[75]

> We hardly know each other
> But we feel the same way.
> That's why we continue ahead
> As brothers hoping for the best
> To Avándaro, heavy place [*lugar de onda*].
>
> With music in our minds
> Our hearts beating together
> And filled with joy
> All we groovy people go
> To Avándaro, heavy place. . . .
>
> Rich kids [*la gente fresa*] join the crowd
> Searching for freedom in their words
> And breathing in deeply.
> Loving the clouds and hating war
> They're going to Avándaro, heavy place.[76]

Meanwhile, at Radio Juventud the live transmission of the festival had resulted in a fine and the temporary imprisonment of the "responsible" disc jockeys. Certainly this in itself could have been expected; laws against abuse of foul language in the United States resulted in similar fines. But castigating the radio announcers, who after all were not directly responsible for someone else's bad language, was only part of the story. In addition, "the hip lexicon pioneered" at the station was declared "definitively over." In the future, disc jockeys would have to "express themselves correctly" or face revocation of their license.[77] This change conformed to another government memorandum that required self-censorship, thus avoiding "the corruption of language, proper customs, traditions, and national characteristics," as required by federal law.[78] Finally, the six hours of material filmed by Telesistema would never reach the public, though at least two different underground films made by participants would later materialize.[79] At any rate, intentions to produce a live sound track of the festival were severely marred by the dismal technical quality of the material itself.[80]

The pressures against La Onda Chicana's production and distribution came precisely at the moment of an intensified marketing strategy by the transnationals. As Rafael González, an artistic director with Polydor at the time, explained to the rock magazine *POP*:

> Look, the idea is the following: We've come to realize that a large amount of money leaves the country as royalties, author's rights, and other stuff. . . . My idea is to try to leave something for Mexico by starting a musical revolution [here]. . . . [I]t's not exactly that we're being nationalistic but that we're trying to understand and support what is ours. Good or bad, it's ours. If we're lacking musically with respect to the level others are at, well we're going to push our [groups] to reach that level. I think what's happening in Mexico is similar to what occurred with the "English Wave."[81]

Polydor's advertising strategy in Mexico had begun to reflect this effort to elevate national rock onto an international plane. Plans, in fact, called for the creation of a separate Mexican rock catalog.[82] Indicative of this new direction was a poster-sized color advertisement included in *Piedra Rodante* featuring album covers by internationally acclaimed artists such as Jimi Hendrix, Crosby, Stills, Nash, and Young, the Rolling Stones, and both volumes from the Woodstock music festival. Partially protruding from each jacket sleeve was a "golden album," emphasizing the international impact of these selected records. Included in this presentation of "superstar" albums was La Revolución de Emiliano Zapata, as if among equals. The text of this poster advertisement succinctly summed up its content: "Esta es la onda gruesa" (This is the heavy scene).[83] In fact, there were already strong indications that all of the transnationals (not just Polydor) were moving in the direction of promoting Mexican rock outside the country, a strategy which coincided with industry reports that "heavier stress would be put on regional campaigns for specific artists rather than aiming at immediate worldwide impact."[84] Support for Mexican rock in southwestern parts of the United States would likely have been strong, where a growing population of Mexican American youth were also searching for their own cultural voice.

As a rule, the four transnational companies with subsidiary operations in Mexico benefited from a diverse musical catalog in addition to economies of scale, which allowed for greater latitude in their investment in native

Table 1. 1971 General Music Catalog for Polydor Records

	Foreign	Mexican / Latin American
Singles:		
Rock/soul	14	6
Folk	3	
Ranchera/norteño		
Balada	17	
Disco	8	
Extended Play:*		
Rock/soul	38	12
Folk	1	
Ranchera/norteño		
Balada	8	
Disco	8	
Other	1	
Long Play:**		
Rock/soul	89	9
Folk	16	
Ranchera/norteño	3	
Balada	3	
Disco	5	
Other	1	

SOURCE: *Catálogo general de discos Polydor, 1971.*

*Four songs.

**Includes composite albums of hits by various artists.

rock. However, this also meant that La Onda Chicana constituted a smaller and ultimately less important part of their overall repertory; native rock could be eliminated without serious market repercussions. This is reflected, for example, in a breakdown of Polydor's 1971 catalog (see Table 1).[85] In fact, as the government could do little to prevent the continued distribution of foreign rock (short of banning it altogether), the companies lost little by cutting loose native rock contracts. Reflecting on Polydor's decision to drop plans for the development of a national rock catalog in the wake of Aván- daro, Herbe Pompeyo commented, "[T]here was a certain amount invested [in La Onda Chicana], but fortunately Polygram [sic] wasn't living from that. It was a project for the future. We continued to live off of other things.

We never placed all of our hope exclusively in the [native rock] project."[86] For the young artistic directors at Polydor Records, enthused by the international success of "Nasty Sex" (La Revolución de Emiliano Zapata), the direct and indirect pressures that restricted further exploitation of the counterculture's commercial potential represented the shattering of a vision of developing a national and international market for Mexican rock. Yet, as Herbe Pompeyo later reflected, "No one wanted to become a martyr in a struggle with the government" over the issue of native rock.[87]

Thus despite the nominal amounts of capital already invested in La Onda Chicana, especially by the transnationals, virtually all of the companies backed off under government pressure. Acting through the guise of the radio industry's chamber of commerce, the Cámara Nacional de la Industria de la Radiodifusión, which had played a consistent game of conflict and cooperation with the state since the 1950s, a memorandum was sent to every recording company asking that it "abstain from producing music interpreted at Avándaro, at the suggestion of the authorities at the Department of Interior Affairs."[88] None of this, however, prevented the companies from seeking to make some profit off the festival. But the resulting efforts were halfhearted and produced little follow-up. For instance, Polydor, having already geared up for a compilation album featuring studio versions of songs performed at Avándaro by its contracted artists, went ahead to produce *Vibraciones del 11 de septiembre*. Similarly, Orfeón produced a studio compilation album of its own entitled *Rock en Avándaro*, which used a photomontage of the event for its cover—but only one of the bands featured had performed at Avándaro. No live sound track of the festival has ever appeared.

Another casualty of the crackdown was the countercultural magazine *Piedra Rodante*. Combining often-daring articles on drugs, politics, and the counterculture in Mexico and abroad with translated material from its parent magazine in the United States, *Piedra Rodante* quickly proved too much for a regime that sought to recontain the rock movement; after eight issues, the magazine was forced to shut down. Claiming a distribution of 50,000, the magazine not only aimed at a national audience but reached Central and South America, Spain, and the "Chicano youth of North America"— indicated as including the borderlands, New York, and Chicago—as well. As editor Manuel Aceves recognized, the survival of such an effort in Mexico "requires an atmosphere of liberty, both in an objective sense and at the level of consciousness," which he believed the apertura democrática under Echeverría would provide. "We sincerely hope we aren't mistaken about this *sexenio* [six-year presidential term]," he wrote in an opening editorial.[89] During the eight issues of its existence, *Piedra Rodante* consistently tested the boundaries of the political opening offered by the new regime. An advertisement in its last issue provocatively queried, "How much freedom of the press exists in Mexico?" To fill this gap, the magazine offered "Youth's viewpoint about their own world versus that of adults. Without inhibition, shame, sweat, or reserve, the sole truth about drugs, politics, sex, rock, art . . . a new type of journalism. Enlightened journalism. And enlightening. . . . The first long-haired news-journal."[90] But its bold testing of political and cultural tolerance—one issue boasted "40 pages replete with drugs, sex, pornography, and strong emotions"[91]—proved too much, especially in the context of an antipornography moralizing crusade spearheaded by conservatives.[92] While called to the attention of the ineffectual Qualifying Commission of Magazines and Illustrated Publications (the government censorship bureau for printed matter) in a letter by a member of Congress, the magazine nonetheless met a quicker fate than what would have been the arduous process of bringing the publisher to court under the rules of the commission: facing threats of physical harm, the editor simply ceased publication.[93]

At the same time that rock's commercialization was halted, live performances were also prohibited. Without concerts, there was little basis for sustaining a native rock movement. A scheduled concert at the National Auditorium featuring "original music" by seven Mexican bands and "lights, fog [that is, dry ice], slide projections, gifts, records, and posters" was forced to cancel.[94] The tocadas organized in the hoyos fonquis of lower-class barrios were especially targeted for police repression. As Joaquín López of La Revolución de Emiliano Zapata recalls the context of the hoyos fonquis around the time of Avándaro: "Well, the bands were popular and began to experiment with these large crowds; people began to call things into question. Potentially, a political hue and cry was in the making. . . . And I believe that exactly at that moment was when [government] repression began to shut down the hoyos fonquis, you see?"[95] Attempts to eliminate rock music in the barrios often led to direct confrontations with the authorities. As Ramón García recounts, "Once the press began to slam Avándaro, there was a total venting of anger directed toward the tocadas. There weren't even tocadas, because the granaderos would arrive and begin to beat up the musicians, carry them and their equipment off, and rough them up some more. And the truth is, people [in the audience] got out of hand . . . and would take on the police, who just stirred them up more."[96] Determined to resist the government crackdown, a "Rock on Wheels" effort was organized in the barrios. Mobile pickup trucks loaded with musicians cruised the streets looking for available spots to set up their equipment and perform in a flash, only to vanish when word of the police reached them. According to Ramón García:

> [T]he response was so tremendous. We all knew these bands and whatever colonia it happened to be, people would come out and gather around. It didn't matter what the time was—morning, afternoon, or night—people came out and joined in. It was really a neat thing. We felt good, and so did the bands. If only a part of the band was playing, the others would pass around a collection hat to help out. It was really a cool thing. . . . But it didn't last all that long. The authorities quickly figured out what was going on and where the [performances] were taking place. And so it was, like, hear a little bit of music and then everyone took off.[97]

The rock critic Víctor Roura would later argue that "everything was shut down simultaneously"[98] after Avándaro. While largely true, to a certain degree this was also an exaggeration that has since lent itself to the myth of rock's total extinction after Avándaro. Though official sanctioning of live performances was out, not all official channels for rock gatherings were eliminated. For instance, in a possible indication of the regime's continued flirtation with rock as a means of reaching out to youth, the Museum of Anthropology in the summer of 1972 offered a presentation of the rock concert film *Monterey Pop Festival*. The screening, shown outdoors on the third night because of crowding, turned into "a mini-Avándaro [with] the three or four thousand kids who showed up behaving totally cool, without causing problems, just enjoying the music and the visual attractions."[99]

As Roura and others have pointed out, live rock went underground, but it by no means disappeared. In spite of the repression, this period gave rise to the reputation of the *hoyos fonquis* as the last bastions of live performance. Roura states that in 1973 "one could easily count some 150 rock groups who played in the capital of Mexico in different urban areas." In contrast to several years earlier, however, only a fraction of these ever made it into a recording studio.[100] Nonetheless, evidence of one such performance suggests the continued vitality of native rock and its significance as an integral element in the popular culture of the lower classes. In June 1972 a twenty-four-hour "festival without permits of rock outdoors" took place in the dry lake of Texcoco, on the margins of the capital district. A letter to the rock magazine *México Canta* responded to the festival with an enthusiasm clearly carried over from Avándaro: "Chicano rock's going forward, right on, with music in Spanish, totally alive. At Lake Texcoco there was rock, rock, and more rock." [101] Moreover, and by means of comparison, in March 1975 another three-day concert took place at the Valle de Bravo, Avándaro site. This time, however, it was on the grounds of an elite sports club. Authorities had granted permission based on satisfaction of three restrictions: (1) that it be limited to the local population; (2) that it not turn into a rock festival; and (3) that no interview be given to the press prior to the event. [102] Clearly, live rock for the masses had become sporadic, underground, and often dangerous in its confrontations with the state.

THE QUESTION OF POPULARITY

One of the most lasting issues concerning the collapse of La Onda Chicana centers on the question of its popularity with a mass audience. After all, if the majority of music was written and performed in English, perhaps it was only natural that its defenders quickly shrank away under the threat of government sanctions. Why defend a product that had only superficial mass support? Víctor Roura, for instance, argues that La Onda Chicana was largely inaccessible because English was the dominant mode of expression, and, in any event, the lyrics generally (but not always) failed to make a connection with everyday concerns. "Rock, therefore, was alien to the feelings of urban youth," he writes, "not so much for its rhythm, but for its inability to communicate." [103] This might make sense, except how then does one explain the popularity of foreign rock to begin with? Indeed, a more common argument for La Onda Chicana's disappearance made at the time (and since then) has been that the music itself was simply not very good. As Iván Zatz-Díaz recalls from a concert by the famed La Revolución de Emiliano Zapata, "I remember thinking actually that they were pretty awful! [laughs] . . . There was nothing special about what they did. Nothing interesting. Nothing particularly good about it. . . . I remember, even by virtue of their name, they were kind of a controversial group. . . . In my opinion, they were pretty anodyne. Their music didn't stand for anything, really." [104]

This was not too far off from a reviewer's opinion of a concert by the same band for a middle-class Mexico City audience in 1971: "By the fifth song one gets the urge to simply leave, for its evident that the concert isn't going anywhere, that it's a disaster, an absolute failure and the group is a fraud. . . . What I don't understand is, why does the audience applaud? Could it be out of inertia, or worse still, out of ignorance? Do they really enjoy this music? This must mean that they've never heard really good rock." [105] And yet, as the former bassist with La Revolución de Emiliano Zapata himself relates somewhat incredulously, the group's hit song "Nasty Sex" was indeed popular: "Playing 'Nasty Sex,' one felt the power of Nasty Sex! [laughs] When you played that piece, the whole atmosphere changed . . . It was a 'hit,' a strange hit. . . . Not a de jure hit, invented by the record company, but a real hit . . . that was popular all over the country. . . . You sensed it. When you played it, you felt the reaction of the audience." [106] Still, in an indication of the bitterness experienced by many band members over the failure of La Onda Chicana to consolidate itself, the former bassist with Love Army would comment in 1974: "The influence of the United States and Britain allows for little originality. Plus, there's a total lack of organization. All of this is based on the fact that we're an underdeveloped country. We lack musical maturity. I haven't encountered anything original. Everything is a poorly made replica of what is produced in other countries." [107] This echoing of the harshest critics of La Onda Chicana reflected the frustrations experienced after Avándaro, but at the same time it may suggest an overly narrow perception of the movement's acceptance on a national scale. If bands' musical creativity was itself inchoate, popular support for what the music stood for most definitely was not.

LATIN AMERICAN PROTEST SONGS

The polemic against rock music was not limited to Mexico but was becoming widely expressed throughout Latin America. Rock was regarded by many on the left as the direct manifestation of an imperialist strategy to depoliticize youth while fortifying transnational capitalist interests. This leftist critique emerged in the context of the nueva canción movement and a renaissance of folk and protest music generally. While its intellectual and artistic origins were rooted in the cultural politics of earlier periods, the New Song movement was semiofficially launched at a 1967 conference held in Havana, Cuba, titled "Encuentro de la Canción Protesta" (Gathering of Protest Song). Reflecting a category of music attuned to the revolutionary and social protest movements that were occurring throughout the continent, New Song—referred to as *nueva trova* in Cuba, but also *canción política* (political song), *canción popular* (popular song), *canción comprometida* (committed song), and other such terms elsewhere—incorporated musicians from across Latin America. Especially prominent were Pablo Milanés, Silvio Rodríguez, and Noel Nicola (Cuba), Víctor Jara, Violeta Parra, and the group Inti Illimani (Chile), Mercedes Sosa and Atahualpa Yupanqui (Argentina), Daniel Viglietti (Uruguay), and Amparo Ochoa and Los Folkloristas (Mexico). [108] This "countersong," as one author dubbed

it,[109] variously used or combined traditional musical repertoires from Latin America to back lyrics that explored political, philosophical, and sentimental themes. It was an eclectic genre of music whose songs "questioned
North American imperialism, economic exploitation, social inequality,
and cultural alienation, along with themes that proclaimed a free and just
future."[110] Pan-American solidarity—not with, but against the United
States—was implied, if not overtly stated, in many of these songs.

As nueva canción gained ascendancy, commercialized popular music,
especially rock, was increasingly slandered for its associations with imperialism.[111] This was ironic, because rock (especially the Beatles) had influenced some New Song musicians, such as Silvio Rodríguez. Nonetheless,
in the context of the politically charged early 1970s, when various regimes
throughout Latin America were openly hostile toward the United States
and faced attacks from right- and left-wing elements, mass culture was
readily conflated with imperialist designs and influence.[112] The critique of
rock in part focused on the links between electronic music and economic
and technological dependencies, ideas expressed, for example, in a round-
table discussion of music, nationalism and imperialism organized in Cuba
in early 1973. As one participant commented, "I'm not against electronic
music, but one has to be conscious of the technological element that creates
dependency. . . . In this sense, one has to stimulate a genuinely Latin American culture with the elements at our disposal. It's necessary to be conscious
that a culture weak in its creation, imprecise in terms of its authenticity, is
always an easy prisoner for whatever type of imperialist penetration."[113]
The various manifestations of "imperialist penetration" were suggested by
an earlier conference also held in Cuba. In the "Final Declaration of the
Meeting of Latin American Music," musical traditions were likened to raw
materials that must be protected from relationships of dependency with the
metropolises: "As with other deeply rooted popular and nationalist expressions, but with particular emphasis on music for its importance as a link between us, the colonialist cultural penetration seeks to achieve not only the
destruction of our own values and the imposition of those from without
but also the extraction and distortion of the former in order to return them,
[now] reprocessed and value-added, for the service of this penetration."[114]

A clear example of this process of "value-added" marketing, which at
the same time pointed to the complicated processes of transnationalism,
was the impact of Simon and Garfunkel's song "El Condor Pasa." The song,
credited as an "arrangement of [an] 18th c. Peruvian folk melody" was popularized by the folk-rock duo through their highly successful album *Bridge
over Troubled Water* (1970). (Re)exported to Latin America at the start of

the revival in folk-protest music, Simon and Garfunkel were, ironically, responsible at one level for the commercial success of Mexico's own resurgence in folk music. As Luz Lozano reflected, "I've thought for a long time, 'How did that folkloric thing get started?' And I would say that it was with that song ['El Condor Pasa']. Or at least, it contributed a lot. It was the image that we had of [Simon and Garfunkel]. It was more than just them, like a triangulation: them, the Andes, and here, us. . . . I didn't know the song before [they recorded it]. I think that after that, the [movement] started to emerge here."[115] In Mexico (as in Cuba, Chile, and Peru) the political regime directly and indirectly supported the New Song movement and a shift toward folkloric cultural expression generally. Institutionalized performance spaces that once restricted rock, or were off limits altogether (such as the Palacio de Bellas Artes), now welcomed national and foreign New Song and folk artists. In one example, the Venezuelan-born singer, Soledad Bravo, whose work was described by *Excélsior* as an "impassioned [reflection] of themes rooted in Latin American folklore," was invited to perform at the Poliforum Siqueiros in Mexico City, a recently opened fine arts space named for the once-imprisoned, communist muralist Alfaro Siqueiros.[116] At the same time, the early 1970s witnessed a proliferation of music cafés called *peñas*, which offered a space for live folk-music performance. Unlike the cafés cantantes of the mid-1960s or the later hoyos fonquis, the peñas did not face the threat of arbitrary closure. On the contrary, the Echeverría regime went out of its way to express its support for this shift toward Latin American folk and protest song. As Federico Arana explains, "there was a clear and convenient symbiosis" between the folk-protest singers and the regime. "The proof that [the performers] weren't dangerous for the government is that they were never censured and never lost the government's support" (see Figure 17).[117]

The most ideologically articulate of the Mexican performers popularized during this period was the group Los Folkloristas, who recorded on the Discos Pueblo label, which became an extension of the group itself. The chosen name of the recording label reflected its broader mission: "[To] [g]ive diffusion to folkloric music and all the new forms of Latin American song, in their most genuine representations, exempt of all concession to the dominant commercialism. . . . [To] [o]ppose the mounting imperialist cultural penetration [with] the voice of our peoples, as a necessity for identification and affirmation."[118] While Los Folkloristas had been in existence since 1966, not until the context of the early 1970s did they gain widespread recognition. To this the state lent a direct hand by donating space previously occupied by the National Symphony for the founding of Discos

Figure 17.   With official sanctioning, folkloric groups such as this one popularized the indigenous sounds of the Andes and other regions in the early 1970s. Source: Federico Arana, *Roqueros y folcloroides* (Mexico City: Joaquín Mortiz, 1988), 48. (Photograph by Olga Durón; reproduced courtesy of Federico Arana)

Pueblo and an indirect one by making concert halls such as the Palacio de Bellas Artes available for performances.[119] Moreover, when a scheduled concert at the National Auditorium was canceled at the last minute by capital-district authorities, President Echeverría intervened personally, stating: "It's very important to me that those young people perform." Echeverría then proposed an additional concert by the group in celebration of Teachers' Day (15 May), an event that was carried live by Telesistema.[120]

As one informant suggested, "One can see how things coincided: El Condor Pasa, the peñas, Los Folkloristas. I mean, they're a group that has been around for a long time. They had plenty of gigs, but they weren't popular. It took the impact of something foreign for them to become accepted."[121] While her statement perhaps overly credits the foreign impact of Simon and Garfunkel, the commercial success of "El Condor Pasa" was not overlooked by the group itself. Before each performance of the song Los Folkloristas "would give this veiled indictment of the commercial forces that had prostituted that wonderful music—meaning, the Simon and Garfunkel thing."[122] Iván Zatz-Díaz, a fan of the folk and New Song movement, recounted: "This sound engineer [my neighbor] . . . his contention was, 'Say what you will, but these guys [Simon and Garfunkel] have made South American music a thousand times more popular than Los Folkloristas ever could. So what's so wrong with that? It's a wonderful version.' And so on and so forth. And I kind of agreed with it, to a certain degree. I still like the Simon and Garfunkel version of 'El Condor Pasa' very much."[123] The radical ideological stance taken by Los Folkloristas was directly extended in their opposition to rock music: "[We are] [p]ledged to spread the best music of our continent, [we are] dedicated to the youth of our country who have discovered their own music [*canción*], [we are] opposing it to the colonizing assault and alienation of Rock and commercial music,"[124] the group announced in a statement.

A confrontation in Peru in late 1971 neatly illustrated this process of rock's politicization and demonstrates perhaps a broader generalization of the Mexican phenomenon. At the time, Peru was in the grips of a nationalist, military-led government that had come to power in a coup in 1968 aimed at preempting guerrilla victory by implementing a radical, leftist policy agenda. Carlos Santana was scheduled to perform eight benefit concerts in Lima for victims of a 1970 earthquake. The rock group was met by 3,000 fans and an official greeting by the mayor of Lima, who "gave [the band] a scroll welcoming them to the city." However, the powerful student union at San Marcos University, where the concerts were to take place at an 80,000-seat soccer stadium, protested that the scheduled event was "an imperialist invasion." Two days before the opening performance, the stadium stage mysteriously burned to the ground. With that warning, the Ministry of the Interior canceled the tour altogether. The band had their luggage and instruments confiscated, and they were promptly ejected from the country, accused of "acting contrary to good taste and the moralizing objectives of the revolutionary government."[125] By comparison, the folk-protest song movement was openly backed by the Peruvian military regime, which actively sponsored performances and media diffusion for national and foreign artists through its National Institute of Culture.[126]

The ramifications of the surge in folk-protest song and the Mexican regime's support for this movement were not the total elimination of rock but rather the further class and cultural bifurcation of rock's reproduction and reception. Native rock, as we saw above, survived by going underground. As Simon Frith might claim, it returned to its working-class roots, where it was sustained into the 1980s.[127] Foreign rock, on the other hand, though dashed by the impact of disco, was reinscribed as vanguard culture among the middle and upper classes, who continued to purchase albums and stay attuned to transformations in the rock-music world. At the same time, Latin American folk music and nueva canción also found a wide reception among middle-class youth, especially among students.[128] As Luz Lozano explained, "[The music] said things more clearly. You knew more of the lyrics from the songs. You knew more about the situation of peasants, workers, and so you liked it more. But that didn't mean you stopped liking the other [rock]. But you related more to the social thing. Besides, it was the fad."[129] What was problematic about folk-protest music in part, however, was that it shifted the attention of protest away from the government and toward the more abstract (at times, less abstract) notion of imperialism generally. Furthermore, it reinforced a concept of cultural authenticity that played directly into populist rhetoric, even while serving to disseminate traditional folk music to a broader audience. Finally, live performances re-inscribed the boundaries of respect and discipline between audience and performer that rock worked to undermine. "Even when they're helped out with their elaborate sound equipment," writes Federico Arana, "the folk performers demand silence and composure from their audience. For rockers, in contrast, the more intense the audience participation, the better."[130]

The polemic against cultural imperialism also served the Mexican regime in its efforts to derail the incipient class-based alliance that native rock had sought actively to forge. Among the middle and upper classes both nueva canción and foreign rock encountered a wide reception at the expense of native rock, música tropical, and Mexican baladistas, all of which became to a significant degree associated with the lumpen, naco classes. As Iván Zatz-Díaz recalled the cultural polemic that developed:

> There were always [student] factions who would reject one form of music or another. For the bulk of us there was a lesser or greater degree of eclecticism, but it was there nonetheless. We did listen to rock, we did listen to folk music. . . . The only music that I poo-pooed, and most of us poo-pooed, were say the cumbias and the boleros. That kind of stuff was the music of the nacos. And God forbid we would be listening to naco music, you know. I guess it also became kind of a 'naco' thing to do to listen to Radio Mil [which played refritos]. So we stopped listening to the Spanish version. We would only listen to the original versions on Radio Exitos or La Pantera. That was really much more of a clash, if you will, than whether you were listening to the music of imperialism or not. Because that was still an open question. Was John Lennon a revolutionary force, or an imperialist force?[131]

Jaime Pontones, later an important rock disc jockey in Mexico City, spoke of "studying Marxism like crazy and listening to rock, not exactly in secret but in my home, because all of my friends didn't listen to rock anymore;

they [only] listened to Latin American music." [132] In an interesting twist, rock in Spanish (that is, refritos) had become inverted from its former status as "high culture" during the early 1960s to become "low culture," or naco, by the 1970s.

But for all of folk and protest music's pretensions of working-class solidarity and peasant struggle in the triumph over the bourgeoisie and imperialism, the music was simply not that popular among lower-class urban youth. This was true even in the case of Chile, a central player in the birth of the New Song movement. One study, for example, concluded that the music was most popular among students, professionals, and state employees; whereas housewives, workers, and the unemployed demonstrated the lowest disposition toward its consumption. [133] In Mexico, student organizers came to discover that folk protest music was not sufficient for attracting large audiences at rallies. As José Enrique Pérez Cruz recalled of student-organized protests during the 1970s: "Sometimes at the rallies, as there wasn't always a heavy draw with protest music, they also invited rock bands. And for those rallies a lot of people definitely came." [134] Indeed, this reflected a deeper class antagonism that the native rock movement had sought to transcend. Ramón García spelled out the impact the New Song movement had on those from the lower classes: "[T]hat was what the students listened to." He continued:

> They listened to that type of music, and so that's where the separation [in the movement] occurred. Because a lot of students also were part of the rock movement, but because rock made them feel special. Maybe it was what they needed, that is, freedom. But they weren't so oppressed. But then when all that protest music came, then the rockers, we stayed on one side, and those who listened to protest music were another class of people. But for the rockers, none of that mattered. Because really, the rhythm didn't interest us very much. [135]

By linking native rock to cultural imperialism, Echeverría hoped to coopt the middle-class, student element of the counterculture, promoting the folk-protest song movement as a Latin American "equivalent." In this way, Echeverría literally tried to *nationalize* La Onda by identifying cultural and social protest with a romanticized, unifying, anti-imperialist discourse. In this he seems to have been at least partially successful. This strategy undermined the mounting interclass alliance that was forming around La Onda Chicana, while marginalizing Mexican rock by driving it into the hoyos fonquis. Ironically, however, the quashing of La Onda Chicana in the name of combating cultural imperialism opened the way for foreign rock to establish itself as a dominant pop idiom. Thus by 1975 nueva canción, folk-

Table 2. 1975 General Music Catalog for CBS Records

	Foreign	*Mexico / Latin America*
Music (cassettes and LPs):		
Rock/soul*	109	1†
Rock 'n' roll**	1	2
Ranchero/balada	1	
Folk	4	
Nueva canción	5	1
Salsa	1	
Jazz	18	
Disco	3	

SOURCE: *Catálogo general de discos CBS,* 1975. (Reviewed with the permission of Sony Records, Mexico)

*Includes Bob Dylan; Simon and Garfunkel.

**Includes Spanish-language refritos.

†45 rpm.

protest, and foreign rock music all coexisted in commodified form, but the commercialization of native rock had virtually disappeared (see Table 2).

In retrospect, it appears that La Onda Chicana was destined to disappear, despite the moderate levels of support by the mass media and fans. Echeverría may have been willing to allow for a greater degree of expression under the terms of his apertura democrática, and perhaps he even viewed the channeling of youth energies toward the counterculture with optimism. But the backlash itself was inevitable. This was true for several reasons. For one thing, middle-class values were still overwhelmingly conservative, especially in the provinces and rural areas. The image of youth openly flaunting buenas costumbres was an affront to parental authority that struck at the heart of the patriarchal family. Second, intellectuals on the left also viewed the counterculture with alarm. While less concerned with the undermining of family values per se, they understood La Onda Chicana as the epitome of cultural imperialism. In a sense, it would have been difficult for them to see otherwise. Given the context of the times, "dropping out" of society suggested the clear imprint of U.S. influence. Finally, the folk-protest revival that was sweeping Latin America overwhelmed the appeal of native rock as vanguard culture, at least among the middle classes. Mexican rock had simply not yet achieved a high enough level of musical respect to assure it a competitive place among popular tastes. (The arrival of disco, cumbia, and salsa music also contributed to the displacement of native rock.) Ironically, the principal supporters of La Onda Chicana seemed to be the mass media. But with the obvious political ramifications of continuing to promote Mexican rock after Avándaro, there was simply little reason for business executives to put their necks on the line. The market was not yet there. President Echeverría's strategy of repression, coupled with a discourse of cultural nationalism, was thus an ingenious means of responding to the crisis of legitimacy facing the PRI in the early 1970s. But Mexican rock had not disappeared as a wedge and mirror lodged within society. Left to ferment in the barrios, rock music would eventually rear its defiant head once more, only this time in the voice of the truly marginalized.

7 A Critique of the "Obvious Imperialist"
The USIA

The U.S. Information Agency was an obvious target for leftist criticism throughout Latin America, and the agency's relationship to music makes an analysis relevant. As a 1970 document produced by the Argentine group Anti-Imperialist Front of Cultural Workers stated: "All musical activity, whether it concerns composition, instrumentation, education, or promotion, is severely controlled by the imperialist enemy."[1] The group specifically accused the USIA of organizing events and sponsoring fellowships that influenced patterns of musical perception and production. But a broader, cultural strategy was also at stake: "The imperialist enemy has comprehended for a long time the necessity of endowing a 'form of seeing the world,' of a culture upon its colonized [peoples], which takes into account the point of view and interests of the colonizer."[2] While local and transnational recording companies served as conduits for commercialized popular music, what role did the U.S. government itself play? If La Onda Chicana came to be seen by leftists as evidence of bourgeois decadence, rote imitation, and the depoliticization of the masses, might there have been a more specific U.S. connection to the Mexican counterculture?

A BRIEF HISTORY OF THE USIA

The USIA is the historical heir to the Office of the Coordinator for Inter-American Affairs (OCIAA), which originated in 1940 as a direct response to the threat of Axis propaganda throughout Latin America. The incorporation of a cultural strategy into the foreign-policy apparatus signaled the recognition that cultural representation and discourse mattered in foreign policy. The OCIAA's tactics involved such actions as subsidizing pro-Allied newspapers and radio stations and screening Hollywood films for export. One of the most acclaimed achievements of the agency was in fact the attention given to film.[3] This strategy focused on the construction of a Pan-American discursive repertory of shared meanings and images that helped link disparate peoples into a common hemispheric alliance, a revitalization of the Western Hemisphere ideal embodied in the Monroe Doctrine. The construction of such a discourse involved the selective incorporation of regional detail into cinematic narratives highlighting local tastes and customs, while emphasizing the material and political benefits associated with U.S. protection.[4] As an integral part of the Good Neighbor Policy, the OCIAA thus sought to project a position of respect for cultural difference which at the same time naturalized political and economic dependencies on the United States that otherwise might have favored an alliance with hostile powers. Following a period of intra-agency conflict and the hostility of congressional conservatives (spearheaded by Joseph McCarthy) after World War II, the USIA evolved out of the OCIAA and officially came into being in 1953.[5]

The USIA was authorized by the U.S. government to engage in overt information gathering and disseminating activities abroad. Covert activities, while not publicly disclosed, were assumed to be a part of its program,[6] and indirect evidence in fact pointed to them. For example, during a congressional hearing on the USIA in 1963, one witness described relations between the USIA and the Central Intelligence Agency as "very close." "We have daily contacts with them at distinct levels," he responded.[7] Throughout the 1960s, the USIA dedicated millions of dollars to information-related activities that worked to achieve the short-, medium-, and long-term strategic policy objectives of the White House. According to policy guidelines established in a 1963 memorandum by President John F. Kennedy, the agency would perform a twofold function within the U.S. government: "[T]o help achieve United States foreign policy objectives by a) influencing public attitudes in other nations, and b) advising the President, his representations abroad, and the various departments and agencies on the implications of foreign opinion for present and contemplated United States policies, programs, and official statements."[8] Clarifying these objectives in terms of information policy, however, proved to be a problem that has plagued the USIA consistently throughout its history. As one author argues, "much disagreement . . . has been integral to the Agency from its controversial birth."[9] Such controversy was often directly related to the question of the agency's clarity of purpose. Was its mission to "inform" or to "convert"? Were its targeted audiences the elites or the masses? In effect, the USIA sought to accomplish all at once. But in doing so, voices in and outside Congress argued, the agency "failed to define its population and program strategy with the precision demanded by the exigencies of the Cold War." [10] By the late 1960s, one of the key arguments used by the agency in its requests for budget increases from Congress was that it specifically targeted youth, thus countering communist propaganda presumably aimed at similar audiences.

Attention to radio as an important medium by which to gauge the composition of urban youth audiences was already apparent in Mexico by the start of the 1960s. A USIA report from 1960, for example, argued for the "[p]ost's dire need for radio audience data, Mexican listening habits, classification of and popularity ratings on radio outlets located in the 20 or so major population centers of Mexico, etc." [11] While a basic objective was to discern "which stations limit themselves strictly to classical music as compared to those which play primarily mariachi," the Mexico City radio stations dedicated to an all-youth format received special mention: "Of course, there are other in-between classifications, i.e., stations of the types of Mexico City's 'Radio Mil' and 'Radio Juventud,' on which U.S. and foreign popular music predominates." [12] Similarly, the draft of a 1964 USIA report entitled "Media Usage by Latin American University Students" compared "opinions and media habits of university students" in Venezuela, Peru, Mexico, and Chile. This report found that there "are variations in the inherent advantages of print, movies, and radio" in conveying USIA messages. "Apparently," the report continued, "the United States can gain through both overt and covert information actions." The effectiveness of USIA activities in Mexico—the location for eleven different USIA installations [13] —was singled out for special praise: "The United States has been fairly effective in building up the image of credibility in Mexico," the report concluded. [14]

THE FOCUS ON YOUTH

The USIA's specific attention to rock and popular music coincided with the agency's greater attention to youth activities in general by the late 1960s. For example, in 1966 the Voice of America (VOA) inaugurated its New Sound programming format. In a report to Congress, the USIA explained that "[t]he style and format of media products must change with the times if they are to hold audiences and attract new ones." The New Sound format was "more typically American," the report explained. "V.O.A. discarded the traditional rigid format of news and commentaries followed by lengthy features, and replaced it with a more diverse and flexible mixture of news, music, and a variety of short pieces." Initiated for English-language broadcasts, the format was extended to other foreign-language areas, including the Soviet Union, Eastern Europe, and Latin America.[15] For example, a half-hour radio show called *Exitos musicales latinamericanos* was inaugurated on Latin American VOA in August 1966. The idea was that each U.S. embassy would forward to VOA's director "the top hit of the week in that nation" for inclusion on the show, thus creating a Pan-American popular-music program structured like the U.S. format of "top hits."[16] "The young particularly respond to the new tempo," the USIA report argued.[17]

This shift in attention toward youth was highlighted by an increase in the number of USIA student affairs officers (SAOs), who were "assigned to work with the important university student audience." Between 1965 and 1968, the number of SAOs increased from twenty-one to thirty-two.[18] Targeting selected "students and youth activists"[19] was a logical extension of the USIA's efforts to reach an elite as well as mass audience, an effort that some argued was undermined by budgetary constraints.[20] Around this same time, the USIA also turned to the rock counterculture as a medium for "relating the American story abroad," as its mission required.

The incorporation of rock music into USIA strategy reflected the agency's multimedia approach to disseminating information while converting audiences to a favorable impression of U.S. intentions. "The sound of American music," one report argued, "does more than create a mood, it carries overseas a message that reflects America."[21] What was the implicit ideological "message" that rock and other avant-garde musical expression carried? In a fundamental respect, the message of rock was similar to that of abstract-expressionist art, which the agency had also propagated (not without congressional controversy) directly and indirectly since the late 1940s: that the United States embodied newness, dynamism, experimentalism, and individualism in artist expression.[22] "Foreign audiences are eager to learn about American music," stated a 1971 USIA report to Congress:

> In American music, these audiences recognize creative freedom at work. . . . Listeners observe in the music of Charles Ives, Henry Cowell, George Crumb, Gunther Schuller, John Cage and other 20th century Americans those same experimental traditions, the same freedom from orthodoxy, the same independence of thought, that has marked American developments in science, medicine, agriculture, and other fields. . . .

> Overseas radio audiences can hear all styles of American music, includ-
> ing musical theater, folk music, concerts, recitals, symphony orches-
> tras, and rock music performed by youth across the United States.[23]

At the same time, rock's direct links to youth rebellion distinguished it as a medium of mass protest. How can we understand the USIA's motives in promoting such music? Was the agency sponsoring rock primarily in an ef-fort to improve its own image among foreign youth audiences? Or did it secretly endorse the value of rock as an arm of bourgeois revolutionary ac-tion by youth—embodied in the pursuit of individualism rather than rev-olutionary confrontation, as leftist critics of rock music often charged?

Based on the available documentation,[24] the latter assertion is quite doubtful. Indeed, the USIA was evidently out of touch altogether with the impact of rock-music culture in Latin America, if not elsewhere. What seems more probable is that the agency saw in rock a possibility for reach-ing out to—if not "converting"—foreign youth audiences to identify posi-tively with North American culture, albeit the emerging counterculture. This strategy, however, completely neglected an understanding of rock's resemantization into local cultural contexts and thus played into a crude analysis of rock's equation with imperialism. "Non-controversial and non-propagandistic, music will often make friends, open doors, influence opin-ion where other programs and other approaches may fail," a USIA report naively argued.[25]

The direct incorporation of rock music into USIA strategy took place at several levels. For one, as mentioned above, VOA programming shifted. Livening up the VOA broadcasts with rock music was basic to the objective of reaching out to a broader youth audience. Peter P. Cecere, a former SAO in Bolivia, also recalled a short-lived program dedicated to youth politics in the United States that was placed specifically on local rock stations (where they existed) throughout Latin America.[26]

A second approach was the direct sponsorship of U.S. rock bands for se-lected concert tours in Eastern Europe and the Soviet Union. For example, the group Blood, Sweat, and Tears became the first foreign rock band to per-form behind the Iron Curtain in a twenty-six-day tour that included dates in Poland, Romania, Yugoslavia, and Czechoslovakia.[27] In an apparent ef-fort to justify the agency's new approach to rock, a 1971 report to Congress explained that "Rock and roll . . . is heard in most foreign countries." This statement, which accompanies a photograph of a performance by the rock band Jefferson Airplane, left it ambiguous, however, whether the agency sought to claim responsibility for the fact that rock was heard "in most foreign countries" or was simply stating a fact of the modern era.[28] At any rate, the USIA would be hard-pressed to claim full responsibility: commercial music traveled best by commercial channels.[29] But in countries where commercialized mass culture was strictly controlled by state apparatuses (such as in the communist bloc), the USIA may indeed have had a significant impact on rock's diffusion.

A third approach was through the publication of articles and images that dealt with various aspects of countercultural and student rebellion in the United States, including the importance of rock music. It is to this approach that we now turn in greater detail. In October 1969 a meeting of all SAOs for Latin America was held in Quito, Ecuador, to discuss ongoing USIA strategies and tactics concerning youth in the hemisphere.[30] This meeting took place in the context of student-led rebellions—met by harsh government repression—and varying degrees of U.S.-influenced, countercultural development in many countries throughout the hemisphere. At the same time, student unrest and the rise of a countercultural movement in the United States framed the discussion for how to approach youth in Latin America generally. For Cecere, a young recruit at USIA, there seemed a need to explain the apparent chaos of student politics and culture in the United States not only to a Latin American audience but to the U.S. field officers as well. As he later recalled:

> Because the pace of change [in the United States] had become so rapid as to be not followable [*sic*] and if you weren't living in the society, watching television everyday and reading newspapers everyday [you wouldn't understand what was happening]. . . . Bolivia in those days didn't even have television, period! . . . So, we decided that one of the things we really needed to do was to look at the student movement in the U.S., which was so much in the headlines, and to explain it to the people in the field, to all officers of all agencies, regardless of what their job was. . . . We wanted them [the "nationals" as well as the Americans] to have some background as to what the hell was going on from an intellectual point of view.[31]

The USIA's mission was to "explain America": to place controversy within the context of democratic process; to demonstrate that modern values and freedom of expression go hand in hand. It was also the USIA's mission to "correct" negative stereotypes and images regarding the United States found around the world. What Cecere and others had in mind, therefore, was a pamphlet that would not only explicate the seeming chaos of student revolt and the counterculture in terms that made sense to a foreign audience but, moreover, framed those changes in a positive light. As a memorandum about the proposed pamphlet explained, "signs of dissent and even turbulence are signs of a healthy society—but these signs must be seen in perspective."[32]

EXPLAINING THE COUNTERCULTURE

One of the central ideas to result from the meeting in Quito was a crash-course pamphlet on dissent in the United States during the late 1960s. This was not the first effort by the agency to discuss controversial domestic topics; the struggle for civil rights and urban rioting had also been "explained" in earlier pamphlets.[33] In fact, the pamphlet that eventually emerged was originally conceived as a "successor issue" to an earlier volume of *America Illustrated,* one of the agency's numerous magazines, which had already dealt with the topic of U.S. youth; that issue had been translated into Spanish, and 50,000 copies were sent to posts abroad.[34] But the seeming repudiation of U.S. values embodied in the counterculture, coupled with the rise of angry student protest on campuses across the country, represented a new and complex challenge for the USIA. How could the agency explain such revolt as the logical outcome of democracy in the United States? After much discussion, a policy memorandum was circulated outlining the following idea:

> Dissent in the United States is highly visible throughout the world, and often misrepresented or distorted by the sensationalism of media treatment. As a result, some of our foreign audiences (and indeed, many here at home!) may be getting the feeling that the United States is coming apart at the seams, that strife and/or far-out life styles are signs of debilitation. We have spent considerable time and energy at the highest levels here in the Agency in recent weeks analyzing these phenomena and their implications, and there is a developing consensus, it seems to us, that the changes now going on in the U.S. should be seen and projected in a positive light. They are part of the real cultural revolution now underway—with relatively little violence—demonstrating the flexibility and adaptability of American society. This can be compared with the static nature of Marxist systems, where rigid inflexibility tends to build up tensions leading to serious explosions.[35]

After considerable delay, the pamphlet that eventually emerged, *Protestas y estilos entre la juventud norteamericana* (Protests and Styles among North American Youth) contained six translated articles (all previously published in mainstream U.S. magazines), covering such themes as student activism, hippies, rock music, and avant-garde movements in film and theater. Color photographs of scenes ranging from the student takeover of Columbia University to the esplanade at Woodstock accompanied the texts. According to a USIA strategy memorandum, the pamphlet would reach "limited key audiences, especially in the educational community." The idea was to provide such audiences "with a much-needed sober, objective treatment of this phenomenon [of rebellion]." "Utilized properly," the memorandum continued, "it could capitalize on the interest awakened by the headlines, and portray dissent as one of the historical sources of strength of the dynamic American society."[36] Nearly 40,000 copies were sent to fifteen countries, including Spain and Brazil (it was also translated into Portuguese); Mexico alone received 10,000 copies.[37] Interestingly, the following warning was struck from the original draft of the memorandum: "Conversely, if placed in the wrong hands, the publication might do harm to the image it was intended to put into perspective." What did "the wrong hands" refer to? (Cecere, too, posed this question in his response to this draft of the memorandum.) One gathers that these "wrong hands" might refer to leftist radicals or even right-wing nationalists, either of whom could conceivably manipulate distribution of the pamphlet as a means of "exposing" U.S. imperialism. But it also may have suggested the fear that student activism in the United States could be used as a pretext for solidarity and activism (or "dropping out," as the case may be) in Latin America, to the distress of local regimes. Might the pamphlet not validate Latin American youth protest? What about the possibility of a "duplicating effect" on foreign audiences? Or perhaps the warning referred to potentially hostile forces in the U.S. Congress who controlled the purse strings of future USIA funding. At any rate, the question was never answered, and the reference itself was struck from the final draft of the memorandum.

A basic assumption reflected in *Protestas y estilos* was that the disparate images of radical protest politics emanating from the United States could be contained under a single rubric, "protests and styles." By reclaiming these images from a global currency of media circulation, the USIA sought to establish a positive identification between protest politics and the theory and practice of democracy. There seemed to be an implicit principle that this information—the text and the photographs—would somehow influence local student leaders and "opinion makers" to take note: to recognize that protest in the United States was not really about making bombs and smoking dope but, rather, that it involved an activist minority with humanist objectives. As the final version of the pamphlet's introductory text read, in part: "Young activists in the U.S. have been described as 'articulate,' 'sophisticated,' 'assertive' and 'committed.' They have given expression to today's generation, which has been called a new kind of generation—

one alive with concern for basic human values, a spirit of questioning and a thirst for experimentation. . . . The activists among America's youth, who are described in this pamphlet, are small in number. Unlike most of their contemporaries, they are dissatisfied with much of what U.S. society offers." [38]

There was controversy within the USIA that the tone of the pamphlet might suggest condoning of the counterculture. To alleviate such concerns, Robert Amerson, head of the Latin American Division of the USIA, sent a memorandum to his superior. The pamphlet, he explained, "attempts to balance the international press distortions about American youth" by providing "articles [that] are sober and scholarly analyses of the youth movement it depicts." He continued, "The pamphlet is *not* designed for mass distribution, but for special audiences in Latin America who are in contact with USIS officers. It is hoped that the pamphlet will serve as a springboard for further discussion between young Latin Americans and youth officers overseas." [39] Another memorandum from the Office of Policy and Planning argued that "[t]he selected articles are essentially explanatory, somewhat detached and on the whole sympathetic, but not committed." [40] Interestingly, this is the only memorandum that again raised the possibility of negative consequences: "[Robert] Amerson points out the risk of misrepresentation in the U.S. [Congress]. I think we should be able to face any such challenges and defend the product. Far more important is the possibility of misrepresentation in Latin America. What would be the reaction of governments to our distributing this material? Would it give to Latin youth the idea that all students in the U.S. are protesting?" [41] The question was again left unanswered.

If one assumption was that the USIA could feasibly (re)present a contained narrative of student and countercultural protest in the United States to a Latin American audience, a second assumption was that the pamphlet would constitute "an effective means of establishing a link between youth abroad and their American counterparts, both of whom are articulate spokesmen of their respective societies." [42] But what exactly was meant by "an effective means" of communicating this relationship, or "a link between" these two youth populations? One interpretation is that the strategy was essentially the same as that dating back to OCIAA days: to create a common discourse and catalog of images that "linked" youth from Latin America (especially) with the United States. *Explaining* the hippies, for example, was understood by the agency as a means for establishing a common series of reference points for future discussions, whether between "student leaders" and SAOs at the USIA (ideally), or between such leaders and their presumed constituencies on the universities. What was fundamentally missing from this strategy perspective, however, was a basic comprehension of the fact that the global circulation of these protest images and the values they embodied had already begun to have a direct impact on the nature of youth protest, certainly in the case of Mexico.

The USIA was clearly concerned that stories of student unrest and the counterculture were undermining an image of collective U.S. strength and resolve as "leader of the Free World." By presenting "sober and scholarly analyses" [43] of these movements for social change, the agency hoped to act as a corrective to the privatized, mass-media representation of the same phenomena. At the same time, the agency could not expect to compete with the commercial mass media in terms of either circulation or content. As a report to the Congress stated, "This is the proper concern of the USIA information and cultural programs—not to influence or compete with the established media, but expertly to supplement their output abroad. Headlines highlight the news of the moment. It is USIA's task to add balance and perspective." [44] But a fundamental flaw was the agency's failure to grasp the multivalenced nature of how images and ideas were being consumed and reproduced by audiences and the cultural industries abroad. Media representations of the counterculture in the United States went beyond the mere suggestion or telling of a story of what was happening in the United States. They were reconfigured in local contexts; they became reference points for other nations' own countercultural reimaginings. Such representations—circulated via a complex network of transnational mass media throughout the world—had already influenced an urban mass audience throughout Latin America. Indeed, if the not-so-hidden agenda of USIA was (ultimately) to encourage the world to follow the U.S. lead in politics and culture, the pamphlet was in many ways "old hat." The impact of U.S. "protests and styles" was already felt in the student-movement culture that was influenced by ideas and images from abroad. [45] The USIA's failure to grasp the impact of transnationalism hence resulted in a pamphlet strategy that, in retrospect, is as equally impressive in its boldness as it is in its ignorance of local student cultural knowledge and politics.

One of the most fascinating aspects of this pamphlet project was the concern and attention given to detail. The danger of "misrepresenting" what was presumably being misrepresented by the media in the first place was a weighty concern. On one hand, according to its introduction, the pamphlet contained images and ideas, "some avowedly Leftist, others almost without ideology." [46] But at the same time, those very images and ideas contained the semiotics of their own sensationalism, which the USIA sought to curb. In the end, certain changes would be made. One important change was a paragraph that was added to the final version of the introduction: "Most young Americans, we must point out, share traditional American values and, while not necessarily maintaining attitudes identical to those of their elders, generally feel at home with the mainstream culture. Most prefer to live and work quietly within the broad consensus of existing social and political institutions."[47] Second, editorial changes were made in several of the articles. In one case, portions removed in translation referred to an extensive discussion of the drug culture; in another, references to the drug culture and to the war in Vietnam were dropped altogether. In yet another, the text for a photograph showing student demonstrators celebrating the takeover of Columbia University was changed from interpreting the "V" sign as meaning "victory" to noting that the "V" was a "signo de la paz" (sign of peace). "The V sign," explained Robert Amerson in a corrective memorandum, "does not refer to victory."[48] Quite clearly, the "V" symbol referred to both. But within a Latin American context, it often referred more to a victory against imperialism, repression, and other injustices. In Mexico, it was specifically referenced to the student movement of 1968. A third change, as Cecere remembers, was that photographs were scrutinized for "offensive gestures, etc." "I remember even in the case of the black protest [photograph]," Cecere noted, "our photo editors going through and blipping out the middle fingers that were up in the air, even in the Woodstock crowd scene—that famous stuff."[49]

Thus the irony of the USIA policy was doubly evident. On one hand, an agency of the U.S. government was sponsoring a large, multicolor pamphlet highlighting the very movements and actors that were defying the political and social power structure, while on the other, the agency felt obliged to "sanitize" the representation to some extent. As an early memorandum from Robert Amerson summed up the contradiction, "There is a major policy issue here: to be credible any publication dealing with American youth has to touch on some themes critical of American society."[50]

There is also significant irony to the fact that *Protestas y estilos* reached Mexico just as La Onda was about to culminate in the rock festival at Avándaro. If anything, the pamphlet would have validated the Mexican counterculture and confirmed, perhaps, that it was "on the right track" in its own development.[51] The subject matter of avant-garde film, student protests against the war and the universities; the emergence of a hippie movement, the significance of rock music: these were all themes that were avidly discussed from a Mexican perspective and that constituted the cultural critique of La Onda as well. Yet the USIA, as evidenced through this pamphlet strategy, failed to recognize this transformation of Mexican youth culture. Further evidence of this lack of an informed perspective at the agency comes from an article coauthored by Peter P. Cecere and Michael Canning, both of whom were SAOs at the time, titled "Student Activism in the Americas: A Comparative View." Here, the authors assert that the equivalent of a countercultural ideology was entirely absent from Latin American protest, which was clearly not the case: "The atmosphere of US campus politics is inseparable from the elements of a new sensibility: drugs, rock music, Eastern religions, commune experiments, psychedelic art, new sexual attitudes, and exotic garb. None of this alternately sincere and fad-laden 'youth culture' manifests itself in Latin America in any way, except perhaps in revolutionary poetry."[52] Hypothetically, if the USIA had recognized the fact that the reappropriation of U.S. popular culture was already an integral aspect of Latin American protest—in terms of music, language, and fashion—then perhaps this pamphlet and other material might have reflected that perspective. Had that been the case, the USIA might conceivably have gone much farther and with greater "success" toward meeting its abstract goal of unifying the hemisphere via a common discourse. Logically, if the U.S. counterculture was indeed "bourgeois"—in that many of its actors were from the middle classes and rock culture was deeply implicated in capitalism—this strategy would have made sense. The USIA might then have also been exposed by leftists and others as an agency of imperialism that was "pushing" the counterculture as a "remedy" for Latin American radicalism, an approach to youth protest perhaps not too dissimilar to that which the Agency for International Development took toward alleviating poverty in the region.

But the USIA was not out to push the counterculture on Latin America. The agency simply hoped to define social protest in the United States on terms at least acceptable to its founding mission, to "tell America's story overseas." With this pamphlet, it thus sought to show the innate "American-ness" of the rock countercultural movement, which, unlike other forms of more radical student protest, the USIA regarded as distinctively of U.S. origin. Indeed, the final version of the pamphlet featured a two-page, full-color photograph of the crowd scene at the 1969 Woodstock festival. The photograph is impressive: the crowd of young people seems endless; their body language expresses calm and creativity, not anger or violence. While most of the faces are male and white (in the lower half of the photo, the faces are clearly discernible), there is also an evident mixture of races and genders. The following paragraph of text was printed over a portion of the sky: "It was the largest concentration in history. According

La cosa no tiene fin. Continúa la búsqueda de cambios. Como en el emblema de la Feria de Música y Arte de Woodstock, la blanca paloma sigue exigiendo paz, en un estilo de vida que vibra con su propio pulso musical. Siguen vivas las esperanzas de la juventud en una nueva comunidad de armonía y comprensión entre los hombres.

Diseño: Joseph Baumer
Preparado por la Sección de Arte
de RSC México

Créditos de las ilustraciones: Portada © 1968, WMCA, distribuida exclusivamente por Darien House, Inc. Nueva York. Segunda de forros: Barry Blackman. Págs. 2-3: United Press International. Pág. 4: Wide World. 5: United Press International. Pág. 6: Ilustración de Paul Salmon. Pág. 7: The Washington Post. Págs. 8 y 11: Paul Salmon. Pág. 14: Ilustración de Tom McCaffrey, tomada de *Mainliner*. Pág. 15: *The Washington Post*. Pág. 16: Paul Salmon. Pág. 17: Peter Larsen, de Nancy Palmer. Pág. 18: Roland Freeman. Pág. 19: *The Washington Post*. Págs. 20-21: Shelly Rusten: Pág. 22: *The Washington Post*. Págs. 23 y 25: Paul Salmon. Págs. 26-27: Arriba: © 1969, Container Corporation of America, distribuida exclusivamente por Darien House, Inc., Nueva York; abajo: Cortesía de Yale University. Pág. 30: Paul Salmon. Pág. 31: Hella Hammid, Rapho-Guillumette. Pág. 32: © Trend Graphics/Wespec Visual Communications, Inc. Pág. 33: Paul Salmon. Pág. 40: Cortesía de Warner Brothers Seven Arts. Tercera de forros: Barry Blackman. Contraportada: Thomas Powell.

Figure 18. "There is no end to it," the last page of the 1971 USIA-produced booklet, *Protestas y estilos entre la juventud norteamericana* (Protests and Styles among North American Youth), which juxtaposes the Woodstock symbol with the Agency's own emblem.

to conservative calculations, 400,000 young pilgrims flocked to the Woodstock Music & Art Fair, celebrated on August 15–17, 1969 on a private farm in the southern part of New York state. They represented a generation 'proud to reject the idea of social conformity, looking for the means by which it can realize itself in a positive way'."[53] Now Woodstock had become a parable for the story of the United States itself, recapturing the spirit of the original colonizing settlers, who "reject[ed] the idea of social conformity" to stake out a new way of life in the New World. Moreover, the concert was described as not simply massive: it was "the largest" gathering of people "in history." Furthermore, that it took place on a "private farm" highlighted the peaceful—and productive—relationship between society and private enterprise. Alas, the private farmer!

On the final page of the pamphlet we also find an enlarged reproduction of the hallmark symbol of the Woodstock festival: a white dove perched on the neck of a guitar (see Figure 18). At the bottom of the page the circular seal of the USIA—an eagle clutching an olive branch in one claw, arrows in the other—balances out the layout. "There is no end to it," begins the closing text just below the Woodstock symbol. "Like in the emblem of the Woodstock Music and Art Fair, the white dove keeps demanding peace, in a lifestyle that vibrates with its own musical pulse. The hopes of youth to form a new community based on harmony and understanding among all humankind are still alive."[54] Peace within capitalism; Woodstock; a new harmonious order organized around youth: these themes became directly associated not only with some abstract notion of "America" but, moreover, with the U.S. government itself. If this was increasingly true, however, one questions the practical impact the USIA pamphlet in fact had. The counterculture was already understood as an "American" phenomenon, reshaping the image of the United States abroad (for better or worse). At the same time, urban middle-class youth around the world were eagerly appropriating the images, language, music, and so forth of that counterculture to suit their own critical projects of rebellion.

Conclusions

For nearly a decade after the Avándaro music festival the rock legacy of La Onda Chicana lay shattered, which is not to say that native rock disappeared altogether. Gone was the momentum of a countercultural movement that had begun to reveal its numbers. In the aftermath of Avándaro, the scores of native bands looking for commercial success either broke up or switched genres—as in the case of the famed La Revolución de Emiliano Zapata, whose remaining members took up cumbia. Several bands did hold together for a few more years, though only Three Souls in My Mind remained viable beyond the 1970s.[1] But the terrain for rock performance was drastically altered. Between state repression and a critical disdain, La Onda Chicana found itself orphaned by the cultural industries that had once nurtured it and rejected by the middle-class fans who had been among its strongest supporters. Avándaro proved an ephemeral moment in Mexican history, its cultural significance now largely forgotten.

Mexican rock found refuge in the hoyos fonquis after Avándaro, where the urban edge of lower-class needs and sensibilities affected the full transformation of rock into a vehicle for desmadre. Gone was the pretense of international acceptance as rock became infused with the nihilistic currents of punk music (influenced by groups such as the Sex Pistols and the Ramones, both of which were idolized in the barrio) and was expressed wholly in Spanish. This musical tendency reflected the increasingly dire economic situation of the urban lower classes and the repressive political conditions that kept them there.

During the 1970s there was a surge of capital infusion into the economy under the populist administration of Luis Echeverría and his successor, José López Portillo. The apparent growth of the economy, however, was chimerical, for it was built on inflationary spending and loans against future sales of still untapped petroleum. Wages rose, but so did prices for basic goods and imports. Meanwhile, the impetus for urban development reflected in massive public-works projects and an influx of social spending further propelled the rural-urban migration patterns already at work. What were once viewed as pockets of urban poverty became veritable *ciudades perdidas* (lost cities), as they became commonly known. From a modern city with cosmopolitan aspirations Mexico City had become a megalopolis. While Echeverría and López Portillo both spoke of economic redistribution and national grandeur, the unprecedented levels of corruption created by oil profits and the wanton inefficiency of the public sector generated cynicism rather than praise, especially from the lower classes. Lacking a political voice for their viewpoint, lower-class youth turned to rock for articulating their frustrations with a system that disempowered them politically, socially, and economically.

The only vibrant link to La Onda Chicana, however, was the group Three Souls in My Mind, which sustained the banner of rock after Avándaro by taking their music directly to the barrios and transforming their message to reflect the needs and concerns of an audience that differed vastly from the relatively privileged origins of the group's lead singer, Alejandro Lora. With a consistent heavy blues rhythm (the group comprised a guitar, bass, and drums), Lora later explained how the band represented "a species of urban Mexican rock and roll, a rock of the streets with words and experiences that reflect Mexicans' lives, especially those who live in the capital."[2] Against the rhetoric of revolutionary promise, their songs exposed the truth of poverty, corruption, and repression. This is reflected, for instance, in their 1975 song "Abuso de autoridad," which takes a jibe at Díaz Ordaz's own roquero son:

To live in Mexico is the worst.	Vivir en México es lo peor.
Our government is really bad	Nuestro gobierno está muy mal
and no one can protest	y nadie puede protestar
because they'll lock him up.	porque lo llevan a encerrar.
No one wants to go out,	Ya nadie quiere ni salir,
or say the truth.	ni decir la verdad.
No one wants to have	Ya nadie quiere tener
more troubles with the police.	más líos con la autoridad
Lots of blue coats [police] in the city	Muchos azules en la ciudad
at every hour wanting to rough you up	a toda hora queriendo agandallar

No!, I don't want to see them any more.	¡No!, ya no los quiero ver mas.
And the rock concerts, they try to take them away. And the only one who'll be left to play is Díaz Ordaz's son.	Y las tocadas del rock ya nos las quieren quitar. Ya sólo va poder tocar el hijo de Díaz Ordaz.[3]

Lora understood the lower classes' need to experience rock as a cathartic release from the repressions of everyday life. He appealed to the desmadre element of lower-class participation and in turn transformed the Three Souls in My Mind into Mexico's premier rock 'n' roll band, sustained almost entirely by support in the barrio rather than the middle classes. As he later reflected:

> I think about it this way, look, when we recorded "Abuso de Autoridad" or "Nuestros Impuestos" we knew that they weren't going to raise people's consciousness. The people aren't conscienticized, or however you might put it. [T]hey don't become more conscious, rather they have a release for a moment. They come out of the hoyo fonqui and now they feel like a guerrilla, but they're not going to take up arms or beat up the president. Yet they feel like they've participated in a political meeting by listening to the Three Souls. It's a psychological escape which I think the government should recognize as such.[4]

By the early 1980s, numerous other barrio bands influenced by punk rhythms and economic poverty proliferated throughout the marginalized zones of urban Mexico. The rest of the nation was still largely unaware of this growing phenomenon, *los chavos banda* (punk-rock youth from the barrios), who soon confronted society with their mounting presence.

Concurrent with this movement in the barrios, among the middle classes by the late 1970s came the experimental sounds of Guillermo Briseño, Jaime López, Jorge Reyes, and others who sought a musical fusion reflecting nueva canción, jazz, indigenous, and rock influences. An important source of inspiration was the evolution of rock in Argentina, where artists such as Fito Páez and Charly García were writing songs that dealt (often in metaphors) with military repression and *los desaparecidos* (extrajudicial kidnappings by military forces).[5] Inspired by such musicians and determined to create a new musical voice for the post-1968 generation, these Mexican artists struggled to re-create a more respectable rock style, one that disassociated itself from some of the colonized overtones of La Onda

Chicana. For instance, a song by Guillermo Briseño from 1978, "Comparaciones (Apariencias)" goes in part:

My country is a child	Mi patria es un niño
that neither cries nor suffers,	que ni llora ni sufre,
that doesn't even remember	que ni siquiera se acuerda
that it was once October 2nd;	que una vez fue dos de octubre;
my sisters always pray	mis hermanas rezan siempre
to get married in San Antonio	por casarse a San Antonio
and in their souls there isn't room	y en sus almas no hay espacio
to speak of the tenth of June.	para hablar de un diez de junio.[6]

Around the mid-1980s, these two musical tendencies—punk-influenced barrio rock and rock-fusion among the middle classes—began to merge, producing an entirely new generation of rock musicians whose material transcended class barriers and brought Mexican rock the international acclaim it had pursued since the 1960s.[7]

There was also a third trend in rock that emerged around 1980 and that Víctor Roura has labeled the "other rock." Highly commercialized and thoroughly sanitized of any offensive gestures, this teenybopper Spanish-language rock movement—catalyzed by the Puerto Rican pop phenomenon Menudo—was far removed from the underground rock scene and experimental fusion. Raúl Velasco, whose show *Siempre en domingo* largely defined the parameters of "proper taste" for Mexico's Televisa, directly launched the movement on commercial television. Intent on putting its earlier affiliation with La Onda Chicana squarely behind it, Televisa now hailed what was viewed by Roura as a "rock repossessed, now by nice people, decent, educated."[8] As Roura continued to describe it, "They invent contests based on youth values designed to show off the new styles: bell-bottomed pants, multicolored sneakers, hair cut short in the style of 'punks,' mini-dresses, androgenous little dances, being in the 'new wave,' living the new romanticism."[9] Federico Arana came sardonically to label this genre "pedarroc," one imagines as in pedophilic rock 'n' roll, so young are its performers with their adult looks and pretensions.[10] Once more, rock was being repositioned by the cultural industries within a hegemonic arrangement that sought to contain it as "entertainment" and profit from its marketing spin-offs. Within this discourse of a circumscribed, commodified rebellion a counterculture was again refashioned as style aimed at an elite who wished to "belong."

The cultural industries were once more caught up in the contradiction of adhering to the state's demands for self-censorship yet seeking to profit from the consumers' demands for a more authentic rock product. In a scene replayed from the famous Doors' appearance in 1969, the rock band the Police gave a concert at the exclusive Hotel de México (in Mexico City) in 1980. Afterward, Sting declared that he would not return to Mexico to "play for the bourgeoisie."[11] Meanwhile, efforts to sponsor concerts for the masses resulted in cancellations and worse. At a 1980 Johnny Winter performance in Pachuca, for instance, the concert "ended in police repression against the audience."[12] Two years later, at a Mexico City opening of the film *Ladies and Gentlemen, the Rolling Stones* police entered the theater and prevented the screening.[13] These were among the scores of similar incidents that affected foreign rock performance in Mexico and characterized to an even greater degree native rock. If the cultural industries were eager to exploit the obvious demand for rock, this would not occur for a few more years.

With economic conditions worsening, moreover, the government was in no mood to allow the commercialization of a more politicized rock. That strategy would do an about-face during the administration of Miguel de la Madrid (1982–1988), but in the meantime rock (as it had during the late 1960s) found its way via semiunderground channels. This was epitomized by the initiation of an open-air, weekly rock "flea market" organized by aficionados outside the Museo del Chopo in Mexico City in 1980. As word of mouth spread, the Chopo market attracted more attention, and it was ejected from the museum's grounds. It wandered in exile, facing constant police harassment, until it finally established itself semi-institutionally next to the railway depot in the northern part of the capital. Known as the Tianguis del Chopo, by the late 1980s it had become, as José Agustín writes, "the capital of the counterculture in Mexico."[14]

The early 1980s marked an important turning point for Mexico as the nation teetered on the brink of bankruptcy. If 1968 had severely damaged the PRI's political credibility, 1982 (when Mexican Finance Secretary Silva Herzog informed the U.S. Treasury Department that there was no money left to continue payment on the national debt) dealt an important blow to the PRI's economic credibility. The "lost decade" of economic growth, which Mexico by no means suffered through alone, proved a severe challenge to the ruling party. The PRI survived intact only after using all of the available techniques of rule at its disposal: symbolism and rhetoric, corporatist influence and repression, electoral dominance and outright fraud. La crisis, as Mexicans called this period, blurred the lines between middle and lower classes as workers of all types invented new strategies of economic survival.

What is particularly significant to the history of rock music's relationship to the state is that after 1982 (with the election of Miguel de la Madrid and the collapse of the peso) there begins a reversal in official policy, embracing what was once deemed anathema. In 1984 the PRI, through its newly created Consejo Nacional de Recursos para la Atención de la Juventud (CREA), actively began to cultivate a relationship with los chavos banda, whose presence could no longer be ignored. Through its official magazine, *Encuentro*, CREA opened up a channel for expression by marginalized youth that, at least initially, appeared relatively free of censorship. *Encuentro* featured stories, interviews, and poetry by chavos banda, as well as music criticism and a calendar of weekly events, including rock concerts (many of which were sponsored by CREA).

But in reality, the PRI was responding to a force that was already widely felt. During the early 1980s, youth in the barrios had begun to organize themselves. This was manifested in the Consejo Popular Juvenil, an organization based in the capital with several thousand members whose aim was to sponsor cultural activities for youth in the barrios and prevent gang violence. The Consejo Popular rejected all political affiliations, despite efforts by the PRI and other parties to eventually seek its endorsement.[15] *Encuentro* not only underwrote its own reporting of the chavos banda, it also drew on material being published through the Consejo Popular, as in this excerpt from a poem that was republished in *Encuentro's* first issue. Here we read the caustic language of a youth rebellion that is anything but bourgeois:

We're more antisocial	Nosotros somos más antisociales
than political, I'm not writing	que políticos, no estoy escribiendo
protest songs, I am the protest!	canciones de protesta, ¡yo soy la protesta!
I am anarchy. . . .	yo soy la anarquía. . . .
This rotten society doesn't accept us, because we won't submit.[16]	Esta sociedad podrida no nos acepta, porque no nos doblegamos.

The contents of *Encuentro* continued to explore various facets of youth culture, both lower and middle class, and featured articles on political themes such as the Sandinistas (supported diplomatically by Mexico), the death of Che Guevara, and the plight of youth living along the U.S. border. But despite its at times radical overtone, the magazine was clearly a propaganda vehicle for the PRI. This created the odd juxtaposition of reports on rock music next to the presidential State of the Union Address (reproduced in full) and other government self-promotions. As the campaign of Carlos Salinas de Gortari began, *Encuentro* pictured the PRI candidate on its cover above the caption: "Carlos Salinas de Gortari: A Young Candidate for a Country of Youth."[17] The PRI by itself could not sanitize the rock movement emanating from the barrios, but by affiliating the party with youth expression it hoped to refashion its reputation as rock-friendly and thus populist. It should not surprise us, then, to find the following language in the 1988 PRI platform: "We will push the authorities of the Federal District to simplify the paperwork, permissions, and licensing for the presentation of artistic and cultural events. In Mexico City and in the rest of the country, we want more rock, theater, cinema, opera, classical and popular music."[18] Indeed, the PRI not only liberalized access to rock but also directly sponsored rock performances, including those by the confrontational TRI. (In 1984 the drummer in Three Souls in My Mind split from the group and sued to keep the original name. Alejandro Lora, the lead performer, adopted the name "TRI" for his own group, which went on to greater fame. The new name was not only a convenient adaptation of the Hispanicized abbreviation for the group—that is, "the Three"—but a clever play on the "PRI" as well, and it was used to great effect in their performances.)

If the PRI now seemed bent on accommodating the demand for rock music at its various levels, from foreign performers to concerts in the barrios, the government was responding to a reality it could no longer effectively repress. But the shift in official policy generated an important cultural opening that reverberated throughout commercial and intellectual channels. For instance, it was in 1984 that the Mexico City rock station, Rock 101, began operation. Rock 101 is remembered as a fundamental contributor to the revival of a middle-class rock consciousness, in that the station played and discussed not only progressive foreign rock but also rock movements emanating from the Southern Cone: "With the arrival of Rock 101 at first place in popularity among young people, all of the radio stations that played rock had to change their attitude and become more concerned about the quality of music they featured."[19] By the late 1980s there was a veritable explosion in rock marketing as well as performance. Foreign artists, for years denied entrance to Mexico, now gained access to large stadium audiences. Several new rock clubs aimed at the middle classes opened up in Mexico City and became the foundation for a rechanneling of rock out of the hoyos fonquis and into more institutionalized locations.[20] From there, it was only a logical next step to record contracts as the transnationals once more began to pursue this nueva onda of rock.

Intellectuals' acceptance of Spanish-language rock performance was another important component of this rock revival. Since rock 'n' roll's initial arrival in Mexico, intellectuals had been generally hostile toward rock music, and Mexican rock in particular. While many intellectuals did regard foreign rock as part of the cultural vanguard, rocanrol and La Onda Chicana were almost uniformly condemned as bourgeois imitation at best, cultural imperialism at worst. When La Onda Chicana retreated to the barrios in the 1970s, it had few followers among leftists who were willing to defend its authenticity as a form of popular culture. This position, however, had begun to change by the mid-1980s, as los chavos banda emerged as a sociological phenomenon and la crisis once more ruptured the close affiliation between intellectuals and the state, which the PRI had recultivated since the early 1970s.[21] Not only had rock music demonstrated its vitality during a decade of underground survival, but the larger theoretical paradigm of what now constituted "popular culture" was itself being challenged by a new level of critique that questioned the validity of a narrowly defined notion of cultural imperialism. The very term *cultura popular* underwent a transformation from its exclusively rural orientation into one that embraced all levels of urban cultural expression. In the realm of popular music, this was expressed in a 1983 conference entitled "¿Qué Onda con la Música Popular Mexicana?" In the very title we find the word *onda* now juxtaposed with the label *música popular*, suggesting the new fusion of urban and rural sensibilities that had occurred. Popular music (which does not mean pop music) had itself become a contested term, as revealed in the conflicting papers presented at the conference, which covered themes ranging from rancheras, corridos, and indigenous music, to cumbias, commercialized pop, and Mexican rock; speakers included Carlos Monsiváis, René Villanueva of Los Folkloristas, and Federico Arana, among others.[22] Even more indicative of this transformation was the opening in 1982 of the Museo Nacional de Culturas Populares (where the conference was held) in Mexico City. Here rural and urban popular cultures became elevated to a similar level of importance, suggesting not only the new intellectual acceptance of urban culture as legitimate but, moreover, the PRI's efforts to affiliate itself directly with that legitimacy through official sponsorship.

If rock had scant direct presence in the student movement of 1968, nearly two decades later, in the student movement of 1986, rock performance was a defining feature of student politics as well as leisure. The 1986 movement came in the aftermath of the 1985 earthquake, which had reduced large portions of the nation's capital to ruins and revealed through tragedy the government's utter incompetence at rescue operations and survivor resettlement.[23] Whereas the 1968 movement challenged the PRI's authoritar-

Figure 19.   The recycling of symbols and discourse from the 1968 student move-ment finds its way into a commemorative march in Mexico City in 1993, now with a clear role for rock music. (Photograph by the author)

ianism on the eve of world attention focusing on the Olympic games, the 1986 movement was oriented more toward university reforms. But its size and energy revealed the ability and desire of youth to take to the streets and make their voices heard, this time seeking to leverage government weakness after the earthquake and in the midst of the worst economic cri-sis since the revolution.[24] Student protest culture now also reflected a much greater synthesis of traditional corridos, nueva canción, and rock (both for-eign and national) than it had in 1968. With the influence of a more po-liticized rock from the Southern Cone and native rock's completed Mexi-canization as it reemerged from the barrios to national prominence, the question of separating rock from social protest had become moot.

Today, the identification between rock music and democratic politics goes almost without question in opposition circles. At a commemorative march marking the twenty-eighth anniversary of the massacre at Tlatelolco, the newspaper *La Jornada* reported that 100,000 people marched on the Zócalo, "awaiting the only speech that mattered to the youth, and that was none other than rock" (see Figure 19).[25] A 1994 album by the band Tijuana No features an image of Emiliano Zapata on its cover, a clear political statement in the context of the Zapatista uprising that had erupted at the beginning of that year; the album's songs, moreover, are filled with attacks on commercial culture and the political system. In a 1995 concert by the band at the U.S.–Mexican border, the lead singer, Teca García (age twenty-seven), shouted: "We dedicate this one to all of us who are Zapatistas," an echo of the stance of "Todos somos Marcos!" ("We're all Marcos") that was popularized throughout the country.[26] Yet as "Pacho" (age thirty-three), drummer for the band La Maldita Vecindad y los Hijos del Quinto Patio, commented:

> Our work is not political, if by political you mean doctrinaire, ideological songs, like the '60s protest songs were and the '70s, with the folkloric Chilean music and nueva canción. We don't intend to educate anyone, we don't believe in ideologies or doctrines. It is political in the broader sense of the word since we speak of the street life, of the everyday person. If you write about them, you're going to confront things that could be considered political.[27]

This new rock period is also marked by musical and cultural fusion as an aesthetic strategy (despite the preponderance of heavy-metal groups), and it has often succeeded in transcending class divisions. In fact, in order to maintain their credibility as being "against the system," the more successful bands must continue to demonstrate their readiness to perform at outdoor festivals (often for free) and in lower-class settings. Mexican rock has once again become the vanguard of a new countercultural movement, one that transcends class in its opposition to the ruling political party and a mounting culture of repression. As Carlos Monsiváis stated, Mexican rock is now the "principal instrument for those who are marginalized in society, the first zone of expression for the under class."[28]

But the stakes in the battle over rock's position in Mexican society have been high. Lost is the musical memory and cultural consciousness integral to La Onda Chicana, though la nueva onda (as one journalist has named the present-day rock movement in Mexico) represents an important development in cultural self-representation and political awareness.[29] Its commercialization process cut off in middevelopment, the fusion represented by La Onda Chicana exists only in direct relationship to the scarce commodity forms—record albums, magazines, photographs—that survived the period, most of which are now in private collections.[30] Indeed, if we are to take the study of rock music in Mexico seriously, it is above all this consideration that we must keep in mind: what is the relationship among capitalism, state power, and popular memory? The commodification of a countercultural movement—often criticized by cultural theorists—becomes an essential factor in the creation and survival of popular memory. Experience, and thus the memory of that experience, is directly tied to the commodified object itself, in this case the rock album, but also films, T-shirts, posters, and whatnot. The paltry availability of Mexican rock in its commodified form from the period of La Onda Chicana—the literal absence of albums and images—is a direct result of state pressures put on the cultural industries in the wake of Avándaro. The U.S. and British rock movements, in contrast, were thoroughly commodified, indeed creating a superabundance of music and images that have made their way into all corners of the globe.[31] Lacking access to the commodity form itself and coupled with the elevation of foreign rock as vanguard culture during the 1960s and 1970s, the articulation of a countercultural memory in Mexico is made almost exclusively in terms of U.S. and British rock. (Though at the same time a political memory, that of 1968, is referenced in various songs and festivals.)

In fact, the entire musical memory from La Onda Chicana has been all but lost. Unlike the Woodstock festival, which continues to influence the styles and consciousness of succeeding generations of youth in the United States, the rock-music culture that generated Avándaro survives only in the underground rock-music scene and in the memory of those who were there.[32] Repressed in the name of cultural imperialism, the memory of Mexico's native rock movement from the early 1970s has been replaced by an imported rock memory of a commercialized counterculture from without. Although today recognized as a familiar term, "Avándaro" has become a reference point absent a shared popular repertoire of images or musical experiences. It is perhaps best seen as a nonmemory, ironically recalled more in terms of the Woodstock experience—which is identified worldwide—than of that experience to which it belongs, La Onda.

Notes

INTRODUCTION

1. The concept of the "Revolutionary Family" became popularized in the social science literature on Mexico by Frank Brandenburg's *The Making of Modern Mexico* (Englewood Cliffs, N.J.: Prentice Hall, 1964 [1967]), esp. chap. 1, "The Revolutionary Family and the Mexican Proposition." He writes: "For the sake of convenience, and to suggest the nature of leadership of this [elite] revolutionary group, it will be assigned the label of 'Revolutionary Family,' or simply 'Family.' The Revolutionary Family is composed of the men who have run Mexico for over half a century, who have laid the policy-lines of the Revolution, and who today hold effective decision-making power" (p. 3). Although the extent to which the term was actually employed by Mexicans themselves is less clear, certainly the imagery of a patriarchally defined revolutionary state was prominent.

2. Popular support, as well as opposition to the students, came from various quarters, a point I address later in the book. The manner in which I am using the plural *middle classes* roughly corresponds with John J. Johnson's preference for the term *middle sectors* (John J. Johnson, *Political Change in Latin America: The Emergence of the Middle Sectors* [Stanford, Calif.: Stanford University Press 1958]).

3. Ulf Hannerz, "Notes on the Global Ecumene," *Public Culture* 1, no. 2 (1989): 66–75. While my subject matter is a mass-produced cultural commodity, I am indebted to the methodological argument presented in Arjun Appadurai, ed., *The Social Life of Things: Commodities in Cultural Perspective* (Cambridge: Cambridge University Press, 1986). See also Ian Ang, "Culture and Communication: Towards an Ethnographic Critique of Media Consumption in the Transnational Media System," *European Journal of Communication* 5 (1990): 239–60.

4. For the revolutionary period see Friedrich Katz, *The Secret War in Mexico* (Chicago: University of Chicago Press, 1981); and Alan Knight, *The Mexican*

Revolution (Lincoln: University of Nebraska Press, 1986), vols. 1–2. For post-revolutionary reconstruction and the institutionalization of presidential rule see Alan Knight, "Mexico, c. 1930–1946," in Leslie Bethell, ed., *Cambridge History of Latin America* (New York: Cambridge University Press, 1990), vol. 7, 3–82.

5. That Mexico did not experience a military coup d'état in 1968 is an important distinction which has much to do as well with the fact that the military was gradually retired from direct participation in politics after the revolution, in contrast to the trend in the Southern Cone, where the military steadily *entered* politics under the guise of providing a stabilizing element.

6. Gilbert M. Joseph and Daniel Nugent, eds., *Everyday Forms of State Formation: Revolution and the Negotiation of Rule in Modern Mexico* (Durham, N.C.: Duke University Press, 1994); Claudio Lomnitz-Adler, *Exits from the Labyrinth: Culture and Ideology in the Mexican National Space* (Berkeley: University of California Press, 1992).

7. Ilene V. O'Malley, *The Myth of the Revolution: Hero Cults and the Institutionalization of the Mexican State, 1920–1940* (New York: Greenwood Press, 1986), 126.

8. Ibid., 47, 85.

9. Octavio Paz, "Return to the Labyrinth of Solitude," trans. Yara Milos, in Octavio Paz, *The Labyrinth of Solitude and Other Writings*, trans. Lysander Kemp, Yara Milos, and Rachel Phillips Balash (New York: Grove Press, 1985), 336.

10. O'Malley, *Myth of the Revolution*, 53. See also Evelyn P. Stevens, "*Marianismo:* The Other Face of *Machismo* in Latin America," in Ann Pescatello, ed., *Female and Male in Latin America: Essays* (Pittsburgh: University of Pittsburgh Press, 1973), 89–101; Parker and others, *Nationalisms and Sexualities* (New York: Routledge, 1992); Jean Franco, *Plotting Women: Gender and Representation in Mexico* (New York: Columbia University Press, 1989).

11. Mathew C. Gutmann, *The Meanings of Macho: Being a Man in Mexico City* (Berkeley: University of California Press, 1996), 224. See also Franco, *Plotting Women*, esp. chap. 7, "Oedipus Modernized."

12. This breakdown of idealized family stability and the power of the state to exercise benign paternalism is hauntingly revealed in Luis Buñuel's classic film, *Los olvidados* (1950), translated as "The Young and the Damned."

13. Jonathan Kandell, *La Capital: A Biography of Mexico City* (New York: Random House, 1988), 486.

14. José Emiliano Pacheco, *Battles in the Desert and Other Stories*, trans. Katherine Silver (Mexico City: Ediciones Era, 1981; New York: New Directions, 1987), 82–83.

15. For a discussion of elite and popular cultures during the Porfiriato see William H. Beezley, *Judas at the Jockey Club and Other Episodes of Porfirian Mexico* (Lincoln: University of Nebraska Press, 1987). For the postwar consumer frenzy see José Agustín, *Tragicomedia mexicana I: La vida en México de 1940 a 1970* (Mexico City: Planeta, 1990), 125 (advertisement for Goodyear Tires).

16. Roger D. Hansen, *The Politics of Mexican Development* (Baltimore, Md.: Johns Hopkins University Press, 1971 [1974]), 41–42.

17. Stephen R. Niblo, *War, Diplomacy, and Development: The United States and Mexico, 1938–1954* (Wilmington, Del.: Scholarly Resources, 1995). Niblo writes that "[n]ot until 1971 did the purchasing power of real wages regain the 1938 level" (p. 147).

18. Carlos Monsiváis, "Muerte y resurrección del nacionalismo mexicano," *Nexos* 109 (January 1987), 13. Unless otherwise noted, all translations from the Spanish throughout this book are mine.

19. Octavio Paz, "The Philanthropic Ogre," trans. Rachel Phillips Balash, in Octavio Paz, *The Labyrinth of Solitude and Other Writings*, trans. Lysander Kemp, Yara Milos, and Rachel Phillips Balash (New York: Grove Press, 1985), 379–98.

20. Stanley R. Ross, ed., *Is the Mexican Revolution Dead?* (New York: Alfred A. Knopf, 1966). See José Luis Cuevas, "The Cactus Curtain," *Evergreen Review* 2 (1959): 111–20. For a discussion of the apogee of Mexico's revolutionary nationalism as a cosmopolitan force in the world see Helen Delpar, *The Enormous Vogue of Things Mexican: Cultural Relations between the United States and Mexico, 1920–1935* (Tuscaloosa: University of Alabama Press, 1992).

21. One might argue that this cynicism had always been there but that the right material conditions for expressing it were not yet available. Hegemony in this view is not something that comes undone (in failing to remake itself) but rather something that is sustained through an implicit acceptance of official lies which are backed by force. Thus, hegemony is always fragile and dependent on the willingness of social actors to play their parts (consciously and unconsciously). The problem with this interpretation, however, is that it does not account for why, when, and how social actors choose to expose the lies sustaining hegemonic relations. The answer to this, in part, lies with the importance of popular culture as a vehicle for both inculcating and contesting hegemonic values. See Derek Sayer, "Everyday Forms of State Formation: Some Dissident Remarks on 'Hegemony,'" in Gilbert Joseph and Daniel Nugent, eds., *Everyday Forms of State Formation: Revolution and the Negotiation of Rule in Modern Mexico* (Durham, N.C.: Duke University Press, 1994), 367–77; William Rowe and Vivian Schelling, *Memory and Modernity: Popular Culture in Latin America* (London: Verso, 1991).

22. See, for example, Linda Martin and Kerry Segrave, *Anti-Rock: The Opposition to Rock 'n' Roll* (New York: Da Capo, 1993); and Dick Hebdige, "Towards a Cartography of Taste, 1935–1962," in *Hiding in the Light* (London: Routledge, 1988), 45–76, about the reception of youth culture in Britain.

23. Alan Knight, "Revolutionary Project, Recalcitrant People: Mexico, 1910–1940," in Jaime E. Rodríguez O., ed., *The Revolutionary Process in Mexico: Essays on Political and Social Change, 1880–1940* (Los Angeles: UCLA, 1990), 263.

24. Ibid., 264.

25. This is not to suggest that the student protests were "caused" by rock music or even necessarily characterized by rock music's presence, though many were. Moreover, in the case of the Cultural Revolution in China as well as other radical movements in parts of the Third World, rock music was regarded as "bourgeois" and "decadent," rather than an "authentic" music of social protest. At the same time, however, the assault on institutional hierarchies, the stress on "communication," and the demand for a democratization of social relations were all values inscribed within the rhythms and later, lyrics, of rock music culture. This is not to argue that contradictions between ideology and practice were not visible; they were often rampant, especially when it came to gender relations. But such contradictions were found among more radical movements as well.

26. See, for example, "Global Report on Rock 'n' Roll," *New York Times Magazine*, 20 April 1958, 24–25; Roger Wallis and Krister Malm, *Big Sounds from Small Peoples: The Music Industry in Small Countries* (New York: Pendragon, 1984); Martin and Segrave, *Anti-Rock;* Timothy W. Ryback, *Rock around the Bloc: A History of Rock Music in Eastern Europe and the Soviet Union* (New York: Oxford University Press, 1990); Charles Hamm, "Rock 'n' roll in a Very Strange Society," *Popular Music* 5 (1985): 159–74; Umberto Fiori, "Rock Music and Politics in Italy," *Popular Music* 4 (1984): 261–78; Lawrence Zion, "Disposable Icons: Pop Music in Australia, 1955–1963," *Popular Music* 8 (1989): 165–75.

27. Ryback, *Rock around the Bloc,* 53; "Crackdown on 'Liberal' Pix, Play and Music in Iron Curtain Countries: Only the Twist Okayed by Russos," *Variety,* 1 May 1963, 25.

28. Rock has been sorely neglected in studies on Latin American culture, which have emphasized the place of "Nueva Canción" and folkloric musical expression over popular music. I wish to thank Susie Trutie of MTV for lending me the tape, "MTV News Latino: Mejor hablar de ciertas cosas, Pequeñas historias del rock argentina," which contains a somewhat frenzied but nevertheless useful musical narrative of rock 'n' roll's early years in that country (Prod. Lily Neumeyer, 12 December 1996, LSPE008). See also Nicolás Casullo, "Argentina: El rock en la sociedad política," *Comunicación y Cultura* 12 (1984): 41–50; Pablo Vila, "*Rock nacional* and Dictatorship in Argentina," *Popular Music* 6 (1987): 129–48; Charles A. Perrone, "Changing of the Guard: Questions and Contrasts of Brazilian Rock Phenomena," *Studies in Latin American Popular Culture* 9 (1990): 65–83; Pilar Riaño-Alcalá, "Urban Space and Music in the Formation of Youth Cultures: The Case of Bogotá, 1920–1980," *Studies in Latin American Popular Culture* 10 (1991): 87–106; Peter Manuel, "Rock Music and Cultural Ideology in Revolutionary Cuba," in Simon Frith, ed., *World Music, Politics and Social Change* (Manchester, U.K.: Manchester University Press, 1991), 161–66.

29. Arjun Appadurai, "Disjuncture and Difference in the Global Cultural Economy," *Public Culture* 2 (Spring 1990): 5. A problem with Appadurai's approach is that it tends to dehistoricize sociocultural change in its emphasis on

the study of contemporary global "flow." See also "Special Issue on Global Culture," *Theory, Culture & Society* 7, nos. 2–3 (June 1990).

30. The term is used in Appadurai, "Disjuncture and Difference." See also Robert J. Foster, "Making National Cultures in the Global Ecumene," *Annual Review of Anthropology* 20 (1991): 235–60. For an interesting study of how by the 1980s First World media shaped and competed with Third World media see Armand Mattelart, Xavier Delcourt, and Michele Mattelart, *International Image Markets: In Search of an Alternative Perspective,* trans. David Buxton (London: Comedia, 1984). For an important introduction to the issues see John Tomlinson, *Cultural Imperialism: A Critical Introduction* (Baltimore, Md.: Johns Hopkins University Press, 1991).

31. Ryback, *Rock around the Bloc,* 26. Ryback points out that a 1958 article in the NATO journal *Revue militaire générale* indeed proposed the argument that jazz, rock, and other modern dance music might be a useful tactic in the global effort to undermine Communism. Soviet response to Presley's military transfer to West Germany reflected these fears. In fact, Voice of America radio and other U.S. information outlets began promoting the youth culture in earnest by the mid-1960s.

32. Thus Herbert Braun writes: "The students may have listened to the Beatles, followed new hair styles from abroad and thought about how their actions related to those of students elsewhere, but their obsession was with Mexico and with their president. . . . They did not see Mexico as part of a World [cultural] economy" (Herbert Braun, "Protests of Engagement: Dignity, False Love, and Self-Love in Mexico, 1968" [paper presented at the Washington Seminar for Historians of Latin America, Georgetown University, Washington, D.C., October 1997], p. 34).

33. Information on marketing strategies comes from interviews with company officials, the business archives at Baker Library (Harvard University), and trade magazines, especially *Variety*. A partial index of *Variety*, covering all references to Mexico for 1957–1971, may be found in my dissertation as a useful source for future research. Eric Zolov, "Containing the Rock Gesture: Mass Culture and Hegemony in Mexico, 1955–1975" (Ph.D. diss., University of Chicago, 1995), vol. 2, 429–442.

34. George Katsiaficas, *The Imagination of the New Left: A Global Analysis of 1968* (Boston: South End Press, 1987); Ronald Fraser, ed., *1968: A Student Generation in Revolt. An International Oral History* (New York: Pantheon, 1988); Robert V. Daniels, *Year of the Heroic Guerrilla: World Revolution and Counterrevolution in 1968* (New York: Basic Books, 1989).

35. An important exception to this lack of historical memory in Mexico is the continued publication of important works of fiction that were written in the context of the counterculture. For example, José Agustín's *Inventando que sueño*, originally published in 1968, is now in its fifteenth edition, and works by other authors of the period can also be found. The music, imagery, and other commodified items, however, are much more difficult to access. At the same time, there are indications that a "revival" of countercultural lore may be un-

der way, for example with the recent publication of José Agustín, *La contracultura en México: La historia y el significado de los rebeldes sin causa, los jipitecas, los punks y las bandas* (Mexico City: Grijalbo, 1996) and the new rock series on Polygram Records, "Las raíces del rock," a collection that features music from La Onda Chicana (Víctor Ronquillo, "El rock tiene su historia," *Reforma*, 22 June 1997, E4). World Wide Web sites, such as [http://www.rockeros.com], also suggest the recovery of a certain historical memory.

CHAPTER 1

1. José Agustín, *Tragicomedia mexicana I: La vida en México de 1940 a 1970* (Mexico City: Planeta, 1990), 147.
2. Alan Bloom, quoted in Trent Hill, "The Enemy within: Censorship in Rock Music in the 1950s," *South Atlantic Quarterly* 90 (Fall 1991): 683.
3. Ibid., 684.
4. Ibid.
5. Mambo was criticized in some quarters for being "music of savages," but this certainly did not seem to affect its broader impact. See Yolanda Moreno Rivas, *Historia de la música popular mexicana* (Mexico City: Promociones Editoriales Mexicanas, 1979; Consejo Nacional para la Cultura y las Artes / Editorial Patria, 1989), 242.
6. *Música tropical* is used to denominate a variety of musical dance styles "in which black or Caribbean influence predominates" (ibid., 236). See also David K. Stigberg, "Foreign Currents during the 60s and 70s in Mexican Popular Music: Rock and Roll, the Romantic Ballad and the Cumbia," *Studies in Latin American Popular Culture* 4 (1985): 170–84.
7. "Baila el rock and roll," by Frank Domínguez. Copyright © 1957 by Peer International Corporation. Copyright renewed. International copyright secured. Used by permission.
8. Moreno Rivas, *Historia de la música*, 243. See also Federico Arana, *Guaraches de ante azul: Historia del rock mexicano* (Mexico City: Posada, 1985), vol. 1, chaps. 1–3.
9. Moreno Rivas, *Historia de la música*, 242.
10. Stigberg, "Foreign Currents."
11. In 1960 the rural sector dropped below 50 percent of the population for the first time (Michael C. Meyer and William L. Sherman, *The Course of Mexican History*, 5th ed. [New York: Oxford University Press, 1995], 655).
12. "El can-rock!" *Impacto*, 2 January 1957, 26.
13. Discos Peerless may have had ties with the U.S. record producer Ralph Peer, who controlled Peer International, a company that marketed "race" and "hillbilly" music in the United States. In 1930 Peer went to Mexico and "gained control of a major catalogue of native popular and classical music for exploitation locally and around the world," possibly a reference to Discos Peerless (Russell Sanjek, *American Popular Music and Its Business: The First Four Hundred Years* [New York: Oxford University Press, 1988], vol. 3, 180). I

thank Deborah Pacini-Hernández for raising this connection and providing the citation.

14. "La primera fábrica de discos en México," *Excélsior*, 2 December 1958. See also "History of the Recording Industry in Mexico," *Discoméxico* 25, (March, 1993). Unfortunately, several dates are cited for the opening of Discos Peerless. *Excélsior* gives 1926. *Discoméxico*, a poorly edited trade journal, states that it was in 1933. An article in *Billboard* (Eliot Tiegel, "Entertainment Fields Sparkle with Diversity!" *Billboard Music Week*, 16 December 1967, M5) gives the date as 1936, which is what I have chosen to keep.

15. This narrative is pieced together from the following sources: Carlos Beltrand Luján, interview with the author, Mexico City, 18 May 1994; Claudia Fernández and Andrew Paxman, "El Tigre" (unpublished manuscript); Marjorie Miller and Juanita Darling, "The Eye of the Tiger: Emilio Azcárraga and the Televisa Empire," in William A. Orme Jr., ed., *A Culture of Collusion: An Inside Look at the Mexican Press* (Miami: North-South Center Press / University of Miami, 1997), 59–70. I am also indebted to Andrew Paxman, Latin American correspondent for *Variety*, for various conversations about the subject.

16. In the late 1960s Audio Devices, Inc. merged with Capitol Records to form Capitol Industries, Inc.

17. *Annual Report*, Audio Devices, Inc., 1957, found in "Capitol Industries–EMI" (Folder 1: Annual Reports, 1950–66), Historical Corporate Records Collection, Baker Library, Harvard University. (Hereafter cited as HCRC–Harvard Collection.)

18. *Annual Report*, RCA Corporation, 1963, 4, Cole-Harvard Collection, Baker Library, Harvard University. (Hereafter cited as Cole-Harvard Collection.)

19. *Annual Report*, RCA Corporation, 1957, 38, Cole-Harvard Collection.

20. *Annual Report*, CBS, Inc., "CBS, Inc., 1944–73," Reel 104, 1958, 62–63, Cole-Harvard Collection.

21. *Annual Report*, CBS, Inc., 1961, 10, Cole-Harvard Collection.

22. *Annual Report*, RCA Corporation, 1959, 24, Cole-Harvard Collection.

23. Kenneth L. Shore, "The Crossroads of Business and Music: A Study of the Music Industry in the United States and Internationally" (Ph.D. diss., Stanford University, 1983), 101.

24. *Annual Report*, CBS, Inc., 1958, 43, Cole-Harvard Collection.

25. In Mexico, the corporations' historical record was so poorly organized that neither RCA (later purchased by Sony Music) nor CBS was able to offer much beyond the scantest of official documents.

26. *Annual Report*, RCA Corporation, 1957, 24, 38, Cole-Harvard Collection.

27. *Annual Report*, CBS, Inc., 1956, 46, Cole-Harvard Collection.

28. Ibid.

29. *Annual Report*, CBS, Inc., 1959, 63, Cole-Harvard Collection; "Col Records 1st LA Convention," *Variety*, 16 April 1958, 45.

30. "Col Expanding South-of-the-Border," *Variety*, 9 November 1960, 49.

31. "Only US, Red China, Brazil Top Mexico in Number of Radio Stations," *Variety*, 21 January 1959, 51. Cheap radio sets were also sold directly by radio stations to low-income families throughout the country.

32. "TV, Radio in Mexico Far Outstrips All Latin American Competish: Conde," *Variety*, 17 August 1960, 89.

33. "Mex TV & Radio See Big Advances, Prosperity in '60," *Variety*, 20 January 1960, 47.

34. In 1962 there were approximately 300,000 homes with record players in the country. "Mexico," *Billboard Music Week: 1962–1963 International Music Industry Buyers' Guide and Market Data Report*, 4 August 1962, 145.

35. Shore, "Crossroads of Business and Music."

36. "Se instalará una fábrica de discos en Argentina para impulsar nuestra música," *Excélsior*, 16 February 1957, B6.

37. "RCA Priming Pump of Mex Subsid to Press Disks for U.S. Lingo Mkt.," *Variety*, 4 February 1959, 59.

38. "Col to Push Hispano Disks in US Market," *Variety*, 17 August 1960, 40.

39. "Mexican-Made Global Disk Gleam," *Variety*, 29 July 1959, 101.

40. "Mex Disk Gross Topping '58 Peak of $30,000,000," *Variety*, 6 January 1960, 209.

41. "Mexican Disk Industry's '60 Exports Hit $1,600,000 Bank's Report Discloses," *Variety*, 2 August 1961, 83; "Se exportaron, en 1960, discos por 20 millones," *Novedades*, 12 July 1961. The principal markets for Mexican music were Venezuela, the United States, El Salvador, Guatemala, and Panama.

42. "Mex Diskeries' Mucho Etcho," *Variety*, 20 January 1960, 65.

43. "Discos Mexicana Preps Major Expansion Via New Studios, Labels," *Variety*, 2 September 1959, 60. The new facilities included "recording studios, presses, printing plant, etc. with latest equipment acquired in U.S." ("Hispavox, Orfeon Accent Mexico's Disk Expansion," *Variety*, 3 December 1958, 73).

44. "Orfeon Mex Disks to Tee Off in Japan," *Variety*, 28 October 1959, 43; "Hispavox, Orfeon Accent Mexico's Disk Expansion."

45. "Mex Diskeries' Mucho Etcho"; Salvador Minjares, "Tres continentes serán invadidos por grabaciones hechas en México," *Excélsior*, 13 January 1957, A18.

46. "Rank in Global Deal for RCA Mexicana Disks," *Variety*, 17 May 1961, 61.

47. "Col Aims at Wider Mkt. for Mex Singers," *Variety*, 6 September 1961, 47.

48. "Victor in Latino Kick in U.S., Bids for $1-Mil. Sales in Genre," *Variety*, 31 October 1962, 44.

49. "Mexico Mulling Ban on Imported Disks," *Variety*, 18 May 1960, 59.

50. "Foreign Diskeries Invading Mexico," *Variety*, 18 February 1959, 41.

51. Eréndira Rincón, interview with the author, Mexico City, 20 August 1996.

52. See chapter 5, chapter 6, and the conclusions.

53. This meaning is not in any Spanish-language dictionary. The closest reference is to *desmadrado,* "an animal abandoned by its mother" (*Diccionario enciclopédico de la lengua castellana,* 3d ed. [Paris: Sarnier Hermanos, 1900], 830). While in contemporary Spanish usage the term is widely known (especially in, though not limited to, Mexico), my perception is that until the mid-to-late 1960s the term itself was used only among the lower classes, and as an extremely vulgar one at that. A synonym for *desmadre* that was available for the middle and upper classes was *relajo,* which has similar connotations but without the offensive, class-oriented overtones. See Jorge Portilla, *Fenomeno-logía del relajo y otros ensayos* (Mexico City: Ediciones Era, 1966); Claudio Lomnitz-Adler, *Exits from the Labyrinth: Culture and Ideology in the Mexican National Space* (Berkeley: University of California Press, 1992), 10.

54. Rincón, interview.

55. cf. Evelyn P. Stevens, "*Marianismo:* The Other Face of *Machismo* in Latin America," in Ann Pescatello, ed., *Female and Male in Latin America: Essays* (Pittsburgh: University of Pittsburgh Press, 1973), 89–101.

56. Rincón, interview.

57. For a wonderful representation of the challenges posed by modernization to patriarchal authority in a middle-class family see the film *Una familia de tantas* (Dir. Alejandro Galindo, 1948). On the question of divorce, see below.

58. Ilene V. O'Malley, *The Myth of the Revolution: Hero Cults and the Institutionalization of the Mexican State, 1920–1940* (Westport, Conn.: Greenwood Press, 1986).

59. See the advertisements in *Excélsior,* 1 January 1957.

60. *Excélsior,* 12 February 1957, A18. Unlike in the United States, where earlier dance steps associated with rock 'n' roll have been largely forgotten, in Mexico rock 'n' roll continues to be recognized as a familiar dance pattern, practiced by young and old alike, and by all classes.

61. Emilio García Riera, *Historia documental del cine mexicano* (Jalisco, Mexico: Universidad de Guadalajara, 1993), vol. 8, 245.

62. Carl J. Mora, *Mexican Cinema: Reflections of a Society, 1896–1988* (Berkeley: University of California Press, 1982 [rev. ed., 1989]), 99.

63. Ibid.

64. See, for example, Anne Rubenstein, "Mediated Styles of Masculinity in the Post-Revolutionary Imagination, or, El Santo's Strange Career" (paper presented at the conference, Representing Mexico: Transnationalism and the Politics of Culture since the Revolution, Woodrow Wilson International Center for Scholars, Washington, D.C., 7–8 November 1997).

65. García Riera, *Historia documental,* vol. 8, 130.

66. Mora, *Mexican Cinema,* 84–85.

67. Interestingly, RCA's Mexican marketing strategy highlighted Presley's darkened, mestizo features ("In Living Cardboard," *New York Times Book Review,* 17 November 1996, 24).

68. A similar plot is developed in the film *Al compás del rock'n roll*, in which the women form their own rock 'n' roll band to compete with their boyfriends and an imitator of Presley, "Elvio Prentis," "sings and dances rock . . . provoking fainting fits among the women" (García Riera, *Historia documental*, vol. 8, 301).

69. See, for example, the advertisements for different schools in *Jueves de Excélsior* during this period. In the short story "Battles in the Desert," by José Emilio Pacheco, this theme of English language within the middle-class family is also explored (José Emilio Pacheco, *Battles in the Desert and Other Stories*, trans. Katherine Silver [Mexico City: Ediciones Era, 1981; New York: New Directions, 1987]).

70. Rafael Solana, "'Celos y revueltos,'" *Excélsior*, 14 February 1957, B4.

71. Linda Martin and Kerry Segrave, *Anti-Rock: The Opposition to Rock 'n' Roll* (New York: Da Capo, 1993), 7. The film was shown in Mexico City theaters in October 1955.

72. *New York Times*, 6 March 1955, B4.

73. *Excélsior*, 26 October 1955, A19.

74. *Juventud desenfrenada* (Dir. José Díaz Morales, 1956). See "Gloria Ríos habla de 'Juventud desenfrenada,'" *Excélsior*, 19 January 1957, B4. I am indebted to Rogelio Agrasanchez Jr. for lending me a copy of this film, for it does not appear in any Mexican film archive.

75. The only female character not prostituted literally, is figuratively "distorted" because she is presented quite obviously as a lesbian. Dressed in trousers and a man's dress shirt, at the end she is shot in the back by a policeman who later exclaims: "It's a woman! If she had worn a skirt, I wouldn't have fired!"

76. *Excélsior*, 20 January 1957, A29.

77. The numbers of registered divorces for the country are as follows: 1940, 42,559; 1950, 67,810; 1960, 119,045. For Mexico City the numbers are: 1940, 6,456; 1950, 16,556; 1960, 30,379. Whether by accident or design, numbers for 1970 show only a slight increase over 1960. *Anuario Estadístico de los Estados Unidos Mexicanos* (Mexico City: Dirección General de Estadísticas, 1951–1970).

78. García Riera, *Historia documental*, vol. 8, 234.

79. "'Juventud desenfrenada' en su 4a semana de exhibición," *Excélsior*, 16 January 1957, B4.

80. I wish to thank Federico Arana for making the original poster available to me.

81. *Excélsior*, 20 January 1957, A29.

82. "Gloria Ríos le enseñará a usted a bailar rock'n roll," *Excélsior*, 6 February 1957, B4.

83. "Un médico y una estudiante ganan el certamen de 'Juventud desenfrenada,'" *Excélsior*, 17 February 1957, B4. See also "'Juventud desenfrenada,' una lección para todos," *Excélsior*, 20 January 1957, B4.

84. Arana, *Guaraches*, vol. 1, 84.

85. Hill, "Enemy within," 688.

86. O'Malley, *Myth of the Revolution*, 111. *The Wild One* was shown in Mexico City in 1954.

87. Not until 1965 did Villa become an "official national hero" (O'Malley, *Myth of the Revolution*, 112).

88. Parménides García Saldaña, *En la ruta de La Onda* (Mexico City: Diógenes, 1972), 65.

89. Ibid. García Saldaña also writes that subtitled translations introduced new terms in an effort to avoid more vulgar Mexicanisms. In *Rebel without a Cause*, for example, "Don't be a chicken" was translated literally as "No seas gallina," rather than the more appropriate "No seas maricón" (p. 63).

90. Johnny Laboriel, interview with the author, Mexico City, 11 August 1996.

91. *Rebel without a Cause* was shown for eight weeks in Mexico City in 1956. Though its permit technically lasted four years, the film faced problems with its renewal, and it is unclear whether it was actually reissued; interviews and a search of the press suggest that the film was banned during much of the late 1950s. However, in mid-1959 one theater in Mexico City was showing it, though with little promotional fanfare. See "James Dean Echoes Still," *Variety*, 28 September 1960, 1.

92. García Saldaña, *En la ruta de La Onda*, 55.

93. "Dos 'niños bien' querían cambiar cheques falsos," *Excélsior*, 12 June 1959, A29.

94. José de Pascual Janet, "Jóvenes de ayer y de hoy," *Jueves de Excélsior*, 24 January 1957, 19.

95. J. Ortiz, "Pavoroso aumento de la delincuencia juvenil," *Jueves de Excélsior*, 14 November 1957, 20–21.

96. Ibid.

97. Quoted in Arana, *Guaraches*, vol. 2, 77. Siqueiros was jailed from 1960 to 1964 but was later commissioned by the government to create a series of murals for the art and exhibition center named after him, Siqueiros Polyforum. By the late 1950s, his art was considered reactionary by a younger generation of artists who sought to break free of the muralist genre, by then closely associated with the official nationalism.

98. "En febrero harán el primer festival 'rock and roll,'" *Excélsior*, 4 January 1957, B6.

99. Arana, *Guaraches*, vol. 1, 72–75.

100. "En febrero harán."

101. "Certero impacto radiofónico de la emisora 'Radio Exitos,'" *Excélsior*, 27 January 1957, A23.

102. Herbe Pompeyo, interview with the author, Mexico City, 8 June 1993.

103. Arana, *Guaraches*, vol. 1, 113.

104. Ibid., 95.

105. "A pesar de todo, hoy se estrena 'Los chiflados por [sic] el rock'n roll,'" *Excélsior*, 27 February 1957, B4; Bill Llano, "Los espectáculos," *Impacto*, 3 April 1957, 44–47.

106. Martin and Segrave, *Anti-Rock*, 81. Banned under Batista for its associations with immorality, rock was again prohibited under Fidel Castro for its alleged ties to imperialism.

107. Carlos Haro, "Elvis Presley dice en su defensa que: 'Jamás he faltado el respecto a la mujer mexicana,'" *Excélsior*, 2 March 1957, B8.

108. I thank Emmy Avilés Bretón for raising this point.

109. "Los discos de Presley han sido retirados de 'Radio Exitos,'" *El Universal*, 22 February 1957, A30.

110. Ibid.

111. "A pesar de todo."

112. "'Los chiflados' pagarán los ritmos rotos por Elvis Presley," *El Universal*, 26 February 1957, A31. Despite initial protests, the film was shown.

113. "Adelita" was the name of a famous revolutionary corrido which told longingly of female companionship during that struggle. The song also popularized the use of the name more generally to identify women who accompanied the male troops in battle, especially among the armies under Pancho Villa. While women participated at various social, intellectual, and military levels during the revolution, the image of the faithful female who followed her man into battle in order to tend to his needs has overshadowed all other historical representations of female participation. See Anna Mathias, *Against All Odds: The Feminist Movement in Mexico to 1940* (Westport: Greenwood Press, 1982), chap. 2, "Women and the Mexican Revolution, 1910–1920."

114. "Hoy será la 'quema' de discos de Elvis Presley," *El Universal*, 7 March 1957, A28. The FEU was formed in 1915 and played a crucial role mediating the relationship between the university and the government. Though still an influential actor in student politics, by the early 1960s the growing size of the university population undermined the monopoly on power the FEU once held. See Donald J. Mabry, *The Mexican University and the State: Student Conflicts, 1910–1971* (College Station: Texas A&M University Press, 1982).

115. *Excélsior*, 9 March 1957, A29.

116. *El Universal*, 27 February 1957, A21.

117. "Hoy será la 'quema.'"

118. Federico de León, "Un hombre de la calle," *Jueves de Excélsior*, 28 February 1957, 33.

119. Pascual Janet, "Jóvenes de Ayer y de Hoy."

120. "'Quema' de Discos de Elvis Presley," *Excélsior*, 2 March 1957, B4.

121. Pascual Janet, "Jóvenes de Ayer y de Hoy."

122. *Excélsior*, 6 May 1959, A29.

123. "Vejaciones y atropellos de 600 'rebeldes sin causa' en un cine," *Excélsior*, 7 May 1959, B1.

124. Ibid.

125. Parménides García Saldaña, *El rey criollo* (Mexico City: Diógenes, 1970; Mexico: Lecturas Mexicanas, 1987), 164. "Me voy al pueblo" is based on a Cuban *son guajiro* (folk song) popularized by the Mexican trio Los Panchos. The original lyrics are, "Me voy para el pueblo / Hoy es mi día / Voy a alegrar

toda el alma mía. (I'm going to the country / Today's my day / I'm going to rejoice with my entire soul). To this day, the song continues to be appropriated by political demonstrators and youth, who similarly twist the lyrics.

126. Ibid., 163–64. The reference to a swastika is glaring, though it most likely was not being displayed with an anti-Semitic intent. If the use of the swastika today is any indication of its earlier display, the symbol was used out of ignorance as a show of rebellion, but without an understanding of its (to us, obvious) racist implications.

127. Ibid., 165–66.

128. Arana, *Guaraches*, vol. 1, 145.

129. Abel Quezada, "Maestro de la juventud," *Excélsior*, 15 May 1959, A7.

130. Abel Quezada, "Al son que le toquen," *Excélsior*, 18 December 1959, A7. For a discussion of Quezada as a social cartoonist see Víctor Alba, "The Mexican Revolution and the Cartoon," reprinted in W. Dirt Raat and William H. Beezley, eds., *Twentieth-Century Mexico* (Lincoln: University of Nebraska Press, 1986), 223–35.

131. "La causa de los 'rebeldes,'" *Excélsior*, 14 May 1959, A7.

132. "Crisis en el hogar," *Excélsior*, 4 June 1959, A6.

133. Arana, *Guaraches*, vol. 1, 15–16.

134. "Nada de 'rebeldes,' dice el procurador: Los mayores de 18 años son pandilleros," *Excélsior*, 9 December 1959, A17.

135. Philip B. Taylor, Jr., "The Mexican Elections of 1958: Affirmation of Authoritarianism?" *Western Political Quarterly* 23, no. 3 (1960): 736.

136. Ibid., 738. See also Evelyn P. Stevens, *Protest and Response in Mexico* (Cambridge, Mass.: MIT Press, 1974).

137. "La causa de los 'rebeldes.'"

138. "La autoridad en crisis," *Jueves de Excélsior*, 3 July 1958, 5.

139. *Juventud* 5, no. 1 (1959), Publicaciones: Galería 3, Administración Pública; López Mateos, 704/159, Archivo General de la Nación. (Hereafter cited as AGN.)

140. "Crisis en el hogar."

141. *Jueves de Excélsior*, 4 June 1959.

142. Anne Rubenstein, *Bad Language, Naked Ladies, and Other Threats to the Nation: A Political History of Comic Books in Mexico* (Durham, N.C.: Duke University Press, 1998).

143. Roger D. Hansen, *The Politics of Mexican Development* (Baltimore, Md.: John Hopkins University Press, 1971 [1974]), 169. Land redistribution under López Mateos accelerated to its highest rate since the time of Lázaro Cárdenas. Meanwhile, friendly ties were maintained with Cuba despite pressures from the United States to rupture them. See Arthur K. Smith Jr., "Mexico and the Cuban Revolution: Foreign Policy-Making in Mexico under President Adolfo López Mateos, 1958–1964" (Ph.D. diss., Cornell University, 1970).

144. Eric Zolov, "Post-War Repackaging of Mexico: The Cosmopolitan-*Folklórico* Axis" (paper presented at the conference, Representing Mexico: Transnationalism and the Politics of Culture since the Revolution, Woodrow

Wilson International Center for Scholars, Washington, D.C., 7–8 November 1997).

145. "Mex $400 Hex on Radio Stations Not Airing 25% in Native Music," *Variety*, 8 April 1959, 55.

146. "Mex Radio-TV Beef: Too Many Foreign Ditties," *Variety*, 15 July 1959, 58. See also, "Mex Ranchero Music in Crisis as Sales Dip Due to Foreign Inroads," *Variety*, 13 May 1959, 56.

147. "Mex's Song Fair for Sept; Oldies," *Variety*, 27 May 1959, 55.

148. "Mexican Folk Music Set for a 'Wax' Museum," *Variety*, 2 September 1959, 61.

149. "Juventudes Musicales de México," 6 December 1958, Publicaciones: Galería 3, Administración Pública; López Mateos, 710.12/1, AGN.

150. "Artistas consagradas ayudarán a nuevos valores que surjan hasta en pueblitos," *Excélsior*, 7 February 1957, B6.

151. "Guerra sin cuartel al vicio," *Jueves de Excélsior*, 22 October 1959, 22–23. The curfew remained in place despite pressures from the musicians' union and club owners over the next several years. See *Variety*, 28 October 1959, 1; 24 January 1962, 47; 28 February 1962, 55.

152. Raúl Vieyra, "La radio mexicana (en todo el mundo) entre las más morales," *Excélsior*, 12 February 1957, B8.

153. Manuel del Castillo, "Prohibidas las películas de nudistas," *Excélsior*, 11 January 1957, B4.

154. "'No más nudismo en el cine,' dice Wallerstein," *Excélsior*, 12 January 1957, B4.

155. Mario J. Sanromán, "El cine y la cultura," *El Universal*, 12 March 1957, A2.

156. "Mex Nat'l Board Bans Yank Pic, 'Daughters,'" *Variety*, 1 January 1958, 2.

157. "Mex Authorities Nix 'Blue Hawaii,'" *Variety*, 7 November 1962, 2; "Beatles' Pic Okayed by Mexico's Censor," *Variety*, 30 June 1965, 54.

158. "Mex Pride Can't Be Denied," *Variety*, 22 June 1966, 13.

159. "Mexicans Find Sinatra Film Insulting, Ban It and Boycott His Disks," *Variety*, 16 March 1966, 1.

160. Anne Rubenstein, "How the Lombardini Brothers Stayed Out of Jail: Conservative Protest, Pornography, and the Boundaries of Expression in Mexico, 1952–1976" (paper presented at the IX Conference of Mexican, United States and Canadian Historians, Mexico City, 27–29 October 1994), 2.

161. November 30, 1959, "Minutario, enero-diciembre, 1959," Secretaría de Gobernación, Comisión Calificadora de Publicaciones y Revistas Ilustradas. (Hereafter cited as CCPRI.)

162. April 3, 1957, "Minutario, enero-diciembre, 1957," CCPRI.

163. July 19, 1957, "Minutario, enero-diciembre, 1957," CCPRI.

164. "Clean-Up Week on Mex TV-Radio," *Variety*, 5 August 1959, 47.

165. The chamber was directly represented by two members on the advisory group created by the new legislation (Article 90). In a speech directed to-

ward Congress, the president of the chamber, Guillermo Morales Blumenkron, noted that private and governmental interests were "[u]nited for the same ideal: the constant improvement of broadcasting" ("Inauguró sus labores la VI Asamblea," *El Nacional,* 5 October 1959). The willingness of the chamber to work closely with the government, especially, for example, in the promotion of public-education campaigns, later led to the resolution of potential conflicts without recourse to judicial sanctions based on a strict interpretation of the law.

166. "Asociación Interamericana de Radiodifusión," 7 August 1959, Comunicaciones: Galería 3, Administración Pública; López Mateos, 512.3/2, AGN.

167. "Ser mexicano es ser libre y la ley de radio y televisión será una plena garantía," *El Nacional,* 5 October 1959, 1.

168. "Cinco discursos con Loas a la ley de radio y TV," *Excélsior,* 8 December 1959, A5.

169. "Ley federal de radio y televisión," *El Diario Oficial,* 19 January 1960, Article 59.

170. Elizabeth Fox, "Media Policies in Latin America: An Overview," in Elizabeth Fox, ed., *Media and Politics in Latin America: The Struggle for Democracy* (London: Sage, 1988), 15.

171. "Ley federal," Article 7.

172. Ibid., Article 58.

173. Ibid., Article 63.

174. Ibid., Article 73.

175. Ibid., Article 75.

176. Ibid., Article 23.

177. "Clean-Up Week."

178. Roberto Velasco, "Prohibido para actores e imitadores que usen amaneramientos en Radio-TV," *Excélsior,* 7 December 1959, B6.

179. "La juventud olvidó el rock'n roll y prefiere lo antiguo," *Excélsior,* 20 December 1959, B6.

180. "Mex Announcers to Get All-Expense U.S. Brushup," *Variety,* 25 December 1959, 43.

CHAPTER 2

1. In using the plural *cultural industries* rather than *culture industry* I am following the position taken by John Sinclair, "Culture and Trade: Some Theoretical and Practical Considerations," in Emile G. McAnany and Kenton T. Wilkinson, eds., *Mass Media and Free Trade: NAFTA and the Cultural Industries* (Austin: University of Texas Press, 1996), 30–60.

2. See Federico Arana, *Guaraches de ante azul: Historia del rock mexicano* (Mexico City: Posada, 1985), vols. 1–2.

3. "The Platters' Mex P.A.s," *Variety,* 4 November 1959, 61.

4. "Warner Bros Pushes Int'l Mkt with Tri-Lingual Recordings," *Variety,* 14 August 1963, 55.

5. "'Los Panchos' empezaron con éxito su gira en el Japón," *Excélsior*, 31 December 1959, B7. This perhaps explains in part the phenomenal popularity of Mexican music in contemporary Japan.

6. "Learning the Lingo of Hits," *Variety*, 7 December 1960, 61.

7. Ibid.

8. "Disk Biz Needs O'Seas Market," *Variety*, 14 September 1960, 61.

9. "Col Expanding South-of-the-Border," *Variety*, 9 November 1960, 49.

10. "Tax & Technology Hit Disks," *Variety*, 20 February 1963, 53.

11. José Cruz Ayala, interview with the author, Mexico City, 13 August 1993.

12. Arana, *Guaraches*, vol. 1, 175.

13. Johnny Laboriel, interview with the author, Mexico City, 11 August 1996.

14. Arana, *Guaraches*, vol. 1, 175–79.

15. Ibid.

16. "RCA's 'New Wave' Disks Clicking in Argentina," *Variety*, 26 October 1960, 57. In Chile, rock 'n' roll music won in several categories at the Third Annual Song Festival, held in 1962 with record-industry sponsorship (*Variety*, 14 March 1962, 57).

17. "Rock 'n' Roll Dominates Mex Disk Biz," *Variety*, 15 February 1961, 55. For a humorous discussion of how a rock 'n' roll style came to dominate the domestic music market for all performers see Arana, *Guaraches*, vol. 2.

18. Manuel Ruiz, interview with the author, Mexico City, 6 August 1991.

19. Arana, *Guaraches*, vol. 2, 175–79, 188–89. According to one count, by 1965 there were some 120 different Mexican rocanrol bands; more than 100 had recorded an album (Arana, *Guaraches*, vol. 4).

20. Laboriel, interview.

21. Laboriel, interview.

22. Carlos Beltrand Luján, interview with the author, Mexico City, 18 May 1994. Violations of copyright protection were outright. In fact, Orfeón's heavy reliance on translations of Paul Anka's ballads led to a lawsuit brought by his publishing firm, Morrow Music. In the settlement, Orfeón agreed to "ask permission to wax Anka's works and submit Spanish lyrics for approval" in the future ("Mex Diskery Settles Row over Spanka Tunes," *Variety*, 14 June 1961, 45).

23. Cruz Ayala, interview.

24. Otto Mayer-Serra, "Rock Still Strong as Sales Fall off by 15%," *Billboard Music Week*, 25 December 1961, 199.

25. "WNEW–TV in Mex Swap on Musicals," *Variety*, 4 January 1961, 126. Efforts to locate this tape proved futile.

26. "Rock 'n' Roll Dominates Mex Disk Biz," *Variety*, 15 February 1961, 55.

27. "Mex Tariff Boost Hits Disk Imports," *Variety*, 3 May 1961, 67. *Variety* cites the tariff at 30 percent and *Billboard* at 40 percent. I have chosen to use the latter. See "Mexico," *Billboard Music Week: 1962–1963 International Music Industry Buyers' Guide and Market Data Report*, 4 August 1962, 145.

28. Otto Mayer-Serra, "Industry Does Well; Maintains '61 Level," *Billboard Music Week*, 29 December 1962, 192.

29. "Importancia económica de la grabación de discos," *El Nacional*, 3 November 1962. Other factors noted in the report as contributing to a decline in exports were trade barriers between Latin American countries, insufficient promotion, pirating, and the recording of Mexican artists by transnationals outside the country, where recording facilities were deemed superior.

30. "Mexico's Orfeon Diskery Inks Bill Haley to 2-Yr. Pact," *Variety*, 2 August 1961, 85. Also under contract with Orfeón were The Platters, who performed on television and in concert in Mexico City in 1959 (*Variety*, 4 November 1959, 61).

31. "Twist Girdles Globe, But Syria Bans It in Deference to Bellydancers," *Variety*, 7 February 1962, 1.

32. "Twisting the Twist," *Variety*, 24 January 1962, 49.

33. Ibid.

34. "Mex Song Fest as Boost for Native Tunes & Tourism," *Variety*, 18 April 1962, 49.

35. Ibid.

36. "Mexican Tooter Union Riled at Rock 'n' Rollers for Undercutting Pros," *Variety*, 26 October 1960, 56.

37. "Mex Radio Exec Nixes Espagnol Rock 'n' Roll," *Variety*, 29 June 1960, 62.

38. "Mexican Tooter Union."

39. Ibid.

40. "Mex Rock 'n' Roll Units Try 'Dignity' Buildup," *Variety*, 7 December 1960, 61.

41. "Tooters' Head Vows Clean Sweep of Mex R 'n R's 'Musical Hoodlums,'" *Variety*, 4 October 1961, 61.

42. "Mexican Tooter Union Accepts R 'n' R Combos, But Strings Attached," *Variety*, 8 November 1961, 57. At one point, claiming that Televicentro (the filming studios of Telesistema) privileged groups performing rocanrol and música tropical, Venus Rey threatened a walkout by union members in an effort to curtail the "inroads in [sic] tv by the smaller combos playing 'exotic' rhythms" ("Mex Tooters' Union in R 'n' R Crackdown," *Variety*, 24 January 1962, 49).

43. Beltrand Luján, interview.

44. Mayer-Serra, "Industry Does Well," 192.

45. "His Label Thriving, Sez Discos Mexicanos Exec," *Variety*, 29 November 1961, 53.

46. Beltrand Luján, interview. This figure may have been an exaggeration, but Orfeón's dominance in the market was still considerable.

47. "His Label Thriving"; "Mexican Disk Industry in Middle of a Price War as LPs Drop to $ Level," *Variety*, 31 August 1960, 43.

48. "Col Steps Up O'Seas Action," *Variety*, 25 April 1962, 45.

49. *Annual Report*, CBS, Inc., 1961, 9, Cole-Harvard Collection.

50. *Annual Report*, CBS, Inc., 1962, 25, Cole-Harvard Collection.

51. "Col Records of Mexico Hiking Capital to $2-Mil," *Variety*, 20 June 1962, 49.

52. "Orfeon Label Quits Mex Assn. of Record Prods," *Variety*, 12 December 1962, 47.

53. "Col's CBS Label Invades Spain via Madrid Distrib," *Variety*, 10 October 1962, 47; "Col Label Goes South-of-Border," *Variety*, 5 September 1962, 43.

54. *Annual Report*, CBS, Inc., 1963, 24, Cole-Harvard Collection.

55. "Orfeon Label Quits."

56. Juventino Flores H., "Los Locos del Ritmo," *México Canta*, 15 October 1965, 6–10.

57. For example, from 1962 to 1964 Los Loud Jets toured Latin America. Afterward they performed in the United States and Europe as "The Mexican Jets" and "The Mexican Jumping Beans." After playing at the Copacabana in New York City for six straight months, where they also appeared on the *Ed Sullivan Show*, the group traveled to the Netherlands and then in 1966 began a tour of Western Europe and Asia ("Los Loud Jets triunfan en América," *Idolos del Rock*, December 1966, 20–25). In an interview with me, Johnny Laboriel, of Los Rebeldes del Rock, later expressed his regret at not having switched companies, complaining that Orfeón was less interested in promoting their music (as the transnationals appeared to be doing for other groups) than in exploiting the group financially.

58. In one interesting example, the company Musart contracted a group to record refritos of another group's (Los Teen Tops) own refritos (Arana, *Guaraches*, vol. 1, 200).

59. "RCA Victor Mexicana Sets TV Musical Series," *Variety*, 28 October 1959, 22; "Programas de mayor duración, 1950–1980," in Fernando González y González, ed. *Historia de la televisión mexicana* (privately published, 1989), p. 373. Although "Orfeón a go-go" continued until 1969, the RCA program does not appear in this source, suggesting that it may have been short-lived.

60. See David Shumway, "Rock & Roll as a Cultural Practice," *South Atlantic Quarterly* 90 (Fall 1991): 753–69; Trent Hill, "The Enemy within: Censorship in Rock Music in the 1950s," *South Atlantic Quarterly* 90 (Fall 1991): 675–707.

61. Víctor Roura, *Apuntes de rock: Por las calles del mundo* (Mexico City: Nuevomar, 1985), 32.

62. Víctor Roura, *Negros del corazón* (Mexico City: Universidad Autónoma Metropolitana, 1984), 22.

63. Beltrand Luján, interview.

64. Roura, *Apuntes*, 32.

65. *Jueves de Excélsior*, 1 February 1962, cover.

66. Conchita Cervantes, interview with the author, Mexico City, 22 August 1996.

67. See chapter 1.

68. Dir. Gilberto Martínez Solares. The film features Los Rockin' Devils. I wish to thank the Sotomayor family for making this film accessible for viewing.

69. Dir. Julián Soler. The film features Los Hooligans. I wish to thank the Sotomayor family for making this film accessible for viewing.

70. Simon Frith, *Sound Effects: Youth, Leisure, and the Politics of Rock 'n' Roll* (New York: Pantheon, 1981), 187.

71. Ibid.

72. Dir. Miguel M. Delgado, 1962.

73. Dir. Julián Soler, 1964.

74. See Evelyn P. Stevens, "*Marianismo:* The Other Face of *Machismo* in Latin America" in Ann Pescatello, ed., *Female and Male in Latin America: Essays* (Pittsburgh: University of Pittsburgh Press, 1973), 96.

75. Emilio García Riera, *Historia documental del cine mexicano* (Jalisco, Mexico: Universidad de Guadalajara, 1993), vol. 9, 342.

76. Dir. Jaime Salvador, 1966. The film features Los Hooligans.

77. "Prohibida su lectura a los muchachos," *México Canta,* 15 October 1965, 37.

78. Víctor Cruz, "Twist con Chubby Checker," *México Canta,* 15 May 1964, 45.

79. Flores H., "Los Locos del Ritmo," 6.

80. 31 January 1962, CCPRI.

81. 2 May 1962, CCPRI.

82. Ibid.

83. Ibid.

84. "Tallahassee Lassie," words and music by Frank C. Slay, Bob Crewe, and Frederick Piscariello. Copyright © 1958, 1959 by Conley Music, Inc. Copyright renewed 1986, 1987 by MPL Communications, Inc. All rights reserved. Used by permission. English translation from the Spanish by the author.

85. *Plaga* can be translated both as *girl* (wild one) and *gang* (raucous group of friends). It also, of course, carries the connotation of a plague.

86. "Good Golly Miss Molly," by Marascalco and Blackwell. Copyright © 1958 by Jondora Music, Robinhood Music, Third Story Music. Reprinted by permission of Jondora Music and Third Story Music. Spanish lyrics by Los Teen Tops. International copyright secured. Used by permission of Jondora Music. All rights reserved.

87. "King Creole," by Jerry Leiber and Mike Stoller. Copyright © 1958 by Elvis Presley Music, Inc. Copyright assigned to Gladys Music (administered by Williamson Music). International copyright secured. Used by permission. All rights reserved.

88. "King Creole," by Jerry Leiber and Mike Stoller. Copyright © 1958 by Jerry Leiber Music, Mike Stoller Music. Spanish lyrics by Los Teen Tops. Copyright renewed. Used by permission. All rights reserved. English translation from the Spanish by the author.

89. Los Locos del Ritmo, *Rock!* (DIMSA, 1960).

90. José Agustín, *Tragicomedia mexicana: La vida en México de 1940 a 1970* (Mexico City: Planeta, 1990), 147.

91. Cervantes, interview.

92. Eréndira Rincón, interview with the author, Mexico City, 20 August 1996.

93. J. Ortiz, "Se pierde la bella tradición de las posadas," *Jueves de Excélsior*, 19 December 1963, 18–19.

94. Cervantes, interview.

95. Rincón, interview.

96. Cervantes, interview.

97. "Carnet de 'Lumiere,'" *Jueves de Excélsior*, 13 September 1962, 30. According to Albert Goldman, Presley never performed abroad—except in Canada—because his manager, Colonel Tom Parker, was actually Dutch-born and not American, as he claimed. Parker refused to allow Presley to perform without his direct supervision and, as Goldman argues, avoided having to apply for a passport in order to conceal his foreign background and likely illegal entry into the United States. See Albert Goldman, *Elvis* (New York: McGraw-Hill, 1981), 146–52, 496–98. I thank Mike Socolow for bringing this information and citation to my attention.

98. "Mex Riot over Avalon," *Variety*, 18 August 1965, 22.

99. "Carnet de 'Lumiere,'" *Jueves de Excélsior*, 8 November 1962, 31.

100. Laboriel, interview. See also the commemorative book edited by Guillermo Chao Ebergenyi, *La caravana corona: Cuna de espectáculo en México* (Mexico City: Corona, Edición Limitada, 1995).

101. See Flores H., "Los Locos del Ritmo."

102. Rincón, interview.

103. Laboriel, interview.

104. See Federico Arana, "Pasión, muerte y milagrosa resurrección de los cafés cantantes," in Carlos Chimal, ed., *Crines: Lecturas del rock* (Mexico City: Penélope, 1984), 45–53.

105. "Cámara Nacional de la Industria de la Radiodifusión," 24 July 1963, Comunicaciones: Galería 3, Administración Pública; López Mateos, 512.3/4, AGN. The following quotations are all drawn from this document.

106. Roura, *Apuntes,* 33.

107. From the liner notes of "Los Rebeldes del Rock: 'Rockin Rebels'" (DIMSA, n.d.). DIMSA was a studio owned by Orfeón Records.

108. "Los Loud Jets triunfan en América."

109. Roura, *Apuntes,* 36.

CHAPTER 3

1. Federico Arana, *Guaraches de ante azul: Historia del rock mexicano* (Mexico City: Posada, 1985), vol. 2, 135–36.

2. From the liner notes of "The Rolling Stones: 'Píntalo de Negro'" (Peerless, 1966). Translation from Spanish.

3. José Agustín, *La nueva música clásica* (Mexico City: Cuadernos de la Juventud, 1968), 67–68.

4. Armando Nava, interview with the author, Mexico City, 5 June 1993.

5. Announcing that the new subsidiary would act "as a launching pad for the company's expansion throughout Latin America," just over a year later Capitol had captured 20 percent of the Mexican market through its distribution of the Beatles, the Animals, the Dave Clark Five, and other well-known British bands. Emilio Azcárraga Milmo was a co-owner of the Capitol subsidiary. See "Cap Spinning into Latino Market via New Mex Diskery," *Variety*, 12 May 1965, 187; Claudia Fernández and Andrew Paxman, "El Tigre" (unpublished manuscript).

6. Nava, interview.

7. Claudio Lomnitz refers to this phenomenon as "staggered distribution" in his essay, "Fissures in Contemporary Mexican Nationalism," *Public Culture* 9 (1996): 55–68.

8. Joaquín ("Chas") López, interview with the author, Mexico City, 7 April 1993.

9. Enrique Partida, interview with the author, Mexico City, 7 June 1993.

10. Armando Blanco, interview with the author, Mexico City, 11 March 1993.

11. For a theoretical discussion see Mark Poster, *The Mode of Information: Poststructuralism and Social Context* (Chicago: University of Chicago Press, 1990), 9–10.

12. Jaime Pontones, interview with the author, Mexico City, 15 August 1991.

13. Manuel Ruiz, interview with the author, Mexico City, 6 August 1991.

14. Eréndira Rincón, interview with the author, Mexico City, 20 August 1996.

15. Iván Zatz-Díaz, interview with the author, New York City, 13 October 1992.

16. Ruiz, interview.

17. Johnny Laboriel, interview with the author, Mexico City, 11 August 1996.

18. Ruiz, interview.

19. Arana (*Guaraches*, vol. 2, 273) suggests that cabaret owners actually opposed the cafés cantantes because they drew away customers, though it seems to me that the clientele, if indeed they overlapped at times, still saw the cabarets and the cafés as distinct types of venues, especially since the latter were prohibited from selling alcohol.

20. Alberto Domingo, "Cafés a go-go," quoted in Arana, *Guaraches*, vol. 4, 92.

21. "Para vigilar los 'cafés cantantes' no hay suficientes inspectores," *Las Ultimas Noticias de Excélsior*, 3 February 1965, 10.

22. Sergio González Rodríguez, *Los bajos fondos: El antro, la bohemia y el café* (Mexico City: Cal y Arena, 1990), 97. Uruchurtu was mayor of the Federal

District from 1952 to 1966, during which time he earned a reputation for often repressive policies aimed at cleaning up the city's image, especially its nightlife.

23. See Federico Arana, "Pasión, muerte y milagrosa resurrección de los cafés cantanes," in Carlos Chimal, ed., *Crines: Lecturas de rock* (Mexico City: Penélope, 1984), 45–53. The essay is reproduced in Arana, *Guaraches*, vol. 2.

24. "Redada y clausuras en más de veinte cafés existencialistas," *El Universal Gráfico*, 1 February 1965, 29.

25. Quoted in Arana, *Guaraches*, vol. 2, 256.

26. Ibid.

27. "Son un peligro para la sociedad los llamados 'cafés existencialistas,'" *El Universal Gráfico*, 6 February 1965, 6.

28. Ramón Gregorio Lara y Chavarría, "Cafés 'existencialistas,'" *El Universal Gráfico*, 10 February 1965, 7.

29. Ruiz, interview.

30. Alma Luzuriaga, "Derechos de la adolescencia," *Jueves de Excélsior*, 27 February 1964, "Jueves Femenino" suppl., n.p.

31. *Jueves de Excélsior*, 12 March 1964.

32. Enrique Alvarez Palacios, "Dioses de barro," *Jueves de Excélsior*, 1 July 1965, 14–15.

33. "'Ay Ay Ay' Giving Way to 'Yeah, Yeah, Yeah' on Mexico's Rockin' Video," *Variety*, 10 November 1965, 1.

34. From the liner notes of "Los Yaki: 'El sonido agresivo de Los Yaki'" (Capitol, 1966).

35. "Los desenfrenados: 5 muchachos que hacen ruido," *México Canta*, 15 October 1965, 42–43.

36. "Reportaje gráfico con LOS SPARKS," *Idolos del Rock* (December 1966), 32–35.

37. "Los Apson: 5 muchachos triunfadores," *México Canta*, 15 October 1965, 48–49.

38. Ibid. *Malinchismo* conveys a notion of cultural treason, of preferring what is foreign to what is native. The term alludes to Doña Marina, Hernán Cortés's aboriginal mistress and translator who abetted his conquest of the Aztecs. When "Mexico became an independent nation and the problem of national identity surfaced . . . Doña Marina, transformed into La Malinche, came to symbolize the humiliation—the rape—of the indigenous people and the act of treachery that would lead to their oppression" (Jean Franco, *Plotting Women: Gender and Representation in Mexico* [(New York: Columbia University Press, 1989], 131). Pulque is an indigenous alcoholic beverage made from the maguey plant.

39. Juventino Flores H., "Los Locos del Ritmo," *México Canta*, 15 October 1965, 6–10.

40. *Jueves de Excélsior*, 3 June 1965.

41. José Agustín, *La contracultura en México: La historia y el significado de los rebeldes sin causa, los jipitecas, los punks y las bandas* (Mexico City: Grijalbo, 1996), 21.

42. Rincón, interview.

43. Ruiz, interview.

44. Rincón, interview.

45. Josefina A. de Gutiérrez, "De las posadas de antaño a las posadas a go go," *Jueves de Excélsior,* 15 December 1966, 18–19. See also chapter 2.

46. Ibid.

47. *Jueves de Excélsior,* 22 September 1966.

48. See Helen Delpar, *The Enormous Vogue of Things Mexican: Cultural Relations between the United States and Mexico, 1920–1935* (Tuscaloosa: University of Alabama Press, 1992). For references to beatnik travels to Mexico see Jack Kerouac, *On the Road* (New York: Signet, 1980; Viking Press, 1957); Carolyn Cassady, *Off the Road: My Years with Cassady, Kerouac, and Ginsberg* (New York: W. Morrow, 1990); D. Wayne Gunn, *Escritores norteamericanos y británicos en México,* trans. Ernestina de Champourcin (Mexico City: Lecturas Mexicanas, 1985; Fondo de Cultura Económica, 1977); Manuel Luis Martinez, "'With Imperious Eyes': Kerouac, Burroughs, and Ginsberg on the Road in South America," *Aztlán* 23, no. 1 (1998): 33–53; Mauricio Tenorio, "Viejos gringos: Radicales norteamericanos en los años treinta y su visión de México," *Secuencia* 21 (September-December 1991): 95–116; Carlos Monsiváis, "Los viajeros y la invención de México," *Aztlán* 15, no. 2 (1984): 201–29.

49. R. Gordon Wasson, "Seeking the Magic Mushroom," *Life Magazine,* 13 May 1957, 100–120. See also R. Gordon Wasson, "Foreword," in Alvaro Estrada, *Vida de María Sabina: La sabia de los hongos,* 9–17 (Mexico City: Siglo XXI, 1977 [1989]).

50. Estrada, *Vida de María Sabina,* 68.

51. "Road to Endsville," *Newsweek,* 9 February 1959, 58.

52. The next few sentences are based on Alvaro Estrada, *Huautla en tiempo de hippies* (Mexico City: Grijalbo, 1996).

53. Estrada, *Vida de María Sabina,* 81.

54. Ibid.

55. Alejandro Ortiz Reja, "Invasión de 'beatniks' en Oaxaca. Parte I," *Excélsior,* 26 August 1967, A1. Locals previously sold mushrooms by the fistful for 5 to 10 pesos (less than U.S. $1.00). At one point, the town mayor tried to capitalize on the hippies' presence by organizing a "Baile a Go-Go" to raise funds for a school. No one showed up, however, and the town lost more than 400 pesos in the effort.

56. The Ballet Folklórico, a traveling dance troupe sponsored by the INBA, directly conveyed this sense of indigenous wonder, as did other, more explicitly tourist-oriented promotions. See Eric Zolov, "Post-War Repackaging of Mexico: The Cosmopolitan-*Folklórico* Axis" (paper presented at the conference, Representing Mexico: Transnationalism and the Politics of Culture since the Revolution, Woodrow Wilson International Center for Scholars, Washington, D.C., 7–8 November 1997); Néstor García Canclini, *Transforming Modernity: Popular Culture in Mexico,* trans. Lidia Lozano (Austin: University of Texas Press, 1993 [1997]), 64–68.

57. "México y las drogas alucinantes," *Jueves de Excélsior,* 7 September 1967, 22–23.

58. Ibid.

59. Estrada, *Huautla en tiempo de hippies,* 64.

60. Marshall Berman, *All That Is Solid Melts into Air: The Experience of Modernity* (New York: Penguin Books, 1982 [1988]), 235.

61. Andreas Huyssen, *After the Great Divide: Modernism, Mass Culture, Postmodernism* (Bloomington: Indiana University Press, 1986), 218. Marshall Berman seeks to frame a discourse of postmodernism within the practices of modernism itself. Compare David Harvey, *The Condition of Postmodernity: An Enquiry into the Origins of Cultural Change* (Oxford: Basil Blackwell, 1989).

62. Huyssen, *After the Great Divide,* 217. Huyssen makes his argument about postmodernism by discussing shifts primarily occurring in the art world. I am applying his argument here to social actors who, I believe, while not being "artists" in the strictest sense, did incorporate a postmodern aesthetic as part of a critique of everyday life.

63. Ortiz Reja, "Invasión de 'Beatniks.'"

64. "Echan del país a los 'hongadictos' de Oaxaca," *Ultimas Noticias,* 7 September 1967, 1.

65. "Ya nos invadieron los 'hippies,'" *Jueves de Excélsior,* 2 May 1968, 22–23. For a description of the hippie/psychedelic scene in Acapulco see José Agustín, *El rock de la cárcel* (Mexico City: Editores Mexicanos Unidos, 1986), passim.

66. "Lo efectivo y lo negativo de la industria turística," *Jueves de Excélsior,* 18 April 1968, 22–23.

67. "Ya nos invadieron los 'hippies.'"

68. Berman, *All That Is Solid,* 194–95.

69. Ruben Salazar, "The Cuevas 'Mafia's' Mexican Mural Revolt," *Los Angeles Times,* 25 June 1967, Calendar Section, 1. The mural was actually a triptych whose strongest visual feature was a self-portrait of the artist signing his own name. It went up in the midst of a congressional political campaign and was removed by Cuevas after a month.

70. "Ya nos invadieron los 'hippies.'"

71. "Pantalla Citadina," *Jueves de Excélsior,* 8 February 1968, 33; 22 February 1968, 37.

72. "Aparecen los 'Mexican Hippies,'" *Jueves de Excélsior,* 3 October 1968, 14–15.

73. Ibid.

74. René Rebetez, "La guerra de las melenas: Unos y otros," *El Heraldo Cultural,* 26 May 1968, 6. Following Moctezuma II's death and the retaking of Tenochtitlán from the Spanish, his nephew Cuitláhuac ascended to the Aztec throne. When Cuitláhuac then contracted smallpox and died, the eighteen-year old Cuauhtémoc became the last Aztec emperor; he died a martyr at the hands of Spanish torturers. A statue of Cuauhtémoc was constructed in the

capital during the Porfiriato as part of an incipient, state-sponsored indigenist movement.

75. Carlos Monsiváis, "México 1967," *La Cultura en México*, 17 January 1968, 7.

76. Domingo, "Cafés a go-go."

77. Carlos Monsiváis, "La nueva generación en Mexico," *El Heraldo de México*, 21 December 1967, D1.

78. Kevin M. Kelleghan, "Image Battle Shapes in Mexico as Firms Gear for 'Tomorrow,'" *Billboard Music Week*, 22 July 1967, 49.

79. "'British Sound' Adds Mucho Momentum to Mexico's Emerging Disk Industry," *Variety*, 20 July 1966, 53.

80. Kelleghan, "Image Battle."

81. "'British Sound.'"

82. Kelleghan, "Image Battle."

83. Todd Gitlin, *The Sixties: Years of Hope, Days of Rage* (Toronto: Bantam, 1987), 205.

84. Agustín, *Nueva música clásica*, 5. For a review of Agustín's book by Carlos Monsiváis see "La Nueva Música Clásica," *La Cultura en México*, 26 June 1968, n.p. Monsiváis argued that rock "seeks to subvert not one, but all structures within its reach." For a later reflection on Agustín's intentions in writing the book see his *Rock de la cárcel*, 43.

85. A 1975 advertisement for Televisa, the television conglomerate, featured its logo (a series of shaded horizontal lines that create the effect of an eye) deep inside the psychedelic effect of spiraling tunnel vision, with the text: "Siempre estamos en onda." This text plays on the term *onda* to mean both "with it" (estar en onda) and "wavelength" ("on the air"). See *Antena*, July 1975, 4.

86. José Agustín, "Cuál es La Onda," *Diálogos* 10, no. 1 (1974), 12.

87. Ibid.

88. Monsiváis, "México 1967," 5.

89. Ibid., 8.

90. Advertisement, *POP*, 20 September 1968, 23. For a historical analysis of the commercialization of countercultural trends during the 1960s in the United States, see Thomas Frank, *The Conquest of Cool: Business Culture, Counterculture, and the Rise of Hip Consumerism* (Chicago: University of Chicago Press, 1997).

91. "Como tú," *POP*, 15 February 1968, 1.

92. "Problemas juveniles," *POP*, 1 March 1968, 6.

93. "Los hippies," *POP*, 15 March 1968, 49.

94. Conchita Cervantes, interview with the author, Mexico City, 22 August 1996.

95. Ruiz, interview.

96. "Mexican Leader Sees No Harm in Hippies," *New York Times*, 19 April 1968. Díaz Ordaz's comments were also quoted in other articles in the Mexican press.

97. Robert Marrow, letter to President Gustavo Díaz Ordaz, 22 April 1968, Comunicaciones: Galería 3, Uncataloged boxes, Box 422, AGN. The letter included a copy of the *New York Times* article.

98. "Night Life Swings, but not for the Peso Counter," *Billboard Music Week*, 16 December 1967, 11 (M).

99. Ibid.

100. Agustín, *Nueva música clásica*, 5.

101. Luis de Llano Jr., interview with Andrew Paxman, Mexico City, 18 December 1997.

102. José Agustín wrote several of the first television scripts for the show before leaving to write for *Happenings a Go-Go*, a show with a similar content theme. During the student movement of 1968 the latter program's constant references to the demonstrators forced a confrontation with Telesistema, which canceled the renewal of its contract. See Agustín, *Rock de la cárcel*, 62–3.

103. Luis Urías, "¡1, 2, 3, 4, 5 a Go-Go! Al borde del efímero electrónico," *Zona Rosa*, 15 March 1968, 8–9.

104. This inversion is also reflected in the Walt Disney cartoon film *The Three Caballeros* (1945), which was distributed by the Office of the Coordinator for Inter-American Affairs throughout Latin America toward the end of World War II. In one of the opening scenes, "Pablo Penguin" repeatedly seeks to leave his "civilized" South Pole habitat in search of "the isle of his dreams," located in the "lazy" tropics. For an interesting analysis of the film see Julianne Burton, "Don (Juanito) Duck and the Imperial-Patriarchal Unconscious: Disney Studios, the Good Neighbor Policy, and the Packaging of Latin America," in Andrew Parker and others, eds., *Nationalisms and Sexualities* (New York: Routledge, 1992), 21–41.

105. "Dug Dugs: Fue o musical! En la pista de hielo," *POP*, 17 May 1968, 24–25.

106. Oscar Chávez, interview with the author, Mexico City, 5 August 1996. The resurgence of folk music in the United States was also noted. Pete Seeger, in fact, had performed in Mexico in 1966. See, for example, Dalibor Saldátic, "Discos," *Punto de Partida* 1, no. 1 (1966), 49–51.

107. "Radio Universidad de México," *Gaceta de la Universidad Nacional Autónoma de México*, 1 July 1968, 15.

108. "El Centro Popular de Cultura," *Gaceta de la Universidad Nacional Autónoma de México*, 1 April 1968, 10.

109. Rincón, interview.

110. "Cream: Disraeli Gears," *Gaceta de la Universidad Nacional Autónoma de México*, 1 July 1968, 14–15. The alternative student literary journal *Punto de Partida* featured several articles on music, ranging from folk to rock. See in particular its first issue, which appeared in 1966.

111. "Beatlemima, una nueva experiencia: Entrevista con Juan Gabriel Moreno," *Gaceta de la Universidad Nacional Autónoma de México*, 1 August 1968, 15. The concept of the performance involved a "search to integrate the aesthetic movements of dance with a utilization of space and human form."

112. Evelyn P. Stevens, *Protest and Response in Mexico* (Cambridge, Mass.: MIT Press, 1974), chap. 6; Sergio Zermeño, *México: Una democracia utópica: El movimiento estudiantil del 68* (Mexico City: Siglo XXI, 1978 [1991]).

113. Gilberto Guevara Niebla, *La democracia en la calle: Crónica del movimiento estudiantil mexicano* (Mexico City: Siglo XXI, 1988), 19–37.

114. Marco Bellingeri, "La imposibilidad del odio: La guerrilla y el movimiento estudiantil en México, 1960–1974," in Ilán Semo, ed., *La transición interrumpida: México, 1968–1988* (Mexico City: Universidad Iberoamericana / Nueva Imagen, 1993), 49–73.

115. Guevara Niebla, *Democracia en la calle*, 45–49.

116. The description that follows is based on the chronologies in Stevens, *Protest and Response;* and Elena Poniatowska, *Massacre in Mexico*, trans. Helen Lane (New York: Viking Press, 1975).

117. Quoted in Stevens, *Protest and Response*, 203. See also "La patria es primero" and related documents, Comunicaciones: Galería 3, Administración Pública; Díaz Ordaz Papers, Box 435, AGN.

118. Guevara Niebla, *Democracia en la calle*, 40.

119. Ibid., 49.

120. Poniatowska, *Massacre in Mexico*, 128. Despite reservations regarding Lane's translation of Poniatowska, I have chosen for simplicity's sake to retain her versions of the Spanish original when citing from that work.

121. Quoted in Bellingeri, "La imposibilidad del odio," 53. Article 145 was not repealed until 1970.

122. César Gilabert, *El hábito de la utopía: Análisis del imaginario sociopolítico en el movimiento estudiantil de México, 1968* (Mexico City: Instituto Mora / Miguel Angel Porrua, 1993), 153–219; Soledad Loaeza, "México 1968: Los orígenes de la transición," in Ilán Semo, ed., *La transición interrumpida: México, 1968–1988* (Mexico City: Universidad Iberoamericana / Nueva Imagen, 1993), 15–47.

123. For an interesting attempt at global analysis see George Katsiaficas, *The Imagination of the New Left: A Global Analysis of 1968* (Boston: South End Press, 1987); see also Ronald Fraser, ed., *1968: A Student Generation in Revolt: An International Oral History* (New York: Pantheon, 1988); Robert V. Daniels, *Year of the Heroic Guerrilla: World Revolution and Counterrevolution in 1968* (New York: Basic Books, 1989).

124. Stevens, *Protest and Response*, 208.

125. Gilabert, *Hábito*, 163–65.

126. Rincón, interview.

127. This term was used several times during my interview with Manuel Ruiz.

128. Pontones, interview.

129. Ruiz, interview.

130. The following discussion is based on the article by Deborah Cohen and Lessie Jo Frazier, "'No sólo cocinábamos . . .': Historia inédita de la otra mitad del 68," in Ilán Semo, ed., *La transición interrumpida: México, 1968–*

1988 (Mexico City: Universidad Iberoamericana / Nueva Imagen, 1993), 75–105.

131. Ibid., 103.

132. Ibid., 99.

133. Poniatowska, *Massacre in Mexico,* 17–18.

134. Stevens, *Protest and Response,* 204. This language, she might have added, was drawn heavily from lower-class slang and was deemed an affront to buenas costumbres.

135. *POP,* 20 September 1968, 3. Reference to "being a citizen" was directly tied to the proposed lowering of the voting age from twenty-one to eighteen, which took effect under Echeverría. The editor of *POP* at the time, Víctor Blanco Labra, later went on to work for Televisa. Subsequent editors would take the magazine in a more radical direction that directly supported La Onda.

136. For examples see Poniatowska, *Massacre in Mexico,* 20–22; and Stevens, *Protest and Response,* 207.

137. Poniatowska, *Massacre in Mexico,* 55.

138. The term *poach* comes from Michel de Certeau, *The Practice of Everyday Life,* trans. Steven Rendall (Berkeley: University of California Press, 1984 [1988]), 37.

139. Gilabert, *Hábito,* 204.

140. Poniatowska, *Massacre in Mexico,* 33.

141. Ibid., 32. Adolfo Gilly later wrote, "In his separation from Cuba and power so that he could begin his struggle anew, in his not belonging to any county but to all, in his gestures, his life, and his death Che Guevara seemed to symbolize the realization of those youth who did not want to substitute for the existing powers that be, but to deny them altogether" (Adolfo Gilly, "1968: La ruptura en los bordes," *Nexos* 191 [1993]: 32).

142. Poniatowska, *Massacre in Mexico,* 41. See also Gilabert, *Hábito,* 217–19.

143. See Carlos Martínez Assad, "La voz de los muros," in Hermann Bellinghausen, ed., *Pensar el 68* (Mexico City: Cal y Arena, 1988), 73–75.

144. "Respuesta al apoyo de intelectuales y artistas mexicanos," Fondo Particular, Movimiento Estudiantil, 1968, Expediente 3, Fichas 101–150, Universidad Nacional Autónoma de México, Hemeroteca, Centro de Estudios sobre la Universidad. (Hereafter cited as CESU.)

145. Poniatowska, *Massacre in Mexico,* 145. "Gustavo" was the president's first name.

146. Ibid., 47.

147. Stevens, *Protest and Response,* 204.

148. Gilabert, *Hábito,* 157.

149. Stevens, *Protest and Response,* 214.

150. For a personal account of the fear and drama surrounding one leader's life in the aftermath of the army incursion see Gilberto Guevara Niebla, "Volver al 68," *Nexos* 190 (1993): 31–43.

151. Ibid., 33.

152. Ibid.

153. According to Guevara Niebla (ibid., 34), an infiltrator must have passed along the information that the march was canceled in favor of a meeting, which presented an ideal situation for a massacre. One suspects, however, that the secrecy of a public meeting would have been difficult to shield from the authorities.

154. Colin M. MacLachlan and William H. Beezley, *El Gran Pueblo: A History of Greater Mexico* (Englewood Cliffs, N.J.: Prentice Hall, 1994), 370.

155. Guevara Niebla, "Volver al 68," 37–42.

156. Stevens, in *Protest and Response,* uses the *New York Times* estimate of around 200, which was probably somewhat conservative in its own right (p. 237). The *Manchester Guardian* reported 325 killed (cited in MacLachlan and Beezley, *Gran Pueblo,* 369).

157. For a dramatic depiction of the massacre's effect on the life of one Mexican family see the film *Rojo amanecer* (Dir. Jorge Fons, 1989). Today the Lecumberri serves as the AGN.

158. See Poniatowska, *Massacre in Mexico;* Cecilia Imaz Bayona, "El apoyo popular al movimiento estudiantil de 1968," *Revista Mexicana de Sociología* 37, no. 2 (1975): 363–92.

159. "El Poder Juvenil—II. Las Parricidas," *El Heraldo Cultural,* 15 September 1968, 8–9.

160. Poniatowska, *Massacre in Mexico,* 82.

161. Jorge Rodríguez Inzunza, "Anónimo 68: Hasta la cirrosis siempre," *Vía Libre* 1, no. 9 (1988), 34. Alfredo Díaz Ordaz, the president's son, was a known *jipi* and an aspiring rock musician. He died in 1994.

162. Gilabert, *Hábito,* 161.

163. Carlos Monsiváis, "Ya nunca nada volverá a ser como antes," *Zona Rosa,* September 1968, 16–17.

CHAPTER 4

1. Quoted in Elena Poniatowska, *Massacre in Mexico,* trans. Helen Lane (New York: Viking Press, 1975), 16.

2. Javier Molina, "Los años perdidos," in Hermann Bellinghausen, ed., *Pensar el 68* (Mexico City: Cal y Arena, 1988), 228.

3. Gilberto Guevara Niebla, *La democracia en la calle: Crónica del movimiento estudiantil mexicano* (Mexico City: Siglo XXI, 1988), 52–56.

4. See Luis González de Alba, *Los días y los años* (Mexico City: Ediciones Era, 1971). This autobiographical account of life in Lecumberri covers such important events as the hunger strike and the attack on political prisoners by common criminals that was instigated by prison officials.

5. Eréndira Rincón, interview with the author, Mexico City, 20 August 1996.

6. Carlos Monsiváis, *Amor perdido* (Mexico City: Biblioteca Era, 1977), 230.

7. Letter to the editor, *POP,* 7 March 1969, 42.

8. Jasmín Solís Gómez, interview with the author, Mexico City, 28 January 1993.

9. Guevara Niebla, *Democracia en la calle,* 52.

10. "Aparecen los 'Mexican Hippies,'" *Jueves de Excélsior,* 3 October 1968, 14–15.

11. "El buen camino de la juventud," *Jueves de Excélsior,* 31 October 1968, 5.

12. Ibid.

13. Carlos Monsiváis, "México 1967," *La Cultura en México,* 17 January 1968, 7.

14. See *Zona Rosa,* June 1968, 6; July 1968, 6; November 1968, 25.

15. Francisco Ortiz, "Jóvenes 'in' y 'Mexican Hippies' en la Zona Rosa," *Jueves de Excélsior,* 1 May 1969, 14–15.

16. "Zonrosadas," *Zona Rosa,* February 1969, 4–5.

17. Gustavo Castañeda, "Spectrum," *Zona Rosa,* September 1970, 30.

18. Fernando Cesarman, "Zona Rosa de lo que pudo haber sido y no fue," *La Cultura en México,* 2 September 1970, 2–4.

19. Carlos Monsiváis, "La cortina de fresa," *Zona Rosa,* April 1969, 14–15.

20. Jasmín Solís Gómez, interview.

21. Carl Franz, *The People's Guide to Mexico* (Santa Fe, N.Mex.: John Muir Publications, 1972 [1979]), 322; passage quoted is from the 1972 edition.

22. Quoted in Elena Poniatowska, "Avándaro," *Plural* 1 (October 1971): 37.

23. Manuel Ruiz, interview with the author, Mexico City, 6 August 1991.

24. Alvaro Estrada, *Huautla en tiempo de hippies* (Mexico City: Grijalbo, 1996), 60.

25. This is not to suggest that foreign hippies were Mexican youths' *sole* inspiration for an indigenous encounter, though I am clearly arguing for its contribution. Another important contribution was Fernando Benítez's multi-volume *Los indios de México* (Mexico City: Ediciones Era, 1967–1972). Benítez directly challenged the government's folkloric appropriation of Mexico's indigenous cultures, which he described as both threatened by modernization and yet of vital significance to the nation's cultural and spiritual identity. He also discussed in detail the use of hallucinogenic plants and fungi by certain indigenous groups, thus providing a native "guidebook" for Mexican jipis.

26. The term is from Monsiváis, "México 1967."

27. Joaquín ("Chas") López, interview with the author, Mexico City, 7 April 1993.

28. López, interview.

29. López, interview.

30. Jasmín Solís Gómez, interview.

31. Mary Louise Pratt, *Imperial Eyes: Travel Writing and Transculturation* (London: Routledge, 1992). Pratt defines *contact zones* as "social spaces where disparate cultures meet, clash, and grapple with each other, often in highly

asymmetrical relations of domination and subordination—like colonialism, slavery, or their aftermaths as they are lived out across the globe today" (p. 4).

32. See Ana M. Alonso, "The Effects of Truth: Re-Presentations of the Past and the Imagining of Community," *Journal of Historical Sociology* 1, no. 1 (1988): 33–57. By *reparticularization* I mean a counterhegemonic strategy that reinscribes local meaning into universalized discourses. Alonso rightly concludes that "National histories are key to the imagining of community and to the constitution of social identity" (p. 50). By introducing the notion of transnationalism, however, I am suggesting that national hegemonic projects are constantly challenged from without, as well as from within. For a review of this literature see Robert J. Foster, "Making National Cultures in the Global Ecumene," *Annual Review of Anthropology* 20 (1991): 235–60.

33. Néstor García Canclini, *Hybrid Cultures: Strategies for Entering and Leaving Modernity*, trans. Christopher L. Chiappari and Silvia L. López (Minneapolis: University of Minnesota Press, 1995), 52.

34. Enrique Marroquín, *La contracultura como protesta: Análisis de un fenómeno juvenil* (Mexico City: Joaquín Mortiz, 1975), 12. Ironically, the spelling *xipiteca*, despite its self-conscious attempt to legitimize the jipi movement on nationalist terms, never caught on.

35. Ibid., 29.

36. López, interview.

37. "Concentración de 'hippies' viciosos en la procuraduría," *El Universal*, 12 July 1969, 1.

38. "Graves peligros," *El Universal*, 14 July 1969, 3.

39. Jasmín Solís Gómez, interview.

40. I thank Claudio Lomnitz-Adler (letter to the author, 30 December 1994) for this important insight.

41. *Jueves de Excélsior*, 21 August 1969. In June 1969 the Nixon administration implemented Operation Intercept, which virtually closed down the U.S.–Mexican border for a three-week period under the pretext of stopping drugs. Mexico's expulsions may have been timed to demonstrate its own show of force as reprisal.

42. "Singapore's Chief Drops Visit to Kuala Lumpur in Dispute over Arrest of 3 Long-Haired Malaysians," *New York Times*, 20 August 1970, 13.

43. "Long Hair Deemed Legal," *Rolling Stone*, 15 April 1971, 12.

44. "Gobernación y los 'jipis alucinógenos,'" *Jueves de Excélsior*, 16 July 1970, 5.

45. Sol Carril, "Badges: I Don't Got to Show You No Steenkin' Badges, Gringo Pothead," *Rolling Stone*, 9 December 1971, 26.

46. Franz, *People's Guide*, 3. In the 1979 edition, this same advice does not appear until pp. 524–25.

47. Ibid.

48. "Archivo de Concentración," 7 October 1971, IV–1280–86, Secretaría de Relaciones Exteriores.

49. Jerry Hopkins, "How Kenya Solved Its Hippie Problem," *Rolling Stone*, 28 September 1972, 12.

50. V. George, Letter to the president, 25 March 1970, Comunicaciones: Galería 3, Uncataloged boxes, Box 422, AGN.

51. Elmer Belew, Letter to the president, 27 March 1970, Comunicaciones: Galería 3, Uncataloged boxes, Box 422, AGN.

52. Ibid.

53. Carl Franz, telephone interview with the author, 23 August 1994.

54. Mitch Blank, interview with the author, New York City, 13 September 1992.

55. Marroquín, *Contracultura como protesta*, 26.

56. Franz, interview.

57. Robert Richter, "Crossing over" (unpublished manuscript, 1972), 3. I wish to thank Robert Richter for lending me his manuscript and allowing me to quote from it.

58. Franz, interview.

59. The number of foreign tourists, largely from the United States, more than tripled between 1960 and 1970, going from 631,000 to 1,986,000 (Mary Lee Nolan and Sidney Nolan, "The Evolution of Tourism in Twentieth-Century Mexico," *Journal of the West* 27, no. 4 [1988]: 21).

60. Franz, interview.

61. Ken Luboff, telephone interview with the author, 1 September 1994. *The People's Guide* is presently in its tenth edition.

62. López, interview.

63. Franz, interview.

64. Steve Rogers, telephone interview with the author, 7 September 1994.

65. Rogers, interview.

66. This comment was made by a friend of Steve Rogers's in the early 1970s (Rogers, interview).

67. Catherine LeGrande, telephone interview with the author, 16 February 1995.

68. Franz, interview.

69. Franz, *People's Guide*, 88.

70. Dean MacCannell, *The Tourist: A New Theory of the Leisure Class* (New York: Schocken, 1976 [1989]), xv.

71. Ibid.

72. Franz, *People's Guide*, 91.

73. Robert Richter, "El Colón," *Tonantzín* (October 1990), 21.

74. "Hippies Flocking to Mexico for Mushroom 'Trips,'" *New York Times*, 23 July 1970, 6. In the United States conflict erupted between hippies from San Francisco and more politically conscious Chicanos over the settlement of a land grant in New Mexico. "To the Chicano," wrote a journalist covering the story, "poverty is not a trip but a pit from which, until recently, he could escape only by extended servitude as a migrant worker" (Peter Nabokov, "La Raza, the Land and the Hippies," *The Nation*, 20 April 1970, 467). For an interesting at-

testation found in literature see Manuel Abreu Adorno, *Llegaron los hippies* (Río Piedras, Puerto Rico: Huracán, 1978).

75. Jim Hougan, "Mexico Raises a Counterculture," *The Nation,* 25 September 1972, 239.

76. This presumed monopoly of English by the upper classes is exemplified in scenes from the 1967 classic film *Los Caifanes* (Dir. Juan Ibáñez). In the film, English is used as a second language by upper-class youth, both as a means of expressing their worldliness with each other and to evade understanding by members of the lower class with whom they are forced to interact. The term *pachuco* refers to the stylistic invention of a separate identity among Mexican American youth during the 1940s and 1950s through language and fashion. For mention of "Tin Tan" and the influence of pachuco styles among Mexicans in the early 1950s see José Agustín, *La contracultura en México: La historia y el significado de los rebeldes sin causa, los jipitecas, los punks y las bandas* (Mexico City: Grijalbo, 1996), 17–20.

77. Parménides García Saldaña, *En la ruta de La Onda* (Mexico City: Diógenes, 1972), 153. The term *pocho* was used as a derogatory expression by Mexicans as well as Anglos to describe Mexican American youth who grew up in-between cultural worlds in the United States. It was later replaced by the more self-affirming *Chicano* in the 1960s, though the latter still conveys an absence of cultural identity when used by Mexicans.

78. The term *fresa* (literally, strawberry) translated as the equivalent of both *square* and *sweet,* depending on one's viewpoint and what was being described. At least two rock bands incorporated the label—Fresa Gruesa and Fresa Acida—which suggested a kind of inverted mockery of the term. Today *fresa* is used to denote youth from the upper class (sheltered) as well as someone or something that is overly stylish (inauthentic).

79. Carlos Monsiváis, "Para todas las cosas hay sasón," in his *Días de Guardar* (Mexico City: Biblioteca Era, 1970 [1988]), 121. The essay originally appeared, in slightly different format, as "Para todas las cosas hay razón," in *La Cultura en México,* 26 March 1969, 7–9.

80. Alejandro Lora, with Arturo Castelazo, *Lora: Vida y rocanrol . . . en sus propias palabras* (Mexico City: Castelazo y Asociados, 1993). Lora's father was a high-ranking military figure. While Lora does not explicitly mention his own role in the tocadas in Las Lomas—he does note playing at the elite Terraza Casino club however—one informant I interviewed claims to have seen him perform in Las Lomas. Over the years, Lora has carefully cultivated his mystique as a rock performer of the lumpenproletariat.

81. Ruiz, interview.

82. López, interview.

83. Monsiváis, "Para todas las cosas," 120. See also Carlos Monsiváis, "No es que esté feo, sino que estoy mal envuelto, je-je," *La Cultura en México,* 14 January 1976, 2–8. Today, *naco* is still used to refer to someone who is "lacking class" in manners or education, though it is also commonly used by the middle classes to refer to ignorance among the upper classes. Claudio Lomnitz

has written an especially revealing interpretation of naco as a sign of the "dismodernity" of Mexico: "Fissures in Contemporary Mexican Nationalism," *Public Culture* 9 (1996): 55–68.

84. See, for example, Joanne Hershfield, *Mexican Cinema / Mexican Woman, 1940–1950* (Tucson: University of Arizona Press, 1996).

85. Ruiz, interview.

86. Ruiz, interview.

87. Dressed in tuxedos, they performed a Latin-style version of the Beatles' song, "Michelle," in English ("The Hollywood Palace," 26 October 1968, Access #T80:0241, Museum of Television and Radio).

88. Armando Molina, "El safarrancho del estadio," *POP,* 25 April 1969, 8.

89. Ibid.

90. For a description of the concert see Monsiváis, "Para todas las cosas," 118–25. According to *Variety,* the riot began when police refused to allow either band to perform after they arrived an hour late for their scheduled appearance ("Plane Delay Causes Mexico City Riot over Union Gap's Late Show," *Variety,* 21 March 1969, 59). This version, however, differs from local sources, which I have chosen to follow.

91. Monsiváis, "Para todas las cosas," 123–24. "Porfirian" refers to the thirty-year reign of Porfirio Díaz, which ended with the start of the Mexican Revolution in 1910.

92. The Castro Brothers were subsequently fined 50,000 pesos (U.S. $4,000) for their negligence in organizing the event ("Popularimiento," *México Canta,* 15 June 1969).

93. Monsiváis, "Para todas las cosas," 125.

94. Jerry Hopkins, "The Doors in Mexico," *Rolling Stone,* 23 August 1969, 29.

95. Ibid.

96. No doubt another factor was pending legislation that threatened the television industry with new state taxes. Azcárraga may have wished to avoid airing the Doors at such a delicate moment in negotiations with the state. Ultimately a compromise was reached on the legislation; to avoid crushing taxes the industry agreed to make available 12.5 percent of air time gratis for public service announcements. I wish to thank Andrew Paxman for our discussion on these and other points concerning Telesistema.

97. Hopkins, "The Doors," 26. See also "Mexico's Pres Takes Bull by the Horns, OKs Breath in the Afternoon for Doors," *Variety,* 4 June 1969, 56. For another account see Jerry Hopkins and Danny Sugerman, *No One Gets out of Here Alive* (New York: Warner, 1980).

98. Hopkins, "The Doors," 26.

99. This contrasted with a performance by Paul Anka that same year at the Sports Palace Arena before a crowd of 20,000, in addition to his performance at the Forum ("From the Music Capitols of the World: Mexico City," *Billboard Music Week,* 12 April 1969, 65).

100. Hopkins, "The Doors," 19.

101. Ibid.

102. "Guatemala prohibe 'Siempre en domingo,'" *Excélsior*, 3 October 1971, B23.

103. Raúl Velasco, "La salúd mental de los jóvenes mexicanos triunfó sobre la proyección sórdida y angustiosa de Morrison y The Doors," *El Heraldo*, 29 June 1969, D2.

104. Ibid.

105. Ibid.

106. Parménides García Saldaña, "Las puertas se han cerrado a las buenas conciencias," *POP*, 1 August 1969, n.p.

107. Margo Glantz, *Onda y escritura en México: Jóvenes de 20 a 33* (Mexico City: Siglo XXI, 1971), 30.

108. Ibid. For works on La Onda as a literary style see June C. D. Carter and Donald L. Schmidt, eds., *José Agustín: Onda and Beyond* (Columbia: University of Missouri Press, 1986); Elena Poniatowska, *¡Ay vida, no me mereces!* (Mexico City: Joaquín Mortiz, 1985 [1992]); Reinhard Teichmann, *De La Onda en adelante: Conversaciones con 21 novelistas mexicanos* (Mexico City: Posada, 1987); Inke Gunia, *¿"Cuál es La Onda"? La literatura de la contracultura juvenil en el México de los años sesenta y setenta* (Frankfurt: Vervuert Verlag, 1994).

109. Poniatowska, *Ay vida*, 176; Danny J. Anderson, "Creating Cultural Prestige: Editorial Joaquín Mortiz," *Latin American Research Review* 31, no. 2 (1996): 3–41.

110. José Agustín, *La nueva música clásica* (Mexico City: Instituto Nacional de la Juventud Mexicana, 1968), 7.

111. José Agustín, *El rock de la cárcel* (Mexico City: Editores Mexicanos Unidos, 1986), 78.

112. For a discussion of this work see José Agustín, "Vera y ondera: Autoentrevista de José Agustín," *La Cultura en México*, 3 September 1969, 7–8.

113. José Agustín, in Carlos Chimal, ed., *Crines: Lecturas de rock* (Mexico City: Penélope, 1984), 40.

114. Parménides García Saldaña, "Three Souls in My Mind," *POP*, July 1973, 72.

115. Poniatowska, *Ay vida*, 188. See also Agustín, *Contracultura en México*, 141–45.

116. For a partial glossary of this vocabulary see Carter and Schmidt, *José Agustín*.

117. Quoted in Glantz, *Onda y escritura*, 33.

118. Agustín, *Rock de la cárcel*, 18.

119. Ibid., 14. *La tumba* was published by Novaro, before Agustín was offered a new contract by Joaquín Mortíz (who republished it in 1966).

120. Parménides García Saldaña, *Pasto verde* (Mexico City: Diógenes, 1968 [1985]), 51–52. García Saldaña originally meant to title the work *La Onda*.

121. José Agustín, "Forty Archetypes Draw Their Swords," in Carter and Schmidt, *José Agustín*, 35. Agustín's father was a pilot who brought him rock 'n' roll and other records from the United States.

122. Bernard Cassen, "La lengua inglesa como vehículo del imperialismo cultural," *Comunicación y Cultura* 6 (February 1979): 77.

123. Advertisement, *Excélsior*, 16 March 1969, 12.

124. For a more detailed discussion of editorial changes at various magazines see Víctor Roura, *Apuntes de rock: Por las calles del mundo* (Mexico City: Nuevomar, 1985), 127–35.

125. Advertisement in *Piedra Rodante*, 30 October 1971, 31. Discoteca Yoko was owned by Manuel Aceves, editor of *Piedra Rodante;* his offices were across the street. Contributors to the magazine were often paid in record albums. See Agustín, *Contracultura en México*, 93.

126. Armando Blanco, interview with the author, Mexico City, 11 March 1993. This was still true up to the late 1980s, before the arrival of imported compact discs. Collections of original rock albums formed a respected treasury of music that was the source (through taped recordings) for diffusion throughout the rock community. Respected rock programs on the radio, for example on Radio Educación (run by the UNAM) or later the commercial station Rock 101, also became important sources for the availability of imported music, where disc jockeys often introduced material from their private collections.

127. Carlos Monsiváis, "Las conquistas juveniles de las [sic] decada," *POP*, January 1970, 44.

128. "Los Dug-Dugs: El grupo de rock revelación (nacional)," *POP*, 15 February 1969, 22.

129. Ramón García, interview with the author, Mexico City, 18 March 1993.

130. Carlos Baca, "Rock subterráneo," *Mexico Canta*, 13 February 1970, n.p.

131. Alberto Macias, "Vibraciones," *Mexico Canta*, 13 February 1970, n.p. For a fuller account of the same incident see Marroquín, *Contracultura como protesta*, 39. Marroquín writes: "Enrique belted out the Beatle chant then in vogue, 'All Together.'" José Agustín (*Contracultura en México*, 78) writes that this incident took place in 1967–that is, before Tlatelolco–but he does not provide documentation to support his claim.

132. Hugo Covantes, "Los estudiantes: Trago amargo para Luis Echeverría," *Zona Rosa*, January 1970, 14–15.

133. Guevara Niebla, *Democracia en la calle*, 55.

CHAPTER 5

1. *Annual Report*, RCA Corporation, 1969, 20, Cole-Harvard Collection.
2. *Annual Report*, RCA Corporation, 1970, 16, Cole-Harvard Collection.
3. *Annual Report*, CBS, Inc., 1966, 28, Cole-Harvard Collection.
4. *Annual Report*, CBS, Inc., 1968, 33, Cole-Harvard Collection. For articles on the company's "revolutionary" advertising campaign and its attendant controversy see *Rolling Stone*, 17 May 1969, 4; 12 July 1969, 10.

5. *Annual Report,* CBS, Inc., 1970, 17, Cole-Harvard Collection.

6. *Annual Report,* CBS, Inc., 1971, 22–24, Cole-Harvard Collection.

7. Kevin M. Kelleghan, "Image Battle Shapes in Mexico as Firms Gear for 'Tomorrow,'" *Billboard Music Week* 22 July 1967, 49.

8. Advertisement, *Billboard Music Week,* 16 December 1967, 16.

9. When Polydor entered the Indian market in 1970, breaking a sixty-three-year monopoly held by the British company His Masters Voice (HMV), *Variety* noted that "[t]hrough the Polydor label, the growing young western-oriented Indian audience will be able to buy records by the Bee Gees, the Cream [*sic*], Jimi Hendrix, et al." ("Polydor Invades Indian Disk Market, Ruled by HMV Label for 63 Years," *Variety,* 26 August 1970, 43).

10. Herbe Pompeyo, interview with the author, Mexico City, 8 June 1993.

11. Enrique Partida, interview with the author, Mexico City, 7 June 1993.

12. Advertisement in *Piedra Rodante,* August 1971, 7. Polydor also launched a "Soul Series" featuring renowned African American artists.

13. Herbe Pompeyo, interview. See also "Polydor lanza la serie 'Rock Power,'" *Piedra Rodante,* August 1971, 8.

14. Carlos Baca, "Los Creedence: Misioneros del rock en México," *México Canta,* 26 February 1971, n.p.

15. Advertisement in *Piedra Rodante,* August 1971.

16. This program, *La respuesta está en el aire* (The Answer's Blowing in the Wind), appeared in 1969. Unfortunately, Radio Educación's extensive archives do not begin until the mid-1970s.

17. Gustavo Castañeda, "Spectrum," *Zona Rosa,* October 1970, 20.

18. Raúl Velasco, "'Hace falta imaginación a nuestros actuales rocanroleros,' Alfredo Gil," *El Heraldo de México,* 22 September 1968, D2.

19. Fred Ohm, "Chihuahua pop cultiva a Los Químicos," *México Canta,* 13 February 1970, n.p.

20. Carlos Santana was born in Jalisco, Guadalajara, but later moved to Tijuana with his family. There he picked up the guitar and befriended Javier Batiz, a blues guitarist, who gave him lessons. Santana left Tijuana as a youth for San Francisco, where he joined the emerging psychedelic rock scene. Batiz, after several recording stints in the United States, stayed in Mexico and became a renowned, if overly pretentious, performer.

21. Ohm, "Chihuahua pop." The word UNDERGROUND was in English.

22. This convergence of musical styles toward an international rock-pop sound was also occurring in other countries outside the United States and Britain (Roger Wallis and Krister Malm, *Big Sounds from Small Peoples: The Music Industry in Small Countries* [New York: Pendragon, 1984], 302–10).

23. Partida, interview.

24. Armando Molina, interview with the author, Mexico City, 17 June 1993. See also Carlos Baca, "Rock subterráneo," *México Canta,* 13 February 1970, n.p.

25. Liner notes from *La Máquina del Sonido* (CBS-Columbia, 1971). The word *underground* was in English.

26. A later study covering the early 1980s found that "the Mexican sub-

sidiaries of major transnational corporations were not necessarily the most modern or most fully-equipped of record producers in the country" and noted that "all studios in the Mexico City metropolitan area were equipped with 16 and 24 tracks." However, in the late 1960s quite likely only Orfeón and possibly Musart had recording facilities comparable to those of the transnationals. The upgrading of Cisne, another important local company, most likely occurred as a result of the acquisition of a majority share by Televisa in 1980. See Annette Riggio F., "The Gate Keepers of Popular Music in Mexico: National and Transnational Record Producers," *Studies in Latin American Popular Culture* 5 (1986): 24.

27. Ibid., 25.

28. Rock musicians were not the only ones now recording in English for a foreign market: a new generation of Mexican baladistas was also composing songs "with international style lyrics that are entirely accessible so that they can be easily transported to other languages without changing their original content and adapted to any country," most notably the United States (Cervantes Ayala, "Nuestros compositores enviarán mayor número de canciones a EU," *Excélsior*, 10 March 1969, B8).

29. Carlos Beltrand Luján, interview with the author, Mexico City, 18 May 1994.

30. Three Souls in My Mind (later, the TRI) became widely popular, especially among the lower and middle classes. In 1980 a 66 percent share of Cisne-Raff was acquired by Televisa. Riggio, "Gate Keepers," 22.

31. Federico Arana lists 122 bands for the year 1971; of that total, some 22 produced at least one album (Federico Arana, *Guaraches de ante azul: Historia del rock mexicano* [Mexico City: Posada, 1985], vol. 4, 115–17).

32. Many of the most important bands of this period in fact originated in cities other than the capital, especially Guadalajara, Monterrey, Tijuana, and Reynosa. Mexican rock magazines increasingly featured articles on the rock scene in the provinces and published letters from fans around the country. For a discussion of rock music in Veracruz see David K. Stigberg, "Urban Musical Culture in Mexico: Professional Musicianship and Media in the Musical Life of Contemporary Veracruz" (Ph.D. diss., University of Illinois at Urbana-Champaign, 1980), chap. 4.

33. According to Armando Molina, this term was first introduced by the disc jockey Felix Ruano Méndez of Radio Juventud (who was later fined and fired for his participation in the live transmission of the Avándaro rock festival). Its usage became widespread among musicians, radio announcers, music critics, and fans alike. Perhaps coincidentally, La Onda Chicana also emerged around 1967 as a label for a new musical fusion of ranchera, jazz, and rock in Mexican American border communities. According to Manuel Peña the movement in the United States, however, was influenced by Chicano activism. While Peña suggested to me that the term may have filtered into Mexico, it is equally plausible that Mexicans invented the term themselves, independent of what was occurring in the United States (Manuel Peña, telephone interview with the au-

thor, 23 April 1997). See also Manuel Peña, "Hispanic and Afro-Hispanic Music in the United States," in Francisco Lomelí, ed., *Handbook of Hispanic Cultures in the United States: Literature and Art* (Houston, Tex.: Arte Público Press; Madrid: Instituto de Cooperación Iberoamericana, 1993–1994), 302–3.

34. Armando Molina, "Rock chicano '71," *POP*, 14 January 1972, 8–10. Molina is the only musician I am aware of who was also actively involved in the promotion of rock in the mass media. More recently he coproduced a radio show that often featured contemporary Mexican rock, *Humo en el agua* (105.7 FM) and is recording a new album under the Máquina del Sonido bandname.

35. Carlos Muñoz Jr., *Youth, Identity, Power: The Chicano Movement* (London: Verso, 1989), 15. The latter-day Chicanos had in fact reappropriated the term from its derogatory usage earlier in the century. For an historical and literary analysis see Tino Villanueva, ed., *Chicanos* (Mexico City: Fondo de Cultura Económica, 1985).

36. On Chicano rock in the United States during this period see David Reyes and Tom Waldman, *Land of a Thousand Dances: Chicano Rock 'n' Roll from Southern California* (Albuquerque: University of New Mexico Press, 1998).

37. Some reference points were directly shared, such as the translated writings of Carlos Castañeda. For a discussion of how U.S. Chicano identity was misinterpreted in Mexico see Jorge A. Bustamante, "El poder chicano en el Distrito Federal," *La Cultura en México*, 3 January 1973, 6–8. See also "A Binational Performance Pilgrimage," in Guillermo Gómez-Peña, *Warrior for Gringostroika*, introduction by Roger Bartra (St. Paul, Minn.: Greywolf Press, 1993), 15–33.

38. See, for example Víctor Roura, *Apuntes de rock: Por las calles del mundo* (Mexico City: Nuevomar, 1985), 123.

39. He writes, for instance, that 1968 was simply "another year" for national rock, without any evident connections to student politics (Víctor Roura, *Negros del corazón* [Mexico City: Universidad Autónoma de México, 1984], 26).

40. The term *monopoly* is often employed by Carlos Monsiváis. See, for example, "Notas sobre el estado, la cultural nacional y las culturas populares en México," *Cuadernos Políticos* 30 (October-December 1981): 33–43.

41. The term *resemanticization* comes from William Rowe and Vivian Schelling, *Memory and Modernity: Popular Culture in Latin America* (London: Verso, 1991), 11.

42. José Agustín, "Cuál es La Onda," *Diálogos* 10, no. 1 (1974): 12. Elena Poniatowska points out, for instance, that no "Onda Manifesto" was ever produced by the principal literary figures of the movement (Elena Poniatowska, *¡Ay vida, no me mereces!* [Mexico City: Joaquín Mortiz, 1985 (1992)], 198).

43. According to Armando Molina, the original manager of La Revolución purposefully had them record in English so that he could present them to Polydor as a band from the United States, which sounds somewhat far-fetched. In

1971 the single of "Nasty Sex" sold some 200,000 copies in Mexico and abroad (Arana, *Guaraches*, vol. 4, 124).

44. *La Revolución de Emiliano Zapata* (Polydor, 1971). "Nasty Sex," by Javier Martín del Campo Muriel and Oscar Rojas Gutiérrez. Copyright © 1971. Copyright renewed 1989. Reprinted by permission of Warner Chapel Music. International copyright secured. All rights reserved.

45. Parménides García Saldaña, "La Revolución mexicana se quita el huarache," *Piedra Rodante*, 1 May 1971, 27.

46. Mario Mora, "La Revolución de Emiliano Zapata: Traducción integra en español del primer L.P.," *México Canta*, 27 August 1971, 6–9. Ironically, the article featured a Spanish-language translation of the album's songs.

47. García Saldaña, "La Revolución." García Saldaña was in general quite deprecatory toward Mexican rock (see chapter 4).

48. Cover of *Piedra Rodante*, 1 May 1971. Venustiano Carranza was leader of the conservative "Constitutional" forces that eventually triumphed over the popular armies of Villa and Zapata.

49. "The [idea] for Three Souls in My Mind was because we were three [musicians], because in our repertoire we had soul tunes [blues] . . . and furthermore, because in those days it was cool to have a long name. So that no one knew what the fuck it meant, we threw in the part, In My Mind" (Alejandro Lora, with Arturo Castelazo, *Lora: Vida y rocanrol . . . en sus propias palabras* [Mexico City: Castelazo y Asociados, 1993], 31). Peace and Love in fact changed their name to Náhuatl in 1973, citing the change as contributing "a first step on the long road of creativity" for the Mexican rock movement, which by that point was in severe crisis (quoted from the liner notes, Cisne-Raff, 1973). In addition to the name change, the majority of song titles and lyrics were now in Spanish; songs written while they were still called Peace and Love were mostly in English.

50. *Peace and Love* (Raff, 1971). The song was written in both English and Spanish.

51. For example, the band 39.4 had a sound resonant of the group Chicago, replete with brass horns.

52. This second album was in fact the sound track of the film *La verdadera vocación de Magdalena* (Dir. Jaime Hermosillo, 1971). An internal debate among band members over the future direction of the group, combined with the pressures against rock in the wake of Avándaro, resulted in a dramatic shift in style to música tropical, even though the band did not change its name (Joaquín ["Chas"] López, interview with the author, Mexico City, 7 April 1993).

53. López, interview.

54. Carlos Baca, "La 'super onda' del Love Army," *México Canta*, 17 April 1970, n.p.

55. Roura, *Negros del corazón*, 134.

56. Before Santana, Latino rock had difficulty breaking into the (White)

mainstream, despite its success on r&b stations (Claude Hall, "Latin-Rock in Sales Upswing," *Billboard Music Week*, 21 January 1967, 1).

57. Numerous expressions emerged to describe the United States: *el gabacho, gabacholándia, gringolándia,* and *la tierra del Tío Sam* among them. Youth in the United States were also sometimes referred to as *nuestros primos* (our cousins).

58. "Entrevista a Carlos Santana," *México Canta,* 17 September 1971, 7–11.

59. John Storm Roberts, *The Latin Tinge: The Impact of Latin American Music on the United States* (New York: Oxford University Press, 1979), 184.

60. *Peace and Love* (Cisne, 1970).

61. "Guadalajara, ¿capital del rock?" *Piedra Rodante,* August 1971, 16.

62. José Enrique Pérez Cruz, interview with the author, Mexico City, 5 March 1993.

63. Quoted in Roura, *Negros del corazón,* 77.

64. Partida, interview.

65. "El buen ROCK aguanta el español," *México Canta,* 12 October 1973, 29–31.

66. Partida, interview.

67. Ramón García, interview with the author, Mexico City, 18 March 1993.

68. Roura, *Apuntes de rock,* 38.

69. Pompeyo, interview.

70. *Los Locos* (Musart, 1971).

71. *Love Army* (Raff, 1971). The translation of "Caminata cerebral" from the Spanish is my own, as I never came across the English-language version.

72. Roura, *Apuntes de rock,* 48.

73. Lora, with Castelazo, *Lora,* 35.

74. Letter to the editor, *POP,* 18 June 1971, n.p.

75. One should add, however, that the compelling necessity to unravel this mystery is an important indicator of U.S. global hegemony.

76. Partida, interview.

77. Pompeyo, interview.

78. Advertisement, *Piedra Rodante,* October 1971, 35.

79. "Mexican-U.S. Rock Groups Competing," *Billboard Music Week,* 25 September 1971, 12.

80. "El grupo 'La Revolución de Emiliano Zapata' actuará en universidades de EU," *Excélsior,* 25 October 1971, B11. Herbe Pompeyo, who accompanied the group, later commented on the "extraordinary" reception they received (Pompeyo, interview).

81. Armando Nava, interview with the author, Mexico City, 5 June 1993.

82. Benedict Anderson, *Imagined Community: Reflections on the Origin and Spread of Nationalism* (London: Verso, 1983). One of the shortcomings of Anderson's analysis is that he fails to discuss the ways in which alternative "imagined communities" arise, often by reappropriating the nationalist discourse, in opposition to official cultures. The transnationalization of the mass

media has introduced a new set of challenges to official nationalism in the latter half of this century.

83. The first political prisoners were released in December 1970, immediately after Echeverría's swearing-in ceremony. However, the principal leaders were not released until that spring and were exiled to Chile. They were let back into Mexico several months later. See Gilberto Guevara Niebla, *La democracia en la calle: Crónica del movimiento estudiantil mexicano* (Mexico City: Siglo XXI, 1988), 67; Yoram Shapira, "The Impact of the 1968 Student Protest on Echeverría's Reformism," *Journal of Interamerican Studies and World Affairs* 19, no. 4 (1977): 557–80.

84. Carl J. Mora, *Mexican Cinema: Reflections of a Society, 1896–1988* (Berkeley: University of California Press, 1982 [rev. ed., 1989]), 112–37; José Agustín, *Tragicomedia mexicana 2: La vida en México de 1970 a 1982* (Mexico City: Planeta, 1992), 59–82; Enrique Cisneros, *'Si me permiten actuar'* (Mexico City: CLETA, n.d.).

85. See Américo Saldívar, *Ideología y política del estado mexicano (1970–1976)* (Mexico City: Siglo XXI, 1980), esp. chap. 3, "La política económica del nuevo gobierno"; Judith Hellman, *Mexico in Crisis* (New York: Holmes and Meier, 1983), chap. 7; Carlos Bazdresch and Santiago Levy, "Populism and Economic Policy in Mexico, 1970–1982," in Rudiger Dornbusch and Sebastian Edwards, eds., *The Macroeconomics of Populism in Latin America* (Chicago: University of Chicago Press, 1991), 223–62.

86. In the 1970 presidential elections, 34 percent of total eligible voters abstained. Of the remaining votes, 25 percent of the ballots were annulled, and another 20 percent were cast for opposition parties (Shapira, "Impact of the 1968 Student Protest," 566–67).

87. Agustín, *Tragicomedia mexicana,* 15.

88. Guevara Niebla, *Democracia en la calle,* 68. Emphasis in original.

89. Hellman, *Mexico in Crisis,* 202–4; Jorge Basurto, "The Late Populism of Luis Echeverría," in Michael L. Conniff, ed., *Latin American Populism in Comparative Perspective* (Albuquerque: University of New Mexico Press, 1982), 93–111.

90. Guevara Niebla, *Democracia en la calle,* 64–88.

91. This point is made, though somewhat too uncritically, by Adrián de Garay Sánchez, who writes that "rock is characterized . . . for its *transcendence of class.* Whether in the popular barrio, or in the wealthiest residential zones of the city, people listen to and participate in the culture of rock" (Adrián de Garay Sánchez, *El rock también es cultura,* Cuadernos de Comunicación y Prácticas Sociales, no. 5 [Mexico City: Universidad Iberoamericana, 1993], 10 [emphasis in the original]).

92. Gustavo Castañeda, "Chapultepec: Festival del naranjazo," *Piedra Rodante,* 1 May 1971, 1. Before the violence of 1968 the regime had sponsored free Sunday entertainment in parks throughout the capital, reportedly offering "[a]n extremely varied format . . . from poetry readings to classical music to mariachi, bolero, tropical and even rock groups both local and foreign" ("Surge

nuevamente el interés en la música folklórica," *Billboard Music Week,* 16 December 1967, M14). It is unclear, however, how the student movement affected the programming of these Sunday performances, though one imagines either that they were canceled or that rock was excluded until the apertura under Echeverría. These *domingos culturales* dated back to the 1920s, when the first postrevolutionary regime began sponsoring cultural events. It is noteworthy, moreover, that guidelines for such events dating from 1924 specified that "foreign music whose morbid character depresses the spirit of the people must be eliminated absolutely" (quoted in Ilene V. O'Malley, *The Myth of the Revolution: Hero Cults and the Institutionalization of the Mexican State, 1920–1940* (Westport, Conn.: Greenwood Press, 1986), 119.

93. Castañeda, "Chapultepec."

94. Ibid., 6.

95. López, interview.

96. Castañeda, "Chapultepec," 1.

97. Ibid., 6.

98. Roura, *Negros del corazón,* 63. Not all bands could or desired to accommodate themselves to this relationship: Armando Nava of Los Dug Dugs said, "Look . . . I have never gotten on stage and told off the audience. And I doubt that I ever will. . . . It's likely that I'm fighting against the current" (p. 72).

99. García, interview.

100. Jasmín Solís Gómez, interview with the author, Mexico City, 28 January 1993.

101. Ana Lau Jaiven, *La nueva ola del feminismo en México* (Mexico City: Planeta, 1987), 75–138. The Echeverría regime responded to feminists' demands by proposing changes in the Constitution but stopped short of legalizing abortion. In 1975 Mexico served as host to the U.N. International Year of the Woman conference. Family planning received government support after 1972, but birthrates were not brought under control until the 1980s.

102. Jasmín Solís Gómez, interview.

103. Lila Orta, interview with the author, Mexico City, 13 January 1993.

104. *La verdadera vocación de Magdalena* (dir. Jaime Hermosillo, 1971).

105. La Revolución de Emiliano Zapata, *La verdadera vocación de Magdalena* (Polydor, 1972).

CHAPTER 6

1. Pilar Riaño-Alcalá ("Urban Space and Music in the Formation of Youth Cultures: The Case of Bogotá, 1920–1980," *Studies in Latin American Popular Culture* 10 [1991]: 87–106) notes that Colombia also had a native rock festival at about this time, but she fails to provide a date. Puerto Rico was used as a backdrop for U.S. rock festivals in July 1970 and April 1972. Yet Saigon can claim credit for being the first Third World city to sponsor its own rock festival. That event featured bands from South Vietnam, Taiwan, Malaysia, the Philippines, Indonesia, and Australia. *Rolling Stone* reported that the one-day con-

cert was "a definite copy of festivals stateside" and cited protest from the opposition press: "This festival legalizes a degenerate foreign culture which is harmful to Vietnamese culture and tradition" ("The Saigon Rock Festival Rolls," *Rolling Stone*, 8 July 1971, 16). Estimates of the number of people at Avándaro vary. Víctor Roura states that 500,000 attended (*Apuntes de rock: Por las calles del mundo* [Mexico City: Ediciones Nuevomar, 1985], 27); Carlos Monsiváis, 300,000 ("No es que esté feo, sino que estoy mal envuelto, je-je," *La Cultura en México*, 14 January 1976, 3); and Federico Arana, 150,000 (*Guaraches de ante azul: Historia del rock mexicano* [Mexico City: Posada, 1985], vol. 3, 100). Meanwhile, *Variety*, calling the festival "a carbon of Woodstock," placed the number at 180,000 ("Rock Festival in Mexico Draws 180,000 Youths in a Carbon of Woodstock," *Variety*, 29 September 1971, 49).

2. According to Armando Molina (interview with the author, Mexico City, 17 June 1993), who was hired to contract bands for the event, the organizers had little intention of promoting rock per se; the idea was simply to organize a "Mexican Night" of revelry to "commemorate and complement" the annual car races held at the Valle de Bravo site. Still, the precedent for Coca-Cola's involvement in a Latin American rock festival was set a year earlier when the soft-drink conglomerate cosponsored the "Rock Festival '70" (featuring U.S. bands) in Puerto Rico ("July 4 Rock Festival Set for Puerto Rico with Coca-Cola Coin," *Variety*, 10 June 1970, 56).

3. Quoted in Eligio Calderón and others, *Avándaro: ¿Aliviane o movida?* (Mexico City: Editorial Extemporáneos, 1971), 85–86. Sections of this book also appeared in "Una guerra sin soldados," *La Cultura en México*, 6 October 1971, 2–7.

4. The film version of Woodstock produced by Warner Brothers and the sound track released by Atlantic Records recuperated losses incurred from the festival itself and in general spurred a closer relationship between capitalist interests and the counterculture. See *Rolling Stone*, 21 January 1970; 7 February 1970; 15 October 1970.

5. Herbe Pompeyo, interview with the author, Mexico City, 8 June 1993.

6. The song was written by Lalo Guerrero and later appeared in the film *Zoot Suit*. The lines from the song go in part, "I like marihuana, you like marihuana, we like marihuana too!" However, Peace and Love apparently added the line: "I want to be a hippie and I want to get stoned." This was all sung in English.

7. Luis de Llano Jr. of Telesistema afterward defended the television station's position by stating: "I went to Avándaro to produce a film for television. I brought my equipment to do this, and I want to clarify that we aren't trying to exalt the negative side which the festival has had" (Roberto Ramírez S., "La reunión de más de cien mil jóvenes en el festival musical de Avándaro sí fue autorizada," *Excélsior*, 20 September 1971, B15). According to Armando Molina, Telesistema filmed during the day on Friday and from around 7:00 P.M. to 1:00 A.M. the night of the festival. The event itself lasted all night long, unlike the Woodstock festival, which paused until morning.

8. Luis González Reimann, "Ceremonia cósmica, poca música," *Piedra Rodante*, 30 October 1971, 18.

9. Marcos Mendoza, "Paz, amor: Cortesía de Coca-Cola," *Piedra Rodante*, 30 October 1971, 26. For a photograph of the Coke banner see Humberto Rubalcaba and others, eds., *Nosotros* (Mexico City: Nosotros, 1972).

10. Javier Batiz famously rejected the amount as too little for his services.

11. While the real political stakes were arguably quite different for Avándaro and Woodstock, I believe a similar rejection of explicit political organizing by those present applied to both festivals. Rock was seen by most bands and fans as an *alternative* to politics rather than as a vehicle for political activism. Political speeches that fell out of line with the anarchic mood of a rock performance were often rejected; Abbie Hoffman was clubbed off stage at Woodstock by guitarist Pete Townshend of the Who. See Abbie Hoffman, *Woodstock Nation* (New York: Vintage, 1969); and Greil Marcus, "The Woodstock Festival," *Rolling Stone*, 20 September 1969, 16–18. On the other hand, politicians have since sought to appropriate rock music as a campaign tactic. This was true also in Mexico beginning in the 1980s, when the PRI, as well as left-wing parties, began to sponsor rock events (see the conclusions).

12. Quoted in Elena Poniatowska, "Avándaro," *Plural* 1, no. 1 (1971), 37.

13. Calderón and others, *Avándaro*, 38.

14. Ibid.

15. In fact, the police would later be criticized for not arresting drug users and allegedly even for distributing marijuana. Reports of the actual number of soldiers and police are mixed. One report put the total number at 530: 120 federal soldiers, 50 judiciales, 350 general police, and various transit agents ("En Avándaro, una juerga increíble," *Excélsior*, 12 September 1971, A17). Another report, cited by *Piedra Rodante* as the official statement by the attorney general, noted the presence of "more than 800 police elements, belonging to the federal and state judiciales, Department of Interior Affairs, General Public Security Agency, State Police, Municipal Police, and elements of the army" ("Fiestas: 21 muertos, 665 heridos, 275 arrestados," *Piedra Rodante*, 30 October 1971, 10). An earlier story in *Excélsior* reported that "Just before arriving in the Valle de Bravo one sees soldiers from the 43d Infantry Battalion, who number [some] 1,200 and were mobilized under the orders of Colonel Javier Vázquez Félix" ("La locura del rock en Avándaro," *Excélsior*, 11 September 1971, A4). Finally, *Variety* claimed that the "fest was guarded by more than 700 soldiers" ("Rock Festival").

16. Quoted in Poniatowska, "Avándaro," 37.

17. González Reimann, "Ceremonia cósmica," 22.

18. Oscar Sarquiz, "Humillacíon, fraude con los músicos," *Piedra Rodante*, 30 October 1971, 16. It was estimated that one-third of all Mexico City youth between the ages of fifteen and twenty were present ("Castigo a los organizadores," *Excélsior*, 18 September 1971, A1).

19. Sol Arguedas, "Lodo sobre lodo," *La Cultura en México*, 6 October 1971, 7–9.

20. Calderón and others, *Avándaro*, 28–29.

21. *Excélsior*, for example, claimed that 93 percent of the audience were men (Raúl Cervantes, "Avándaro, insuficiente para albergar a los espectadores del festival 'Pop,'" *Excélsior*, 12 September 1971, B25).

22. Poniatowska, "Avándaro," 39.

23. Lila Orta, interview with the author, Mexico City, 13 January 1993.

24. Orta, interview.

25. *Piedra Rodante*, 30 October 1971, 24. The Spanish text reads: "¡Qué buen patín agarró la torta ésa!"

26. Quoted in Poniatowska, "Avándaro," 40.

27. José Enrique Pérez Cruz, interview with the author, Mexico City, 5 March 1993.

28. Catherine LeGrande, telephone interview with the author, 16 February 1995. In the interview, LeGrande mispronounced "Avándaro" (stressing the fourth syllable), reflecting how she probably remembered her pronunciation at the time, when she was just learning to speak Spanish.

29. Rubalcaba and others, *Nosotros*. This commemorative collection of photographs and text from the event was apparently published with the collaboration, at least in part, of Telesistema. Jacobo Zabludovsky, creator and anchorman for Telesistema's nightly news broadcast, *24 horas*—which first aired on 7 September 1970—wrote the opening editorial for the book. Also noteworthy were the high production quality of the photographs and the fact that 10,000 copies were printed, an extraordinary quantity for any print run in Mexico. In an interview, Luis de Llano Jr. stated categorically that Telesistema was not directly responsible for the book's publication, thus countering a rumor that was widely circulated during the period of my research. Luis de Llano Jr., interview with Andrew Paxman, Mexico City, 18 December 1997.

30. Pérez Cruz, interview.

31. A 1967 Mexican law prohibited all nonofficial usage of the national flag, anthem, and coat of arms ("Respeto a la bandera, al himno y al escudo nacionales," *Jueves de Excélsior*, 28 December 1967, 5). For an instance of an individual's being prosecuted for illegal appropriation of the U.S. flag see "19-Yr. Old Busted in Mass. for Using Flag as Patch on Pants," *Rolling Stone*, 2 April 1970, 4. Jimi Hendrix's widely commodified, acid-rock rendition of the national anthem at Woodstock became a landmark reference point for the counterculture in the United States and elsewhere.

32. U.S. and British flags were present, both on T-shirts and hanging from posts. And at least one Canadian flag can also be spotted in photographs. One observer commented on "the large numbers of foreigners, above all from the U.S. and Britain." However, this remark should be taken in the context of negative reaction to the festival as "colonialist." Although some foreigners were indeed present, my sense is that the foreign flags belonged overwhelmingly to Mexicans. See Cervantes, "Avándaro."

33. See also "El símbolo de la paz," *POP*, 25 February 1971, 3.

34. A fifteen-minute color video of Avándaro (transferred from 8 mm) is

available from Sergio García, at the Tianguis del Chopo rock flea market in Mexico City. A 16 mm black-and-white film is in the Filmoteca Archives of the UNAM. Both make reference to the use of the U.S. flag. See also Rubalcaba and others, *Nosotros.* While this book was in press I also received news of a newly released documentary, *A 25 años de Avándaro.* See Hugo Lazcano, "Muestran Avándaro," *Reforma,* 14 September 1996, E5.

35. Armando Molina, "Rock chicano '71," *POP,* 14 January 1972, 8–10.

36. Enrique Marroquín, "'Dios quiere que llueva para unirnos,'" *Piedra Rodante,* 30 October 1971, 12. Marroquín was a liberal priest who publicly supported the youth counterculture. See also Enrique Marroquín, *La contracultura como protesta: Análisis de un fenómeno juvenil* (Mexico City: Joaquín Mortiz, 1975), 47–51. Significantly, on the Día de la Raza (celebrated in the United States as Columbus Day) a native rock festival has been held annually for many years. This takes place at the base of the National Monument to the Revolution in Mexico City.

37. For a reproduction of the promotional pamphlet for Avándaro see Luis Carrión and Graciela Iturbide, *Avándaro* (Mexico City: Diógenes, 1971). The original promotional pamphlet from Woodstock was photocopied, with permission, from the personal archives of Mitch Blank of New York City.

38. See Marroquín, "Dios quiere," 11. References to Woodstock abounded in the criticism and support of the festival that followed. See for example, José Emilio Pacheco, "Woodstocktlán: Pintar el coco y luego tenerle miedo," *Excélsior,* 18 September 1971, A7. While Polydor distributed the live album (pressed in Mexico), the film of Woodstock was banned for several years.

39. Calderón and others, *Avándaro,* 17.

40. "Festival de rock y ruedas en Avándaro," in Carrión and Iturbide, *Avándaro,* n.p.

41. From the movie *Woodstock* (Dir. Michael Wadleigh, 1970).

42. Compare Fredrick B. Pike, *The United States and Latin America: Myths and Stereotypes of Civilization and Nature* (Austin: University of Texas Press, 1992), esp. chap. 9.

43. Editorial, "Culpables de la orgía de Avándaro," *Jueves de Excélsior,* 23 September 1971, 5.

44. "Moya reprueba lo de Avándaro; la procuraduría investiga," *Excélsior,* 14 September 1971, A1.

45. Jesus Pavlo Tenorio, "Avándaro 1991: Veinte años después," *Jueves de Excélsior,* 23 September 1971, 14–15.

46. Quoted in "Avándaro y el fascismo," *Siempre,* 29 September 1971, 55. Interestingly, no author was given for the article (which in fact denounced the Puebla meeting as "fascistic").

47. "Moya reprueba lo de Avándaro."

48. "Avándaro '71, gobierno, iglesia, padres de familia: Todos hemos sido culpables de esto!" *Siempre,* 29 September 1971, 9.

49. Letter to the editor, *Siempre,* 22 September 1971, 4.

50. Alberto Domingo, "Avándaro: ¿Una conjura política?" *Siempre,* 29 Sep-

tember 1971, 22–23. According to Domingo, attacks on Hank González were instigated by local political interests threatened by reforms González was instituting as governor.

51. Quoted in Calderón and others, *Avándaro*, 19–20.

52. Ramírez, "Reunión." Advertisements for lots on which to build private country estates at Avándaro first appeared in Mexico City newspapers in the early 1950s; one labeled it "The Dream City" (*Excélsior*, 21 May 1954, A15).

53. Pérez Cruz, interview.

54. Arana, *Guaraches*, vol. 3, 109.

55. "Medidas de seguridad," from the pamphlet "Festival de rock."

56. This more conspiratorial view came through in several interviews. One informant, Armando Blanco (interview with the author, Mexico City, 11 March 1993), went so far as to suggest that Echeverría had assembled the nation's leading social and cultural critics for a "private live screening" of the concert at the president's office. A more cynical but certainly no less fantastic view is that Echeverría authorized the festival precisely in order to produce a backlash that warranted a full-fledged crackdown on the rock movement itself.

57. From the provincial newspaper, *El Diario de Puebla*, quoted in Arana, *Guaraches*, vol. 3, 136.

58. Pedro Ocampo Ramírez, "Los jóvenes y el anti-Avándaro," *Jueves de Excélsior*, 30 September 1971, 8.

59. Luis Cervantes Cabeza de Vaca, "La fuga de la realidad, la nausea," *Siempre*, 29 September 1971, 43.

60. Carlos Monsiváis, *Amor perdido* (Mexico City: Biblioteca Era, 1977), 251.

61. Carrión and Iturbide, *Avándaro*, n.p.

62. Pacheco, "Woodstocktlán." *Relajo* was a more printable expression for desmadre. See chapter 1 for a discussion of these terms.

63. Rubalcaba and others, *Nosotros*.

64. Enrique Marroquín, "Cultura pop y represión," *Piedra Rodante*, 15 November 1971, 29. His phrase, "por nuestra gente hablará el rock" was an explicit reappropriation of José Vasconcelos's famous statement: "Por mi raza hablará el espíritu." (Alan Knight translates this as, "By virtue of my race the spirit shall speak" ["Racism, Revolution, and *Indigenismo:* Mexico, 1910–1940," in Richard Graham, ed., *The Idea of Race in Latin America, 1870–1940* (Austin: University of Texas Press, 1990), 92].)

65. Ricardo Garibay, "Dar juntos la batalla: Urgencia del diálogo entre la juventud y el poder," *Excélsior*, 28 October 1971, 6.

66. Quoted in José Agustín, *La contracultura en México: La historia y el significado de los rebeldes sin causa, los jipitecas, los punks y las bandas* (Mexico City: Grijalbo, 1996), 88–89.

67. Carlos Monsiváis, "Carlos Monsiváis refuta a C.M.," *La Edad del Rock*, 30 November 1971, 25.

68. *Three Souls in My Mind* (Discos Cisne-Raff, 1971).

69. "Colonialismo cultural," *Excélsior*, 14 September 1971, A6.

70. Cervantes Cabeza de Vaca, "Fuga de la realidad."

71. Quoted in Arana, *Guaraches*, vol. 3, 127. For the magazine's earlier criticism of the government in 1968 see "Esta es ¡la verdad!," *¿Porqué?* Special issue, 1968, n.p.

72. José Agustín, *Tragicomedia mexicana 2: La vida en México de 1970 a 1982* (Mexico City: Planeta, 1992), 17.

73. *Jueves de Excélsior*, 24 February 1972. Charro means, roughly, "cowboy."

74. Pompeyo, interview.

75. Agustín Salmón, "Prohibieron la grabación de la música que se tocó en Avándaro," *Excélsior*, 23 September 1971, B10.

76. The song was written in English and Spanish by the group Rosario. The English version actually loses much of the sentiment conveyed by the Spanish version, and it contains several grammatical errors. Thus the version I have used incorporates my translation from the Spanish, which I based on the linguistic structure of the original version in English.

77. "Telecomentarios," *Excélsior*, 19 September 1971, B21; Salmón, "Prohibieron la grabación"; Roberto Ramírez S., "'Radio Juventud' aclara su intervención en Avándaro," *Excélsior*, 18 September 1971, B11.

78. "Exhortó a locutores para que hagan buen uso del lenguaje," *Excélsior*, 27 September 1971, B15. The Federal Radio and Television Law, dating from 1960, required programming to "conserve national characteristics, the country's customs and traditions, the essence of language, and to exalt the values of Mexican nationality" (*El Diario Oficial*, 19 January 1960, 2). See also chapter 1.

79. Ramírez, "Reunión." Ten minutes of the festival were actually shown on Telesistema's *24 horas* news program the following night, but Emilio Azcárraga Milmo confiscated the tapes and locked them away in a company vault. Luis de Llano Jr. tried on several occasions to persuade Azcárraga to release the tapes, but he always refused to do so (de Llano, interview).

80. Luis de Llano Jr. later explained in an interview: "It was all shot on videotape. At the time our technology was not that advanced, as well. We didn't have the lighting equipment that was necessary, and we didn't have the consoles to mix the sound correctly. So the sound was pretty bad, and the video was not that good, either" (de Llano, interview). Armando Molina was compensated for his organizing efforts with the rights to record an album from the festival, but a combination of government censorship and poor technical quality kept the album from being produced (Molina, interview).

81. Vivianne Klein, "Cotorreando con las grabadoras," *POP*, 14 January 1972, 44–46.

82. Pompeyo, interview.

83. Advertisement in *Piedra Rodante*, 30 October 1971.

84. "Expanding Int'l Disk Mkt. Still Strongly Regional in Tastes, Sez RCA's

Soria," *Variety*, 11 June 1969, 73. CBS Records, for example, used a bilingual advertising strategy to promote Carlos Santana's new album in the United States (*Rolling Stone*, 23 November 1972, 40).

85. I reviewed this catalog at Polygram Studios in Mexico City. Unfortunately, it was the only available catalog for this entire period for all companies and the earliest one archived for Polygram. Outdated catalogs were simply thrown away. Not one company kept careful records of the quantity or market destinations of records sold.

86. Pompeyo, interview.

87. Pompeyo, interview.

88. Salmón, "Prohibieron la grabación."

89. *Piedra Rodante*, 15 May 1971, 4–5.

90. *Piedra Rodante* (January 1972). This issue did not have a specific date.

91. *Piedra Rodante* (October 1971). This issue did not have a specific date.

92. See Anne Rubenstein, *Bad Language, Naked Ladies, and Other Threats to the Nation: A Political History of Comic Books in Mexico* (Durham, N.C.: Duke University Press, 1998).

93. "Minutario, January-April 1972," 29 March, CCPRI; Roura, *Apuntes de rock*, 137–39. Curiously, *Rolling Stone* never mentioned the creation of a Mexican counterpart. When later queried on the issue, editors at *Rolling Stone* responded that they had no knowledge of the Mexican version (Eric Etheridge, senior features editor of *Rolling Stone*, letter to the author, 18 November 1992).

94. Marcos Mendoza, "Un chavo consigue el auditorio nacional," *Piedra Rodante*, October 1971, 25.

95. Joaquín ("Chas") López, interview with the author, Mexico City, 7 April 1993.

96. Ramón García, interview with the author, Mexico City, 18 March 1993.

97. García, interview. The "Rock sobre Ruedas" effort was organized by the bands Three Souls in My Mind (now the TRI) and Tinta Blanca.

98. Víctor Roura, *Negros del corazón* (Mexico City: Universidad Autónoma Metropolitana, 1984), 29.

99. Carlos Baca, "Rock subterráneo," *México Canta*, 16 June 1972, 4–5.

100. Roura, *Apuntes de rock*, 28. At the same time, however, Mexican rock performances still took place abroad. One year after Avándaro the group Three Souls in My Mind performed for a month in El Salvador with several other bands, including Peace and Love. To their surprise, songs by both Three Souls in My Mind and Peace and Love were already on the "Hit Parade" charts and were featured constantly on local radio (Alejandro Lora, with Arturo Castelazo, *Lora: Vida y rocanrol . . . en sus propias palabras* [Mexico City: Castelazo y Asociados, 1993], 46–48).

101. "Páginas de la chaviza ondera," *México Canta*, 16 June 1972, 14.

102. Roura, *Apuntes de rock*, 44.

103. Roura, *Negros del corazón*, 28.

104. Iván Zatz-Díaz, interview with the author, New York City, 13 October 1992.

105. David Ramón, "¿Rock meshica? Un concierto Zapatista," *Diorama de la Cultura* (Sunday Supplement), *Excélsior,* 26 September 1971, 3.

106. López, interview.

107. Quoted in Roura, *Apuntes de rock,* 42.

108. See Fernando Reyes Matta, "The 'New Song' and Its Confrontation in Latin America," in C. Nelson and L. Grossberg, eds., *Marxism and the Interpretation of Culture* (Urbana: University of Illinois Press, 1988), 447–60; Patricia Oliart and José A. Lloréns, "La nueva canción en el Perú," *Comunicación y Cultura* 12 (1984): 73–82; Jan Fairley, "La Nueva Canción latinoamericana," *Bulletin of Latin American Research* 3, no. 2 (1984): 107–15; Jan Fairley, "Annotated Bibliography of Latin-American Popular Music with Particular Reference to Chile and to Nueva Canción," *Popular Music* 5 (1985): 305–56; Jeffrey F. Taffet, "'My Guitar Is not for the Rich': The New Chilean Song Movement and the Politics of Culture," *Journal of American Culture* 20, no. 2 (1997): 91–103.

109. Reyes Matta, "'New Song,'" 448.

110. Oliart and Lloréns, "Nueva canción," 77.

111. Citing "new forms of alienation probably influenced by Western music and fashions," the Cuban government abruptly banned all U.S. and British pop music from the airwaves in 1973 (*Rolling Stone,* 21 June 1973, 5). But even prior to this the slogan "Inside the Revolution, everything; Outside the Revolution, nothing" severely limited access to and popularization of "Western" music and fashions. See also Michele Mattelart, "El conformismo revoltoso de la canción popular," *Cine Cubano* 69/70 (1972): 144–55.

112. See Ariel Dorfman and Armand Mattelart, *How to Read Donald Duck: Imperialist Ideology in the Disney Comic* (New York: International General, 1991). Originally published in Chile in 1971, *How to Read Donald Duck* launched a leftist crusade against the influence of U.S.-inspired mass culture. Based on a structuralist interpretation of how mass culture "works," this early cultural-imperialist critique came under attack in the 1980s as new interpretations emerged. For an extremely useful discussion of the origins and historical development of the discourse on cultural imperialism see John Tomlinson, *Cultural Imperialism: A Critical Introduction* (Baltimore, Md.: Johns Hopkins University Press, 1991).

113. "Música y Liberación (mesa redonda)," *Cine Cubano* 13, no. 76 (1973): 19–20.

114. "Declaración final del Encuentro de Música Latinoamericana," *Casa de las Américas* 13, no. 75 (1972). See also Leonardo Acosta, *Música y descolonización* (Havana: Editorial Arte y Literatura, 1982).

115. Luz Lozano, interview with the author, Mexico City, 2 March 1993. The song included an instrumental track by the Peruvian group Los Incas. Its commercial appropriation by Simon and Garfunkel created considerable

controversy in Peru, where the duo was widely denounced in the press for their imperialism. I am indebted to Iván Hinojosa and Elizabeth Howorth for our conversations on radical responses to rock music in Lima during this period.

116. "Soledad Bravo habla de la canción con mensaje social," *Excélsior,* 7 November 1974, B8. For an important discussion of the cultural politics behind the creation of the Polyforum, see Leonard Folgarait, *So Far from Heaven: David Alfaro Siqueiros' The March of Humanity and Mexican Revolutionary Politics* (Cambridge: Cambridge University Press, 1987).

117. Federico Arana, interview with the author, Mexico City, 13 August 1991. Arana was a guitar player and band leader for several different rock 'n' roll, rock, and, later, folk-music groups dating from the late 1950s. In 1973 he was awarded the Xavier Villaurrutia Prize for his novel *Las jiras* (Mexico City: Joaquín Mortiz, 1973), which chronicles the travails of a Mexican rock group touring in the United States. The author of several books on rock music in Mexico, Arana teaches biology and methodology at the UNAM. See also his *Roqueros y folcloroides* (Mexico City: Joaquín Mortiz, 1988).

118. From the album cover of *Los Folkloristas: Repertorio, 1967–1970. Vol. 3* (Discos Pueblo, 1970).

119. René Villanueva, *Cantares de la memoria: 25 años de la historia del grupo Los Folkloristas, alma y tradición de la música popular mexicana* (Mexico City: Planeta, 1994), 225 and passim.

120. Ibid., 156–57.

121. Lozano, interview.

122. Zatz-Díaz, interview.

123. Zatz-Díaz, interview.

124. Quoted in Arana, *Roqueros y folcloroides,* 26.

125. "Santana Concert Undermined by Leftists/Government," *Rolling Stone,* 6 January 1972, 4. During a tour of Central America in late 1973, the band encountered "crowds [that] were so huge in El Salvador that the group had to be escorted to their plane by the Red Cross" (*Rolling Stone,* 22 November 1973, 33).

126. Oliart and Lloréns, "Nueva canción."

127. Simon Frith, "'The Magic That Can Set You Free': The Ideology of Folk and the Myth of the Rock Community," *Popular Music* 1 (1981): 159–68.

128. New Song and folk music performances and discussions were widely sponsored by the UNAM, for instance. See the poster archive, "Difusión Cultural / UNAM," CESU. See also Lucía Martínez Villegas and Hilda Rivera Delgado, *La Extensión Universitaria en la Universidad Nacional Autónoma de México: Información General, 1973–1978* (Mexico City: Universidad Nacional Autónoma de México, 1979), vol. 6.

129. Lozano, interview.

130. Arana, *Roqueros y folcloroides,* 122.

131. Zatz-Díaz, interview.

132. Jaime Pontones, interview with the author, Mexico City, 15 August 1991.

133. Anny Rivera and others, *El público del canto popular* (Santiago, Chile: CENECA, 1980), 14. See also Armand Mattelart and Michele Mattelart, *Juventud chilena: Rebeldía y conformismo* (Santiago, Chile: Editorial Universitaria, 1970).

134. Pérez Cruz, interview.

135. García, interview.

CHAPTER 7

1. "De como U.S.A. usa la música como arma de penetración," *Cine Cubano* 66/67 (1970), 70.

2. Ibid., 68.

3. Gerald K. Haines, "Under the Eagle's Wing: The Franklin Roosevelt Administration Forges an American Hemisphere," *Diplomatic History* 1 (1977): 373–88.

4. For an analysis of how this worked with cartoons see Julianne Burton, "Don (Juanito) Duck and the Imperial-Patriarchal Unconscious: Disney Studios, the Good Neighbor Policy, and the Packaging of Latin America," in Andrew Parker and others, eds., *Nationalisms and Sexualities* (New York: Routledge, 1992), 21–41.

5. Robert E. Elder, *The Information Machine: The United States Information Agency and American Foreign Policy* (Syracuse, N.Y.: Syracuse University Press, 1968), 34–44.

6. Ibid., 6–7.

7. "De como U.S.A.," 72.

8. Quoted in Elder, *Information Machine*, 3.

9. Ronald I. Rubin, *The Objectives of the United States Information Agency: Controversies and Analysis* (New York: Praeger, 1968), 9.

10. Ibid., 61.

11. USIA Record Group no. 306, Country Project Correspondence, Box 15, "1952–1963," 16 December 1960, National Archives and Records Administration, Suitland Reference Branch. (Hereafter cited as Suitland Archives.)

12. Ibid.

13. This count is based on a conservative interpretation (that is, counting overlapping installations only once) of total USIA activity in Mexico taken from the agency's 1965 semiannual report to Congress. That report lists installations at the following locations: Mexico City, Guadalajara, Hermosillo, Monterrey (mission post, information center, branch post, or subpost); Mexico City, Guadalajara, Monterrey, Mérida, Morelia, San Luís Potosí, Veracruz (binational centers); Mazatlán, Puebla, Tampico (reading room or distribution outlet) (*USIA 24th Semiannual Report to the Congress*, January–June 1965, 33).

14. USIA Record Group no. 306, S-30–64, Box 1, December 1964, Suitland Archives.

15. *USIA 30th Semiannual Report to the Congress,* January-June 1968, 16. The article does not specifically mention Latin America, but judging from other evidence it would be apparent that this was the case for Spanish-language broadcasts as well.

16. "Latinos to Get Own 'Hit Parade' on VOA," *Variety,* 3 August 1966, 52.

17. *USIA 30th Semiannual Report,* 16.

18. Ibid., 6.

19. Ibid.

20. Rubin, *Objectives,* 48–61.

21. "Music Opens Doors," *USIA 36th Semiannual Report to the Congress,* January-June 1971, 17. For an article on VOA's programming of rock in the 1980s see "Voice of America: Rock & Roll with Uncle Sam," *Rolling Stone,* 18 August 1983, 37.

22. Frank Ninkovich, "The Currents of Cultural Diplomacy: Art and the State Department, 1938–1947," *Diplomatic History* 1 (1977): 215–37.

23. "Music Opens Doors," 13–14.

24. In the course of my research I filed for access under the Freedom of Information Act, and as I was finishing writing, much of the official documentation from the period under discussion became declassified. I hope to explore this newly released archival material in future projects.

25. "Music Opens Doors," 14.

26. Peter P. Cecere, interview with the author, Mexico City, 20 April 1993.

27. "Blood, Sweat & Tears in Iron Curtain Tour," *Variety,* 6 May 1970, 1. Significantly, the tour coincided with a USIA psychedelic poster exhibit held in Poland (*USIA 36th Semiannual Report,* 6). In both Poland and Czechoslovakia, local rock movements had developed by the late 1960s. See "Czechoslovakia Has Own Pop Festival," *Rolling Stone,* 24 February 1968, 6; "Would You Believe . . . Polish Rock & Roll," *Rolling Stone,* 17 September 1970, 34–37; Timothy W. Ryback, *Rock around the Bloc: A History of Rock Music in Eastern Europe and the Soviet Union* (New York.: Oxford University Press, 1990); Sabrina Petra Ramet, ed., *Rocking the State: Rock Music and Politics in Eastern Europe and Russia* (Boulder, Colo.: Westview Press, 1994).

28. "Music Opens Doors," 15.

29. A USIA official also made this point, noting that the philosophy of the agency was, "Don't do things that commercial traffic can handle" (William J. Dieterich, interview with the author, Mexico City, 20 September 1993).

30. The information for the following discussion comes from the folder entitled, "Publications: Estilos y protestas entre la juventud norteamericana," which was given to me by Peter Cecere of the USIA (hereafter cited as Estilos y protestas Folder). This folder contains original and carbon copies of documents relevant to the development and authorization of the full-color pamphlet, *Protestas y estilos entre la juventud norteamericana,* produced in large part by Peter Cecere and distributed by the USIA to posts in Latin America and

Spain in late spring 1971. I am very indebted to Peter Cecere for letting me see and later keep these documents and for our discussions regarding his role at the USIA.

31. Cecere, interview.

32. Memorandum, Robert Amerson, Seth Isman, and Peter Cecere to all posts, 15 January 1971, Estilos y protestas Folder, 2.

33. *USIA 29th Semiannual Report to the Congress*, July-December, 1967, 9.

34. Memorandum, Robert Amerson to William H. Weathersby, 13 November 1969, Estilos y protestas Folder. I have not yet gained access to a copy of this earlier pamphlet, but, judging from the controversy surrounding the publication of the "successor issue," it is unlikely that it dealt specifically with countercultural values, which at any rate were still incipient at the time of its publication.

35. Memorandum, Amerson and others to all posts, 15 January 1971, 1.

36. Ibid, 2. It is interesting to note that the pamphlet used the term *norteamericano*, or *North American*, in its title to refer to youth in the United States, which is the appropriate way of referring to the United States in Latin America. At the same time, however, the term *American* is used repeatedly in the pamphlet itself, which reflects an important inconsistency and an oversight on the part of the agency.

37. According to Peter Cecere, the numbers were based on actual requests made by country operatives. The breakdown of distribution according to a handwritten note found in the file was as follows: Mexico, 10,000; Brazil, 10,000, in Portuguese translation; Argentina, 5,000; El Salvador, 5,000; Paraguay, 1,000; Venezuela, 1,000; Guatemala, 1,000; Uruguay, 1,000; Peru, 1,000; Spain, 1,000; Nicaragua, 600; Honduras, 500; Dominican Republic, 500; Ecuador, 500; and Equatorial Guinea, 100.

38. Memorandum, Amerson and others to all posts, 15 January 1971, 3. This quotation reflects the original English, before it was translated into Spanish for the final product.

39. Draft memorandum, Robert Amerson to Mr. Halsema, 15 December 1970, Estilos y protestas Folder (emphasis in the original). Abroad, the agency was called the U.S. Information Service (USIS).

40. Memorandum, 19 November 1969, Estilos y protestas Folder.

41. Ibid.

42. Memorandum, Amerson to Weathersby, 13 November 1969.

43. Draft memorandum, Amerson to Halsema, 15 December 1970.

44. *USIA 30th Semiannual Report to the Congress*, 37.

45. See chapter 3.

46. This is the original English text from the introduction that was later translated into Spanish.

47. Memorandum, James Meyer to Robert Amerson, 28 December 1970, Estilos y protestas Folder.

48. Memorandum, Robert Amerson to Mr. Bielak, 6 January 1971, Estilos y protestas Folder.

49. Cecere, interview.

50. Memorandum, Amerson to Weathersby, 13 November 1969. In reply, Weathersby agreed that the "material can be used for a creditable approach to this widely discussed topic." He argued, ultimately unsuccessfully, for "the addition of one article which shows that there are many students, indeed, the majority, who are not political activists but who are simply pursuing their studies and the usual interests of the young." This criticism was eventually added to the introduction. Memorandum, William H. Weathersby to Robert Amerson, 23 December 1969, Estilos y protestas Folder.

51. I did not meet a single person who had actually seen or heard of this pamphlet.

52. Michael Canning and Peter P. Cecere, "Student Activism in the Americas: A Comparative View," *Foreign Service Journal* (May 1970): 17. This article was republished by the USIA in Spanish and Portuguese for mass distribution. (Information on this project comes from the folder, "Publications: Article on Student Activism in the Americas," also given to me by Peter Cecere of the USIA.) In conversations with Cecere it was revealed that he was unaware of the existence of a Mexican counterculture, much less the Avándaro music festival.

53. *Protestas y estilos,* 20.

54. Ibid, 40.

CONCLUSIONS

1. Nuevo México, Peace and Love (who changed their name to Náhuatl), Enigma, Los Dug Dugs, and Javier Batiz, among others, managed to retain a recording foothold through the 1970s. But only Three Souls in My Mind produced new albums in succession and developed a mass following. By the 1990s, Los Dug Dugs were playing at a restaurant owned by Armando Nava, the only remaining member of the band. Javier Batiz was performing for government-sponsored events.

2. Rafael Molina Domínguez, "La entrevista de encuentro: Alejandro Lora," *Encuentro,* May 1987, 36.

3. *Chavo de Onda* (Cisne-Raff, 1975).

4. Quoted in Víctor Roura, *Negros del corazón* (Mexico City: Universidad Autónoma Metropolitana, 1984), 51.

5. Pablo Vila, "Rock *nacional* and Dictatorship in Argentina," *Popular Music* 6, no. 2 (1987): 129–48; Nicolás Casullo, "El Rock en la sociedad política," *Comunicación y Cultura* 12 (October 1984): 41–50; Jorge Reyes, "Guillermo Briseño: ¿Un rock de izquierda?" *El Machete,* no. 12 (April 1981): 53–55.

6. *Briseño, Carrasco y Flores* (CBS, 1978). Interestingly, one of the tracks on this album ("Try") is written in English.

7. These bands included Maldita Vecindad y los Hijos del Quinto Patio, Los Caifanes, and Café Tacuba.

8. "El otro rock nacional," directed by Víctor Roura, series *Bellas artes en*

radio, no. 284, aired 15 August 1983 (Radio Educación, Fonoteca de Programas). For the same text see Víctor Roura, *Apuntes de rock: Por las calles del mundo* (Mexico City: Nuevomar, 1985), 99.

9. Roura, *Apuntes de rock*, 99.

10. See Federico Arana, *Guaraches de ante azul: Historia del rock mexicano* (Mexico City: Posada, 1985), vol. 4, chap. 1.

11. "Los últimos tiempos de rock en México," series *Bellas artes en radio*, no. 438, aired 6 August 1986 (Radio Educación, Fonoteca de Programas).

12. Ibid.

13. Ibid.

14. José Agustín, *La contracultura en México: La historia y el significado de los rebeldes sin causa, los jipitecas, los punks y las bandas* (Mexico City: Grijalbo, 1996), 105. Carlos Monsiváis had earlier labeled the Tianguis del Chopo "a temple to the Mexican counterculture" (Carlos Monsiváis, "Tianguis del Chopo," *Aullido* (Revista del Tianguis Cultural del Chopo), n.d., 2. The Chopo operates every Saturday from 10:00 A.M. to 2:00 P.M. alongside the Railway Station of the North, near the Monument of the Revolution. The word *tianguis* is an indigenous term meaning open-air market.

15. Ernesto Fajardo, interview with the author, Mexico City, Fall 1987. The group Fajardo represented was autonomous of all government or other political affiliation, but it is not entirely clear whether the Consejo Popular Juvenil (which existed as early as 1984) was indeed the organizational basis for the group he represented, the Consejo Popular Juvenil de Ricardo Flores Magón (which was based in Santa Fe, a marginalized barrio of the city).

16. From "¡Cámara!" by Victorino, republished in *Encuentro*, February 1984, n.p.

17. *Encuentro*, October 1987.

18. Cited in Federico Reyes Heroles, ed., *Los partidos políticos mexicanos en 1991* (Mexico City: Fondo de Cultura Económica, 1991), 168. I wish to thank John Coatsworth for bringing this citation to my attention.

19. Santiago Pérez, "El rock en México," *Universidad de México*, September 1988, 36.

20. Ibid. See also Adrián de Garay Sánchez, *El rock también es cultura*, Cuadernos de Comunicación y Prácticas Sociales, no. 5 (Mexico City: Universidad Iberoamericana, 1993), 53–79.

21. See, for example, Jorge García-Robles, *¿Qué transa con las bandas?* (Mexico City: Posada, 1985).

22. *¿Qué onda con la música popular mexicana?* (Mexico City: Ediciones del Museo Nacional de Culturas Populares; Cultura/SEP, 1983).

23. Elena Poniatowska, *Nothing, Nobody: The Voices of the Mexico City Earthquake*, trans. Aurora Camacho de Schmidt and Arthur Schmidt (Philadelphia: Temple University Press, 1995).

24. Gilberto Guevara Niebla, *La democracia en la calle: Crónica del movimiento estudiantil mexicano* (Mexico City: Siglo XXI, 1988), 103–61.

25. Jaime Avilés, "Cien mil en la marcha del 2 de octubre," *La Jornada*,

3 October 1996, 1. Other recent examples of this relationship, which took place during the course of my research, were the "Rock the Plebiscite" concert held in Mexico City in the summer of 1993 and a series of concerts at the UNAM in protest against government repression of the rebellion in Chiapas.

26. María Elena Fernández, "Meckseecahnose! Tijuana No Blasts Across the Border," *Los Angeles Weekly*, 2–8 June 1995, 39. "Marcos" is the nom de guerre of one of the subcommanders who compose the Zapatistas' revolutionary army. Due to a combination of intellect, media scrutiny, and commodification of his image, Marcos has come to stand for the Zapatista struggle itself.

27. Ed Morales, "Rock Is Dead and Living in Mexico," *Rock & Roll Quarterly*, supplement to the *Village Voice*, Winter 1993, 17.

28. Carlos Monsiváis, interview with the author, Mexico City, 20 August 1991.

29. Morales, "Rock Is Dead."

30. An important source for this material is the Tianguis del Chopo rock flea market. For a description see ibid. The commodification of Mexico's refrito period, on the other hand, has meant continued access to the music from the early 1960s, which continues to be played on the radio and heard at parties.

31. This commercialization strategy was repeated with crass effectiveness with the mass promotion of the Woodstock 94 festival. See, for example, *Woodstock 94: 3 More Days of Peace & Music* (New York: St. Martin's Press, 1994); and *Woodstock 94: The Guide* (New York: Entertainment Weekly Custom Publishing, 1994), which was distributed at the festival and features numerous advertisements for concert paraphernalia. I wish to thank Andrew Zolov for lending me the concert guide.

32. A clear example of this is found on Mexico radio. During the time of my field research, 1993–1994, Mexico City's principal rock station, Rock 101, dealt exclusively in foreign rock, itself a shift away from the Spanish-language rock emphasis on which the station had built its early reputation. One featured program, "Radio Alicia" (conducted by Jaime Pontones), though a deliberate effort to re-create the mood of the 1960s and 1970s, lacked any reference to a Mexican rock movement at that time, while explicitly appropriating U.S. countercultural references as belonging to Mexico's own experience. The recommodification of La Onda Chicana is nonetheless partially visible in the recent release of a compact disc, *Vibraciones de Avándaro: 25 aniversario* (Polygram) (Víctor Ronquillo, "El rock tiene su historia," *Reforma*, 22 June 1997, E4). Also, a twenty-two-minute color video, "A 25 años de Avándaro" (Víctor Vallejo), was recently produced (Hugo Lazcano, "Muestran Avándaro," *Reforma*, 14 September 1996, E5). Information on certain bands from the era is available at the World Wide Web site [http://www.rockeros.com].

Bibliography

PRIMARY SOURCES

Archives and Institutes

Mexico City (Public)

Archivo General de la Nación
    Hermanos Mayo Photo Archive
    Ramo Presidentes
Banco Nacional de Comercio Exterior
Biblioteca Miguel Lerdo de Tejada
    Archivo Cortes de Periódico
Dirección General de Radio, Televisión y Cinematografía
Filmoteca de San Ildefonso
Fundación Manuel Buendía
Instituto Mexicano de la Radio
Museo Nacional de Culturas Populares
Radio Educación
    Fonoteca de Programas
Secretaría de Comunicaciones y Transportes
    Dirección General de Normas de Sistemas de Difusión
Secretaría de Gobernación
    Comisión Calificadora de Publicaciones y Revistas Ilustradas
Secretaría de Relaciones Exteriores
    Archivo de Concentración
Universidad Nacional Autónoma de México, Hemeroteca
    Centro de Estudios sobre la Universidad (CESU)

Mexico City (Private)

Cámara Nacional de la Industria de Radio y Televisión
Cecere, Peter P. (U.S. Information Agency)
García, Ramón (Tianguis del Chopo)

Polygram Records
Sony Records

United States (Public)

Museum of Broadcast Communications (Chicago)
Museum of Television and Radio (New York City)
National Archives and Records Administration
  Suitland Reference Branch

United States (Private)

Blank, Mitchell (New York City)
Cecere, Peter P. (U.S. Information Agency)
Harvard Business School, Baker Library (Cambridge, Mass.)
  Cole-Harvard Collection
  Historical Corporate Records Collection

Personal Interviews

Arana, Federico. Novelist and former member of the band Los Sinners, Los Tequilas, and Naftalina. Mexico City. 13 August 1991.
Beltrand Luján, Carlos. Former sales agent for Discos Orfeón. Mexico City. 18 May 1994.
Blanco, Armando. Former rock concert promoter and founder of the Hip-70 music store / club. Mexico City. 11 March 1993.
Blank, Mitch. Musical archivist for the Bob Dylan estate. New York City. 13 September 1992.
Cecere, Peter P. Former student affairs officer in the U.S. Information Agency. Mexico City. 20 April 1993.
Cervantes, Conchita. Upper-middle-class participant in the youth culture. Mexico City. 22 August 1996.
Chávez, Oscar. Renowned folk singer who also starred in the film *Los Caifanes* (1966). Mexico City. 5 August 1996.
Cruz Ayala, José. Former artistic director for CBS Records. Mexico City. 13 August 1993.
De Llano, Luis, Jr. Producer of "La Onda de Woodstock" for Telesistema and in charge of film production at Avándaro. Interview with Andrew Paxman. Mexico City. 18 December 1997.
Dieterich, William J. Advisor for cultural affairs in the U.S. Information Agency. Mexico City. 20 September 1993.
Fajardo, Ernesto. Cultural coordinator of the Consejo Popular Juvenil de Ricardo Flores Magón. Mexico City. Fall 1987.
Franz, Carl. Author of *The People's Guide to Mexico*. Telephone interview. 23 August 1994.

García, Ramón. Cofounder of Tianguis del Chopo. Mexico City. 18 March 1993.

García Michel, Sergio. Independent rock cinematographer. Mexico City. 12 February 1993.

Gaytán, Eddie. Linguist from Guatemala. New York City. 6 November 1992.

Hernández, Severiano. Editor of the trade magazine *Discoméxico*. Mexico City. 31 May 1993.

Laboriel, Johnny. Member of the band Los Rebeldes del Rock. Mexico City. 11 August 1996.

LeGrande, Catherine. Latin American historian. Telephone interview. 16 February 1995.

López, Joaquín ("Chas"). Former member of the band La Revolución de Emiliano Zapata. Mexico City. 7 April 1993.

Lozano, Luz. Mexican university student in the early 1970s. Mexico City. 2 March 1993.

Luboff, Ken. Vice president of John Muir Publications. Telephone interview. 1 September 1994.

Medina Rodríguez, Leticia. Archivist for CESU and university student in the 1970s. Mexico City. 2 March 1993.

Molina, Armando. Founder of the band La Máquina del Sonido and coorganizer of the Avándaro rock festival. Mexico City. 17 June 1993.

Monsiváis, Carlos. Cultural critic and author. Mexico City. 20 August 1991.

Nava, Armando. Founder of the band Los Dug Dugs. Mexico City. 5 June 1993.

Orta, Lila. Participant in La Onda. Mexico City. 13 January 1993.

Partida, Enrique. Former sales agent for Polydor Records. Mexico City. 7 June 1993.

Peña, Manuel. Musicologist at the Center for Mexican-American Studies, University of Texas, Austin. Telephone interview. 23 April 1997.

Pérez Cruz, José Enrique. Archivist at the Hemeroteca and former student activist at the Universidad Nacional Autónoma de México. Mexico City. 5 March 1993.

Pompeyo, Herbe. Former artistic director for Polydor Records. Mexico City. 8 June 1993.

Pontones, Jaime. Former disk jockey at Rock 101. Mexico City. 15 August 1991.

Rincón, Eréndira. Cofounder of the children's musical group Los Hermanos Rincón. Mexico City. 20 August 1996.

Rogers, Steve. Member of the production staff for *The People's Guide to Mexico*. Telephone interview. 7 September 1994.

Ruiz, Manuel. Rock 'n' roll and refrito aficionado. Mexico City. 6 August 1991.

Septien, Alejandro. Coordinator for special events of the Coca-Cola Co. Mexico City. 20 February 1993.

Solís Gómez, Gustavo. Mexican rock aficionado. Mexico City. 12 January 1993.

Solís Gómez, Jasmín. Participant in La Onda. Mexico City. 28 January 1993.

Zatz-Díaz, Iván. Folk and New Song aficionado. New York City. 13 October 1992.

Newspapers, Popular Magazines, and Reports

Annual Corporate Reports
  Capitol Industries–EMI
  Columbia Broadcasting System
  Radio Corporation of America
Antena (Cámara Nacional de la Industria de la Radio y la Televisión)
Aullido (Revista del Tianguis Cultural del Chopo)
Billboard Music Week
La Cultura en México
El Diario Oficial
Discoméxico
La Edad del Rock
Encuentro
Excélsior
Gaceta de la Universidad Nacional Autónoma de México
El Heraldo
El Heraldo Cultural
El Heraldo de México
Idolos del Rock
Impacto
La Jornada
Jueves de Excélsior
Life en Español
México Canta
El Nacional
New York Times
Novedades
Piedra Rodante
POP
Punto de Partida
Revista Mexicana de Comunicación
Rock-Press
Rolling Stone
Siempre
Las Ultimas Noticias de Excélsior
El Universal
El Universal Gráfico
U.S.I.A. Semiannual Reports to the Congress
Variety
Zona Rosa

SECONDARY SOURCES

Printed Materials

Abreu Adorno, Manuel. *Llegaron los hippis.* Río Piedras, Puerto Rico: Huracán, 1978.

Acosta, Leonardo. *Música y descolonización.* Havana: Editorial Arte y Literatura, 1982.

Agustín, José. *Abolición de la propiedad.* Mexico City: Joaquín Mortiz, 1969 [1983].

―――. *La contracultura en México: La historia y el significado de los rebeldes sin causa, los jipitecas, los punks y las bandas.* Mexico City: Grijalbo, 1996.

―――. "Cuál es La Onda." *Diálogos* 10, no. 1 (1974): 11–13.

―――. "Forty Archetypes Draw Their Swords." In June C. D. Carter and Donald Schmidt, eds. *José Agustín: Onda and Beyond,* 24–36. Columbia: University of Missouri Press, 1986.

―――. *Inventando que sueño.* Mexico City: Joaquín Mortiz, 1968 [1992].

―――. *La nueva música clásica.* Mexico City: Instituto Nacional de la Juventud Mexicana, 1968.

―――. *El rock de la cárcel.* Mexico City: Editores Mexicanos Unidos, 1986.

―――. *Tragicomedia mexicana 1: La vida en México de 1940 a 1970.* Mexico City: Planeta, 1990.

―――. *Tragicomedia mexicana 2: La vida en México de 1970 a 1982.* Mexico City: Planeta, 1992.

Agustín, José, José Buil, and Gerardo Pardo. *Ahí viene la plaga.* Mexico City: Joaquín Mortiz, 1985.

Alba, Víctor. "The Mexican Revolution and the Cartoon." Reprinted in W. Dirt Raat and William H. Beezley, eds., *Twentieth-Century Mexico,* 223–35. Lincoln: University of Nebraska Press, 1986.

Alisky, Marvin. "Mexico's Broadcasting: Private and Public Stations with Assistance from Gobernación." In Marvin Alisky, ed., *Latin American Media: Guidance and Censorship,* 51–66. Ames: Iowa State University Press, 1981.

Alonso, Ana M. "The Effects of Truth: Re-Presentations of the Past and the Imagining of Community." *Journal of Historical Sociology* 1, no. 1 (1988): 33–57.

Anderson, Benedict. *Imagined Communities: Reflections on the Origin and Spread of Nationalism.* London: Verso, 1983.

Anderson, Danny J. "Creating Cultural Prestige: Editorial Joaquín Mortiz." *Latin American Research Review* 31, no. 2 (1996): 3–41.

Ang, Ian. "Culture and Communication: Towards an Ethnographic Critique of Media Consumption in the Transnational Media System." *European Journal of Communication* 5 (1990): 239–60.

Anuario del Comercio Exterior. Mexico City: Banco Nacional de Comercio Exterior, 1955–1976.

Anuario Estadístico de los Estados Unidos Mexicanos. Mexico City: Dirección General de Estadísticas, 1951–1970.

Appadurai, Arjun. "Disjuncture and Difference in the Global Cultural Economy." *Public Culture* 2 (1990): 1–24.

———, ed. *The Social Life of Things: Commodities in Cultural Perspective.* Cambridge: Cambridge University Press, 1986.

Arana, Federico. *Guaraches de ante azul: Historia del rock mexicano.* Vols. 1–4. Mexico City: Posada, 1985.

———. *Las jiras.* Mexico City: Joaquín Mortiz, 1973.

———. "Pasión, muerte y milagrosa resurrección de los cafés cantantes." In Carlos Chimal, ed., *Crines: Lecturas de rock,* 45–53. Mexico City: Penélope, 1984.

———. *Roqueros y folcloroides.* Mexico City: Joaquín Mortiz, 1988.

Attali, Jacques. *Noise: The Political Economy of Music.* Minneapolis: University of Minnesota Press, 1985.

Atwood, Rita, and Emile G. McAnany. *Communication and Latin American Society: Trends in Critical Research, 1960–1985.* Madison: University of Wisconsin Press, 1986.

Baciu, Stefan. "Beatitude South of the Border: Latin America's Beat Generation." *Hispania* 49 (1966): 733–39.

Bartra, Roger. "Mexican Oficio: The Miseries and Splendors of Culture." *Third Text* 14 (1991): 7–15.

Basurto, Jorge. "The Late Populism of Luis Echeverría." In Michael L. Conniff, ed. *Latin American Populism in Comparative Perspective,* 93–111. Albuquerque: University of New Mexico Press, 1982.

Bayón, Damián, ed. *Arte moderno en América Latina.* Madrid: Taurus, 1985.

Bazdresch, Carlos, and Santiago Levy. "Populism and Economic Policy in Mexico, 1970–1982." In Rudiger Dornbusch and Sebastian Edwards, eds., *The Macroeconomics of Populism in Latin America,* 223–62. Chicago: University of Chicago Press, 1991.

Beezley, William H. *Judas at the Jockey Club and Other Episodes of Porfirian Mexico.* Lincoln: University of Nebraska Press, 1987.

Bellingeri, Marco. "La imposibilidad del odio: La guerrilla y el movimiento estudiantil en México, 1960–1974." In Ilán Semo, ed., *La transición interrumpida: México, 1968–1988,* 49–73. Mexico City: Universidad Iberoamericana / Nueva Imagen, 1993.

Bellinghausen, Hermann, ed. *Pensar el 68.* Mexico City: Cal y Arena, 1988.

Benítez, Fernando. *Los indios de México.* Vols. 1–4. Mexico City: Ediciones Era, 1967–1972.

Berman, Marshall. *All That Is Solid Melts into Air: The Experience of Modernity.* New York: Penguin Books, 1982 [1988].

Blanco, Armando. *20 años de aventuras hip 70: El nuevo rock and roll en México desde 1968.* Mexico City: Posada, 1994.

Blanco Labra, Víctor. *Elvis en el bosque: Psicografía de Elvis Presley.* Mexico City: Diana, 1988.

Blum, Stephen, Philip V. Bohlman, and Daniel M. Neuman, eds. *Ethnomusicology and Modern Music History*. Urbana: University of Illinois Press, 1991.

Brandenburg, Frank. *The Making of Modern Mexico*. Englewood Cliffs, N.J.: Prentice Hall, 1964 [1967].

Braun, Herbert. "Protests of Engagement: Dignity, False Love, and Self-Love in Mexico, 1968." Paper presented at the Washington Seminar for Historians of Latin America, Georgetown University, Washington, D.C., October 1997.

Burton, Julianne. "Don (Juanito) Duck and the Imperial-Patriarchal Unconscious: Disney Studios, the Good Neighbor Policy, and the Packaging of Latin America." In Andrew Parker, Mary Russo, Doris Sommer, and Patricia Yaeger, eds., *Nationalisms and Sexualities*, 21–41. New York: Routledge, 1992.

Burton, Julianne, and Jean Franco. "Culture and Imperialism." *Latin American Perspectives* 5 (1978): 2–12.

Calderón, Eligio, Vicente Anaya, Carla Zenzes, and José Luis Fernández. *Avándaro: ¿Aliviane o movida?* Mexico City: Edit. Extemporáneos, 1971.

Caletti Kaplan, Rubén Sergio. "Communications Policies in Mexico: An Historical Paradox of Words and Actions." In Elizabeth Fox, ed., *Media and Politics in Latin America: The Struggle for Democracy*, 67–81. London: Sage, 1988.

Canning, Michael, and Peter P. Cecere. "Student Activism in the Americas: A Comparative View." *Foreign Service Journal* (May 1970): 15–18.

Cardoza y Aragón, Luis. *Pintura contemporánea de México*. Mexico City: Ediciones Era, 1974 [1988].

Careaga, Gabriel. *Mitos y fantasías de la clase media en México*. Mexico City: Cal y Arena, 1990.

Carrión, Luis, and Graciela Iturbide. *Avándaro*. Mexico City: Diógenes, 1971.

Carter, June C. D., and Donald L. Schmidt, eds. *José Agustín: Onda and Beyond*. Columbia: University of Missouri Press, 1986.

Cassady, Carolyn. *Off the Road: My Years with Cassady, Kerouac, and Ginsberg*. New York: W. Morrow, 1990.

Cassen, Bernard. "La lengua inglesa como vehículo del imperialismo cultural." *Comunicación y Cultura* 6 (February 1979): 75–84.

Castro Leal, Antonio. "El pueblo de México espera: Estudio sobre la radio y la televisión." *Cuadernos Americanos* 26 (1967): 75–102.

Casullo, Nicolás. "Argentina: El rock en la sociedad política." *Comunicación y Cultura* 12 (October 1984): 41–50.

Catálogo de la Fonoteca Alejandro Gómez Arias, Radio UNAM. Mexico City: Dirección General de Radio UNAM, 1987 [1988].

Chao Ebergenyi, Guillermo. *La caravana corona: Cuna de espectáculo en México*. Mexico City: Corona, Edición Limitada, 1995.

Chimal, Carlos, ed. *Crines: Lecturas de rock*. Mexico City: Penélope, 1984.

———. *Crines: Otras lecturas de rock*. Mexico City: Era, 1994.

Cisneros, Enrique. *'Si me permiten actuar.'* Mexico City: CLETA, n.d.

Cockcroft, James. D. "Coercion and Ideology in Mexican Politics." In James D. Cockcroft, André Gunder Frank, and Dale L. Johnson, *Dependence and Underdevelopment: Latin America's Political Economy*, 245–67. New York: Anchor Books, 1972.

Cohen, Deborah, and Lessie Jo Frazier. "'No sólo cocinábamos . . .' : Historia inédita de la otra mitad del 68." In Ilán Semo, ed., *La transición interrumpida: México, 1968–1988*, 75–105. Mexico City: Universidad Iberoamericana / Nueva Imagen, 1993.

Comaroff, Jean, and John Comaroff. *Of Revelation and Revolution*. Vol. 1. Chicago: University of Chicago Press, 1991.

Cuevas, José Luis. "The Cactus Curtain." *Evergreen Review* 2 (1959): 111–20.

———. *José Luis Cuevas. Self Portrait with Model*. Translated by Kenneth Lyons. New York: Rizzoli, 1983.

Daniels, Robert V. *Year of the Heroic Guerrilla: World Revolution and Counterrevolution in 1968*. New York: Basic Books, 1989.

De Certeau, Michel. *The Practice of Everyday Life*. Translated by Steven Rendall. Berkeley: University of California Press, 1984 [1988].

"De como U.S.A. usa la música como arma de penetración." *Cine Cubano* 66/67 (1970): 68–89.

"Declaración final del Encuentro de Música Latinoamericana." *Casa de las Américas* 13, no. 75 (1972).

Delpar, Helen. *The Enormous Vogue of Things Mexican: Cultural Relations between the United States and Mexico, 1920–1935*. Tuscaloosa: University of Alabama Press, 1992.

Denselow, Robin. *When the Music's Over: The Story of Political Pop*. London: Faber and Faber, 1989.

Diccionario enciclopédico de la lengua castellana. 3d ed. Paris: Sarnier Hermanos, 1900.

Dickstein, Morris. *Gates of Eden: American Culture in the Sixties*. New York: Basic, 1977.

Dorfman, Ariel, and Armand Mattelart. *How to Read Donald Duck: Imperialist Ideology in the Disney Comic*. New York: International General, 1991.

Douglas, Ann. "On the Road Again." *New York Times Book Review*, 9 April 1995, 2.

Eclaire, René. *Elvis Presley*. Mexico City: Publicaciones Liverpool, n.d.

Elder, Robert. *The Information Machine: The United States Information Agency and American Foreign Policy*. Syracuse, N.Y.: Syracuse University Press, 1968.

"¡Esta es la verdad!" *¿Porqué?* Special issue, 1968.

Estrada, Alvaro. *Huautla en tiempo de hippies*. Mexico City: Grijalbo, 1996.

———. *Vida de María Sabina: La sabia de los hongos*. Mexico City: Siglo XXI, 1977 [1989].

Fairley, Jan. "Annotated Bibliography of Latin-American Popular Music with Particular Reference to Chile and to Nueva Canción." *Popular Music* 5 (1985): 305–56.

————. "La Nueva Canción latinoamericana." *Bulletin of Latin American Research* 3, no. 2 (1984): 107–15.

Feld, Steven. "Notes on World Beat." *Public Culture* 1 (1988): 31–37.

Fernández, Claudia, and Andrew Paxman. "El Tigre." Unpublished manuscript.

Fernández, María Elena. "Meckseecahnose! Tijuana No Blasts across the Border." *Los Angeles Weekly*, 2–8 June 1995, 39.

Fiori, Umberto. "Rock Music and Politics in Italy." *Popular Music* 4 (1984): 261–78.

Florescano, Enrique, ed. *El patrimonio cultural de México*. Mexico City: Fondo de Cultura Económica, 1993.

Folgarait, Leonard. *So Far from Heaven: David Alfaro Siqueiros' The March of Humanity and Mexican Revolutionary Politics*. Cambridge: Cambridge University Press, 1987.

Foster, Robert J. "Making National Cultures in the Global Ecumene." *Annual Review of Anthropology* 20 (1991): 235–60.

Fox, Elizabeth. "Media Policies in Latin America: An Overview." In Elizabeth Fox, ed. *Media and Politics in Latin America: The Struggle for Democracy*, 6–35. London: Sage, 1988.

Franco, Jean. "From Modernization to Resistance: Latin American Literature, 1959–1976." *Latin American Perspectives* 5 (1978): 77–97.

————. *Plotting Women: Gender and Representation in Mexico*. New York: Columbia University Press, 1989.

————. "What's in a Name? Popular Culture Theories and Their Limitations." *Studies in Latin American Popular Culture* 1 (1982): 5–14.

Frank, Thomas. *The Conquest of Cool: Business Culture, Counterculture, and the Rise of Hip Consumerism*. Chicago: University of Chicago Press, 1997.

Franz, Carl. *The People's Guide to Mexico*. Santa Fe, N.Mex.: John Muir Publications, 1972 [1979].

Fraser, Ronald, ed. *1968: A Student Generation in Revolt: An International Oral History*. New York: Pantheon, 1988.

Frith, Simon. "'The Magic That Can Set You Free': The Ideology of Folk and the Myth of the Rock Community." *Popular Music* 1 (1981): 159–68.

————. *Sound Effects: Youth, Leisure, and the Politics of Rock 'n' Roll*. New York: Pantheon, 1981.

————, ed. *World Music, Politics and Social Change*. Manchester, U.K.: Manchester University Press, 1989.

Garay Sánchez, Adrián de. *El rock también es cultura*. Cuadernos de Comunicación y Prácticas Sociales, no. 5. Mexico City: Universidad Iberoamericana, 1993.

García Canclini, Néstor. *Hybrid Cultures: Strategies for Entering and Leaving Modernity*. Translated by Christopher L. Chiappari and Silvia L. López. Minneapolis: University of Minnesota Press, 1995.

————. *Transforming Modernity: Popular Culture in Mexico*. Translated by Lidia Lozano. Austin: University of Texas Press, 1993 [1997].

García Riera, Emilio. *Historia documental del cine mexicano.* Vols. 8–12. Jalisco, Mexico: Universidad de Guadalajara, 1993.

García-Robles, Jorge. *¿Qué transa con las bandas?* Mexico City: Posada, 1985.

García Saldaña, Parménides. *En la ruta de La Onda.* Mexico City: Diógenes, 1972.

———. *Pasto verde.* Mexico City: Diógenes, 1968.

———. *El rey criollo.* Mexico City: Diógenes, 1970; Lecturas Mexicanas, 1987.

Gifford, Barry, ed. *As Ever: The Collected Correspondence of Allen Ginsberg and Neal Cassady.* Berkeley, Calif.: Creative Arts Book Co., 1977.

Gilabert, César. *El hábito de la utopía: Análisis del imaginario sociopolítico en el movimiento estudiantil de México, 1968.* Mexico City: Instituto Mora / Miguel Angel Porrua, 1993.

Gilly, Adolfo. "1968: La ruptura en los bordes." *Nexos* 191 (November 1993): 25–33.

Gitlin, Todd. *The Sixties: Years of Hope, Days of Rage.* Toronto: Bantam, 1987.

Glantz, Margo. *Onda y escritura en México: Jóvenes de 20 a 33.* Mexico City: Siglo XXI, 1971.

"Global Report on Rock 'n' Roll." *New York Times Magazine,* 20 April 1958, 24.

Goldman, Albert. *Elvis.* New York: McGraw-Hill, 1981.

Goldman, Shifra. *Contemporary Mexican Painting in a Time of Change.* Austin: University of Texas Press, 1981.

Gómez-Peña, Guillermo. *Warrior for Gringostroika.* Introduction by Roger Bartra. St. Paul, Minn.: Greywolf Press, 1993.

González de Alba, Luis. *Los días y los años.* Mexico City: Ediciones Era, 1971.

González Casanova, Pablo. *La democracia en México.* Mexico City: Era, 1965 [1989].

González y González, Fernando, ed. *Historia de la televisión mexicana.* Privately published, 1989.

González Rodríguez, Sergio. *Los bajos fondos: El antro, la bohemia y el café.* Mexico City: Cal y Arena, 1990.

Goodall, H. L., Jr. *Living in the Rock & Roll Mystery: Reading Context, Self, and Others as Clues.* Carbondale: Southern Illinois University Press, 1991.

Granados Chapa, Miguel Angel. "El estado y los medios de comunicación." In Jorge Alonso, ed., *El estado mexicano,* 341–56. Mexico City: Nueva Imagen, 1982.

Gronow, Pekka. "The Record Industry: The Growth of a Mass Medium." *Popular Music* 3 (1983): 53–75.

Grossberg, Lawrence. "Another Boring Day in Paradise: Rock & Roll and the Empowerment of Everyday Life." *Popular Music* 4 (1984): 225–60.

———. *We Gotta Get Out of This Place: Popular Conservatism and Postmodern Culture.* New York: Routledge, 1992.

Guevara Niebla, Gilberto. *La democracia en la calle: Crónica del movimiento estudiantil mexicano.* Mexico City: Siglo XXI, 1988.

———. "Volver al 68." *Nexos* 190 (October 1993): 31–43.

Gunia, Inke. ¿"Cuál es La Onda"? La literatura de la contracultura juvenil en el México de los años sesenta y setenta. Frankfurt: Vervuert Verlag, 1994.

Gunn, D. Wayne. Escritores norteamericanos y británicos en México. Translated by Ernestina de Champourcin. Mexico City: Lecturas Mexicanas, 1985; Fondo de Cultura Económica, 1977.

Gurevitch, Michael, Tony Bennett, James Curran, and Janet Woollacott. Culture, Society and the Media. London: Routledge, 1982 [1988].

Gutmann, Mathew C. The Meanings of Macho: Being a Man in Mexico City. Berkeley: University of California Press, 1996.

Haines, Gerald K. "Under the Eagle's Wing: The Franklin Roosevelt Administration Forges an American Hemisphere." Diplomatic History 1 (1977): 373–88.

Hamilton, Nora, and Timothy F. Harding, eds. Modern Mexico. Beverly Hills, Calif.: Sage, 1986.

Hamm, Charles. "Rock 'n' Roll in a Very Strange Society." Popular Music 5 (1985): 159–74.

Hannerz, Ulf. "Notes on the Global Ecumene." Public Culture 1, no. 2 (1989): 66–75.

Hansen, Roger D. The Politics of Mexican Development. Baltimore, Md.: Johns Hopkins University Press, 1971 [1974].

Harvey, David. The Condition of Postmodernity: An Enquiry into the Origins of Cultural Change. Oxford: Basil Blackwell, 1989.

Hebdige, Dick. Hiding in the Light. London: Routledge, 1988.

———. Subculture: The Meaning of Style. London: Routledge, 1979.

Hellman, Judith. Mexico in Crisis. New York: Holmes and Meier, 1983.

Hernández García, M. Guadalupe, Y. Reyes Vázquez, and G. Rubio Zárate. "Lenguaje coloquial en la llamada 'literatura de La Onda.'" B.A. thesis, Mexico City: Universidad Intercontinental, 1989.

Hershfield, Joanne. Mexican Cinema / Mexican Woman, 1940–1950. Tucson: University of Arizona Press, 1996.

Hill, Trent. "The Enemy within: Censorship in Rock Music in the 1950s." South Atlantic Quarterly 90 (Fall 1991): 675–707.

Hoffman, Abbie. Woodstock Nation. New York: Vintage, 1969.

Hopkins, Jerry, and Danny Sugerman. No One Here Gets out Alive. New York: Warner, 1980.

Hougan, Jim. "Mexico Raises a Counterculture." The Nation, 25 September 1972, 238–41.

Huyssen, Andreas. After the Great Divide: Modernism, Mass Culture, Postmodernism. Bloomington: Indiana University Press, 1986.

Imaz Bayona, Cecilia. "El apoyo popular al movimiento estudiantil de 1968." Revista Mexicana de Sociología 37, no. 2 (1975): 363–92.

Jiménez, Lucina I. "Notas sobre cultura nacional y cultura popular." Hómines 13 (February-July 1989): 47–51.

Johnson, John J. *Political Change in Latin America: The Emergence of the Middle Sectors.* Stanford, Calif.: Stanford University Press, 1958.

Joseph, Gilbert, and Daniel Nugent, eds. *Everyday Forms of State Formation: Revolution and the Negotiation of Rule in Modern Mexico.* Durham, N.C.: Duke University Press, 1994.

Jud, Donald G. "Tourism and Economic Growth in Mexico since 1950." *Inter-American Economic Affairs* 28 (1974): 19–43.

Kandell, Jonathan. *La Capital: A Biography of Mexico City.* New York: Random House, 1988.

Katsiaficas, George. *The Imagination of the New Left: A Global Analysis of 1968.* Boston: South End Press, 1987.

Katz, Friedrich. *The Secret War in Mexico.* Chicago: University of Chicago Press, 1981.

Kerouac, Jack. *On the Road.* New York: Signet, 1980 [Viking Press, 1957].

Knight, Alan. *The Mexican Revolution.* Vols. 1–2. Lincoln: University of Nebraska Press, 1986.

———. "Mexico, c. 1930–1946." In Leslie Bethell, ed., *Cambridge History of Latin America,* vol. 7, 3–82. New York: Cambridge University Press, 1990.

———. "Racism, Revolution, and *Indigenismo:* Mexico, 1910–1940." In Richard Graham, ed., *The Idea of Race in Latin America, 1870–1940,* 71–113. Austin: University of Texas Press, 1990.

———. "Revolutionary Project, Recalcitrant People: Mexico, 1910–1940." In Jaime E. Rodríguez O., ed., *The Revolutionary Process in Mexico: Essays on Political and Social Change, 1880–1940,* 227–64. Los Angeles: University of California Press, 1990.

Laing, David. "The Music Industry and the 'Cultural Imperialism Thesis.'" *Media, Culture & Society* 8 (1986): 331–41.

Lau Jaiven, Ana. *La nueva ola del feminismo en México.* Mexico City: Planeta, 1987.

Lazcano, Hugo. "Muestran Avándaro." *Reforma,* 14 September 1996, E5.

Lipsitz, George. "Cruising around the Historical Bloc—Postmodernism and Popular Music in East Los Angeles." *Cultural Critique* 5 (1986): 157–77.

Loaeza, Soledad. "México 1968: Los orígenes de la transición." In Ilán Semo, ed., *La transición interrumpida: México, 1968–1988,* 15–47. Mexico City: Universidad Iberoamericana / Nueva Imagen, 1993.

Lomnitz-Adler, Claudio. *Exits from the Labyrinth: Culture and Ideology in the Mexican National Space.* Berkeley: University of California Press, 1992.

———. "Fissures in Contemporary Mexican Nationalism." *Public Culture* 9 (1996): 55–68.

Lora, Alejandro, with Arturo Castelazo. *Lora: Vida y rocanrol . . . en sus propias palabras.* Mexico City: Castelazo y Asociados, 1993.

Mabry, Donald J. *The Mexican University and the State: Student Conflicts, 1910–1971.* College Station: Texas A&M University Press, 1982.

MacCannell, Dean. *The Tourist: A New Theory of the Leisure Class.* New York: Schocken, 1976 [1989].

MacLachlan, Colin M., and William H. Beezley. *El Gran Pueblo: A History of Greater Mexico.* Englewood Cliffs, N.J.: Prentice Hall, 1994.

Malm, Krister, and Roger Wallis. *Media Policy and Music Activity.* London: Routledge, 1992.

Manuel, Peter. "Rock Music and Cultural Ideology in Revolutionary Cuba." In Simon Frith, ed., *World Music, Politics, and Social Change,* 161–66. Manchester, U.K.: Manchester University Press, 1991.

Marroquín, Enrique. *La contracultura como protesta: Análisis de un fenómeno juvenil.* Mexico City: Joaquín Mortiz, 1975.

Martin, Linda, and Kerry Segrave. *Anti-Rock: The Opposition to Rock 'n' Roll.* New York: Da Capo, 1993.

Martinez, Manuel Luis. "'With Imperious Eyes': Kerouac, Burroughs, and Ginsberg on the Road in South America." *Aztlán* 23, no. 1 (1998): 33–53.

Martínez, Rubén. *The Other Side: Fault Lines, Guerrilla Saints and the True Heart of Rock 'n' Roll.* London: Verso, 1992.

Martínez Assad, Carlos. "La voz de los muros." In Hermann Bellinghausen, ed., *Pensar el 68,* 73–75. Mexico City: Cal y Arena, 1988.

Martínez Villegas, Lucía, and Hilda Rivera Delgado. *La Extensión Universitaria en la Universidad Nacional Autónoma de México: Información general, 1973–1978.* Set 2, vol. 6. Mexico City: Universidad Nacional Autónoma de México, 1979.

Mathias, Anna. *Against All Odds: The Feminist Movement in Mexico to 1940.* Westport, Conn.: Greenwood Press, 1982.

Mattelart, Armand. "Notas al margen del imperialismo." *Comunicación y Cultura* 6 (1979): 7–27.

Mattelart, Armand, and Michele Mattelart. *Juventud chilena: Rebeldía y conformismo.* Santiago, Chile: Editorial Universitaria, 1970.

Mattelart, Armand, Xavier Delcourt, and Michele Mattelart. *International Image Markets: In Search of an Alternative Perspective.* Translated by David Buxton. London: Comedia, 1984.

Mattelart, Michele. "El conformismo revoltoso de la canción popular." *Cine Cubano* 69/70 (1972): 144–55.

McAnany, Emile, and Kenton T. Wilkinson, eds. *Mass Media and Free Trade: NAFTA and the Culture Industries.* Austin: University of Texas Press, 1996.

Memoria del Instituto Nacional de Bellas Artes, 1958–1964. Mexico City: Instituto Nacional de Bellas Artes, 1964.

"Mexico: Prospering Pacesetter." *Fortune Magazine,* May 1968, 68–92.

Meyer, Michael C., and William L. Sherman. *The Course of Mexican History.* 5th ed. New York: Oxford University Press, 1995.

Miller, Marjorie, and Juanita Darling "The Eye of the Tiger: Emilio Azcárraga and the Televisa Empire." In William A. Orme Jr., ed., *A Culture of Collusion: An Inside Look at the Mexican Press,* 59–70. Miami: North-South Center Press / University of Miami, 1997.

Molina, Javier. "Los años perdidos." In Hermann Bellinghausen, ed., *Pensar el 68,* 227–31. Mexico City: Cal y Arena, 1988.

Monsiváis, Carlos. *Amor perdido*. Mexico City: Biblioteca Era, 1977.
———. "De algunos problemas del término 'cultura nacional' en México." *Revista Occidental* 2 (1985): 37–48.
———. "Del muralismo al ballet folklórico." *Deslinde* 1 (1982): 3–11.
———. *Días de guardar*. Mexico City: Biblioteca Era, 1970 [1988].
———. "Los viajeros y la invención de México." *Aztlán* 15, no. 2 (1984): 201–29.
———. "Muerte y resurrección del nacionalismo mexicano." *Nexos* 109 (January 1987): 13–22.
———. "1968–1978: Notas sobre cultura y sociedad en México." *Cuadernos Políticos* 17 (1978): 44–58.
———. "No con un sollozo, sino entre disparos (notas sobre cultura mexicana, 1910–1968)." *Revista Iberoamericana* 148–49 (1989): 715–35.
———. "Notas sobre cultura popular en México." *Latin American Perspectives* 5 (1978): 98–118.
———. "Notas sobre el estado, la cultura nacional y las culturas populares en México." *Cuadernos Políticos* 30 (October-December 1981): 33–43.
Montalvo, Enrique. 1986. *El nacionalismo contra la nación*. Mexico City: Grijalbo, 1986.
Mora, Carl J. *Mexican Cinema: Reflections of a Society, 1896–1988*. Berkeley: University of California Press, 1982 [rev. ed. 1989].
Morales, Ed. "Rock Is Dead and Living in Mexico." *Rock & Roll Quarterly*, supplement to the *Village Voice*, Winter 1993, 13–19.
Morales, Mariano. *Locutopia: Crónica, poesía y música del rock*. Sinaloa, Mexico: Alebrije, 1990.
Moreno Rivas, Yolanda. *Historia de la música popular mexicana*. Mexico City: Promociones Editoriales Mexicanas, 1979; Consejo Nacional para la Cultura y las Artes / Editorial Patria, 1989.
Mowitt, John. "The Sound of Music in the Era of Its Electronic Reproducibility." In Richard Leppert and Susan McClary, eds., *Music and Society*, 173–97. Cambridge: Cambridge University Press: 1987.
Muñoz, Carlos, Jr. *Youth, Identity, Power: The Chicano Movement*. London: Verso, 1989.
"Música y Liberación (mesa redonda)." *Cine Cubano* 13, no. 76 (1973): 19–20.
"Música de rock: Idolos rocanroleros." *Historia ilustrada de música popular mexicana*, chap. 10. Mexico City: Promexa, 1979.
Nabokov, Peter. "La Raza, the Land and the Hippies." *The Nation*, 20 April 1970, 464–68.
Niblo, Stephen R. *War, Diplomacy, and Development: The United States and Mexico, 1938–1954*. Wilmington, Del.: Scholarly Resources, 1995.
Ninkovitch, Frank. "The Currents of Diplomacy: Art and the State Department, 1938–1947." *Diplomatic History* 1 (1977): 215–37.
Nolan, Mary Lee, and Sidney Nolan. "The Evolution of Tourism in Twentieth-Century Mexico." *Journal of the West* 27, no. 4 (1988): 14–25.

Ocampo, Tarsicio V., ed. *México: Conflicto estudiantil 1968.* Cuernavaca, Mexico: Centro Intercultural de Documentación, 1969.

Oliart, Patricia, and José A. Lloréns. "La nueva canción en el Perú." *Comunicación y Cultura* 12 (1984): 73–83.

O'Malley, Ilene V. *The Myth of the Revolution: Hero Cults and the Institutionalization of the Mexican State, 1920–1940.* Westport, Conn.: Greenwood Press, 1986.

Pacheco, José Emiliano. *Battles in the Desert and Other Stories.* Translated by Katherine Silver. Mexico City: Ediciones Era, 1981; New York: New Directions, 1987.

Paredes Pacho, José Luis. *Rock mexicano: Sonidos de la calle.* Mexico City: Aguirre y Beltrán, 1993.

Parker, Andrew, Mary Russo, Doris Sommer, and Patricia Yaeger, eds. *Nationalisms and Sexualities.* New York: Routledge, 1992.

Paz, María Emilia. *Strategy, Security, and Spies: Mexico and the U.S. as Allies in World War II.* University Park: Pennsylvania State University Press, 1997.

Paz, Octavio. *The Labyrinth of Solitude and Other Writings.* Translated by Lysander Kemp, Yara Milos, and Rachel Phillips Balash. New York: Grove Press, 1985.

Peña, Manuel. "Hispanic and Afro-Hispanic Music in the United States." In Francisco Lomelí, ed., *Handbook of Hispanic Cultures in the United States: Literature and Art,* 291–311. Houston, Tex.: Arte Público Press; Madrid: Instituto de Cooperación Iberoamericana, 1993–1994.

Pérez, Santiago. "El rock en México." *Universidad de México* 43 (September 1988): 86–87.

Perrone, Charles A. "Changing of the Guard: Questions and Contrasts of Brazilian Rock Phenomena." *Studies in Latin American Popular Culture* 9 (1990): 65–83.

Peterson, Richard A. "The Unnatural History of Rock Festivals: An Instance of Media Facilitation." *Popular Music and Society* 2 (1973): 97–123.

Pike, Fredrick B. *The United States and Latin America: Myths and Stereotypes of Civilization and Nature.* Austin: University of Texas Press, 1992.

Piñero Loredo, Carlos. "Música y Liberación (mesa redonda)." *Casa de las Américas* 13, no. 76 (1973): 116–21.

Poniatowska, Elena. "Avándaro." *Plural* 1, no. 1 (1971): 34–40.

———. *¡Ay vida, no me mereces!* Mexico City: Joaquín Mortiz, 1985 [1992].

———. *Massacre in Mexico.* Translated by Helen Lane. New York: Viking Press, 1975.

———. *Nothing, Nobody: The Voices of the Mexico City Earthquake.* Translated by Aurora Camacho de Schmidt and Arthur Schmidt. Philadelphia: Temple University Press, 1995.

Portilla, Jorge. *Fenomenología del relajo y otros ensayos.* Mexico City: Ediciones Era, 1966.

Poster, Mark. *The Mode of Information: Poststructuralism and Social Context.* Chicago: University of Chicago Press, 1990.

Pratt, Mary Louise. *Imperial Eyes: Travel Writing and Transculturation.* New York: Routledge, 1992.

Prince, Caroline Lee. "The Music Industry in Light of NAFTA." M.A. thesis, University of Texas, Austin, 1994.

¿Qué onda con la música popular mexicana? Mexico City: Ediciones del Museo Nacional de Culturas Populares; Cultura/SEP, 1983.

Ramet, Sabrina Petra, ed. *Rocking the State: Rock Music and Politics in Eastern Europe and Russia.* Boulder, Colo.: Westview Press, 1994.

Ramón, David. "¿Rock meshica? Un concierto zapatista." *Diorama de la Cultura,* 26 September 1971, 3.

Randall, Margaret. 1968. *Los 'Hippies': Expresión de una crisis.* Translated by Felipe Ehrenberg. Mexico City: Siglo XXI, 1968.

Rejas, O. "Santana o, El pasado nunca vuelve." *Caretas,* 3 August 1995, 83.

Reyes, David, and Tom Waldman. *Land of a Thousand Dances: Chicano Rock 'n' Roll from Southern California.* Albuquerque: University of New Mexico Press, 1998.

Reyes, Jorge. "Guillermo Briseño: ¿Un rock de izquierda?" *El Machete,* no. 12 (April 1981): 53–55.

Reyes Heroles, Federico, ed. *Los partidos políticos mexicanos en 1991.* Mexico City: Fondo de Cultura Económica, 1991.

Reyes Matta, Fernando. "The 'New Song' and Its Confrontation in Latin America." In C. Nelson and L. Grossberg, eds., *Marxism and the Interpretation of Culture,* 447–60. Urbana: University of Illinois Press, 1988.

Reyna, José Luis. "Redefining the Authoritarian Regime." In José L. Reyna and Richard S. Weinert, eds., *Authoritarianism in Mexico,* 155–71. Philadelphia: Institute for the Study of Human Issues, 1977.

Riaño-Alcalá, Pilar. "Urban Space and Music in the Formation of Youth Cultures: The Case of Bogotá, 1920–1980." *Studies in Latin American Popular Culture* 10 (1991): 87–106.

Richter, Robert. "El Colón." *Tonantzín,* October 1990, 20–22.

———. "Crossing over." Unpublished manuscript, 1972.

———. "Fieldnotes in Mexico: On the Ferrocarril del Pacífico." Unpublished manuscript, 1969.

Riggio F., Annette. "The Gate Keepers of Popular Music in Mexico: National and Transnational Record Producers." *Studies in Latin American Popular Culture* 5 (1986): 19–30.

Rivera, Anny, and others. *El público del canto popular.* Santiago, Chile: CENECA, 1980.

"Road to Endsville." *Newsweek,* 9 February 1959, 58.

Roberts, John Storm. *The Latin Tinge: The Impact of Latin American Music on the United States.* New York: Oxford University Press, 1979.

Rodríguez Inzunza, Jorge. "Anónimo 68: Hasta la cirrosis siempre." *Vía Libre* 1, no. 9 (1988): 33–34.

Ronquillo, Víctor. "El rock tiene su historia." *Reforma,* 22 June 1997, E4.

Ross, Stanley, ed. *Is the Mexican Revolution Dead?* New York: Alfred A. Knopf, 1966.

Roura, Víctor. *Apuntes de rock: Por las calles del mundo.* Mexico City: Nuevomar, 1985.

———. *Negros del corazón.* Mexico City: Universidad Autónoma Metropolitana, 1984.

Rowe, William, and Vivian Schelling. *Memory and Modernity: Popular Culture in Latin America.* London: Verso, 1991.

Rubalcaba, Humberto, Karen Lee de Rubalcaba, Alfredo González, and Mario Ongay. *Nosotros.* Mexico City: Nosotros, 1972.

Rubenstein, Anne. *Bad Language, Naked Ladies, and Other Threats to the Nation: A Political History of Comic Books in Mexico.* Durham, N.C.: Duke University Press, 1998.

———. "How the Lombardini Brothers Stayed Out of Jail: Conservative Protest, Pornography, and the Boundaries of Expression in Mexico, 1952–1976." Paper presented at the IX Conference of Mexican, United States and Canadian Historians, Mexico City, 27–29 October 1994.

———. "Mediated Styles of Masculinity in the Post-Revolutionary Imagination, or, El Santo's Strange Career." Paper presented at the conference, Representing Mexico: Transnationalism and the Politics of Culture since the Revolution, Woodrow Wilson International Center for Scholars, Washington, D.C., 7–8 November 1997.

Rubin, Ronald I. *The Objectives of the United States Information Agency: Controversies and Analysis.* New York: Praeger, 1966.

Ryback, Timothy W. *Rock around the Bloc: A History of Rock Music in Eastern Europe and the Soviet Union.* New York: Oxford University Press, 1990.

Sainz, Gustavo. *Obsesivos días circulares.* Mexico City: Joaquín Mortiz, 1969; Secretaría de Educación Pública, 1986.

Salazar, Ruben. "The Cuevas 'Mafia's' Mexican Mural Revolt." *Los Angeles Times,* 25 June 1967, Calendar Section, 1.

Saldátic, Dalibor. "Discos." *Punto de Partida* 1, no. 1 (1966), 49–51.

Saldívar, Américo. *Ideología y política del estado mexicano (1970–1976).* Mexico City: Siglo XXI, 1980.

Sanjek, Russell. *American Popular Music and Its Business: The First Four Hundred Years.* Vol. 3. New York: Oxford University Press, 1988.

Sayer, Derek. "Everyday Forms of State Formation: Some Dissident Remarks on 'Hegemony.'" In Gilbert Joseph and Daniel Nugent, eds., *Everyday Forms of State Formation: Revolution and the Negotiation of Rule in Modern Mexico,* 367–77. Durham, N.C.: Duke University Press, 1994.

Semo, Ilán. *El ocaso de los mitos (1958–1968).* Vol. 6 of Enrique Semo, ed., *México, un pueblo en la historia.* Mexico City: Alianza Editorial Mexicana, 1989.

———, ed. *La transición interrumpida: México, 1968–1988.* Mexico City: Universidad Iberoamericana / Nueva Imagen, 1993.

Shapira, Yoram. "The Impact of the 1968 Student Protest on Echeverría's Reformism." *Journal of Interamerican Studies and World Affairs* 19, no. 4 (1977): 557–80.

Shore, Kenneth L. "The Crossroads of Business and Music: A Study of the Music Industry in the United States and Internationally." Ph.D. diss., Stanford University, 1983.

Shumway, David R. "Rock & Roll as a Cultural Practice." *South Atlantic Quarterly* 90 (Fall 1991): 753–70.

Simon, Kate. *Mexico: Places and Pleasures.* New York: Dolphin Books, 1962 [1965].

Sinclair, John. "Culture and Trade: Some Theoretical and Practical Considerations." In Emile G. McAnany and Kenton T. Wilkinson, eds., *Mass Media and Free Trade: NAFTA and the Cultural Industries,* 30–60. Austin: University of Texas Press, 1996.

Smith, Anthony. *The Geopolitics of Information: How Western Culture Dominates the World.* New York: Oxford University Press, 1980.

Smith, Arthur K., Jr. "Mexico and the Cuban Revolution: Foreign Policy-Making in Mexico under President Adolfo López Mateos, 1958–1964." Ph.D. diss., Cornell University, 1970.

"Special Issue on Global Culture." *Theory, Culture & Society* 7, nos. 2–3 (June 1990).

Stevens, Evelyn P. "*Marianismo:* The Other Face of *Machismo* in Latin America." In Ann Pescatello, ed., *Female and Male in Latin America: Essays,* 89–101. Pittsburgh: University of Pittsburgh Press, 1973.

———. "Protest Movement in an Authoritarian Regime." *Comparative Politics* 7 (1975): 361–82.

———. *Protest and Response in Mexico.* Cambridge, Mass.: MIT Press, 1974.

Stigberg, David K. "Foreign Currents during the 60s and 70s in Mexican Popular Music: Rock and Roll, the Romantic Ballad and the Cumbia." *Studies in Latin American Popular Culture* 4 (1985): 170–84.

———. "Urban Musical Culture in Mexico: Professional Musicianship and Media in the Musical Life of Contemporary Veracruz." Ph.D. diss., University of Illinois at Urbana-Champaign, 1980.

Szemere, Anna. "Some Institutional Aspects of Pop and Rock in Hungary." *Popular Music* 3 (1983): 121–42.

Taffet, Jeffrey F. "'My Guitar Is not for the Rich': The New Chilean Song Movement and the Politics of Culture." *Journal of American Culture* 20, no. 2 (1997): 91–103.

Tatum, Chuck. "From Sandino to Mafalda: Recent Works on Latin American Popular Culture." *Latin American Research Review* 29 (1994): 198–214.

Taylor, Philip B., Jr. "The Mexican Elections of 1958: Affirmation of Authoritarianism?" *Western Political Science Quarterly* 23, no. 3 (1960): 722–44.

Teichmann, Reinhard. *De La Onda en adelante: Conversaciones con 21 novelistas mexicanos.* Mexico City: Posada, 1987.

Tenorio, Mauricio. "Viejos gringos: Radicales norteamericanos en los años treinta y su visión de México." *Secuencia* 21 (September-December 1991): 95–116.

Tomlinson, John. *Cultural Imperialism: A Critical Introduction*. Baltimore, Md.: Johns Hopkins University Press, 1991.

Trejo Delarbre, Raúl, ed. *Televisa: El quinto poder*. Mexico City: Claves Latino-americanas, 1985 [1991].

Vila, Pablo. "*Rock nacional* and Dictatorship in Argentina." *Popular Music* 6, no. 2 (1987): 129–48.

Villanueva, René. *Cantares de la memoria: 25 años de la historia del grupo Los Folkloristas, alma y tradición de la música popular mexicana*. Mexico City: Planeta, 1994.

Villanueva, Tino, ed., *Chicanos*. Mexico City: Fondo de Cultura Económica, 1985.

Wallis, Roger, and Krister Malm. *Big Sounds from Small Peoples: The Music Industry in Small Countries*. New York: Pendragon, 1984.

Wasson, R. Gordon. "Foreword." In Alvaro Estrada, *Vida de María Sabina: La sabia de los hongos*, 9–17. Mexico City: Siglo XXI, 1977 [1989].

———. "Seeking the Magic Mushroom." *Life Magazine*, 13 May 1957, 100–120.

Wise, Sue. "Sexing Elvis." *Women's Studies International Forum* 7 (1984): 13–17.

Woodstock 94: The Guide. New York: Entertainment Weekly Custom Publishing, 1994.

Woodstock 94: 3 More Days of Peace & Music. New York: St. Martin's Press, 1994.

Yúdice, George, Jean Franco, and Juan Flores, eds. *On Edge: The Crisis of Contemporary Latin American Culture*. Minneapolis: University of Minnesota Press, 1992.

Zermeño, Sergio. *México: Una democracia utópica: El movimiento estudiantil del 68*. Mexico City: Siglo XXI, 1978 [1991].

Zion, Lawrence. "Disposable Icons: Pop Music in Australia, 1955–1963." *Popular Music* 8 (1989): 165–75.

Zolov, Eric. "Containing the Rock Gesture: Mass Culture and Hegemony in Mexico, 1955–1975." 2 vols. Ph.D. diss., University of Chicago, 1995.

———. "Post-War Repackaging of Mexico: The Cosmopolitan-*Folklórico* Axis." Paper presented at the conference, Representing Mexico: Transnationalism and the Politics of Culture since the Revolution, Woodrow Wilson International Center for Scholars, Washington, D.C., 7–8 November 1997.

Films and Videos Consulted

Ah verda' (Dir. Sergio García, 1973)
Al compás del rock'n roll (Dir. José Díaz Morales, 1956)
Amnistía (Dir. Oscar Menéndez, 1978)
Los años verdes (Dir. Jaime Salvador, 1966)

Avándaro (Dir. A. Gurrola, 1971)

Betty Rock (Dir. Sergio García, 1989)

Los caifanes (Dir. Juan Ibáñez, 1966)

Las caras de la banda (Dir. Jorge Cana, 1992)

Los chiflados del rock'n roll (Dir. José Díaz Morales, 1956)

Cinco de chocolate y uno de fresa (Dir. Carlos Velo, 1967)

¿Cómo ves? (Dir. Paul Leduc, 1984)

Comunicados 1 & 2 (Prod. Comité Nacional de Huelga, 1968)

Concierto de Avándaro (Dir. Candiani, 1971)

2 de octubre — aquí México (Dir. Oscar Menéndez, 1968–1970)

La edad de la tentación (Dir. Alejandro Galindo, 1958)

La edad de la violencia (Dir. Julián Soler, 1963)

Una familia de tantas (Dir. Alejandro Galindo, 1948)

El fín (Dir. Sergio García, 1970)

El grito (Dir. Leobardo López, 1968)

Juventud desenfrenada (Dir. José Díaz Morales, 1956)

Juventud rebelde (Dir. Julián Soler, 1961)

La juventud se impone (La nueva ola) (Dir. Julián Soler, 1964)

Juventud sin ley (Rebeldes a go-go) (Dir. Gilberto Martínez Solares, 1965)

King Creole (Dir. Michael Curtiz, 1958)

Una larga experiencia (Dir. Sergio García, 1982)

La locura del rock'n roll (Dir. Fernando Méndez, 1956)

México '68 (Dir. Oscar Menéndez, 1993)

"MTV News Latino: Mejor hablar de ciertas cosas, 'Pequeñas historias del rock argentino'" (Prod. Lily Neumeyer. Aired 12 December 1996, LSPE008)

"MTV News Latino: Nunca digas que no, '3 décadas de la historia de rock mexicano'" (Prod. Sebastián Portillo. Aired 12 December 1996, LSPE009)

Los olvidados (Luis Buñuel, 1950)

Paloma herida (Dir. Emilio Fernández, 1962)

La provocación (Dir. Sergio García, 1976)

Rebel without a Cause (Dir. Nicholas Ray, 1955)

Rojo amanecer (Dir. Jorge Fons, 1989)

Simón del desierto (Dir. Luis Buñuel, 1965)

Twist, locura de la juventud (Dir. Miguel M. Delgado, 1962)

Unete pueblo (Dir. Oscar Menéndez, 1968)

La verdadera vocación de Magdalena (Dir. Jaime Hermosillo, 1971)

Vírgen de medianoche (Dir. Alejandro Galindo, 1941)

Viva la juventud (Dir. Fernando Cortés, 1955)

The Wild One (Dir. Laslo Benedek, 1953)

Woodstock (Dir. Michael Wadleigh, 1970)

Permission Credits

Note: Credits for figures appear in their accompanying captions.

Portions of chapter 2 are reproduced from "*Rebeldismo* in the Revolutionary Family: Rock 'n' Roll's Early Challenges to State and Society in Mexico," *Journal of Latin American Cultural Studies* 6, no. 2 (1997): 201–16 (Carfax Publishing, United Kingdom).

Excerpts from "Crossing over" (unpublished manuscript, 1972) used by permission of Robert Richter.

"Baila el rock and roll," by Frank Domínguez. Copyright © 1957 by Peer International Corporation. Copyright renewed. International copyright secured. Used by permission.

"Good Golly Miss Molly," by Marascalco and Blackwell. Copyright © 1958 by Jondora Music, Robinhood Music, Third Story Music. Reprinted by permission of Jondora Music and Third Story Music. Spanish lyrics by Los Teen Tops. International copyright secured. Used by permission of Jondora Music. All rights reserved.

"King Creole," by Jerry Leiber and Mike Stoller. Copyright © 1958 by Elvis Presley Music, Inc. Copyright assigned to Gladys Music (administered by Williamson Music). International copyright secured. Used by permission. All rights reserved.

"King Creole," by Jerry Leiber and Mike Stoller. Copyright © 1958 by Jerry Leiber Music, Mike Stoller Music. Spanish lyrics by Los Teen Tops. Copyright renewed. Used by permission. All rights reserved.

Index

Acapulco, 109

Aceves, Manuel, 221–22. See also *Piedra Rodante* (Rolling Stone)

adelita, 44, 272n113

Agustín, José, 159–63; on *cafés cantantes*, 104; on Echeverría, 216–17; on rock music, 84, 94, 99, 113, 117; role in student movement, 160

Alameda Park, 193 fig 14

Al compás del rock'n roll (1956), 31

Allende, Salvador, 180, 191

"Americanization," 6, 8, 217; of film industry, 30; and threat to parental authority, 40, 49–51. See *also* cultural imperialism; La Onda Chicana; United States Information Agency (USIA)

Anka, Paul, 91, 276n22, 294n99

Los años verdes (1966), 77–78

Appadurai, Arjun, 14

Arau, Alfonso, 117

Argentina: "Anti-Imperialist Front," 234; record industry in, 23, 65, 70; rock music of, 10, 176, 251

Asociación Interamericana de Radiodifusión (AIR), 58

Avalon, Frankie, 88

Avándaro (music festival, 1971), 13, 16, 244, 308n52; censorship of, 202, 217–19, 221–24, 259; critique of, 209, 211–17; film versions of,

199, 206, 218–19, 304n7, 306n34, 309n80, 318n32; and *hoyos fonquis*, 222–23; impact of Woodstock on, 210–11, 244; participation at, 204–7, 306n21; popular nationalism and, 207–11 figs 15, 16; program of, 201–4. *See also* La Onda Chicana

Azcárraga, Rogelio, 20–21, 63–64

Azcárraga Milmo, Emilio Jr., 20, 157

Azcárraga Vidaurreta, Emilio Sr., 20

Ballet Folklórico, 53, 147

"La Bamba" (song), 64

Batiz, Javier, 94, 159, 316n1

The Beatles: "Beatlemima" (UNAM), 118; and British Invasion, 93–99, 102; censorship of films, 55; mentioned, 91, 112, 114, 117, 137, 226

Benítez, Fernando, 290n25

Berman, Marshall, 108–9, 110

Berry, Chuck, 82, 160

Blackboard Jungle (1955), 34–37

Los Black Jeans (rock band), 65, 88, 91

Blanco, Armando, 97

Blanco Labra, Víctor, 173

border: and hippies, 110, 143–46 fig 10; "Operation Intercept," 291n41; and rock music origins, 93–96, 98

Compositor: G & S
Text: 10/13 Aldus
Display: Aldus
Printer and binder: Thomson-Shore